FIVE MILES AWAY, A WORLD APART

FIVE MILES AWAY, A WORLD APART

*One City, Two Schools, and the Story of
Educational Opportunity in Modern America*

JAMES E. RYAN

OXFORD
UNIVERSITY PRESS
2010

OXFORD
UNIVERSITY PRESS

Oxford University Press, Inc., publishes works that further
Oxford University's objective of excellence
in research, scholarship, and education.

Oxford   New York
Auckland   Cape Town   Dar es Salaam   Hong Kong   Karachi
Kuala Lumpur   Madrid   Melbourne   Mexico City   Nairobi
New Delhi   Shanghai   Taipei   Toronto

With offices in
Argentina   Austria   Brazil   Chile   Czech Republic   France   Greece
Guatemala   Hungary   Italy   Japan   Poland   Portugal   Singapore
South Korea   Switzerland   Thailand   Turkey   Ukraine   Vietnam

Copyright © 2010 by Oxford University Press, Inc.

Published by Oxford University Press, Inc.
198 Madison Avenue, New York, New York 10016

www.oup.com

Oxford is a registered trademark of Oxford University Press.

Library of Congress Cataloging-in-Publication Data
Ryan, James E. (James Edward)
Five miles away, a world apart : two schools, one city, and the story of educational
opportunity in modern America / James E. Ryan.
p.   cm.
Includes bibliographical references and index.
ISBN 978-0-19-532738-0
1. Segregation in education—Law and legislation—United States.   2. Education—United States—Regional
disparities   3. Discrimination in education—Law and legislation—United States.
4. School integration—Law and legislation—United States.   I. Title.
KF4155.R93 2010
344.73'0798—dc22   2009033219

2 4 6 8 9 7 5 3 1

Printed in the United States of America
on acid-free paper

For my parents

ACKNOWLEDGMENTS

I received a great deal of help on this book, from beginning to end. I would like to start by thanking the roughly eighty individuals I interviewed. This group included principals, teachers, parents, students, legislators, school board members, newspaper reporters, school finance experts, and attorneys. Except when they asked to remain anonymous or speak off the record, adults I interviewed are cited by name in the endnotes. I have not identified any students by name, in order to protect their privacy. To a person, those I interviewed were gracious and informative, for which I remain extremely grateful.

I am especially indebted to the principals, teachers, students, and parents at Thomas Jefferson and Freeman High Schools. Edward H. Pruden was the principal at Freeman High during most of the time I was researching the book. He was always willing to answer questions, and his insights into Tee-Jay and Freeman were unparalleled. Indeed, I would not have written about Tee-Jay and Freeman were it not for him. Barbara Ulschmid was the principal at Tee-Jay during the same time period and she, like Dr. Pruden, was very generous with her time. This was also true of their successors: Anne L. Poates, who took over as principal at Freeman, and Tanya Roane, who became principal at Tee-Jay, found time in their hectic schedules to answer my questions and accommodate my visits.

William Russell Flammia, who taught at Tee-Jay from 1966 until 2000, was an invaluable resource on the history of Tee-Jay. Barry Gabay was equally helpful in providing insight into present-day Tee-Jay, allowing me to observe him teach and to speak with his students, who were a remarkably thoughtful, insightful, and delightful group. The students and teachers I met and interviewed at Freeman were also welcoming and informative, as were the parents of students at both schools. I could not have written this book without their help.

I received outstanding research assistance from a large group of talented law students at the University of Virginia, my home institution, and Harvard University, where I visited for a semester during the course of writing this book. This group included: Doug Bouton, Joseph Caissie, Lisa Chadderdon, Kate Foss, Jenna Gallagher, Ross Goldman, John Kabealo, Mike Lecaroz, Matt Madden, Nick Matteson, David Mordkoff, Louise Raines, Mike Riordan, Abby Shafroth, Megan

Strackbein, and Katherine Twomey. Stephen W. Murphy proofread the entire manuscript twice and spared me some embarrassing mistakes. Angela Ciolfi, a former student who is currently a first-rate child advocacy attorney, helped me untangle the politics and mechanics of school funding in Virginia.

The reference librarians at the University of Virginia Law School, who as a group are unrivaled in higher education in their combination of talent, speed, professionalism, and good cheer, were their usual perfect selves. Jon Ashley, Ben Doherty, Kristin Glover, Kent Olson, and Cathy Palombi went above and beyond on numerous occasions to track down references and help find data. Michelle Morris deserves special mention for, among countless other things, putting together a team of undergraduate research assistants who pored through the Richmond papers to help tell the story of the first two chapters. Michelle also produced a research memorandum that was longer—and bet-ter—than the chapters they supported.

I presented portions of the book at a number of faculty workshops and con-ferences, including those at Harvard Law School, the University of California, Berkeley, School of Law, the University of Chicago Law School, the University of Michigan Law School, Stanford Law School, and the University of Virginia School of Law. Thanks to those who invited me and to those who attended and asked questions or offered suggestions.

A number of friends and colleagues at Virginia and elsewhere read all or portions of the manuscript and provided very useful feedback. Steve Gillon offered help with the book proposal itself and provided support at every stage, consistently pressing me make the book more accessible to a general audience. Toby Heytens offered some very good suggestions regarding the chapter on standards and testing. Rich Schragger and Risa Goluboff did the same with regard to the first three chapters and helped convince me to weave more of Tee-Jay and Freeman into the narrative. Scott Shapiro read portions of the manu-script and entertained hours of conversation about the book, which benefited me greatly. Michael Heise and Martha Minow each read relatively early versions of the manuscript and offered advice and encouragement. Jack Martin of Rich-mond also read the manuscript and offered suggestions from the perspective of someone who has lived through some of the experiences I describe.

Ted White read a rough draft of the manuscript and suggested, with his charac-teristic combination of insight and honesty, that I needed to figure out what the books was about. John Jeffries then read the manuscript and *told me* what the book *should* be about, which was right on the money. He also offered, as usual, some elegant writing suggestions. James Forman read the entire manuscript and focused like a laser beam on the weak points and inconsistencies in my argument, forcing me to confront what I had chosen to ignore.

Daryl Levinson read the entire manuscript, endured countless questions and discussions, and offered a number of insightful suggestions and incisive comments. Perhaps most usefully, he suspended his critical judgment just long enough to provide enthusiastic support at some key moments. Mike Klarman read the manuscript with a tremendous amount of care, and he spared neither criticism nor praise, both of which were welcome. Mike is the primary reason I am a law professor in the first place, and his own scholarship, to me, remains the gold standard. His help and encouragement on this project were invaluable. Last but not least, Liz Magill read the manuscript and rightfully focused my attention on the beginning and end of the book. She also provided strongly needed help at the very end of the editing process. I am not sure I would have finished the book without her help.

David McBride and Jessica Ryan at Oxford were wonderful editors. I am grateful for their support and for their expert advice. I am especially thankful for the patience, flexibility, and good humor they showed a first-time author.

Thanks to Katie for serving as sounding board, editor, and best friend, and for invariably saying "that sounds good" (instead of "please stop talking about this") whenever I ran yet another idea past her. Most of all, thanks for caring about this book and for handling a million and one different things so that I could focus on just this one. Thanks to Will, Sam, Ben, and Phebe for reminding me why public education matters so much and why my own work does not, at least as compared to some of my other responsibilities.

This book is dedicated to my parents, Jim and Sheila Ryan. My father died before I began writing the book, and my mother died before I finished it. Although neither attended college, they valued education more than anyone I know. They would not agree with everything written in the book, but they would certainly understand—and, I hope, appreciate—the motivation behind it.

CONTENTS

FIVE MILES AWAY, A WORLD APART

INTRODUCTION

Freeman and Tee-Jay

Equal educational opportunity is a foundational principle of our society, embraced as an ideal by school officials, citizens, parents, and politicians alike. Not all would agree on what makes educational opportunities equal, but most would agree, at least at a sufficient level of abstraction, that it remains a worthy—indeed, a primary—goal. Most would also agree that the goal remains elusive. Educational opportunities are far from equal in this country and too often depend on where students live, on how much money their parents earn, or on the color of their skin. This book tries to explain why.

More precisely, this book tells the story of how law and politics have structured educational opportunity in this country for the last half century. The story is a national one, but it has played out across fifty states and within thousands of school districts and schools throughout the country. To make the story more concrete, and to give it some life, throughout the book I use as illustrative examples the experiences of two schools (Freeman and Tee-Jay High Schools), their respective school districts (Henrico County and Richmond), and the state—Virginia—in which the districts are located. I cannot claim that the experiences in these places capture perfectly what has happened elsewhere; there are too many schools, districts, and states for any one set to be completely representative. But there are enough similarities across states and localities to make these examples useful and, with appropriate caution, generalizable.

Freeman High School sits near an intersection on a busy road in Henrico County, a suburb of Richmond, Virginia. The school opened in 1954, the same year that the Supreme Court decided *Brown v. Board of Education*. The school's mascot was, and remains, the Rebel. When it opened, the school population was 100 percent white. Today, the school is still predominantly white but increasingly diverse: 73 percent of the students are white, 13 percent are African-American, 7 percent are Hispanic, and 6 percent are Asian. The majority of students, roughly 75 percent, come from middle-class families, although socioeconomic diversity, like racial and ethnic diversity, has increased in recent years.[1]

When I first visited Freeman, the students had just finished a round of state tests for the day. They could expect to do well, as they had in the past. Freeman students typically perform better than the state average, consistent with Freeman's reputation as one of the more academically rigorous high schools in the state. Most students graduate in four years and go to college. The principal, on the day I met him, described the school as successful and challenging but also as one that prides itself on fostering a sense of community. Although it is fairly large, at just over sixteen hundred students, I was told the school is a place where teachers know the names of students and students know that they can trust the teachers.

Thomas Jefferson High School, or "Tee-Jay," as it is known to students and teachers alike, is in the Richmond City School District and sits about five miles away from Freeman. Described by one author as "the school that refused to die," Tee-Jay has a history that stretches back to the 1930s. It was once segregated and home to the affluent white residents of Richmond's West End. Since the 1970s, its student body has been predominantly African-American. Indeed, the composition is nearly the mirror opposite of Freeman's: 82 percent of the students are black, 16 percent are white, and 2 percent are Asian or Hispanic. Most are from poor families.[2]

The students at Tee-Jay were also being tested on the first day I visited. Their prospects for success were not quite as bright. But this is not a failing school, at least not according to these tests, which form the primary basis for judging schools under both state and federal accountability schemes. Roughly 90 percent of Tee-Jay's students score at the "proficient" level on the state reading and math tests.

These results seem impressive at first glance, but the tests themselves are quite basic, a point driven home by the fact that a 90 percent passage rate is still below the statewide average for high schools. Other measures of academic achievement, moreover, reveal troubling signs. Fewer than half of the eligible Tee-Jay students take the SAT, for example, compared to two-thirds of the students at Freeman. Only about 15 percent of Tee-Jay's students take AP tests, and very few of these do well on them. By contrast, more than a quarter of Freeman's students take AP exams, and more than three-fourths of them receive passing scores. Dropout rates are higher at Tee-Jay than at Freeman, and college attendance rates are lower.[3]

Tee-Jay is a smaller school than Freeman, enrolling roughly 840 students. The administrators and teachers I met were, for the most part, caring and hardworking. But the overall atmosphere seems tense and apprehensive. A metal detector marks the entrance to the school and police officers monitor the halls and the cafeteria; during one visit to the school, I watched an officer break up a fight in the cafeteria and drag a student away. Teachers and administrators are justly proud of the students' improved performance on state tests, but they seem less secure about their students' academic achievement and the school's reputation.

If you hit the lights at the right time, the trip from Freeman to Tee-Jay takes about ten minutes by car. The route leads along Monument Avenue, a wide and famous boulevard that memorializes Confederate heroes Robert E. Lee, Stonewall Jackson, and Jefferson Davis, among others. (In 1996, city officials added a memorial in honor of Richmond native Arthur Ashe, the path-breaking African-American tennis player.) Along the way, you cross the border that separates the mostly suburban Henrico school district from the Richmond city school district. In doing so, you leave a world that, while becoming more diverse, is still largely white and middle-class, and you enter a world that is mostly black and poor. In suburban Henrico, adults generally expect academic success and children seem to understand and appreciate their opportunities and potential. In urban Richmond, academic success is hard-won and measured primarily by scores on state tests, and far fewer students seem as certain of their own opportunities or potential for success.

The line that separates Tee-Jay and Freeman represents the most important boundary in public education: the boundary between city and suburban schools. This boundary has been the fault line of public education for half a century, doing more than anything else to define and shape the educational opportunities of public school students. On one side stand predominantly white, middle-income, and relatively successful schools. On the other side stand predominantly minority, poor, and relatively unsuccessful schools. The urban-suburban divide is not as stark today as it once was. The blurring of this line, as described in the final chapter of this book, offers unprecedented opportunities to reshape educational opportunities for urban students. For now, however, the line remains significant in Richmond and elsewhere.

I chose Freeman and Tee-Jay because they are good examples of the past and interesting harbingers of the future of educational opportunity. Both schools have been shaped by school desegregation in ways typical of many urban and suburban schools and districts. At one time, both schools fit the classic pattern of suburban and urban schools, with Freeman nearly completely white and middle-class and Tee-Jay nearly completely black and poor. But both schools are slowly becoming more racially and socioeconomically diverse. The increased diversity at Freeman is consistent with demographic trends in other metropolitan areas, where some suburbs are experiencing a marked increase in minority residents. In addition to these demographic changes, there is a nascent movement in the Richmond metropolitan area, led by business and religious leaders, to consider ways to integrate suburban and urban schools along socioeconomic lines.

I also chose these schools because of the experience of Dr. Edward H. Pruden, who became principal of Freeman in 2000 and served in that role throughout most of the period during which this book was written. Most important, before coming to Freeman in 2000, Dr. Pruden served for four years as the principal of Tee-Jay. With over twenty years of experience as a teacher and administrator in both school systems, Dr. Pruden is uniquely qualified to assess the differences between these two schools and between suburban and urban schools more generally.

Freeman and Tee-Jay are also fairly representative of a large group of urban and suburban schools that tend to be hidden in plain sight. Neither school is at the extreme end of the spectrum in terms of student composition, funding, performance, or facilities. Freeman is not a lily-white, gold-plated suburban school; indeed, it spends less per pupil than Tee-Jay. In turn, Tee-Jay is predominantly black and poor but not exclusively so. The facilities are old but not decrepit. The City of Richmond, moreover, is a middle-sized city, not a mammoth one like New York, Chicago, or Los Angeles. Henrico County is prosperous but not extremely wealthy like Scarsdale, New York, or Greenwich, Connecticut.

Freeman and Tee-Jay, in short, are not the type of schools depicted in Jonathan Kozol's well-known book *Savage Inequalities*, which paints a shocking portrait of urban-suburban disparities that are certainly real in some places but hardly the norm. To be sure, disparities exist between these schools, just as they do among most suburban and urban schools. The students who attend Freeman and Tee-Jay have unequal opportunities and face different futures. The divide that separates them is large and important. But the differences are more subtle than those that jump off the pages of Kozol's book or other accounts that contrast high-flying suburban schools with completely dysfunctional urban ones. The future is also less bleak for Tee-Jay, and more uncertain for Freeman, than one might believe from reading accounts that depict urban schools as vermin-infested centers of misery and suburban schools as Shangri-Las.[4]

The main plot line of this story follows the construction and maintenance of the boundary that separates urban schools like Tee-Jay from suburban schools like Freeman. The full story stretches back at least to 1954, but for immediate purposes, we can begin in 1972. That was the year in which President Richard Nixon offered a "solution" to urban-suburban segregation that has proven remarkably durable, if not especially effective.

NIXON'S COMPROMISE

It might seem odd to identify President Nixon as the (accidental) architect of modern education law and policy, but the label fits. In March 1972, he took the unusual step of delivering a televised address devoted exclusively to school desegregation. In this speech, Nixon offered a basic roadmap for education policy that we are still following today.

A few months before Nixon delivered his address, federal district courts in Detroit and Richmond had ordered suburban districts to participate in metropolitan-wide desegregation plans. The Richmond court decision would have merged the city district with those of neighboring Henrico and Chesterfield counties; in particular, it would have meant that some students attending Freeman would attend Tee-Jay, and vice versa. The courts in Richmond and Detroit favored a metropolitan-wide solution because urban school districts were already dominated by poor and minority students, as they are today. Without including the suburbs, which were mostly white and middle-class, meaningful integration would not be possible.[5]

The lower court decisions were eventually overturned on appeal, but at the time of Nixon's speech, the possibility of cross-district busing or consolidation seemed very real. Nixon denounced this possibility and proposed legislation that would prohibit busing to achieve racial balance. He suggested that such legislation reflected the preferences of both black and white parents to keep their children in neighborhood schools. He then offered an alternative approach to the problems in urban schools:

> It is time for us to make a national commitment to see that the schools in central cities are upgraded so that the children who go there will have just as good a chance to get a quality education as do the children who go to school in the suburbs.

Nixon's compromise was clear: poor and minority students would remain in the city and would not have access to suburban schools, but efforts would be made to improve education in city schools. In other words, save the cities, but spare the suburbs.[6]

To say that this compromise is all one needs to know in order to understand the basic structure of educational opportunity would oversimplify a complex area of law and policy. But only a little. Nixon's compromise, broadly conceived to mean that urban schools should be helped in ways that do not threaten the physical, financial, or political independence of suburban schools, continues to shape nearly every modern education reform. This compromise is evident in every major attempt—whether through court decision or legislation—to enhance or equalize educational opportunities, including desegregation decisions, school finance reform, school choice plans, and the current emphasis on standards and testing, embodied most visibly in the federal No Child Left Behind Act (NCLB).

Indeed, to a large extent, providing some type of aid to urban students while maintaining the sanctity of suburban schools is the defining feature of modern education law and policy in the United States. The bulk of this book documents this feature and assesses its consequences.

DESEGREGATION AND THE SUBURBS

Start with desegregation. Less than two years after Nixon's 1972 address, the U.S. Supreme Court, in *Milliken v. Bradley*, halted efforts to integrate public schools across district lines. The Court was closely divided: the decision was five to four, with all four of Nixon's appointees in the majority. But the outcome aligned with dominant political sentiment on both the left and the right; liberal and conservative politicians alike had been working before the decision to limit cross-district busing. The decision essentially confined desegregation to urban school districts and relieved most suburban districts of any obligation to participate in integrating city schools. This was certainly true in Richmond. After the brief threat of district consolidation disappeared, desegregation in Richmond took place solely within district boundaries, while students in Henrico County remained free to attend schools in their own district.[7]

Combined with intense residential segregation on the basis of race and class, *Milliken* also helped preserve a set of schools in urban areas nationwide that were and continue to be attended primarily by poor children. In Richmond, for example, nine in ten public school students are black, and seven in ten are eligible for free and reduced-price lunch (the most commonly used measure of poverty in the school context). Most schools in Richmond, not surprisingly, are predominantly poor. High-poverty schools, if not destined to perform poorly, are exceedingly unlikely to excel—especially if their performance is measured against that of middle-class suburban schools.

Having endorsed the first half of Nixon's compromise in *Milliken*, a few years later the Court tried to make good on the second half, in the same case out of Detroit. In *Milliken v. Bradley* (widely referred to in legal circles as *Milliken II*), the Court ordered the state to provide compensatory aid to formerly segregated school districts. Echoes of *Plessy v. Ferguson* and its embrace of "separate but equal" were audible to some but obviously unintended by the Court. Compensatory aid was supposed to remedy the educational harms of segregation, not provide justification for a new era of legally segregated schools. Whatever the symbolic import of the decision, the practical effect of the *Milliken* decisions was clear. Together, they transformed many desegregation cases from fights over student assignments to fights over money. Urban districts with few white students and no access to the suburbs had little hope of integrating their schools and went after *Milliken II* funding instead. Notice the ultimate impact: school desegregation was tamed and confined to urban areas, where it became largely about providing compensatory funding to urban schools.

SCHOOL FINANCE REFORM

School finance litigation, which began in the late 1960s, went after money by design rather than necessity. Indeed, the premise of school finance litigation is that students do not need to be moved from one school or district to another to receive a decent education; they simply need access to well-financed schools. The early goal of school finance reformers was to gurantee equal funding for all schools, or atleast equal access to funding. If this approach had succeeded, it might have tied schools together financially. Students from different racial and economic backgrounds would have attended different schools, but legislatures, parents, and citizens from cities and suburbs alike would have had reason to care about the financial fate of all schools because all would be drawing from a common pool of money.[8]

Things did not work out as planned. School finance reform never got off the ground in the U.S. Supreme Court. In *San Antonio v. Rodriguez*, decided in 1973, the Court upheld Texas's funding scheme against an equal protection challenge. (The Court also divided five-to-four in this case, with the same justices in the majority and dissent as in *Milliken*.) The Court recognized that the funding scheme led to inequalities but refused to intervene because doing so would interfere with local control over education. The Court had used the same justification in *Milliken* when it refused to extend desegregation across school district lines. In the desegregation context, local control protected the ability of suburban schools to reserve their seats for local students. In the school finance context, local control protected the ability of wealthy suburban districts to spend greater resources on their own schools.

School finance litigation has since moved to state courts. Advocates in nearly every state have filed claims based on state constitutional provisions that guarantee a right to education.[9] They have succeeded in roughly twenty states, though not in Virginia. Even successful suits, however, have not equalized resources. Most legislatures have responded to court orders by providing a bit more money for poorer districts while leaving wealthier districts largely free to devote locally raised funds to their own schools. Indeed, most advocates no longer even seek to equalize resources. The favored strategy these days is to seek "adequate" funding, which is the amount thought necessary to ensure that all students receive a decent education. In embracing this strategy, advocates have abandoned the idea of tying the financial fate of districts together, as the goal of adequacy presupposes that wealthier districts will be able to devote more than adequate resources to their own schools. The end result is that suburban districts are largely left untouched by school finance reform, just as they were left untouched by school desegregation.

This is not to say that all suburban districts spend more per pupil than urban ones. Indeed, Richmond spends a good deal more per student than Henrico County. But the truth is that no one really knows how much it costs to provide a good education to poor students in high-poverty schools, which places urban schools like Tee-Jay in a difficult bind. They may receive more money than their suburban counterparts, but it still might not be enough. The state legislature in Virginia, however, is not especially sympathetic to pleas by urban school systems for more money. State legislatures, in Virginia and most other states, tend to be dominated by suburban representatives, for the simple reason that most people live in the suburbs. The prevailing incentive among suburban legislators, whose constituents have no immediate stake in urban schools, is to not to increase spending on city schools but to limit it.[10]

This political dynamic has naturally attracted legislators to alternative reforms that do not revolve around money. The most important to have emerged over the last two decades are school choice and standards and testing.

SCHOOL CHOICE

Like school desegregation and school finance reform, school choice has offered some relief to urban students while preserving the sanctity of suburban schools. Although typically associated with conservatives, the idea of school choice is potentially quite radical, insofar as the logic of choice is in tension with the idea of neighborhood schools, which cater exclusively to local residents. After all, if students should be given a choice of schools, either because it is fair to do so or because choice creates competition, there is no logical reason why choice should be limited either to public schools within a single district or confined to private schools and voucher programs. Indeed, the fairness and efficiency rationales that supposedly justify school choice point toward opening *all* schools to those who live within a reasonable distance, regardless of district lines or existing neighborhood attendance zones.[11]

But this is not how choice plans have evolved. To the contrary, the (often implicit) principle that suburban independence must be respected has curtailed school choice. Most public school choice plans offer students choices solely among schools within their home district. Richmond, for example, has an "open" enrollment policy, which allows students some choice among public schools *within city limits*. Such plans are typical of those in other states. Limiting choice to schools within a particular district is also a feature of the school choice provision contained in the NCLB. This law gives students the right to transfer out of persistently "failing" schools, which are defined as schools that do not meet certain benchmarks on state tests. But choices are limited to "successful" public schools located in the same district. In many urban districts, this effectively means no choice at all, because there are too few successful schools within the district and suburban schools are off limits.

Other school choice programs are similarly constrained. Most states have interdistrict school choice plans on paper, but these plans either make district participation voluntary or require schools to accept out-of-district students only when space is available. In addition, only a few states provide transportation across district lines, and very few require school officials to inform parents about the plan. Because of these limitations, very few students—less than 1 percent of all public school students—cross district lines to attend public school.

Charter schools and voucher programs, the two newest and most widely discussed forms of school choice, also tend to be confined geographically. Charter schools, which are public but given more autonomy than traditional public schools, are usually located in urban districts and enroll local students. The location and enrollment patterns are the product of both law and popular demand. Many state laws explicitly direct or gently nudge charters toward urban areas, where they tend to be more popular in any event. In many suburban districts, charters are viewed by residents as either unnecessary or threatening alternatives to traditional public schools.

There are relatively few publicly funded voucher programs, but these, too, are confined mostly to urban areas and do not allow city students to choose suburban schools. In Milwaukee and Washington, D.C., for example, vouchers may only be used at private schools that are located within city limits. In Cleveland, vouchers can be used at private city schools and at suburban public schools, provided that the suburban school agrees to accept the voucher student. Not a single suburban school has volunteered.

Teachers' unions are often identified as the reason why broad voucher programs have not been adopted. A closer look at political campaigns for universal voucher programs, however, reveals that they have failed primarily because suburbanites have not supported them. This is not surprising, given that many suburbanites already "chose" schools for their children when they purchased their homes, and most are satisfied with the schools they selected. From a typical suburbanite's perspective, broach voucher programs are unnecessary at best and potentially threatening at worst, as voucher programs could open up suburban public schools to city students. President George W. Bush, who favored vouchers, apparently recognized as much while the NCLB legislation was being considered. Unaware that his comments were being broadcast to the press, Bush acknowledged before a White House event that "there are a lot of Republicans who don't like vouchers. They come from wealthy suburban districts...and their schools are good."[12]

Despite their radical potential, voucher programs have been tamed and constrained. Like other choice programs, vouchers have been made to cohere with the basic theme of modern education reform: some aid (this time in the form of school choice) is provided primarily to urban students, but the aid does not threaten the autonomy of suburban schools.

STANDARDS, TESTING, AND THE NCLB

At first blush, the standards and testing movement does not seem to fit so well with earlier reforms. The movement was created in part to raise expectations in low-performing schools, and in this sense was another example of an effort to help city schools. Instead of being structured in a way that leaves suburban schools alone, however, the standards and testing movement has affected all public schools. Because of federal and state laws, all students in each state are subjected to the same academic standards and judged by the same tests. One might think that standards and testing have done what no other reform has managed to do: tie the fate of all students together by subjecting them to the same standards and requiring them to pass the same tests. The rhetoric of "leaving no child behind" conveys the same impression.[13]

A closer look reveals something else entirely. The key point to recognize is that the academic bar has been set quite low, which is partially a product of the perverse incentives created by the NCLB and partially a product of the same political dynamic that has shaped school finance reform and school choice. The NCLB requires states to impose sanctions on schools that do not meet certain testing benchmarks, but it lets states decide for themselves how hard their tests will be to pass. State officials are not dumb. They quickly realized that setting a high bar would lead to more schools being sanctioned, which would be costly, both financially and politically. Challenging standards would reveal the large gap between suburban and urban schools, creating pressure to close it.

Challenging standards might also call into question the quality of some suburban schools, which would anger suburbanites. Neither possibility was attractive, so most states set the bar quite low.

As a result, the standards and testing movement, in practice, is primarily about ensuring that students learn the basics. It is not about closing the gap between urban and suburban schools in educational opportunities or results. Students in many high-poverty schools, especially in urban areas, still struggle to pass the tests. This struggle and the penalty for failure tend to concentrate attention in these schools on little more than the tests themselves. Middle-class schools in suburban areas, by contrast, have relatively little trouble with the tests and provide an education that goes well beyond test preparation. Getting city kids to master the basics, to be sure, represents an improvement from the past in some schools. But the standards and testing movement, if it continues along the same path, will do little to disrupt the current pattern of separate and unequal schools. Indeed, standards and testing do more to create an illusion of equity than they do to equalize opportunities.

At the end of the day, therefore, the standards and testing movement is of a piece with earlier reforms. It does not pose much of a threat to good suburban schools, which generally do fine on the requisite tests without having to significantly alter their curriculum or current practices. At the same time, it offers some assistance to poor, urban schools in the form of greater accountability for failure and thus (hopefully) increased incentives for teachers to ensure that students learn the basics. Save the cities, but spare the suburbs.

The reality of the standards and testing movement becomes obvious when one contrasts the approaches to testing at Freeman and Tee-Jay. Test results are important at both schools, to be sure. But teachers and administrators at Freeman tend to see testing as an annoyance that often detracts from their core mission of teaching challenging, enriching material. If anything, they try to downplay the amount of time spent specifically preparing for the tests. They also emphasize that the tests cover fairly basic material. Freeman students not only perform well on the tests but receive an education that goes well beyond them. At Tee-Jay, by contrast, all eyes are focused on the test, and teachers and administrators do not suggest that test preparation just happens along the way. Instead, they focus intensely on the test itself and devote large chunks of classroom time to practice questions and test-taking strategies. There is little sense that students are being prepared to go beyond what is tested. Thus, while suburban districts have not been completely spared from the standards and testing movement, it represents a far less significant intrusion for them than it does for urban districts, where it tends to dominate what happens in the classroom.[14]

PROTECTING THE SUBURBS

The thread that links these seemingly disparate forms, from desegregation to the NCLB, is the notion that school district lines are sacrosanct and, more specifically, that the physical, financial, and political independence of suburban schools must not be overly compromised. Each major reform has had the potential to link the fate of urban and suburban schools, or urban and suburban students, but that potential has not been realized. Instead, the reforms themselves have been altered and shaped in ways that conform to Nixon's basic compromise: some aid is offered to urban schools, but suburban schools remain largely untouched.

Along the way, it appears that our conception of what schools should do has narrowed. From the beginning of public education, schools were seen as both academic and socializing institutions. A key idea of the common school movement in the mid-nineteenth century was to provide education to rich and poor students alike, equally and together in the same schools. Throughout the first half of the twentieth century, and continuing through the struggle for desegregation, schools were seen as places where students would not only gain academic knowledge but also learn to be better citizens. This socializing aspect of public education, along with the important tradition of preparing students to be responsible citizens, has faded from view. Today, the conversation is dominated by test scores, and the predominant criterion of a school's success is how well its students perform on standardized tests. In this environment, the idea that schools should also expose students to others from different backgrounds, in order to prepare them to live and work in a diverse society, is usually dismissed as softheaded.[15]

Courts have played an important but largely misunderstood role in the story of educational opportunity in this country. It is in the area of education, as much as if not more than any other, that courts have been accused of "liberal activism." School "busing" cases, for example, usually compete with abortion and school prayer as exhibit A in the case against court "activism." School finance litigation is high on the list as well. A closer look at court decisions, however, reveals that both federal and state courts have been fairly moderate to conservative in their rulings. More precisely, courts have respected suburban independence nearly as much as legislatures have. Part of the reason, as I will explain, may have something to do with the theories pressed and the remedies requested by advocates. But whatever the reason, courts, like most of the advocates who appear before them, have generally accepted Nixon's compromise.

The continued separation of urban and suburban students has been the most dominant and important theme in education law and policy for the last fifty years. In short, the failure in the early 1970s to integrate urban and suburban schools has helped preserve a set of city schools that face nearly insurmountable obstacles. Most urban schools are schools of concentrated poverty, where the majority of students are poor, sometimes the vast majority. These high-poverty schools remain the largest challenge in the field of education policy; they almost always perform worse than middle-income schools, and they usually perform a lot worse. The poor performance of these schools is not just a product of the students, as middle-income students also perform worse in high-poverty schools than they do in predominantly middle-income schools.[16]

Most major education reforms since the beginning of the 1970s, whether in the form of compensatory desegregation aid, school finance reform, school choice, or standards and testing, have been responses to the predictable academic consequences of separating poor minority students into their own schools and districts. These reform efforts, however—and this is the key point— have themselves been shaped by the political consequences of this separation. This is just as true of reforms supported by the right, such as vouchers, as of those proposed by the left. Conservatives and liberals alike have seen their favored programs curtailed to conform to the principle that the sanctity of suburban schools must not be overly threatened. Urban schools, meanwhile, are caught in a Catch-22: because they educate disadvantaged students, they need more resources and assistance. But because they educate disadvantaged students, they are less likely to get the assistance and resources they need.

There are other stories to tell about educational opportunity, including pedagogical and governance reforms, the explosion of special education, the role of teachers' unions, the continued controversies over bilingual education, and the general neglect of rural schools. I will touch on some of these topics, but my focus will remain on the ways law and policy have patrolled the borders that separate schools and school districts, and on the costs of that separation.

THE POLITICS OF SEPARATION

Understanding this story is important not only for what it reveals about the past, but also for what it suggests about the future. Past experience indicates that schools separated by race, ethnicity, and class will not offer equal educational opportunities. Past experience also indicates that high-poverty urban schools will rarely provide a genuinely adequate education. If city and suburban schools continue in the future to look the way they do now, we should expect little change in this pattern.

The reason has everything to do with politics, both internal to urban districts and external to them. There is not enough pressure within urban districts, from parents, to ensure that existing resources are used wisely and that expectations remain high for all students. And urban districts lack the political muscle on the state and federal levels to ensure that workable policies are implemented wisely and that they are accompanied by sufficient resources. The lackluster track record of urban districts also makes them unsympathetic to many legislators. Education policy, at the moment, is largely something that happens *to* urban districts, not something that comes from them.

This is not to suggest that the substance of education policy is irrelevant. Some policies are certainly better than others, and it makes all the sense in the world to choose smart policies. My point is simply that politics matter as much as policy, and education politics do not currently work to maximize the potential of urban education reform; they work to protect suburban districts. For educational opportunities to be more equal, and to correlate less with class and race than they do now, the politics of educational opportunity have to change. And the only way education politics will change, I believe, is if school districts and schools become more diverse by race and class. Thus, in the last chapter, I consider whether there are ways to bridge the current gap between urban and suburban schools by increasing racial and socioeconomic diversity within urban and suburban schools and districts.[17]

IN SEARCH OF TIES THAT BIND

It is unfashionable, I realize, to suggest that integration might be a useful strategy for improving educational opportunities. Indeed, anyone who raises the issue risks being branded a throw-back, an elitist, or even a racist for suggesting that poor minority kids might need the company of white middle-income kids to succeed. So let me explain up front what I mean and do not mean in calling for greater integration.

I do not mean to suggest that courts should order integration or that legislatures should force it, nor do I think either is a real possibility. We are past the days of court-ordered integration, and local or state legislatures are not likely to adopt coercive programs that their constituents oppose. In calling for more integration, I also emphatically do not mean to suggest that integration is a panacea. The sort of education provided within integrated schools, and the academic policies those schools follow, will still matter a great deal. Many integrated schools had, and continue to have, segregated classrooms because of tracking, and students in integrated schools still tend to self-segregate in social settings and lunchrooms. More generally, an integrated school without reasonable class sizes, good teachers, decent facilities, high expectations, and a sense of personal accountability on the part of students, teachers, and principals, will be a lousy school.

The point instead is that predominantly middle-income schools, especially if located in predominantly middle-income districts, are more likely to have the ingredients that make for successful schools. They are more likely to have good teachers, strong principals, reasonable class sizes, parental involvement, decent facilities, high expectations and real accountability—the kind that comes from parents monitoring what happens in schools and school districts and pressuring teachers, principals, and students to work hard and do well. Teachers and principals who work in such schools are also less likely to feel overwhelmed by the challenge, and more likely to have the time and energy to help those students in real need. In addition, diverse schools provide opportunities to increase understanding and friendships across lines of race, class, and ethnicity; these opportunities simply do not and cannot exist in homogenous schools.

In short, integrated schools are superior to segregated ones both as a matter of education policy and as a matter of political strategy. Integrated schools offer more potential for educational opportunities to be equal, adequate, and full. Students who attend racially diverse and predominantly middle-income schools have a greater chance at succeeding academically than those who attend high-poverty, high-minority schools. And all students who attend diverse schools have an opportunity to obtain a fuller and richer education than those who attend schools isolated by race, class, and ethnicity. There is no guarantee that students in integrated schools will receive all of these benefits, but the potential is there in a way that is not in segregated schools. At the same time, integration along lines of race and class can reshape the politics of educational opportunity by linking the fate of politically weak families with that of politically powerful ones.

A skeptical reader, especially an older skeptic who remembers the 1970s, might well object at this point, pointing out that integration might be ideal in theory but it is not practical. Segregation by class and race, the skeptic might continue, is ubiquitous and inexorable, and past attempts to integrate largely failed. Working to improve high-poverty urban schools might be a second-best solution, but why not stick with second-best solutions rather than pie-in-the-sky dreams? Why not push for smaller class sizes, better teachers, and preschool, afterschool or summer school programs? Why waste time, in other words, fretting about the impossible?

This is a fair question, but there is an answer: the world is changing, and quickly. So, too, are the attitudes among the people who count the most: young adults. To be more specific, we are in the midst of some important demographic shifts, as well as some generational shifts in attitudes about racial and ethnic diversity, which have the potential to alter the composition of urban schools and districts.

The public school population, which is already 40 percent minority, is becoming more diverse and is projected to be majority-minority within two decades. Suburbs are becoming more diverse economically, racially, and ethnically, especially inner-ring suburbs. Some cities are attracting and retaining a larger share of white, middle-income residents, including families with children. Growth at the outer fringes of suburbia, also known as the exurbs, is slowing. At the same time, polls reveal a greater attraction to and acceptance of diversity among young adults than any previous generation has ever exhibited.

The blurring of the urban-suburban boundary, and especially the reversion toward the urban core, are still in their early stages. Polling, moreover, does not directly correlate with behavior. If these trends continue, however, greater opportunities will exist for socioeconomic and racial diversity within school districts. If that were to happen, the effect on education politics would be transformative, and those in charge of schools and districts should realize this. Indeed, responding wisely to these demographic changes might be the most important step school district leaders could take to ensure the long-term health of their districts and schools.

In particular, school districts should be thinking now of ways to nudge these demographic changes in a productive direction. Urban districts should be thinking of ways to attract and retain more middle-income families, while suburban districts should be thinking of ways to avoid a flight of middle-income families from the suburbs to the exurbs. For urban districts, this might mean instituting a universal choice plan, which would allow all parents to choose among neighborhood, charter, or private schools. Parents with options about where to live want to be able to choose a good school for their children. At the moment, there are not enough good neighborhood schools in urban districts, which means that more options—including charter *and* private schools—need to be made available. I recognize that this proposal combines a liberal goal (integration) with a conservative method (vouchers), which might irk ideological partisans on both sides of the divide. But my hope is that those less wedded to ideology will be most interested in what might actually work.

Suburban districts, meanwhile, need to focus on ways to make diverse schools successful. This task was clearly on the mind of Dr. Pruden at Freeman High, as he realized that his biggest challenge was to maintain academic success in the face of an increasingly diverse student body. If he failed, he knew he risked the departure of middle-income families. Dr. Pruden's goal—to prove that diverse schools can remain academically rigorous—should be the goal of all suburban districts with increasingly diverse student populations.[18]

At the same time, efforts must also be made to reclaim the full purpose, or perhaps the ideal, of public education. Academic achievement should remain the paramount goal, but the conversation needs to broaden beyond the reporting of test scores. School districts with increasingly diverse student populations, whether urban or suburban, should celebrate their diversity rather than downplay it. They should champion diversity as a supplement to, not a substitute for, academic rigor. And they should highlight schools that are both academically successful and diverse, making the case that these schools are providing a more complete education than those that are socioeconomically and racially isolated.

Broadening the discussion about the purpose of public education is important because white, middle-class parents must come to see some benefit to *their* children attending diverse schools. If they do not, attempting to increase school or even district diversity will remain a difficult struggle. The past fifty years have shown that white, middle-class parents usually get what they want when it comes to education. If they do not want diverse schools or districts, we are unlikely to see many. If they do, we will see plenty. In the final chapter of the book, I offer some specific suggestions about how to alter the incentives of middle-class parents, one of which includes calling on colleges and universities to give a boost in admissions to any student who has attended a diverse high school.

For those who remain pessimistic about the possibilities for increased diversity through demographic changes, there is a flip side to my argument, which is sufficiently bleak to satisfy the gloomiest of readers. It is the simple point that educational opportunities and outcomes will remain unequal if the current structure of education remains unchanged, and suburban schools continue to educate mostly white, middle-income and affluent students while urban schools educate mostly poor, minority students. The fact of racial and socioeconomic isolation cannot be finessed through second-best alternatives, and unless resolved it will continue to cast a long shadow over the ideal of equal educational opportunity.

A final note about the limits of educational reform. This book focuses on schools and, in particular, on the gap in opportunity and results between urban and suburban schools. This focus should not be construed to imply that life outside schools is irrelevant to life inside them, or that school reform can remove all of the obstacles confronting children living in poverty. If we want children to realize their potential as students, we need to pay attention to their health, nutrition, housing, and family life. But improving child welfare is not an either-or proposition, and schools will always remain a crucial part of preparing children for productive lives as adults. At the moment, too many urban schools are failing in that task. Why they are failing, how this came to be, and what can be done about it are thus important questions in their own right, and these are the questions this book tries to answer.

PART I

PAST: SCHOOL DESEGREGATION
AND MIDDLE AMERICA

CHAPTER 1

Buying Time

"Why didn't Richmond ever desegregate?"

An African-American high school student posed this question at a public forum in 2004 in Richmond. Religious and business leaders organized the forum to allow community members the chance to discuss ways to increase racial and socioeconomic integration in their metropolitan area. The student's question was simultaneously unsurprising and startling. It brought home the reality that for someone unburdened by history, who simply looked around neighborhoods or into classrooms in Richmond and Henrico, it would be easy to think that desegregation had indeed never touched the area. Single-race settings still predominated. At the same time, it is remarkable that Richmond's long, convoluted experience with court-ordered desegregation would be largely forgotten in the space of two generations. It seems odd that students in Richmond and Henrico probably learn more about the Civil War than they do about the local and relatively recent experience with desegregation.

As the student's question suggests, the desegregation effort in Richmond failed—at least if the goal of desegregation was to produce schools with stable, racially integrated student bodies. That goal was not realized in Richmond or in any but a handful of metropolitan areas in the country. Indeed, like most places across the country, Richmond never really came close to succeeding. In Richmond and elsewhere, schools that were integrated in the late 1960s and early 1970s appear in hindsight to have been schools in transition from all-white to mostly minority. A snapshot in time might reveal an integrated student body, if not necessarily integrated classrooms. But a series of photos taken over a decade would show a school with a fairly rapidly changing student composition. Desegregation, from this perspective, marked the relatively brief time between the arrival of the first black students and the departure of most white students. This is certainly the picture painted by the student yearbooks at Tee-Jay.

The student's question also hints at the lack of public discussion about desegregation today. Among those who *do* know the history, one detects a shared, implicit understanding that desegregation was attempted, it did not work, and there is little use in rehashing the experience. There seems especially little interest in seriously considering new ways to promote integration. As the principal of an 88 percent black elementary school in Richmond said in *1980*: "We don't think about desegregation anymore; it just doesn't seem to matter." That sense of fatigue and futility seems only to have heightened over the last twenty-five years.[1]

But the question remains. What happened? Why *didn't* Richmond ever (really) desegregate?

The answer is fairly straightforward and, in its general outline, relatively well known. State and local officials first completely resisted desegregation, which courts did not tolerate. Officials then accepted degregation but moved very slowly, which courts did tolerate. By the time the Supreme Court finally issued a clear and forceful order to integrate schools, in 1968, it was too late: Richmond city schools were predominantly African-American, which made meaningful integration nearly impossible. What was true in Richmond was generally true throughout the South, though there were variations in terms of the length and intensity of resistance, and in some places, though not in Richmond, desegregation prompted violence.

This much, as I say, is fairly well known. Less appreciated is the role played by white, middle-class parents in Richmond and other metropolitan areas throughout the South. In the usual tale told about school desegregation, the role played by white parents living in southern cities and suburbs is rarely front and center. The Court, the NAACP, black students and their parents, white politicians, angry white mobs, and rural and working-class whites are the institutions, groups, and individuals that usually dominate the narrative. But urban, middle-class white parents—a group I will call "metropolitan whites" for ease of reference—played a crucial role in shaping school desegregation, and they did so from the very beginning.[2]

Metropolitan whites, for example, helped end massive resistance, the name given to the effort by southern school officials and legislators to nullify *Brown v. Board of Education*. These officials refused to desegregate absent a specific court order and tried to evade orders when issued. In case those tactics failed, legislators in some states enacted laws effectively requiring schools to shut down if forced to integrate. When President Eisenhower ordered troops to Little Rock in September 1957 to enforce a court order to desegregate Central High School, it became clear that court orders could not be evaded forever, which meant that the only option left for those intent on blocking all racial mixing was school closure.[3]

School closure, however, was too high a price to pay for most metropolitan whites. When the threat of closure became a reality in places like Norfolk and

Charlottesville, Virginia, the parents in those cities hopped off the massive-resistance bandwagon and formed groups specifically dedicated to keeping schools open—even if doing so meant tolerating some integration. Most metropolitan white parents, if given their first choice, would have chosen not to integrate. But this same group strongly preferred some integration to closing schools altogether. Without the support of this group, massive resistance eventually crumbled, first in the Upper South and eventually in the Deep South.[4]

In place of massive resistance came a relatively long period of token compliance, which was supported by most metropolitan whites. Instead of simply refusing to desegregate, southern states and school districts formally complied with the command not to assign students to schools on the basis of race, while simultaneously relying on a variety of ruses designed to perpetuate single-race schools. Pupil placement boards were given authority over student assignments and used race-neutral but vague criteria to perpetuate segregation. "Freedom-of-choice" plans formally offered parents the option to choose schools, but southern officials correctly predicted that no white parents would choose traditionally black schools and few black parents would choose white schools. Token compliance mechanisms were not perfect at maintaining segregation, but they kept integration to a minimum while also keeping schools open.[5]

Token compliance also received the blessing of most courts, including the U.S. Supreme Court. The Court did not tolerate outright defiance. It intervened in the Little Rock case and rejected the notion that opposition to a court order justified delaying its implementation. And the Court eventually intervened in Prince Edward County, Virginia, to make clear that closing schools to avoid desegregation would not be tolerated. But the Court explicitly upheld or let stand measures that were clearly designed to perpetuate school segregation for as long as possible. These measures included a pupil placement statute that allowed racial minorities to transfer to schools where they would be in the majority (so whites sent to a formerly all-black school under a desegregation order could transfer back), and a law that called for desegregation of one grade per year, which meant it would take twelve years before each grade in the school system was desegregated.[6]

The early struggle over school desegregation foreshadowed the dominant role metropolitan whites would play in modern education law and policy. Metropolitan white parents clearly preferred token compliance to massive resistance, and desegregation policies and court decisions bent toward these preferences. Indeed, for more than a decade after *Brown v. Board of Education*, school desegregation unfolded on terms most agreeable to one group: metropolitan whites, whose overriding desire was to promote the education of their own children. Later education reforms followed the same pattern, as described in subsequent

chapters. The only difference is that since the 1970s, most metropolitan white parents have lived in the suburbs rather than the cities.

The Supreme Court eventually lost its patience with southern foot-dragging and in 1968, in *Green v. New Kent County*, made clear that school districts had to achieve more than token levels of integration. By that point, however, demographic changes had altered the complexion of many school districts. Rural school districts remained home to white and black students, but urban districts were increasingly dominated by minority students and suburban districts by white ones. Meaningful integration within urban or suburban districts alone would be a real challenge, even in the late 1960s. Metropolitan whites, it turns out, used the period of token compliance to buy time—time to make other plans about education, which meant sending their children to private school or moving to the suburbs.[7]

The big question looming in the early 1970s was whether courts would follow white parents to the suburbs and pull them back within the orbit of school desegregation. That question is addressed in the next chapter. This chapter starts at the beginning, with *Brown v. Board of Education*, and it starts in Richmond. The Richmond experience, as suggested, was not precisely repeated in cities throughout the South. But Richmond nonetheless serves as a useful example insofar as it was something like the median city, occupying the middle ground between cities that complied sooner and with less resistance and those that resisted longer and with violence.

RICHMOND AND HENRICO, 1954

It was hot and sunny in Richmond on Monday, May 17, 1954, the day the Court announced its decision in *Brown*. Shoppers took advantage of low prices at the 250 stores participating in the third annual Richmond Day sale, which featured boys' shirts for 88 cents and girls' dresses for $4.49. One shopper, Robert McConnell, claimed a place in front of an appliance store on West Broad Street at four o'clock on Sunday afternoon in order to be first in line on Monday morning, which would entitle him to buy a twelve-and-a-half-inch television for $5.99. The Colonial movie theater at Eighth and Broadway featured the thriller *Miami Story*. White kids in Richmond could pay 25 cents for the Saturday morning special, which included a main feature, several cartoons, and—as a bonus—no newsreels. The Colonial did not admit black kids, nor did the State or the Grand movie theaters. Blacks could watch movies at their own theaters—the Booker T., the Hippodrome, or the Walker.[8]

Segregated movie theaters, like segregated lunch counters, schools, and other public facilities, seemed to many in Richmond a fact of life so ordinary and basic that it was almost invisible. Greenhow Maury recalled the life of a white elementary school student in Richmond in the 1950s: "We didn't ask about it, just like we didn't ask about why we go to church on Sunday [and] not Monday or Tuesday. It was just the way it was." Margaret Bigger had a similar recollection. Bigger traveled eighteen miles by bus to Virginia Randolph High School, Henrico's only high school for blacks. The route took her past three white high schools closer to her home. She says she never really thought about the fact that she traveled past white schools to get to her own school. "That's what you grew up with," she said. "So it didn't faze you."[9]

Richmond and Henrico County each had separate schools for whites and blacks. The Virginia Constitution commanded as much in plain terms: "White and colored children shall not be taught in the same school." On the eve of *Brown*, Richmond enrolled roughly 34,500 students, a record-breaking number. Forty-two percent of them attended "colored" schools, and 58 percent attended "white" schools. Enrollment in Henrico was much smaller and predominantly white. Roughly 11,500 students attended public schools in Henrico, and slightly less than 90 percent of these students were white. Not all students who could attend school actually enrolled. To the contrary, only 34 percent of children in the fourteen-to-nineteen age group attended high school—the lowest percentage in the country. Virginia came in second to last in school attendance by children of all ages.[10]

Thomas Jefferson High School was one of two white high schools in Richmond. The other, John Marshall, was Tee-Jay's rival. Blacks also had two high schools, Armstrong and Maggie Walker. Tee-Jay opened in 1930 and catered to the predominantly wealthy, white residents of Richmond's West End. Tee-Jay offered students a rigorous education and a wide-ranging choice of extracurricular activities, including numerous clubs, two orchestras, a band, a choir, two glee clubs, a newspaper and literary magazine, and an array of athletic teams. White Richmonders generally believed their schools to be among the region's finest, and Tee-Jay stood atop the system, considered one of the best high schools in the Southeast. Tee-Jay routinely sent most of its graduating seniors to college, and Richmonders boasted that college attendance rates among Tee-Jay graduates matched or exceeded any high school on the East Coast.[11]

Despite its smaller population, Henrico County also operated four high schools, three for whites and one for blacks. Freeman High School, which opened a few months after *Brown* was decided, was named after Douglas Southall Freeman, the South's premier historian of the Civil War. A Richmond native and the son of a Confederate soldier, Freeman was also an influential newspaper editor and a Pulitzer Prize–winning biographer of George Washington and Robert E. Lee. The site for Freeman High is near the border of the city of Richmond and, as noted, about five miles away from Tee-Jay. Freeman opened its doors, after *Brown*, as a school for whites only. Reflecting the interests of its namesake, the school's colors were (and remain) blue and grey, and the school's mascot was (and remains) the Rebel.[12]

Separate and Unequal

Separate facilities were supposed to be equal. At least that was the legal rule, established by the U.S. Supreme Court in its infamous 1896 decision in *Plessy v. Ferguson*, in which the Court upheld a law that required separate-but-equal railway accommodations. The reality was different, especially when it came to schools. In Richmond and surrounding counties, white schools surpassed black ones on nearly every measure, including facilities, course offerings, teacher salaries, and extracurricular activities. Black schools lacked science labs, auditoriums, lunchrooms, and classroom space. Maggie Walker High School offered classes in double shifts to accommodate all the students, which meant that students went to school for half a day. Black teachers received an annual salary that ranged between $300 and $900; white teachers received between $1,000 and $1,900. Students at black schools often received basic supplies and equipment when white schools discarded them. A student at all-black Armstrong High School recalled receiving many of his books from Tee-Jay: "The first Latin book I ever used was one that had been thrown out by Thomas Jefferson, with several pages torn out. That kind of thing was quite common."[13]

The unequal treatment was the heritage of an era in the early twentieth century, in Virginia and elsewhere, when many whites argued against educating blacks at all. Paul Barringer, the chair of faculty at the University of Virginia, argued in 1900 against schools for blacks because they tended "to make some Negroes idle and vicious" and "others able to compete with whites." The *Richmond Times-Dispatch* editorialized that black education was "a needless expense that made hotbeds of arrogance and aggression out of black schools" and pointed out that "many families distinctly prefer nurses and cooks who cannot read and write." The *Farmville Herald* was blunter in identifying the problem of educating blacks: "When they learn to spell dog and cat they throw away the hoe."[14]

Given this attitude, it should come as no surprise that black schools were shortchanged. For the first few decades of the twentieth century, Virginia segregated tax revenues by the race of the taxpayers, and it funded black schools only with taxes raised from black taxpayers. Because black taxpayers generated much less revenue, their schools received significantly less funding. Even as the state increased its share of funding, very little of the money went to black schools.[15]

The discrepancies that characterized schooling in Richmond pervaded the South and existed in northern school districts as well, where school segregation was more often a function of residential segregation than direct legal command. In the two decades prior to *Brown*, southern states spent between two and ten times more per capita on white students than on blacks. These figures did not include expenditures on facilities, where the inequalities were, in Gunnar Myrdal's words, "as spectacular as [they are] well known."[16]

Those challenging segregation, chiefly lawyers associated with the NAACP Legal Defense Fund, initially focused on these disparities in an effort to enforce the "equal" part of the separate-but-equal bargain. They hoped that doing so would make dual school systems too expensive to operate. As Oliver Hill, a Richmond attorney who worked for the NAACP, explained: "Our initial approach was to tackle the problem of inferior facilities at Negro schools, and to try to force whites to make the schools equal; we felt that if we did that, then maybe they would get sense enough to recognize the fact that it would be simpler and cheaper to operate one school than two—but it didn't work out that way."[17]

Court victories in these early equalization cases were sporadic, and southern school districts proved sluggish or resistant in response. Where courts seemed either impatient with the separate-but-equal doctrine or determined to enforce both halves of the equation, some school officials would respond with more generous funding and improvements in an effort to forestall desegregation. This was especially true in the early 1950s, when it appeared that the Supreme Court might make a move against school segregation. In these years, Virginia and other southern states took larger steps to improve black schools. More often than not, however, school officials would make a token gesture to improve education facilities in an attempt to paper over a system that was fundamentally unequal. This included, at times, constructing hastily built, flimsy facilities that some blacks derided as "Supreme Court schools." As Hill recalled, "all we were doing was getting [slightly] better segregated schools[.] They were never equal."[18]

Desegregation as a Tying Strategy

Many African Americans who opposed segregation and hoped for its demise were primarily interested in improving educational opportunities for black students. *Brown* is now an iconic case about racial justice, but at the time many saw desegregation primarily as a way for blacks to obtain a better education. As civil rights attorney and now federal judge Robert L. Carter recalled, "the basic postulate of our strategy and theory in *Brown* was [that] the elimination of enforced, segregated education would necessarily result in equal education."[19]

As long as blacks were in separate schools, many believed, they would always be shortchanged. Separate was never going to be equal, and the equalization suits tended to confirm this impression. The best and perhaps only way for blacks to receive an education equal to whites was to attend the same schools. That way, white-dominated legislatures and school officials could not benefit white students without also benefiting black ones, or harm black students without also harming whites. Desegregation, from this perspective, was not so much an end in itself as a means to an end. It was a tying strategy, essentially, where black students would tie their fates to white students because, as the saying went, green follows white.[20]

Lawyers challenging segregation became more aggressive toward the end of the 1940s, a product of their disappointment over equalization suits and their hope that the country might be ready for a more direct challenge to *Plessy*. When advocates first brought equalization suits, they did so in large part because a more direct challenge to segregation seemed destined to fail. By the late 1940s, however, such challenges seemed more plausible. Demographic changes after *Plessy*, combined with post–World War II politics, generated both internal and external pressure for change. The black migration from south to north before and during the war improved the economic standing of many blacks and increased their political strength. Black soldiers returning from the war wondered aloud why they were good enough to fight and die for their country, but not good enough to participate as equal and full citizens in their own country. The burgeoning Cold War with the Soviet Union and the battle for the allegiance of developing countries, populated by people of color, placed increasing pressure on Jim Crow laws and customs, which were an embarrassing anomaly in a country supposedly committed to the ideals of equal opportunity and fair treatment.[21]

Political and legal activists, like the African-American community generally, did not all agree with the shift in strategy from enforcing *Plessy* to seeking its internment. This disagreement foreshadowed debates that continue today about the best way to improve educational opportunities for black students. Some doubted that the Court would go along. Others feared what desegregation would mean in practice and worried, in particular, about the fate of black schools and black schoolteachers. Still others believed that blacks needed the resources necessary to provide a decent education, not access to white schools and students. As W. E. B. Du Bois contended, as early as 1935, "theoretically the Negro needs neither segregated schools nor mixed schools. What he needs is Education."[22]

Disagreement within the black community in Richmond over the wisdom of desegregation showed in letters to the *Richmond Afro-American*, the weekly African-American newspaper at the time. One woman wrote in a letter to the editor that "we should strive to have everything we can of our own. This means churches, schools, hotels, and everything else." Others expressed similar sentiments, but the editors at the *Afro-American* tried to dismiss these as the product of false consciousness. One editorial, for example, compared prosegregationist blacks to brainwashed prisoners of war in Korea. Prosegregationist blacks may have been in the minority, and Du Bois's view about the irrelevance of integration did not command majority support among black leaders. Over time, however, and in light of the disappointing experience with desegregation, more and more black leaders would come to agree with Du Bois's sense of priorities. Indeed, some would come to view those who *favored* integration as themselves brainwashed into thinking all-black institutions were necessarily inferior to white ones.[23]

BROWN V. BOARD OF EDUCATION

The Road to *Brown*

In the decade or so preceding *Brown*, the Supreme Court offered signs that it might be ready to overrule *Plessy*. The clearest signal came in a pair of decisions released on the same day in 1950. In *Sweatt v. Painter*, the Court ruled that a separate law school created for blacks was not equal to the University of Texas Law School and unlikely ever to become so. The decision marked the first time the Court had determined that a black school was unequal and the first time the Court ordered that a black student be admitted to a formerly all-white school. The decision left *Plessy* formally intact, but the Court's reasoning placed *Plessy* in serious jeopardy, at least as it applied to law schools. The Court focused on "intangible" differences between the white and black schools and on the inability of a black law student to receive an equal education without exposure to white students, who would comprise the bulk of practicing attorneys in Texas. This line of reasoning seemed to foreclose any chance of creating separate but equal law schools.[24]

The second decision, *McLaurin v. Oklahoma*, barred the graduate education school at the University of Oklahoma from segregating a black student *within* the school. The University of Oklahoma had admitted George McLaurin but required him to use separate seating in classrooms, the cafeteria, and the library. This segregation, the Court ruled, inhibited McLaurin's ability to learn his profession. Access to white students, the Court seemed to be saying in both *Sweatt* and *McLaurin*, was necessary for black law or graduate students to receive an equal education. On that reasoning, separate could never be equal.[25]

This does not mean that *Brown v. Board of Education* was preordained. Far from it. Legal and practical differences existed between graduate and grade schools. Intangible qualities like the prestige of schools or interaction among students, so important to the *Sweatt* and *McLaurin* decisions, seem less important in grade school. This made it easier to imagine grade schools that were separate but truly equal, assuming similar facilities, curricular offerings, and teachers. On a practical and political level, moreover, everyone knew that desegregating graduate schools would be less controversial and provoke less resistance than desegregating grade schools. Indeed, this is one reason why lawyers for the NAACP focused on graduate schools first. Graduate schools enrolled relatively few students, and those students were older, less impressionable, and came primarily from more elite families, whose racial views were generally more progressive than those of lower-income families. Grade schools, by contrast, educated huge numbers of both white and black students from all economic backgrounds. Moreover, attendance at grade school, unlike graduate school, was compulsory.[26]

Justices and Lawyers

The justices knew that desegregating grade schools would involve a social revolution in the South. The rest of the country might be prepared for the South to take this step, but the South was not, as the ensuing resistance to *Brown* illustrated with painful clarity. The justices themselves were apparently divided over the issue after hearing arguments in 1952, with two voting to uphold segregation, four voting to invalidate it, and three undecided. Justice Felix Frankfurter convinced his colleagues to postpone a decision and hear another round of arguments in December 1953. In the meantime, Chief Justice Fred Vinson died and was replaced by Earl Warren. Vinson was one of the two justices who had voted to uphold segregation, and his death and replacement by Warren may well have tipped the scales against segregation. Indeed, Frankfurter later commented uncharitably that Vinson's death was "the first indication I have ever had that there is a God."[27]

The *Brown* ruling actually involved consolidated cases from four different states: Kansas (home to the named plaintiff, Linda Brown), Delaware, South

Carolina, and Virginia. The Virginia case involved a challenge to segregation in Prince Edward County. The Court also considered a companion case from Washington, D.C., *Bolling v. Sharpe*, which raised a somewhat different legal issue, given that the Fourteenth Amendment's equal protection clause applies only to states, not to the federal government. Although scores of lawyers were involved in the case, the two main oral advocates were Thurgood Marshall, then of the NAACP Legal Defense Fund and later a Supreme Court justice, and John W. Davis, arguing for South Carolina. Davis was eighty by the time of the last *Brown* argument in 1953 and by that point had argued more cases before the Supreme Court than any other living person. He was an excellent advocate, some say the best of his time. He offered a passionate and emotional defense of segregation, contending that South Carolinians, both white and black, were "convinced that the happiness, the progress, and the welfare of these children are best promoted in segregated schools."[28]

Davis would lose this case to Marshall, whose track record before the Court was remarkable. Marshall won twenty-eight out of the thirty-one cases he argued before the Supreme Court, first as chief lawyer for the NAACP and later as solicitor general of the United States. Marshall's argument in *Brown* was less emotional than Davis's but obviously not less effective. Marshall's presence in the Court had to draw attention to the idiocy of white supremacy, and white supremacy was the ideology on which segregation rested. Indeed, Earl Warren told his colleagues after the argument that separate but equal "rests on [the] basic premise that the Negro race is inferior," and the "argument of Negro counsel proves that they are not inferior."[29]

Warren worked to convince a majority of his colleagues to strike down segregation and then helped persuade the remainder of the importance of a unanimous decision. There was no way to avoid controversy altogether, of course. The result was inherently controversial. A splintered decision might nonetheless weaken the legitimacy of the opinion and encourage resistance by offering proof to skeptics that the outcome was not consistent with the Constitution. What Warren perhaps did not foresee was that unanimity would extract its own price in clarity, which in turn would give room to those intent on resisting desegregation.[30]

The Opinion

Warren's opinion in *Brown* was short and plain, equally devoid of legal jargon and moral condemnation. Instead of stressing the evil of segregation, he emphasized the importance of education. In a passage often cited, he wrote:

Today, education is perhaps the most important function of state and local governments.... It is required in the performance of our most basic public responsibilities, even service in the armed forces. It is the very foundation of good citizenship. Today it is a principal instrument in awakening the child to cultural values, in preparing him for later professional training, and in helping him to adjust normally to his environment. In these days, it is doubtful that any child may reasonably be expected to succeed in life if he is denied the opportunity of an education.[31]

Warren described the contemporary importance of education to blunt the argument that the framers of the Fourteenth Amendment, which was ratified in 1868, did not intend to outlaw school segregation. Whatever the framers might have believed, Warren argued, they lived at a time when the importance of public education was only dimly perceived. To answer the question presented in *Brown*, Warren claimed, "we cannot turn the clock back to 1868 when the Amendment was adopted.... We must consider public education in light of its full development and its present place in American life throughout the Nation."[32]

Warren used the societal importance of education as the basis for recognizing— some would say inventing—a right to equal educational opportunity. Educational opportunity, he wrote, "where the state has undertaken to provide it, is a right which must be made available to all on equal terms." States, in other words, might not be required by the Constitution to offer public education. But if they did offer it, Warren seemed to suggest that the equal protection clause mandated that educational opportunities be equal for "all."[33]

It remained to explain why segregation was inconsistent with this mandate, even when separate facilities were in fact equal. Here Warren avoided moral judgments by invoking social science evidence—amassed since the Court's decision in *Plessy*—to buttress the claim that segregation harmed minority students. "To separate [black students] from others of similar age and qualifications solely because of their race," Warren wrote, "generates a feeling of inferiority as to their status in the community that may affect their hearts and minds in a way unlikely ever to be undone." This sense of inferiority, in turn, "affects the motivation of a child to learn" and "has a tendency to [retard] the educational and mental development of Negro children and to deprive them of some of the benefits they would receive in a racial[ly] integrated school system." Segregation, therefore, deprived students of their right to an equal educational opportunity.[34]

The Court did not explicitly overrule *Plessy*, nor did it reject the separate-but-equal doctrine in its entirety. Instead, the court banished the principle from the field of public education. As Warren stressed, "separate *educational* facilities are inherently unequal."[35]

Strategy more than legal or moral conviction explains the structure and reasoning of the *Brown* opinion. (This is equally true of the Court's opinion in *Bolling*, the companion case from Washington, D.C. In that case, the Court struck down segregation primarily because it found it "unthinkable" to countenance segregation in the nation's capital while outlawing it in the states.) Warren and the other justices did not want to antagonize the South by casting blame or by deciding any issue other than school segregation. The Court was especially careful to avoid any implication that striking down school segregation might call into question anti-miscegenation laws, which had a great deal of popular support and existed in both the North and South. (It took the Court more than a decade after *Brown* to confront this issue, finally ruling in 1967 in *Loving v. Virginia* that interracial marriage bans violated the Constitution.) The Court thus focused on the importance of education to confine the reach of *Brown* to that sphere, at least initially.[36]

The Court also sought to avoid controversy by relying on social science rather than moral judgments when outlawing school segregation. But the strategy backfired. The social science studies were plagued by methodological problems that critics as well as supporters of *Brown* quickly identified. In addition, the studies focused solely on *psychological* harms, and solely on harm to *black* students. Many who supported desegregation, as mentioned, hoped it would reduce the *material* inequality that inevitably accompanied segregation. In focusing on psychological harms, the Court ignored this point and unintentionally made the case for desegregation seem weaker than it was. Instead of describing it as a basic issue of material fairness, the Court placed the claim for desegregation on the more intangible, if not exotic, foundation of psychology.

The Court's singular focus on harm to black students also suggested that they needed to sit next to white students in order to feel good about themselves and to learn, a suggestion critics ridiculed and supporters found troubling. The Court's limited focus was not surprising given the posture of the case; black students were challenging segregation, not white students. Nonetheless, in later years some commentators, as well as Supreme Court justice Clarence Thomas, would argue that the Court's rationale for *de*segregation rested on the same belief that motivated segregation—black inferiority. The Court's formulation of the harm also implicitly suggested that desegregation held no benefit for white students, which played into fears among whites that it would hurt their children. The only ones who would gain, the Court seemed to be saying, were black students. White students, at best, would not be harmed by desegregation; they certainly would not be helped by it.[37]

Lingering Questions and *Brown II*

The *Brown* opinion left at least two important questions unanswered. First, the scope of the newly minted right to equal educational opportunity was not entirely clear. Segregation, the Court ruled, violated this right, but it was easy to imagine other inequalities that might interfere with such a right, including inequalities in funding. Was the Court really prepared to recognize and enforce a broad, general right to equal educational opportunity?

Some cases decided shortly after *Brown* suggested not. In a series of one-paragraph per curiam opinions, the Court struck down segregation in a host of public facilities, including beaches, bathhouses, and public golf courses. This extension of *Brown*, which occurred without any explanation, was hard to reconcile with *Brown*'s emphasis on the unique importance of education. This tension, in turn, cast doubt on the notion that the Court meant to create a free-standing right to equal educational opportunity in *Brown*, which would transcend the context of desegregation. By extending the rule in *Brown* to beaches, buses, and other public facilities, the Court transformed what looked like a case largely about education into a case primarily about race. The Court eventually returned to the general question of equal educational opportunity nearly two decades after *Brown*. In the 1973 case of *San Antonio v. Rodriguez*, involving school funding, the Court rejected the claim that education was a fundamental right, confirming what many had suspected: the Court did not mean what it said in *Brown* about a general right to equal educational opportunity.[38]

The Court also left unanswered the question of remedy and instead scheduled another oral argument devoted solely to that topic. The Court ultimately issued a separate opinion in 1955, which became known as *Brown II*. Like the first *Brown* opinion, *Brown II* was unanimous and written by Chief Justice Warren. Unfortunately, it offered little clarification. The Court emphasized that district courts should fashion flexible remedies in order to vindicate "the personal interests of plaintiffs in admission to public schools as soon as practicable on a nondiscriminatory basis." To do so, the Court reasoned, might require "the elimination of a variety of obstacles in making the transition to school systems operated in accordance with the constitutional principles set forth in" the first *Brown* opinion. Accordingly, school districts were to operate "with all deliberate speed" to take steps to admit students to public schools on a nondiscriminatory basis.[39]

Brown II is most famous for its oxymoronic phrase "all deliberate speed," which is confusing enough. Less noted, however, is the more fundamental uncertainty over the meaning of desegregation. Did desegregation require integration or simply prohibit school assignments based on race? On the one hand, admitting students to schools on a nondiscriminatory basis might require little more than repealing segregation laws. This might not result in much integration but also presumably would not take much time. Yet the Court seemed to envision something more when referring to the need to remove "a variety of obstacles," by which the Court must have meant obstacles to integration. But even if the Court imagined that some integration was required, it remained silent about the degree of integration necessary to cure the constitutional violation. The Court offered no benchmarks that lower courts could use to determine whether states and school districts had satisfied their remedial obligations. The omission proved fateful.

REACTION TO THE *BROWN* DECISIONS

Most political leaders in Virginia reacted with calm to the Court's announcement of its decision in *Brown*. Governor Thomas B. Stanley expressed disappointment at the Court's decision but promised "to work toward a plan which will be acceptable to our citizens and in keeping with the edict of the Court." Attorney general and future governor J. Lindsay Almond, Jr., expressed a similar thought, acknowledging that the "highest Court in the land has spoken" and expressing his hope "that Virginia will approach the question realistically and endeavor to work out some rational adjustment." Stanley and Almond could afford to be magnanimous because the Court in *Brown* did not actually require Virginia—or any other state—to do anything. Stanley emphasized this point on the day after *Brown*, making clear his view that the decision would not have any impact whatsoever the following school year. By the end of the month, the State Board of Education had announced that no desegregation would occur in the fall of 1954.[40]

The white newspapers in Richmond, the *Richmond Times-Dispatch* and the *Richmond News Leader*, also reacted with restraint. The day after the decision in *Brown*, the *Richmond Times-Dispatch* urged readers: "this is a time for calm and unhysterical appraisal of the situation" and reminded them that "full integration throughout the 17 [southern and border] states will take a long time," perhaps "a decade or two." Editors at the *Richmond News Leader* repeated their belief in segregated schools, but added: "we believe also in abiding by the law." They expressed their hope that a reasonable solution could be achieved. In just a short period of time, it would become clear that the only solution favored by these papers was the continuation of segregation. But for the moment they could afford, like Virginia's politicians, to appear moderate.[41]

Student reactions were more mixed, and perhaps more honest, than those of the politicians and news editors. The *Richmond News Leader* interviewed white and black students for an article that appeared the day after *Brown*. The article presaged some of the trouble that lay ahead and the inevitable disappointment among those who were optimistic in the early aftermath of *Brown*. The white students interviewed expressed disapproval of *Brown* and of integrated schools. "I just don't like it at all," said sixteen-year old Jimmy Traylor, a student at John Marshall High School. His classmate James Reedy predicted "an awful lot of trouble if they come here." The black students expressed more optimism. Leroy Henderson of Maggie Walker High School recognized that white students would not "jump right at" the chance to integrate but believed that "eventually they will come around all right." Jane Bates, another Maggie Walker student, explained that "the whole thing is strictly a matter of ignorance" and predicted that there might be "a little trouble" at first "but things will work out."[42]

The Byrd Machine and Massive Resistance

Unfortunately, one person who was dead set against making "things work out" was also the most powerful man in the state: U.S. senator Harry Flood Byrd. To a degree difficult to appreciate today, Byrd and his political machine dominated state politics for four decades. His political support was fairly strong but somewhat uneven across the state. His real strength came from Southside Virginia—the rural and poor southern part of the state. Most important, Southside was also 40 percent black, just about double the percentage for the entire state. Blacks in Southside were essentially disenfranchised, so Byrd had no need to court their vote; he cared instead about the whites there.[43]

Whites in Virginia, just like whites in other states from Florida to Maine, tended to support or oppose desegregation depending on the percentage of blacks in their community. The higher the percentage, the less enthusiasm for desegregation. The correlation was not perfect, but it was a safe bet. Opposition to desegregation ran high in Southside, Virginia, just as it did in so-called Black Belt counties across the South, where the African-American population was at least one-third of the total.

These overwhelmingly rural counties exercised disproportionate political strength within their states because of electoral malapportionment. Rural areas in many states retained the same amount of representation for decades despite population growth in cities and suburbs. Given the disenfranchisement of blacks in the South, this effectively meant that a relatively small number of rural southern whites, who tended to be the most committed to segregation, exercised enormous influence over state politics. This structural political defect remained until the 1960s, when the U.S. Supreme Court finally required states to apportion representation evenly on the basis of population.[44]

Senator Byrd's senate seat did not depend directly on malapportionment, but the Byrd machine nonetheless drew its strength from Southside. Byrd thus had every reason to ensure that the rest of the state followed Southside's lead on school segregation. On June 20, 1954, twenty legislators from Southside, under the leadership of state senator Garland Gray, met in Petersburg to declare themselves "unalterably opposed" to school integration. Five days later, on June 25, Governor Stanley promised to "use every legal means at my command to continue segregated schools in Virginia." Gone was any hint of moderation or the earlier promise to devise a plan that would "be in keeping with the edict of the Court." In its place was the first sign of commitment to what would eventually be called "massive resistance," the goal of which was simple: preserve segregated schools.[45]

The Gray Commission

Stanley began, in August 1954, by appointing a thirty-two-member, all-white legislative commission to formulate a response to *Brown*. Heading the commission was Senator Gray, who had led the anti-desegregation meeting in Petersburg a few months earlier. Southsiders in general dominated the commission, which seemed fair to Stanley, given that they had the most at stake. The Gray Commission, as it was called, met for over a year and finally issued a report and recommendations in November 1955.[46]

In the meantime, two important court decisions were released. The first, discussed earlier, was *Brown II*. Released on May 31, 1955, the opinion did nothing to suggest that the Gray Commission should recommend aggressive steps toward desegregation. To the contrary, *Brown II* had the effect of encouraging those in Virginia and elsewhere in the South who were intent on resisting desegregation. Attorney General Almond felt "that we got about all we could ask for" from the Court in terms of the pace of desegregation. The *Richmond News Leader* aggressively claimed that *Brown II* "ended nothing" and "changed nothing," pointing out that some would interpret the Court's admonition to desegregate "'as soon as practicable'" to mean "never at all." Meanwhile, on the ground, school officials in both Richmond and Henrico County forged ahead with segregated school construction programs just days after *Brown II* was announced.[47]

The other noteworthy case was decided by the Virginia Supreme Court on November 7, 1955. It is as forgotten as *Brown II* is well known, but at the time it was quite important. In *Almond v. Day*, the court held that providing public funds to private schools violated section 141 of the Virginia Constitution, which prohibited appropriations "to schools not owned or exclusively controlled by the State" or a state subdivision. The program at issue in *Almond* provided tuition assistance to allow the orphans of veterans killed in action to attend private schools.[48]

On the surface, the *Almond* decision had nothing to do with desegregation, but its relevance to that fight was not lost on anyone. Closing public schools and offering tuition assistance to students attending private schools had been floated in Virginia as a way of avoiding school desegregation. To the extent that Virginia officials were interested in this route, *Almond* made clear that they would need to amend the state constitution to allow public aid to flow to private schools.[49]

That is precisely what the Gray Commission proposed, just days after *Almond* was decided. The commission first recommended that decisions about assignment be left to local school boards, who would consider a number of nonracial factors—including the "welfare and best interests of all other pupils attending a particular school"—when assigning students. Structuring student assignments this way meant that Virginia could claim compliance with the *Brown* decisions while ensuring that segregation remained in place. After all, the *Brown* decisions did not explicitly require integration; they outlawed forced segregation. As long as student assignments were not based explicitly on race, it was argued, the *Brown* rulings were satisfied. The weak link in this argument was its transparent duplicity. The criteria for student assignment might have been neutral, but they were clearly designed and used to preserve segregated schools. It was inevitable that courts would see through this ruse, which was repeated in various forms during the long period of token compliance with the *Brown* decisions. But it bought Virginia and other southern states some time.[50]

The proposal also contained an escape hatch for students in the event that local school boards somehow missed the point of the ruse and voluntarily integrated, or in the more likely scenario that a court ordered integration. Students who found themselves in integrated schools would receive tuition vouchers from the state that would enable them to attend (segregated) private schools. This was the part of the plan that, after the Virginia Supreme court's decision in *Almond v. Day*, would require a change to the state constitution. This is also the part of the plan, it bears mentioning, that still reverberates today. As discussed in more detail in chapter 5, traditional civil rights groups, as well as a majority of African Americans over sixty, oppose vouchers. The historical connection between vouchers and massive resistance surely helps explain why.[51]

Constitutional Amendment

The General Assembly, in what one newspaper described as a "hasty, almost hysterical four-day special session" in December 1955, approved all of the Gray Commission's proposals. The legislators then set in motion the machinery to change the state constitution in order to allow aid to flow to private schools. In general, state constitutions can be changed more easily than the federal one, but amendments to state constitutions are nonetheless relatively rare, highly publicized, and significant political events. All of which is to say: the fact that the General Assembly was willing to push for a constitutional amendment was remarkable, especially when one considers how controversial the issue of aid to private schools was (and remains).[52]

Perhaps more amazing is how popular the amendment proved to be. Voters approved the measure by a two-to-one margin in early January 1956. In the years to come, many whites would complain that desegregation, especially busing for that purpose, threatened to destroy public education. The same fear, obviously, did not prevent them in 1956 from approving a constitutional amendment that in theory could literally empty the public schools. To be sure, the vote on this issue was split precisely because some whites saw tuition vouchers as a threat to public education. And it may be that few of those who voted for the provision imagined that vouchers would be widely used, probably because they remained confident that little integration would occur. If so, much support for the amendment might have been symbolic, a supposition bolstered by the fact that middle-class whites later opposed school closures in response to desegregation orders. Nonetheless, this is not the last time that a small bit of history will prove useful in evaluating the sincerity of arguments about the dangers desegregation posed to the health of public education.[53]

With this constitutional change in place, it appeared that Virginia's defenses against desegregation were secure. Some integration might occur here and there, but very little, and only slowly. In the meantime, Virginia could plausibly, if not in entirely good faith, claim to be complying with the *Brown* rulings.

But this was not enough for Senator Byrd, who did not want to take any chances with even token integration. Nor was it enough for James Jackson Kilpatrick, the increasingly voluble editor of the *Richmond News Leader*.[54]

Interposition

Beginning in late 1955 and continuing into 1956, Kilpatrick worked to revive the seemingly obsolete doctrine of "interposition." This doctrine held that states could assert their own sovereignty to defend against illegal acts by the national government. Here, the illegal act was the Supreme Court's decision in *Brown*.

The idea had a patina of legitimacy. Thomas Jefferson and James Madison had toyed with the concept, as had John C. Calhoun of South Carolina, a staunch defender of states' rights. But the Civil War had discredited the notion that the Constitution was a compact among independent states, each of which retained the right to secede as well as the lesser power to determine which federal laws to follow. Kilpatrick, perhaps in a fit of wishful thinking, simply ignored the impact of the Civil War. For months, the editorial pages of his newspaper strove to create an intellectually respectable defense of a morally and legally bankrupt position. The effort endeared Kilpatrick to segregationists across the South, turning him into both intellectual leader and folk hero.[55]

Kilpatrick succeeded in persuading others; whether they were swayed by the merits of his position or its usefulness is not clear. Regardless, the General Assembly adopted an interposition resolution on February 1, 1956. It claimed that Virginia had a right to interpret the Constitution for itself and had no obligation to follow the Court's incorrect decision in *Brown*. Virginia legislators thus proposed to "take all appropriate measures, legally and constitutionally available to us, to resist this illegal encroachment upon our sovereign powers." It was not entirely clear what specific measures the legislators had in mind, but it was clear that allowing even limited integration was not in keeping with this strong statement of defiance. The Gray Commission's plan, which contemplated token integration, was only two months old but already outdated.[56]

Massive resistance was now picking up steam. In late February, Senator Byrd gave the movement its name and expressed optimism about its goals: "If we can organize the Southern States for massive resistance to this order I think that in time the rest of the country will realize that racial integration is not going to be accepted in the South." A few weeks later, Byrd helped introduce a resolution in Congress that became known as the "Southern Manifesto." Signed by 101 southern Congressmen, the manifesto sounded a lot like the interposition resolution in Virginia. It denounced the *Brown* decisions "as a clear abuse of judicial power" and encouraged states "to resist forced integration by any means."[57]

Over the course of the spring and summer of 1956, Governor Stanley and state senator Gray met secretly with Byrd, first in Washington, D.C., and later in Richmond. To Byrd, the glaring weakness in the Gray plan was the fact that control over student assignments was left to local school boards. What if racial liberals got control over just one school board and decided to integrate their schools? In an era when falling dominoes was familiar Cold War imagery, Byrd believed that the integration of one school district could set off a chain reaction across the state and then, ultimately, across the South—just as whole regions might fall into the grip of Communism if one country fell.[58]

To prevent that first domino from falling, Byrd persuaded Stanley that Virginia needed a safer fallback than vouchers for private schools. The state needed what one might call the nuclear option: school closure. With Byrd's urging, Stanley proposed and the General Assembly passed a thirteen-bill legislative package intended to seal any cracks in the wall separating black and white schools. The centerpiece of the package, which came to be known as the Stanley Plan, was the school closing law.[59]

The Stanley Plan

Under the Stanley Plan, localities would no longer have control over student assignments. That power was handed over to a state body called the Pupil Placement Board, which was staffed with hard-core segregationists. That took care of voluntary integration. It also took care of what some, including the U.S. Supreme Court, have called the most "deeply rooted tradition" in public education: local control over public schools. That "tradition" was conveniently brushed aside here, only to be resurrected by opponents of desegregation when crosstown busing and district consolidation were proposed. Local control was a fine tradition, it appeared, as long as localities exercised that control to resist rather than promote integration.[60]

If a court ordered a school to integrate, the Stanley Plan required the state to cut off funding, which would effectively shut down the school. Localities might try to keep schools open with local funding, but this would be next to impossible for all but a few localities. Where public schools were closed, students would be eligible for state-funded tuition vouchers. For good measure, the General Assembly also passed legislation designed to harass and cripple the NAACP in Virginia.[61]

Not all legislators endorsed this extreme legislative package. Two major figures, Democratic state senator Armistead L. Boothe and Republican state senator Ted Dalton, led an important minority group that opposed the plan. These senators and their supporters saw the plan as an obvious threat to public education. To this contingent of moderates, keeping public schools open outweighed the importance of ensuring that all schools remained segregated. In a relatively short period of time, this view would be echoed across the state by white, middle-class parents and would ultimately prevail. For the moment, however, Byrd and others committed to defiance ruled the day.[62]

Middle-class Whites and the End of Massive Resistance

For two years, the legislation calling for school closures sat on the books in Virginia, waiting to be tested. In the meantime, a confrontation in Little Rock made it clear that school closure would eventually have to be used if schools were to remain segregated, as simply ignoring court orders was not an option. In September 1957, Governor Orville Faubus called out the Arkansas National Guard to block nine African-American students from entering, per court order, the all-white Central High School. Two weeks later, a federal judge ordered Faubus to allow the Little Rock Nine, as they came to be known, to enter. Faubus removed the troops but did nothing to stop the mob that formed and awaited the students. The students managed to enter the building, but violence ensued outside, with whites attacking black spectators as well as reporters and photographers. Fearing for their safety, the Little Rock Nine fled school at midday.[63]

The confrontation in Arkansas drew national and international attention, and television crews caught many of the uglier scenes, all of which increased pressure on President Eisenhower to act. Reluctantly, he sent in over a thousand troops to clear the way for the Little Rock Nine. A smaller contingent of troops remained throughout the school year, but that did not spare the Little Rock Nine from being cursed, spat at, pushed, and kicked by some of their white classmates. It also did not stop the violence. Fires were set, the school suffered through more than forty bomb scares, and segregationists shot at the home of Daisy Bates, the president of the local NAACP branch. At the end of the school year, the Little Rock School Board asked the district court to delay desegregation until 1960 in light of the violence and unrest.[64]

The district court agreed, but the U.S. Supreme Court emphatically did not. In a strongly worded opinion in *Cooper v. Aaron*, issued in September 1958, the Court emphasized that *Brown* was the law of the land. Desegregation could not be avoided or delayed because of opposition, the Court concluded. Together, Eisenhower's actions and the Court's decision in *Cooper v. Aaron* took away one option from massive resisters: outright defiance of court orders. Court orders might take time to secure, and they might not call for much desegregation, but they could not be ignored.[65]

Those intent on preventing any integration were thus left with school closure as their only option. Faubus himself exercised this option in response to the Court's decision in *Cooper*. In September 1958, he ordered all four high schools in Little Rock to close for the upcoming school year.[66]

Schools were closed in Virginia the very same month. In three different cases, all decided in September 1958, federal courts ordered school desegregation in Warren County, Charlottesville, and Norfolk. The state responded by closing schools in each place. In Norfolk, for example, six high schools were closed, which left nearly ten thousand students without a school to attend. Parents, teachers, and politicians in each locale tried to provide makeshift alternatives and in some cases succeeded. Overall, however, thousands of students went without education for the fall semester.[67]

As often happens, a confrontation inspired reconsideration. Threatening to close schools might have been popular, but actually closing them proved too much for all but the most dedicated segregationists. Popular and political support for massive resistance began to collapse as the reality of school closings replaced the heady rhetoric of state sovereignty and interposition. Local citizens across the state protested school closings and formed "committees for public schools" to fight against or prevent them. The Richmond Area Committee for Public Schools, formed in 1959, was dedicated to "free public education for every child in Virginia." Most of these committees were created and led by white, middle-class women who thought closing school was too high a price to pay for segregation. They might not have favored integrated schools, but they certainly favored some integration over school closures.[68]

A similar phenomenon occurred elsewhere in the South, as white middle-class parents resisted the efforts of state governments to use school closure to avoid desegregation. The Women's Emergency Committee to Open Our Schools (WEC) fought to keep schools open in Little Rock. In New Orleans, women reformers, religious leaders, and university faculty formed Save Our Schools (SOS) for the same purpose. Similar groups formed in Atlanta (Help Our Public Education), and eventually in Alabama (Alabamians Behind Local Education) and Mississippi (Mississippians for Public Education). These groups did not embrace integration; they simply chose some integration over school closures. As the founders of the WEC explained, in terms that ironically echoed W. E. B. Du Bois's argument decades earlier: "[we are] dedicated to the principle of free public school education and to law and order. We stand neither for integration nor for segregation, but for education." Groups like the WEC sought to follow a tactic that had been pioneered in North Carolina in 1957, where three cities had assigned a handful of carefully selected black students to white schools as a way of keeping schools open while gesturing toward compliance with the *Brown* rulings.[69]

Virginia's powerful business community joined parent groups in turning against massive resistance, for similar reasons: they did not think it was worth the cost. So, too, did Virginia's major white newspapers, the *Richmond Times-Dispatch* and the *Richmond News Leader*, abandon massive resistance once schools were closed. Even James Kilpatrick admitted that actually closing schools—instead of just threatening to do so—went too far: "I believe the [school-closure] laws we now have on the books have outlived their usefulness, and I believe that new laws must be devised—speedily devised—if educational opportunities are to be preserved and social calamity is to be avoided."[70]

An important holdout was Lindsay Almond, who replaced Stanley as governor in 1957. Although not oblivious to the fact that massive resistance was increasingly unpopular by late 1958, he remained committed to Byrd, who himself was unrepentant. At a private dinner in December 1958, some members of the Virginia Industrial Group, which represented Virginia's business community, met with Almond in an attempt to persuade him to abandon massive resistance. They told him what he surely knew already: it was just a matter of time before the school closing laws were struck down by the courts, and in the meantime these laws were hurting Virginia. Why stick with a harmful policy that was destined to fail in any event? Almond, however, was not moved and vowed never to allow school integration.[71]

Or at least he would not move until forced to do so, as he was just a few weeks later. On the same day in January 1959, both the Virginia Supreme Court and a federal district court struck down Virginia's school closing law, the former on state constitutional grounds and the latter on federal ones. Almond, it seemed, would have to abandon massive resistance whether he wanted to or not.

The Virginia Supreme Court's opinion, and Almond's reaction to it, are noteworthy for what they reveal about the influence of middle-income whites on education law and policy. In a five-to-two decision, the state court concluded in *Harrison v. Day* that closing public schools violated section 129 of the constitution, which required the state to "maintain an efficient system of public free schools throughout the state." The state argued that "efficient" in section 129 necessarily meant "segregated." It followed that when segregated schools were deemed in *Brown* to violate the federal Constitution, section 129 was effectively repealed. There was no way, in other words, to maintain a system of public schools that was both "efficient" and integrated, which rendered section 129 a legal nullity.[72]

The court disagreed. The state had a plain obligation to operate public schools, regardless of whether they were segregated or integrated. Section 129 operated independently of any other provision in the constitution, and its meaning was clear. The state, said the court, must "support such public free schools in the state as are necessary to an efficient system, including those in which pupils of both races are compelled to be enrolled and taught together, however unfortunate that situation may be."[73]

The last bit of editorializing reveals that the Virginia Supreme Court did not have its heart in desegregation. Indeed, it ended its opinion with a denunciation of *Brown* that echoed the interposition resolution and the Southern Manifesto. The court "deplore[d] the lack of judicial restraint by *that court* [otherwise known as the U.S. Supreme Court] in trespassing on the sovereign rights of this Commonwealth reserved to it in the Constitution of the United States." The Virginia Supreme Court then actually blamed *Brown* for inducing the lawless behavior of the Virginia legislature, calling the school closing law "an understandable effort to diminish the evils expected from the decision in the *Brown* case."[74]

So why did a majority of the Virginia Supreme Court justices strike down the school closing laws, given their views about *Brown*? After all, the state's argument was a bit of a stretch but not entirely implausible. It seems at least debatable that those who ratified section 129 would have agreed that "efficient" meant, among other things, "segregated." If so, then outlawing segregated schools would nullify the obligation to provide "efficient" schools on the grounds of impossibility. Two of the seven justices accepted this argument.

Perhaps even more intriguing, the same court later upheld Prince Edward County's infamous decision to close its schools rather than comply with a desegregation order. The state did not force this closure or other ones made by local decision; it merely tolerated them. The Virginia Supreme Court decided that this made all of the difference, in an opinion whose reasoning can most charitably be described as nuanced. The relevant constitutional language required the state to "maintain an efficient system of public free schools throughout the state." The court concluded that this obligation was satisfied as long as the state created a "system" of local option, such that localities could decide for themselves whether to operate schools or not. Suffice it to say that a less determined reading of the relevant language would suggest that the state had a duty to ensure schools remained open "throughout the state." It is a little nonsensical to speak of "*maintain[ing]*" a "*system* of public free schools *throughout* the state" by leaving their existence to local discretion. Indeed, the chief justice of the Virginia Supreme Court, who had written the earlier opinion that struck down the school closing laws while blasting *Brown*, dissented on this very point.[75]

Clearly, then, the Virginia Supreme Court was not without the ability or will to stretch constitutional language to reach the outcomes it desired. So why not uphold the school-closure law? One can never know for sure, but it seems quite possible that a majority of justices shared the views of a majority of Virginians, especially those middle- and upper-class Virginians most like the justices themselves in background and temperament. By 1959, it was clear that most white Virginians, especially middle-class whites in metropolitan areas, did not have the stomach for massive resistance. It was telling, for instance, that 1950s housewives—not a group typically known for their political activism—led the campaign against the school-closure laws. To them, as well as to business leaders, closing schools to prevent even token integration was not worth the cost.

It would not be surprising if the Virginia justices felt the same way and ruled accordingly—a possibility that seems more plausible when one considers the court's subsequent decision to allow Prince Edward County to close its schools. The difference the court saw between local and state school closings is difficult to justify as a matter of state constitutional law, but it is easy to understand politically. It may have been distasteful to metropolitan whites for rural localities to close their schools, but local autonomy was obviously less threatening than a state law requiring all schools to close. It is impossible, of course, to know for sure what motivated the justices, but the more important point to keep in mind is that this is not the last time one will see a correlation between court decisions regarding public education and the preferences of middle-class white parents.[76]

Indeed, one detects in this period the early influence of the principle that would eventually come to dominate modern education law and policy: above all else, white middle-class schools must be preserved and protected from outside interference. Here, this principle worked, somewhat surprisingly, to limit the scope and duration of massive resistance, both in Virginia and elsewhere in the South. Middle-class white parents in Virginia and elsewhere worked *against* massive resistance by trying to prevent or overturn school closing laws. They did so in part because they believed that keeping schools open was, on balance, a better option for their children, and in part because they could be confident that measures short of school closings could work to limit the amount of actual integration. Whites in cities and those in the suburbs—especially those in the suburbs—knew that residential segregation would limit the amount of actual integration that would occur if massive resistance were abandoned.[77]

The extent to which the Virginia Supreme Court's decision in *Harrison v. Day* reflected dominant political sentiment was evident in the subsequent actions of Governor Almond. Shortly after the court's decision, he delivered one last fiery segregationist speech and then bowed to the inevitable. On January 28, 1959, less than ten days after the court decisions, Almond broke with the Byrd machine. He went to the General Assembly to introduce a token integration plan that would replace massive resistance as the legislative response to desegregation. Five days later, twenty-one black students entered previously all-white schools in Arlington and Norfolk. Nearly five years after *Brown* was decided, massive resistance ended in Virginia, and desegregation finally began.[78]

It would take another year for desegregation to reach Richmond schools. When it finally came, desegregation in Richmond and elsewhere in Virginia was not accompanied by the violence experienced in places like Little Rock, Arkansas or Charlotte, North Carolina, where fifteen-year-old Dorothy Counts was spat on and pelted with sticks when she enrolled in a previously all-white school in 1957; or Nashville, Tennessee, where white mobs engaged in violent protests and even bombed a school in August 1957. At the same time, it should not escape notice that desegregation began later in Virginia than it did in some other southern states. Virginians, and Richmonders in particular, may have been more polite in their response to the advent of desegregation, but they were just as determined as those in other states to prevent and then limit it. And they were just as effective, if not more so.[79]

What followed the relatively brief period of massive resistance in Virginia, and throughout the South, was a decade of token integration. This period featured a mixture of resignation, cleverness, and claimed innocence on the part of southern officials. They resigned themselves to some integration, explored clever ways to limit its extent, and claimed innocence when their schemes were identified as discriminatory and obstructionist. Token integration was more attractive to middle-class whites than was massive resistance, which helps explain why token integration proved more durable. It may also explain why both state and federal courts were much more receptive to token integration than they were to massive resistance.

Token Integration

Before serving as an associate justice on the U.S. Supreme Court, Richmond native Lewis F. Powell, Jr., served as chair of the Richmond School Board for eight years, from 1952 to 1960. In 1959, he expressed the dominant attitude of whites in Richmond and in other metropolitan areas of the South when he promised that "public education will be continued in our city—although every proper effort will be made to minimize the extent of integration when it comes." In his capacity as chair of the school board and as a private citizen, Powell fought against the extreme measures proposed by diehard segregationists, and he argued publicly against the doctrine of interposition that Kilpatrick espoused. Powell recognized that Richmond would have to choose "between some integration and the abandonment of our public school education," and he clearly favored the former.[80]

Powell sincerely believed in the importance of public education, which undoubtedly influenced his stance against massive resistance. But choosing "some" integration over school closings was made easier by the fact of residential segregation. The simplest race-neutral way to assign students is to rely on geography and send students to neighborhood schools.By the 1950s, Richmond's neighborhoods—like Henrico County's—were heavily segregated, so if students were assigned to neighborhood schools, the schools would be as segregated as the neighborhoods. This is why, in 1959, Powell could state that there "are sound reasons to believe that a majority of the elementary schools [in Richmond] will have no more than a negligible percentage of integration for many years."[81]

The Pupil Placement Board and Conversion

Residential segregation, however, was not the only tool at the disposal of local and state school officials in Virginia; hence Powell's careful use of the plural when speaking about "sound reasons" to expect little integration. Where residential segregation alone did not minimize integration, the Pupil Placement Board would step in to complete the task.

There was no question that this board understood its mission. Its three original members acknowledged that their policy was "to fight, with every legal and honorable means, *any* attempted mixing of the races in public schools." And so they did. By 1960—six years after *Brown*—only a handful of black students had attended white schools. Indeed, the 1961–62 *Directory of the Richmond, Virginia, Public Schools*, a public document produced by the school district, continued to list "white" schools and "black" schools.[82]

The Pupil Placement Board, in cooperation with Richmond school officials, relied mostly on attendance zones for elementary schools that tracked neighborhoods and reinforced residential segregation in the schools. Past decisions about school sitings made this task easier, because schools were purposefully built squarely in the middle of white or black neighborhoods, as opposed to near the boundaries between them. Richmond then relied on a "feeder" system under which all black elementary schools would feed into only black middle schools, and all black middle schools would feed into only black high schools. White students were part of a separate feeder system. Individual students could request a transfer from the schools to which they were assigned, but the Pupil Placement Board retained a great deal of discretion to reject applicants for a host of reasons, including academic qualifications and the distance from home to school.[83]

In some areas of the city, attendance zones for white and black schools were completely separate. But residential segregation was not complete, so in other areas the attendance zones had to overlap in order to ensure that white students went to white schools and black students to black schools. This meant that in some areas, two schools, one white and one black, drew from the same neighborhood. Where this happened, the Pupil Placement Board assumed that white students wished to go to white schools and blacks to black schools, and they assigned students accordingly. The only way to avoid this automatic assignment was to request a transfer, which in turn triggered the board's broad discretion over transfer requests.[84]

Even this system, however, was not perfect because of the changing demographics in the Richmond School District, which by 1960 had become predominantly black. Assigning all black students to traditionally black schools and white students to traditionally white ones led to overcrowded black schools. One might think this would have put pressure on the Pupil Placement Board to assign some of the students in overcrowded black schools to white schools, especially in areas where attendance zones overlapped. It might be hard for the Richmond School Board and the Pupil Placement Board to explain why, in a single neighborhood all the white students were being sent to a school that had extra room, while all the black students were being sent to a school that had more students than desks.[85]

But the Richmond School Board had an answer for this problem: conversion. Where overcrowding in black schools was a problem, a formerly all-white school would be converted into a black one. The white students at school A would be transferred to another all-white school B, and school A would then be opened to (only) black students.[86]

The Pupil Placement Board and the Richmond School Board in the early 1960s were thus doing all they could to continue segregation. This meant that they took actions with every intent of assigning students to school on the basis of race. Doing so, in turn, plainly violated even the narrowest reading of *Brown*, which might not have required integration but certainly prohibited intentional segregation. Local and state school officials pleaded innocence and claimed racial neutrality. Their pleas might have been accepted if they had relied solely on a combination of residential segregation and neighborhood school assignments. But with each additional step taken to ensure segregation, it became harder to deny that race discrimination remained at the heart of student assignments.

The Court of Appeals for the Fourth Circuit recognized as much, and in 1963 it ruled that the Richmond School Board had to stop discriminating on the basis of race in student assignments. In saying so, the court simply repeated what the U.S. Supreme Court had said about a decade earlier in *Brown*, but the message bore repeating in Richmond. Beyond admonishing Richmond not to ignore *Brown*, however, the appeals court said relatively little. To the contrary, it made clear that Richmond was not required "to effect a general intermixture of races in the schools" but only to stop being so blatantly discriminatory in student assignments.[87]

Freedom of Choice

Richmond's school officials responded to this ruling by adopting various "freedom-of-choice" plans, which the lower federal courts upheld as constitutional until 1970. The earliest version of the freedom-of-choice plan still funneled students through the Pupil Placement Board but gave them and their parents a bit more room to choose schools. The plan changed in 1966, when the Virginia legislature disbanded the Pupil Placement Board and local officials regained complete control over student assignments. In Richmond, officials eliminated some of the more vague criteria that had been used to deny transfer requests. This meant that fewer requests would be denied on the basis of pretext, and students would be more able to exercise choice. But even as the ability to choose a school became more of a reality, its usefulness as a means of actually integrating schools remained limited.[88]

White students, as expected, virtually never chose to attend black schools. The burden of integration thus fell entirely on black students and their parents, many of whom were understandably reluctant to choose a white school. Their request might be granted, but that often signaled the beginning rather than the end of their hardship. The first hurdle involved transportation. Students could get to school by walking, getting their parents to take them, or paying to ride a city bus. There was no free transportation for city students. Given the degree of residential segregation, any black student who chose a white school was usually choosing a school outside of her neighborhood. As a result, for all but the few blacks who lived within walking distance of white schools, transportation was a problem.[89]

Even if the transportation problem were solved, black students did not always face a warm and welcoming environment when they enrolled at mostly white schools. Parents who believed strongly in the benefits of integration might be willing to push their children into a hostile environment. But it took a great deal of conviction about such benefits, which might not be immediately apparent, for parents to ignore the costs of such an education, which usually were front and center. A sense of the determination required is apparent from an exchange between Bill Brock, the principal of Tee-Jay, and the first black student to attend that school. "I hope you are happy here," Brock said to the student, who was reported to be "quiet and dignified." "I am not here to be happy," she answered.[90]

Most black students and their parents decided not to take a chance in white schools. Indeed, Richmond's freedom-of-choice plan was nearly as effective as the actions of the Pupil Placement Board had been in maintaining segregated schools. Integration began in Richmond in the fall of 1960, a full six years after *Brown*, when Carol Irene Swann and Gloria Jean Mead were admitted to the previously all-white Chandler Junior High School. In the fall of 1963, when freedom of choice was first adopted, only 312 of Richmond's 26,000 black students—roughly 1 percent—were attending school with white students. After seven years of freedom of choice, little had changed. Most schools, in 1970, remained overwhelmingly white or overwhelmingly black.[91]

In the meantime, the demographics of the district changed significantly. In 1954, the year *Brown* was decided, Richmond was a majority white district, though just barely. It became majority black in 1958, and by 1964, school enrollment there was 38 percent white and 62 percent black. By 1970, when freedom of choice was abandoned in compliance with a court order, the proportion of whites enrolled in the Richmond schools had fallen below 30 percent.[92]

Virginia Crockford, a white member of the Richmond School Board, acknowledged years later that token integration was an effort by state and localities "to buy time." One might ask: Buy time for what? Apparently, it was to buy time for those not interested in desegregation to make other plans—which they did. While Richmond toyed with integration, many middle-class families, overwhelmingly white, decamped for the suburbs. This meant that by the time courts got serious about desegregation in the early 1970s, it was essentially too late in Richmond. The same was true in many other cities across the country.[93]

Indeed, the pattern in Richmond was repeated elsewhere in the South. School districts throughout the region relied on pupil placement boards and freedom-of-choice plans to avoid or limit desegregation. Some relied on "minority-to-majority" plans that allowed students to transfer from a school in which they were a racial minority to one where they would be in the majority, a device that offered white parents an exit option if their children were reassigned by court order to a traditionally black school. Still others relied on grade-a-year plans, where desegregation would begin in either the first or twelfth grade and then expand by one additional grade each year. All the while, cities across the South were losing white residents, and urban public schools were becoming increasingly dominated by minority students. By 1968, the median percentage of blacks in southern city school districts was 42 percent; it would climb to 53 percent by 1976.[94]

Tentative Courts

Prior to 1968, most state and federal courts seemed content to move slowly when it came to enforcing *Brown*. Courts did not tolerate outright defiance of the *Brown* rulings, but they certainly did not push for much actual integration. Many courts instead endorsed what became known as the Briggs Dictum, which referred to the 1955 decision in *Briggs v. Elliot* by the United States Court of Appeals for the Fourth Circuit. In a widely noted and influential opinion, the court in *Briggs* sought to limit the reach of *Brown* by reading it narrowly: "the Constitution," the court wrote, "does not require integration.... It merely forbids the use of governmental power to enforce segregation."[95]

The Fourth Circuit reaffirmed this position in its 1963 decision involving Richmond, discussed above, when it reminded Richmond officials not to discriminate on the basis of race in student assignment, while simultaneously making it clear that *Brown* did not require integration.[96] Some federal judges disagreed with this narrow reading of *Brown* and took a more aggressive stance, but they were in the minority. The majority agreed that the *Brown* rulings prohibited intentional racial discrimination but did not mandate integration. With that distinction firmly in hand, most judges approved all but the most blatantly discriminatory methods of assignment, even if those methods, like freedom-of-choice plans, led to very little integration and therefore produced very little change on the ground.[97]

Even when courts struck down discriminatory assignment policies, they were reluctant to order widespread remedies. They might order the admission of the few black students who brought the case. But they refrained from issuing an order to admit other blacks who were similarly situated. Two cases out of Richmond illustrate the point.

In the first, a black girl and her parents sued in 1958 to challenge the Pupil Placement Board's decision to send her to a school five miles away instead of the school in her neighborhood. The plaintiffs also requested an order from the court prohibiting the school board from discriminating on the basis of race. The case was not decided until 1961. The District Court granted relief, concluding that the plaintiff had the right to attend a white school, but the court limited its order to *a single black girl*. The court refused to issue a broader injunction, emphasizing that the plaintiff "is admitted... as an individual, not as a class or a group." The clear signal: if black students wanted to challenge their school assignments, they would have to do it one at a time, case by case. Obviously, that would take quite a long time, which may have been the District Court's point.[98]

The second example comes from the early stages of *Bradley v. School Board*, a long running case that is the subject of the next chapter. Eleven African-American students in Richmond sued the school board and the Pupil Placement Board in 1961, requesting that they be admitted to white schools. They argued that the Pupil Placement Board had discriminated on the basis of race when it had rejected their requests to transfer from black to white schools. The District Court agreed and ordered the admission of these eleven plaintiffs to white schools. But the court refused to issue a broader injunction or to require Richmond to develop any kind of plan regarding school desegregation. A comprehensive plan was unnecessary, the court reasoned, because Richmond had made "a reasonable start toward a non-discriminatory school system." This was 1962, eight years after *Brown*. A total of 23,177 black students were enrolled in the Richmond school district that year, and all but 127 of them were still in all-black schools.[99]

In many ways, the slow pace of desegregation was the Supreme Court's fault, and it was a problem the Supreme Court eventually would try to fix. Scholars at the time and ever since have debated whether the Court was right to allow the South some time to get used to the *Brown* rulings and transition out of segregated schools. If the Court had instead required swift action, some argue, the South would have put up some resistance but then would have buckled and become used to integrated schools. Quite the contrary, others say: pushing the issue would have led to greater and fiercer resistance. Better to go slowly than to incite violence.[100]

That debate is beyond resolution but also beside the point in some respects. One could defend the Court's decision to move somewhat slowly initially, but it is hard to defend the Court's virtual absence from the field of desegregation from *Brown II* until the late 1960s. *Brown II* itself, decided in 1955, provided very little concrete direction to school districts or lower court judges. The Court subsequently issued a few decisions making it clear that outright defiance of the *Brown* rulings was prohibited. So Little Rock was not exempt from those rulings simply because people there did not like them. And schools in Prince Edward County, the Court concluded, could not remain closed to avoid desegregation. But these decisions simply marked what was clearly forbidden; they did not provide any more guidance as to what was required of school districts.[101]

This left district court judges with virtually unlimited discretion to fashion desegregation remedies. Some personally opposed integration and therefore were inclined to move slowly. Others faced intense community pressure to do so, and under the circumstances the pressure was difficult to resist. Federal judges are appointed for life and are for that reason immune from political pressure, at least in theory. But judges live in the same communities affected by their rulings, and life tenure on the bench does not guarantee that life off the bench will be pleasant. Because the Supreme Court left the issue so open-ended, judges who ordered more integration would take the blame for doing so. They could not point to a ruling from the Supreme Court and claim that their hands were tied.[102]

The Court made matters worse by giving tacit approval to the various ploys southern officials used to limit desegregation. In *Shuttlesworth v. Birmingham Board of Education*, decided in 1958, the Court upheld a pupil placement statute against a facial challenge. The Court made clear that plaintiffs might prevail if they could show that the law, as applied, discriminated, but the decision nonetheless left the law on the books. Southern politicians were gleeful at the result. Senator Russell Long from Louisiana captured the sentiment of many when he opined that the decision "shows a willingness of the Court to settle for token integration."[103]

The following year, in 1959, the Court declined to review a lower court decision that upheld Nashville's desegregation plan, which allowed both the grade-a-year approach and minority-to-majority transfers. Technically, when the Court declines to review a decision, it implies no view as to the merits of the case. But in this case, *Kelley v. Board of Education of Nashville*, three justices dissented, indicating that they believed the case should be heard and signaling that the justices had considered the issue. Moreover, southern officials, who watched the case closely, interpreted the Court's actions as approval of Nashville's plans and a further sign that the Court was willing to tolerate token gestures toward desegregation.[104]

The South took full advantage of these decisions, and the legal uncertainty they helped create, by enacting schemes that seemed on the surface to comply with the *Brown* rulings but in reality led to little change. For years, most judges went along with this wink-and-nod approach to compliance, which meant that very little desegregation occurred in the decade after *Brown*. As of 1964, only about 2 percent of all black students in the South attended schools with whites. As historian James Patterson points out: "virtually all southern black children who had entered first grade in 1954 and who remained in southern schools graduated from all-black schools twelve years later."[105]

Southern politicians and southern judges, however, did not know when to quit. Perhaps if they had tolerated a bit more integration, or perhaps if their assignment plans had not been so obviously discriminatory, the Supreme Court would have continued to allow the South to go its own way on desegregation. But southern officials seemed content to block desegregation as long as southern judges would tolerate it, and southern judges seemed quite tolerant. In hindsight, the Supreme Court's return to the field appears inevitable. Indeed, it seems fair to say that the South invited a response, and a forceful one, by the Supreme Court.[106]

SIGNS OF CHANGE: THE 1964 CIVIL RIGHTS ACT AND *GREEN V. NEW KENT COUNTY*

When the Court did return to the field in 1968, in *Green v. New Kent County*, it finally had the support of the other branches of the federal government. The Civil Rights Act of 1964 contained two provisions that bolstered efforts to desegregate schools. One authorized the federal government to bring desegregation suits, which took some pressure off the NAACP Legal Defense Fund and added the weight and prestige of the Justice Department. The other allowed the Department of Health, Education, and Welfare (HEW) to cut off federal funds to schools that did not desegregate. The HEW guidelines outlined the steps required for schools to remain eligible for funding. Timid at first, these guidelines became increasingly insistent that school districts actually desegregate their schools. The guidelines also provided lower courts with political cover, as district court judges could and did incorporate the regulations into their own decrees.[107]

Here, again, the South could look to itself for blame. Southern resistance to *Brown* helped trigger the Civil Rights Act of 1964. As legal historian Michael J. Klarman has described, the *Brown* rulings pushed racial politics in the South, especially in the Deep South, hard to the right. Politicians interested in attaining or keeping office could not appear to be soft or moderate on racial issues, and many tolerated or invited harsh responses to those pushing against segregation and in favor of voting rights. In this climate, violence was inevitable. When police beat civil rights demonstrators and blasted them with fire hoses in Alabama and Mississippi, television cameras documented the images for a shocked and disgusted northern audience. No longer complacent, many northerners and their representatives in Congress became supporters of federal legislation protecting civil rights. Other factors motivated passage of the Civil Rights Act, to be sure, and *Brown* may have also influenced passage of the Act by encouraging civil rights demonstrations in the first place. But southern resistance to *Brown* undoubtedly played a role, albeit perverse and unintended, in securing passage of the Act.[108]

The Civil Rights Act, in turn, may have encouraged the Supreme Court to put some muscle into its desegregation jurisprudence. Prior to the Act, the other branches of the federal government sent mixed signals, at best, about desegregation. President Eisenhower was ostentatiously lukewarm about *Brown*, and Congress was split largely, though not entirely, along sectional lines. President John F. Kennedy was not much better, at least at first. He ultimately proposed the framework for the Civil Rights Act in 1963, shortly after watching—along with the rest of the country—the violence that greeted civil rights demonstrators in Birmingham.[109]

The Court's decision in *Green v. New Kent County* changed everything. The case was simple enough. Rural New Kent County, which borders Henrico County in Virginia, had two schools. Watkins, on the west side, served blacks; New Kent, on the east, served whites. Whites and blacks lived in the same neighborhoods, which was not uncommon in rural areas. Segregated housing patterns were more prevalent in southern (and northern) cities than in rural parts of the South. For years, white and black students were bused across New Kent County in order to maintain segregated schools. For the first decade after *Brown*, the county did nothing to change assignments, and the schools remained totally segregated. In 1965, the county adopted a freedom-of-choice plan in order to comply with HEW guidelines and remain eligible for federal funds. As anyone would have predicted, the plan led to very little integration. No whites chose to attend Watkins, and relatively few blacks chose to attend New Kent.[110]

The plaintiffs argued that New Kent County had not done enough to comply with *Brown*. The lawyer for New Kent County, Frederick T. Gray, disagreed. He insisted during oral argument before the U.S. Supreme Court that freedom-of-choice plans satisfied the *Brown* rulings because those decisions only required that states "take down the fence" keeping students apart. They did not mandate integration. Chief Justice Warren expressed skepticism: "Isn't the net result that while they took down the fence, they put booby traps in place of it, so there won't be any white children going to a Negro school?" Gray was unbowed: "If the free choice of an American is a booby trap," he replied, "then this plan has booby traps."[111]

In an opinion written by Justice Brennan, the Court declared the end of "all deliberate speed" and spoke as if the duty of school districts had been clear all along. *Brown II* charged school boards, Brennan wrote, "with the affirmative duty to take whatever steps might be necessary to convert to a unitary system in which racial discrimination would be eliminated root and branch." The school board must "come forward with a plan that promises realistically to work, and promises realistically to work *now*." What the Court meant by a plan that would "work" was relatively clear: the plan had to result in integration and convert the district "promptly to a system without a 'white' school and a 'Negro' school, but just schools."[112]

Despite Brennan's suggestion to the contrary, the Court in *Green* did more than just reinforce *Brown II*. The Court converted *Brown II*'s vague mandate to desegregate into a clear charge to integrate—and to do so immediately. By claiming that *Brown II* required as much, the Court relieved itself of the obligation to explain why it was shifting course, though the Court hinted at one obvious cause: impatience with southern intransigence. As the Court explained: "In determining whether [the board satisfied *Brown II*] by adopting its 'freedom-of-choice' plan, it is relevant that this first step did not come until some 11 years after *Brown I* was decided and 10 years after *Brown II* directed the making of a 'prompt and reasonable start.'" The Court may also have been emboldened by the increasingly stringent HEW guidelines, which had been altered in 1966 to require not simply the cessation of segregation but the achievement of some integration.[113]

Although clearer than it had been in *Brown II*, the Court in *Green* nonetheless left some important questions unanswered. How much integration, exactly, would be required? Perfect racial balance? How long would the "affirmative obligation" to integrate last? And what steps, exactly, would districts have to take to satisfy this obligation? In New Kent County, this last question, at least, was easy to answer. Given the lack of residential segregation, the district could simply institute a policy of neighborhood schools and *stop* busing students across the county. If everyone who lived on the east side attended one school, while those on the west side attended the other, the schools would be integrated because neighborhoods were integrated.

From this perspective, *Green* was also easy to justify as a remedy for past school segregation. Legal remedies generally share the goal of restoring the victim, as best possible, to the state of affairs that existed before the illegal act. In New Kent County, there was never a period where the schools were integrated; as long as there were public schools, essentially, there were laws requiring segregation. It was nonetheless plausible to imagine that, absent the law commanding school segregation, the schools would have been integrated because the neighborhoods were integrated. Requiring integration was thus a way, at least in New Kent County, to establish the state of affairs that would have existed absent the (now unconstitutional) law that required segregation.

But what about urban areas in the South where whites and blacks did not live in the same neighborhoods? In those districts, it was not so easy to imagine that schools would have been integrated but for laws requiring segregation, for the simple reason that a race-neutral policy of sending students to neighborhood schools would have produced mostly segregated schools. Indeed, widespread school segregation in the North demonstrated that neighborhood attendance policies in combination with residential segregation could produce significant school segregation on their own, without any assistance from a law specifically requiring school segregation. Would urban districts in the South be required to overcome the effects of residential segregation in order to achieve integrated schools? And if they were, would school districts in the North have a similar obligation, or would this burden fall only on the South because of its history of laws explicitly commanding school segregation?

The Court did not answer any of these questions in *Green*, but the impatient tone of the opinion and the emphasis on results provided clues to how they eventually would be answered. The Court in *Green* vowed—to the South and perhaps to itself—that evasion and delay would no longer be tolerated. Most white southerners would not acknowledge that they bore some responsibility for the Court's reaction. To the contrary, many clung to the notion of "freedom of choice" as if it were a fundamental right and an anchored tradition in public education. "One would find," one HEW official said, "that freedom to choose one's school was being talked about in the South in the same breath as the freedoms of speech and assembly under the First Amendment." White southerners ignored the fact that school segregation, in place for decades, itself violated the supposedly sacrosanct principle of free choice. They also refused to admit that freedom-of-choice plans were always meant to be a subterfuge to avoid desegregation, and that they were popular precisely because they were so effective in this regard.[114]

Too Late?

Green opened a new chapter in the desegregation story, and many southerners predicted, with alarm, only one possible conclusion: massive integration, including busing where housing patterns were segregated. Georgia's governor, Lester Maddox, responded to the *Green* decision by ordering all state flags to be flown at half-mast. The alarmed predictions about the importance of *Green* were accurate as a measure of the Court's newfound determination. The Court did turn a corner in *Green* and, indeed, later authorized the use of busing for desegregation in 1971 in *Swann v. Charlotte-Mecklenburg Board of Education*. But there were already signs at the time of *Green* that the Court might be acting too late and that integrated schools might yet prove elusive.[115]

As described earlier, many urban school systems in the South had by 1968 already lost a lot of white students, some to private academies but most to the suburbs. (The same was true in the North, where desegregation cases were just getting under way.) This demographic trend showed little sign of abating. The Richmond school district was typical of many. It had been losing white students since the year that *Brown* was decided, and by the time of *Green* the district was two-thirds black. Even if a court were to order busing, a predominantly black school district might be difficult to integrate, and busing might become self-defeating by spurring even more white flight. Indeed, in 1968, the Richmond school district sponsored a study of school attendance patterns. The authors of the report concluded that the only realistic way to integrate Richmond schools would be to merge Richmond and surrounding Henrico and Chesterfield counties, which were overwhelmingly white.[116]

In addition, by 1968 a visible cleavage in black opinion had emerged over school desegregation. This was the era of black nationalism and the repudiation, by some, of the idea of integration. Stokely Carmichael and Charles V. Hamilton, for example, wrote in *Black Power* in 1967 that school and housing integration rested on "the idea that 'white' is automatically superior and 'black' is by definition inferior. For this reason, 'integration' is a subterfuge for the maintenance of white supremacy." This was also the era of black riots, a violent manifestation of the same frustration expressed by black intellectuals tired of trying to court white favor. Indeed, *Green* was argued the day before Martin Luther King was assassinated on April 4, and King's assassination touched off rioting in 125 American cities over the course of the summer. The Court could say all it wanted about integration, but in urban areas throughout the country, blacks questioned the very idea of integration while whites recoiled at the self-destructive behavior among blacks in inner cities.[117]

The same year, 1968, was also the year of Richard Nixon, who was elected in the fall following the *Green* decision. He campaigned on a platform to restore law and order and to block aggressive efforts by courts and federal agencies to desegregate schools, especially through busing. The timing could hardly have been worse from the perspective of those who equated desegregation with meaningful integration. Nixon's election signaled the end of the remarkably brief period of time when all three branches of the federal government pushed hard to desegregate schools. Desegregation is usually depicted as a long saga. But in many respects desegregation was like an unreliable car: it took forever to warm up, ran well for a brief period, and then sputtered and eventually died.[118]

Consider the overall timing. During the first decade after the *Brown* rulings, little happened. Movement began in 1964 when the Civil Rights Act was passed, but the first steps were tentative. In 1966, HEW issued guidelines that required school districts to take meaningful steps to achieve integration, and some courts incorporated those guidelines into their decrees. Two years later, the Court decided *Green* and signaled that it, too, was getting serious about integration. Less than one year later, however, Richard Nixon occupied the White House, where he kept his promise to slow down school desegregation. He instructed the Justice Department and HEW officials to ease their efforts and directed them to oppose the NAACP in some desegregation cases.

Thus, just as the Court was getting on the integration bus, the executive branch was getting off. Many activists and commentators lament the lost promise of *Brown* and contend, with justification, that *Brown* was something of a failure if measured by the extent of lasting school integration sparked by the decision. What is rarely noticed, however, is how little chance the federal government, including the Court itself, gave *Brown* to succeed. For the mere seven months between the Court's decision in *Green* and Nixon's inauguration, one could fairly say that all three branches of government were committed not just to desegregation but to integration. At every other point, from the time of *Brown* until today, at least one branch of the federal government either acted to limit the reach of *Brown* or did next to nothing to enhance the likelihood that black and white students would actually attend school together.

CONCLUSION

So "why didn't Richmond ever desegregate?"

Some would say, as Eisenhower said of the *Brown* decision, that it is because "it is difficult through law and through force to change a man's heart." The implication is that the Supreme Court, with help from Congress and the president, tried its best to integrate the schools but simply could not. The lesson to be drawn is that, as the saying goes, "stateways can't change folkways." Whatever general truth may be contained in that saying, it is an inapt lesson to be drawn from the desegregation experience because, in reality, the state did not actually do all that much to force change. It was not so much a case of trying and failing as a case of not really trying in the first place. Whether the Court, Congress, and the president lacked the *ability* to affect change on this front is unknown and perhaps unknowable. What we do know is that, save for a brief few years, they lacked the will.[119]

This was true of lower federal courts and state courts as well. For more than a decade after the *Brown* rulings, most of these courts acted in accordance with the interests of middle-class whites, who had no real interest in integration. Middle-class whites wanted to protect their schools from closure while avoiding any significant influx of black students for as long as possible. To do so, they opposed school-closure laws—willing to risk a small bit of integration if that was the only way to avoid the destruction of their schools. Courts aided them in this task by declaring state school-closure laws unconstitutional. But middle-class whites were not interested in meaningful integration, nor were the courts, at least at first. By the time the Supreme Court ordered integration in *Green*, many middle-class whites had given up on their urban schools and had instead headed for private schools or, more commonly, the suburbs.

If one had to pick a winner in the early contest over school desegregation, it would have to be southern, metropolitan white parents. They did not win every battle, to be sure. *Brown* and the end of legally mandated segregation was certainly a loss. But from 1955 until 1968, desegregation proceeded on their terms. They defeated massive resistance by pushing for schools to remain open, and they supported efforts, endorsed by courts, to limit desegregation to token numbers. And they used the years between *Brown* and *Green* to make alternative arrangements.

These parents did not subscribe to a particular political ideology, nor did they endorse extremists at either end of the spectrum. They rejected the cause of massive resistance as well as that of massive integration. They acted instead to protect their own interests. Desegregation was less threatening to their interests than shuttering schools, so they chose the former over the latter. Massive integration was more threatening than token integration, so they chose the latter over the former. They won both times, both in legislative arenas and in the courts.

The initial fights over desegregation presaged ensuing contests over cross-district busing, school funding, school choice, and standards and testing. Middle-class, mostly suburban whites would participate in all of these fights, as later chapters describe, and their motivation would remain the same throughout: to protect their children and the schools they attended. Reforms that helped other children might be fine, provided that those reforms did not threaten the interests of their own children. Once reforms threatened their interests, middle-class parents fought back, and they usually won.

A perfect example of this trend came in the next battle over school desegregation. After middle-class whites decamped for the suburbs, they circled the wagons to shield their children and their schools from the reach of desegregation orders. In the early 1970s, it appeared that courts might reach across district lines and pull suburban students back into city schools in order to desegregate them. One of the most important contests occurred in Richmond, where a district court judge, Robert R. Merhige, ordered the consolidation of the Richmond school district with two neighboring suburban districts, Henrico and Chesterfield. In the end, Judge Merhige's ruling was overturned. The story of that case, and the larger story of what might have been, are the subjects of the next chapter.

CHAPTER 2

Don't Cross That Line

In early January 1970, *Time* announced that "Middle Americans" were the magazine's "Man and Woman of the Year." This group of middle-class, mostly suburban whites had been rediscovered in the 1968 election when Nixon famously appealed to the "silent majority." *Time* did its best to capture the mindset of this amorphous group, which in *Time*'s description included teenagers who watched John Wayne movies, mothers who feared rising crime rates and declining moral standards, policemen who arrested and sometimes beat political and antiwar protestors, members of the Chamber of Commerce, and followers of the Reverend Billy Graham. Neither rich nor poor, these ordinary men and women believed firmly in America and the American dream but felt like they were losing their grip on the country. Surrounded by signs of dysfunction in cities, confusion and death in Vietnam, and a burgeoning drug culture among the youth, Middle Americans felt like their way of life was under siege.[1]

Nowhere was this more true than in the field of public education. In the early 1960s, the Supreme Court prohibited prayer and Bible reading in the schools, and a few years later it began pushing hard for school integration. As one southern congressman said crudely, the Court "put Negroes in the schools and now they're driving God out." By the turn of the new decade, it seemed clear that courts would order busing for desegregation, and it also seemed clear that school desegregation would no longer be confined to southern schools. Forced busing thus became a national issue and a looming threat to the Middle American's way of life, where buying a house in the suburbs in a good school district was the reward for hard work and playing by the rules.[2]

Now it seemed like the rules were changing, and most middle-class whites could not—or would not—understand why. They refused to accept responsibility for the actions of those who had preceded them or for present-day injustices, because the idea that inequalities pervaded American society did not fit their image of America. As *Time* described it, the Middle American "cannot believe that the society he has come to accept as the best possible on earth, the order he sees as natural, contains wrongs so deeply built-in that he does not notice them." This was especially true when it came to issues of race. The nation was moving, in the words of the federal Kerner Commission, "toward two societies, one white, one black—separate and unequal." But most white Americans chose not implicate themselves: "What white Americans have never fully understood—but what the Negro can never forget—is that white society is deeply implicated in the ghetto. White institutions created it, white institutions maintain it, and white society condones it."[3]

Instead of focusing on historical or present injustices, Middle Americans expressed outrage at attempts to correct them, and busing to desegregate schools became a primary target. As *Time* reported, Middle Americans would quite sincerely protest that they were not prejudiced against blacks and would support efforts to improve the education of black students. But the idea of sacrificing their own children's educations in order to improve opportunities for black students "appall[ed] them."[4]

Middle Americans might have favored integration over the closing of public schools, but this did not mean that they favored busing over neighborhood schools. This was as true in Richmond as it was elsewhere, in both the North and the South, with little exception. When it came to the issue of busing, Middle Americans revolted. They pleaded with politicians and judges, arguing in Richmond and elsewhere that busing would destroy public education, by which they meant their neighborhood schools. They demonstrated in the streets, appropriating the symbols and songs of the civil rights era, marching to the sounds of "We Shall Overcome." And when all else failed, those who could, fled—either to private schools or to the suburbs.

The big question in the early 1970s was whether the urban school bus would follow those who fled to the suburbs. Would busing for desegregation cross school district lines? If busing was inherently controversial, busing across district lines was radioactive, especially when this meant crossing from city to suburb and back again. Nonetheless, for a very brief moment in time, it looked as if this might actually happen, and the place where it was supposed to begin was Richmond, Virginia. To the dismay of suburbanites across the country, who followed case of *Bradley v. Richmond School Board* in national papers, Judge Robert Merhige ordered the consolidation of the Richmond, Henrico, and Chesterfield county school districts for the purpose of desegregating the entire metropolitan area. In doing so, Judge Merhige became the first federal judge to order urban and suburban districts to participate in a metropolitan-wide desegregation plan.

He was also one of the last. The Court of Appeals for the Fourth Circuit overruled Judge Merhige, and the appellate court's decision was affirmed by an equally divided Supreme Court, which tied four-to-four because Justice Powell recused himself. The tie meant that the decision had no effect beyond Richmond, which in turn meant that a rule for the entire country had to await another case. In 1974, the Court took a case from Detroit, *Milliken v. Bradley*, and in a well-known five-to-four opinion ruled against interdistrict busing, essentially confirming the Fourth Circuit's position in the Richmond case. Although the Richmond case has been all but lost to history, it is a fascinating and crucially important episode in the history of Richmond and school desegregation generally. In many ways, *Bradley v. Richmond School Board* was a dry run for *Milliken v. Bradley*, helping to set the stage not just for that later decision but for the future of school desegregation in the Richmond area and beyond.[5]

When the dust finally settled in the summer of 1974, Middle Americans were (again) the clear winners. Members of the same group had fought a decade earlier to avoid school closures and then to limit the amount of desegregation that occurred. Courts had assisted them in achieving both goals, and they did so again on the issue of interdistrict integration. The Supreme Court, first in *Bradley v. Richmond School Board* and then in *Milliken v. Bradley*, spared the suburbs—where most white, middle-class parents now lived—from school desegregation. The Court continued to require all-out desegregation in the cities but made it virtually impossible to include suburban schools in the effort. *Bradley v. Richmond School Board* and *Milliken v. Bradley* essentially told parents that they and their children would be safe once they reached the suburbs.

In other cases, the Supreme Court shielded the suburbs against legal challenges to zoning policies that explicitly kept out the poor and implicitly kept out minorities. In so doing, as one scholar described, "the Supreme Court began to lift from white America responsibility for the ghetto." The Court's decisions played to the self-image of Middle Americans by exonerating them from charges that they were responsible for the continued separation of white and black students, and by assuring them that they had earned the right to remain quartered in their suburban sanctuaries, safely beyond the reach of court orders and urban schools.[6]

The end result was to leave urban public schools to poor, mostly minority students. Of all the various consequences of school desegregation, this was perhaps the most significant and the longest lasting. Indeed, in some ways, the *Milliken* decision marked the beginning of the modern and still current era of urban public education. We have been living with the aftermath of *Milliken* ever since and trying, with little success, to make urban schools of concentrated poverty equal to schools of relative affluence. Those efforts are the subject of future chapters. This chapter continues the story of how we got here and begins, like chapter 1, in Richmond.

CIRCA 1970: ON THE EVE OF BUSING

As the new decade began, metropolitan Richmond looked a lot like other areas around the country. The city itself was losing population and becoming predominantly minority. In 1950, the population in Richmond was two-thirds white. By 1970, it was split evenly between blacks and whites. Meanwhile, the population in the neighboring suburbs of Henrico and Chesterfield counties was exploding, having tripled during the same twenty-year period. These counties remained overwhelmingly white.[7]

Residential Segregation: Where and Why

There is no single explanation for this dramatic demographic shift in Richmond, which was repeated in metropolitan areas across the country, whether in the South, North, East, or West. Instead, a mix of factors were responsible, some private and some public. Economics caused some of the shift. Housing in the suburbs often cost more, which meant that it was available primarily to the middle-class residents of Richmond looking to leave the city. Given that blacks were disproportionately poor, middle-class flight often meant white flight. Preferences also undoubtedly played a role in shaping residential patterns; some whites simply preferred to live near other whites and some blacks preferred to live near other blacks.[8]

But economics and preferences only partially explained the segregation that existed between Richmond and its surrounding suburbs. Public and private discrimination in housing also played a crucial role in keeping blacks in the city and out of the suburbs. The Federal Housing Authority (FHA) had for decades promoted residential segregation by subsidizing mortgages only in racially homogenous neighborhoods and by refusing to finance the rehabilitation of older housing in blighted urban neighborhoods. Banks followed the lead of the FHA and refused to lend money to those looking to buy homes in integrated neighborhoods or in dilapidated urban areas. The end result was to nudge whites into all-white suburban areas. The federal government also provided money for highway construction, which made travel between city and suburb easier. The federal government thus subsidized suburbanization by effectively lowering housing costs in the suburbs and making transportation from home to work easier.[9]

Suburban governments and white suburbanites, in turn, did their part to make sure that blacks did not follow them. Public housing, for example, was concentrated in the city. Local governments could seek federal money for public housing, but they were not required to do so. Richmond sought the money; Henrico and Chesterfield did not. As a result, public housing was built in Richmond and was simply unavailable in Henrico and Chesterfield. The public housing that was built in Richmond, moreover, was built exclusively in black neighborhoods and was occupied almost exclusively by black residents. Making matters worse, urban renewal projects, also funded by the federal government, cleared away slums but offered little replacement housing, thus displacing black neighborhoods without creating new ones. As blacks resettled in different parts of the city, whites in those neighborhoods began to leave.[10]

Local governments, like Henrico and Chesterfield, also used exclusionary zoning to keep out the poor. By allowing only single-family housing in many areas, for example, and by requiring minimum lot sizes, zoning laws drove up the price of housing. Single-family houses on ample lots were beyond the reach of the poor, which effectively meant that they were beyond the reach of many minority residents as well.

Those black residents who could afford single-family houses in the suburbs were unlikely to be guided to white neighborhoods. Real estate agents openly discriminated on the basis of race, steering white purchasers to white neighborhoods and blacks to black ones. Newspapers played along, allowing advertisements for "black" homes and "white" homes. Real estate agents also engaged in blockbusting: they would help "flip" a neighborhood from white to black by playing on fears among white homeowners who worried that one black neighbor would lead to another, and then another. When one black homeowner purchased a house in a white neighborhood, real estate agents would contact other homeowners and encourage them to sell before it was too late.[11]

Private individuals played a part as well. Racially restrictive covenants could not be enforced by courts after 1948. The Supreme Court, in the famous case of *Shelley v. Kraemer*, held it unconstitutional for courts to enforce private covenants that prohibited the sale of housing to a black buyer. But the fact that courts would not enforce covenants did not make them disappear, and houses throughout the Richmond metropolitan area continued to have restrictive covenants into the 1970s. Local residents also resorted to intimidation and sometimes violence to deter black buyers from seeking to move into white neighborhoods.[12]

Richmond, even more so than other cities, also faced obstacles to expanding its boundaries to include at least some portion of the surrounding suburbs. Rules about annexation differ among the states, but most require consent from the citizens or property owners in the areas to be annexed. In Virginia, annexation is more significant than elsewhere because counties and cities are distinct rather than overlapping. Land annexed by cities is thus lost for tax purposes to the counties. Annexation battles in Virginia consequently have been waged for higher stakes than in other states, though cities like Richmond nonetheless managed to grow through annexation in the early part of the twentieth century.[13]

Annexation in the Richmond area became caught up in racial politics in the 1960s and 1970s. White business and political leaders in the city favored annexation of mostly white residents in order to maintain power and a healthy tax base. But an odd couple of white suburbanites and black political leaders opposed annexation. White suburbanites opposed annexation because they did not wish to be a part of Richmond; black political leaders opposed it because they feared dilution of political power.

Annexation also fell victim to the struggle over school desegregation. After a lengthy court battle, Richmond annexed a portion of Henrico County in 1970 and substantially increased the percentage of whites (and especially white students) in the city. One year later, however, at precisely the same time that Judge Mehrige began ordering busing in Richmond, the Virginia legislature imposed a five-year moratorium on annexation. Annexing suburban areas would have meant including them in busing plans, a fact not lost on the legislators who ordered the moratorium. When the moratorium was finally lifted in 1979, large counties like Henrico and Chesterfield were granted immunity from annexation. As part of the same legislative package, the legislature provided more financial aid to Richmond. School desegregation, as we shall see, followed the same course of keeping the suburbs and cities separate while offering more aid to the cities.[14]

All of these factors combined, in ways impossible to untangle, to keep the suburbs mostly white and cities like Richmond mostly minority. Some middle-class blacks managed to find housing in the suburbs, usually at an inflated price, but they tended to locate in small, mostly black enclaves. The vast majority of blacks in the Richmond area, like the vast majority of blacks in most metropolitan areas, resided in the city itself.

The Federal Government's Tepid Response

For a brief period of time, the federal government considered affirmative efforts to integrate the suburbs. More precisely, one member of the Nixon administration, George Romney, pursued this agenda. Romney, the father of 2008 Republican presidential candidate Mitt Romney, was a liberal Republican and former governor of Michigan before Nixon appointed him secretary of housing and urban development (HUD). Romney seemed to operate in "an orbit all his own," while and HUD secretary he tried to force open the suburbs.[15]

The program was called the Open Communities initiative, and through it HUD was trying to put some teeth into the 1968 Fair Housing Act, which prohibited housing discrimination but had little remedial bite. Romney proposed cutting off federal highway funds and other infrastructure subsidies for suburban municipalities that used exclusionary zoning to block low-income housing and maintain residential segregation. Romney worried about the "ominous trend toward stratification of our society by race and by income." His colleagues in the Nixon administration worried instead about political backlash from powerful suburbanites. In a memorandum to the president, John Ehrlichman wrote that Romney "keeps loudly talking about [suburban integration] in spite of our efforts to shut him up." Nixon wrote in the margins simply: "Stop this one."[16]

Stop him they did. The White House released a statement on housing segregation in June 1971, in which the administration pledged to prosecute individuals who violated the Fair Housing Act, but not to push hard for integration. Nixon bizarrely likened suburbanization to exploring the frontier, stating that "through the ages, men have fought to defend their homes; they have struggled and often dared the wilderness." He then made clear that in his view, economic segregation was a natural outgrowth of this freedom to explore and that "forced integration of the suburbs is not in the national interest." Two years later, Romney was forced out of HUD, and Nixon instructed his replacement not to pursue challenges to exclusionary zoning in the suburbs.[17]

The Need for Interdistrict Remedies

The public school population tended to reflect overall residential patterns, in Richmond and elsewhere. The two did not match perfectly because some affluent parents, who were an overwhelmingly white group, remained in cities like Richmond and sent their children to private schools. City populations were thus often whiter than the public school population. In Richmond, for example, public school enrollment was predominantly minority by 1970, even though the city itself was half white and half black. Public school enrollment in Chesterfield and Henrico, by contrast, was over 90 percent white.[18]

Freeman High School in Henrico County reflected this demographic trend. In 1970, it enrolled only a handful of black students. Thomas Jefferson High School in Richmond was something of an outlier at the time, as it remained an island of white students in a predominantly minority district. In 1970, only

8 percent of Tee-Jay's students were black. The school had changed relatively little since the *Brown* rulings, reflecting the city's determination to move slowly and the desire of those connected with Tee-Jay to resist change. In addition to remaining mostly white, Tee-Jay continued to be academically rigorous, boasting more national merit semifinalists than any school in the Richmond metropolitan area—except Freeman.[19]

There was little doubt in 1970 that Richmond and Henrico would have to increase their efforts to desegregate their schools. The Court's 1968 decision in *Green v. New Kent County* made it clear that districts like Richmond and Henrico needed to come forward immediately with plans that promised real integration. Many foresaw, correctly, that courts would order students bused in order to desegregate the schools. All of that said, the demographics in each district made meaningful integration an unlikely prospect. It is hard to have much integration in a district, like Henrico, that is over 90 percent white. There was greater opportunity for integration in Richmond, given that the ratio of black to white students was sixty-five to thirty-five. But there was no guarantee that whites would remain in the district once previously all-white schools, like Tee-Jay, were integrated and white students found themselves in the minority.[20]

For integration to be both meaningful and stable, it seemed to many by 1970 that district lines would have to be crossed. Indeed, those who studied the issue came to this conclusion in the late 1960s. A 1969 report prepared for the Richmond School Board, which came to be known as the Sartain Report, concluded that school segregation within Richmond was due largely to housing patterns. The authors urged the passage of a meaningful open housing law, the construction of low-rent housing throughout the city rather than simply in minority neighborhoods, and better enforcement of a code of ethics for real estate agents. But they also recognized that only so much could be done with a school population that was close to two-thirds black. The study therefore concluded that "Richmond's public school system must be combined in some way with those of predominantly white Chesterfield and Henrico counties."[21]

Lewis Powell apparently reached a similar conclusion the same year. On his retirement from the Virginia Board of Education in 1969, just three years before he joined the U.S. Supreme Court, he said:

> In our larger metropolitan areas, there are income deficiencies and a racial mix which result in serious educational disadvantages. The injustice, as well as the potentially disastrous social consequences of this situation, have prompted action by government at all levels as well as the private segment of our communities. There is no longer any debate as to the need for vigorous action to right this educational imbalance.

As the *New York Times* later reported, Powell's colleagues interpreted his state-ment "as an endorsement of the proposal [in the Sartain Report] to achieve racial balance by merging the city and suburban schools."[22]

As Powell's statement suggested, suburban participation promised more than just racial integration. It also promised integration by class. The flight to the suburbs was predominantly white, but it was overwhelmingly middle-class. City schools, as a result, were becoming poorer. Desegregation remedies limited to urban school districts would thus involve mostly poor students, and high-poverty schools—whether white, black, or integrated—rarely performed well. Including the suburbs would thus benefit disadvantaged urban whites as much as disadvantaged blacks.[23]

Suburban participation also held out the promise of more equitable fund-ing. If districts were consolidated, funding would be more equitable because suburbanites would be required to share their property tax revenues with urban schools. Even if districts were not consolidated but buses crossed district lines, suburbanites would still have an incentive to spend money on urban schools because students from the suburbs would be attending them. In effect, interd-istrict integration would be a way to tie the fate of urban and suburban stu-dents together, much in the same way that the *Brown* lawyers had hoped deseg-regation would tie the fate of white and black students together.[24]

Under an interdistrict integration plan, enrollment in metropolitan schools might also stabilize because there would be fewer places for whites to flee. Most jobs remained in city centers, and most housing opportunities remained either in the cities or in nearby suburbs. Whites looking to avoid a metropolitan-wide desegregation decree would have to move far away from employment and choose among limited housing stock. Private schools were an option, obviously, but there were not enough to absorb more than a small fraction of white stu-dents. Not all parents, moreover, could afford both private school tuition and property taxes. The impetus to flee to a private school, or to a far-flung suburb, would also be reduced because public schools under a metropolitan-wide desegregation decree would remain predominantly white.[25]

For similar reasons, housing integration might increase. Whites would have less reason to flee the cities, and blacks might have more opportunities to move into the suburbs. There would be less incentive for whites to leave when blacks moved into a particular city neighborhood, because their arrival would not her-ald the transition to an all-black neighborhood school. Similarly, there might be reduced opposition—though it would not disappear altogether—to the move-ment of blacks into the suburbs if excluding them did not keep them out of suburban schools. More generally, families tend to make decisions about where to live in part based on school assignments. If all schools in a metropolitan region were to have roughly the same racial balance, race would be less of a factor when choosing a place to live.[26]

The need for suburban participation became clear at the same time that the Court awakened from its slumber and grew aggressive about school integration. The Court in *Green* required school boards and states to devise desegregation plans that would "work *now*." Three years later, in *Swann v. Charlotte-Mecklenburg Board of Education*, the Court concluded that lower courts could and should order busing when necessary to desegregate schools. More generally, the Court required school officials to "achieve the greatest possible degree of actual desegregation." For desegregation to "work" and for it to result in the "greatest possible degree" of actual racial mixing, the suburbs would have to be included.[27]

This was precisely the conclusion that Judge Merhige reached in 1972 in the Richmond school desegregation case, *Bradley v. Richmond School Board*. By that point, the case was more than a decade old, and Judge Merhige had already become one of the most unpopular men in Richmond.

BRADLEY V. RICHMOND SCHOOL BOARD

As mentioned in the previous chapter, *Bradley v. Richmond School Board* was originally filed in 1961. It began as a suit by eleven black students in Richmond who were denied permission by the Pupil Placement Board to transfer to white schools. The students succeeded in their challenge, but the judge, John D. Butzner, refused to order widespread relief. The Fourth Circuit affirmed the decision and mildly suggested (but did not require) that Richmond make a more concerted effort to desegregate its schools.[28]

As noted, Richmond then adopted a "freedom-of-choice" plan that supposedly offered students greater opportunity to choose schools than had been possible under the direction of the Pupil Placement Board. The change was more cosmetic than substantive; students' requests could still be denied on the basis of vague and broad criteria. Judge Butzner nonetheless upheld the plan in a 1964 decision, trusting the school board to administer it impartially. The plaintiffs appealed.[29]

The Fourth Circuit affirmed Judge Butzner's decision and endorsed Richmond's freedom-of-choice plan in 1965, holding that Richmond had no duty to promote integration and embracing neighborhood schools as the proper vehicle for educating children. The court did encourage Richmond to make greater efforts to integrate faculties, threatening more compulsion if those efforts did not succeed. But freedom of choice was allowed to continue for the time being.[30]

From 1966 to 1970, *Bradley v. Richmond School Board* lay dormant, but integration remained front and center in Richmond. White Richmonders, and especially the white papers, clung to freedom of choice and castigated those who demanded more. The *Richmond News Leader* published an editorial advocating racial cooperation to maintain good schools within Richmond. "For their part," the editorial advised, "Richmond's white parents should understand that affirmative integration of the public schools is here to stay." But the editors also issued a warning to those interested in "instant" integration. If blacks "press unreasonably for faculty integration, regardless of merit; if they insist upon the 'preferential' advantage granted by the court order; if they abuse the system of 'freedom of choice' in order to achieve instant integration under artificial circumstances, they probably will get what they ask—but they could trigger a disastrous flight of white families to the suburbs." So far as the Richmond establishment was concerned, "freedom of choice" was enough. Doing more would risk harm to everyone.[31]

But freedom of choice was not enough for the Supreme Court in 1968. The *Green* decision did not prohibit the use of freedom of choice per se, but the Court made its use contingent on its effectiveness. The goal now, clearly, was integration, and that would be the sole measure of desegregation plans. Braced by this development, the *Bradley* plaintiffs went back to court in March 1970.

Judge Merhige

When the plaintiffs returned to court, a new judge awaited them: Robert H. Merhige. A transplanted northerner who had attended law school in Richmond and returned there to practice after World War II, Merhige was appointed to the bench by President Lyndon Johnson in 1967. Merhige took over *Bradley v. Richmond School Board* when Judge Butzner was elevated to the U.S. Court of Appeals for the Fourth Circuit.[32]

Merhige was not a crusader for civil rights during his twenty-year career as a practicing lawyer. He showed basic kindness and respect toward black lawyers, which was exceptional for the time but not exactly heroic. In his early years as a judge, he continued his moderate ways, particularly in his approach to desegregation cases.[33]

This would change in the 1970s, and Merhige would become one of the most forceful proponents for meaningful and far-reaching desegregation measures. As a result, by the middle of the decade, he required twenty-four-hour protection by U.S. marshals. Segregationists spat in his face, threatened his family, shot his dog, and bombed the cottage on his property where his mother-in-law was living. The Ku Klux Klan held weekly parades outside his home and repeatedly threatened to abduct him. State and federal legislators called for his impeachment. The U.S. attorney uncovered not one but two plots to raise money to finance Merhige's assassination. His involvement in desegregation cases, not all concerning Richmond, earned him the unofficial title "commissioner of education." It also earned him the less vaulted title "the most hated man in Richmond."[34]

The First Busing Order

It all began when Merhige ordered busing in Richmond in 1970. On March 10, 1970, the plaintiffs filed a motion with a general request that the court order Richmond to create a unitary system as required by *Green*. The Richmond School Board admitted that Richmond schools were not unitary, according to the constitutional standards announced in *Green*. Judge Merhige gave the school board two months to develop a plan and scheduled hearings for June. The *Richmond Times-Dispatch* immediately sounded the alarm over busing, while Merhige toured Richmond to get a firsthand look at housing patterns.[35]

The school board prepared a desegregation plan with the assistance of HEW. Reflecting Nixon's determination to stall on desegregation and avoid busing, the HEW plan did not require busing. Editors at the *Richmond Times-Dispatch* immediately expressed doubt that the HEW plan would satisfy the court, as did the plaintiffs. The Fourth Circuit then issued its decision in *Swann v. Charlotte-Mecklenburg Board of Education* on May 26, 1970, in which it endorsed court-ordered busing to facilitate desegregation. This ruling, which would eventually be affirmed by the U.S. Supreme Court, cast a further shadow over the HEW plan.[36]

The plaintiffs submitted their own desegregation plan, prepared by noted desegregation expert Gordon Foster, which became known as the Foster plan. In contrast to the HEW plan, the Foster plan called for extensive busing. It also called for the pairing of white and black schools, which would involve, for example, all students in first through third grades attending one of the schools and all fourth- and fifth-grade students attending the other.[37]

At the hearing in June, Judge Merhige heard testimony about a range of issues: discriminatory housing practices in Richmond; the effect on Richmond's city budget if busing were ordered; the middle-class flight to the suburbs that a busing order would trigger; and the increasing amount of housing segregation across the nation. Ultimately, Merhige rejected the HEW plan and directed the school board to produce a new plan by late July. He warned board members that if they failed to produce an acceptable plan, he would have no choice but to rely on the plaintiffs' proposal. He clearly wanted the board to include busing in their new plan. Without busing, too many schools would remain segregated. He also rejected—implicitly at first and later explicitly—the notion that school segregation that occurred because of residential segregation was simply "de facto" and not the responsibility of the state or localities. "Negroes live where they live," Merhige said, "because they have no other choice."[38]

A wave of applications by whites to private schools followed the ruling, and some Richmond parents tried unsuccessfully to send their children to Henrico County public schools. By the summer, however, it was estimated that only a few hundred of Richmond's 53,000 public school students would actually transfer to private schools, most of which were already at capacity. In the meantime, protests began and antibusing rhetoric grew more heated. Opponents of busing portrayed children as the victims of meddlesome federal courts and made emotional pleas to keep children in their own neighborhoods. They picketed the courthouse, protesting that "our children are not cattle." Some parents became overwrought; one exclaimed that "the collar of governmental control has tightened around my neck so that I am about to strangle" and invoked Patrick Henry's words: "Give me liberty or give me death."[39]

Merhige Raises the Possibility of Consolidation

Before the July deadline, Judge Merhige sent a letter to the lawyers in the case that proved to be a bombshell. He suggested that "the Richmond School Board discuss with Henrico and Chesterfield county officials 'the feasibility or possibility of consolidation of school districts.'" Henrico and Chesterfield counties, up until that point, had not been parties to the case. Merhige's suggestion was just that; it had no legal force behind it. Nonetheless, and not surprisingly, it made a big splash. The *Richmond Times-Dispatch* called the letter "profoundly shocking" and "an incredible, gratuitous act that is likely to complicate the Richmond situation in particular [and] introduce a disturbing new element into the school integration controversy in general." In truth, they had not seen anything yet.[40]

At a closed meeting in late July, the Richmond School Board devised a revised desegregation plan that involved some busing of older students. It passed by a vote of four to three. In a separate vote, which was unanimous with two abstentions, the board directed its attorneys to ask that the Henrico and Chesterfield county school boards be joined as defendants in *Bradley v. Richmond School Board*. The board also directed its attorneys to request that the court order the consolidation of the three school districts. Judge Merhige's letter, it seems, had found a receptive audience. Three days after this meeting, the Richmond School Board submitted to the court its new desegregation plan along with its "surprise motion" requesting consolidation.[41]

Protests followed. The *Richmond Times-Dispatch* reacted with predictable alarm, calling the consolidation motion a "dangerous proposal." Lawyers for Chesterfield County moved to stay the case until the Supreme Court decided the *Swann v. Charlotte-Mecklenburg* appeal. The Richmond city attorney filed a motion claiming that busing violated the equal protection clause because some students were allowed to attend neighborhood schools while others were not. (The Richmond School Board was and remains an independent municipal agency, not formally controlled by the Richmond City Council; the two entities disagreed on consolidation, at least at first.) A group called Citizens Against Busing (CAB) organized rallies to protest both the board's busing plan as well as the merger proposal. The leader of the group, fundamentalist minister John Book of Chesterfield County, declared that "the combining of all races by force is Communism." Several thousand whites attended a freedom-of-choice rally at the Richmond Arena, sponsored by CAB, where they were greeted by banners proclaiming "Busing—Never" and "United We Stand—Divided We Fall."[42]

Another, more temperate, group formed in the affluent West End section of Richmond. Called the West End Concerned Parents Group, this organization opposed "busing without parental consent" and endorsed "the preservation of a strong neighborhood public school system." These antibusing activists strongly resisted the charge that they were against all integration. But they were not willing to sacrifice neighborhood schools. As one parent explained, "I think freedom of choice is a good idea. I have no objection to my children going to school with colored children, but I think anybody normally wants to go to school nearest their home."[43]

Nonetheless, worries about the *kind* of "colored children" who might participate in a busing plan were never far from the surface. The issue was one of class as much as of race. A West End mother, for example, explained that she supported the sort of "reasonable integration" that occurred through freedom of choice, whereby some middle-class black students attended West End schools. But she did not favor integrating students with "different socioeconomic values," and she worried that busing would bring her child into contact with a "different type of black child."[44]

It is easy from a distance to dismiss objections to busing as thin veils over the ugly face of racism, and often they were nothing more. But not always, and this is why busing was such a complicated issue. It is not as if all black parents were wild about busing; some were just as opposed as white parents. Moreover, a white or black parent without a trace of racism might nonetheless object to transporting her children away from local schools. As one father wrote to Judge Merhige: "I have never resisted the logical integration of public schools.... Although raised and educated in the South, I have always tried to judge a man on his merits." Busing, however, left this father with what he saw as three unpalatable alternatives: move to the suburbs, send his daughter to a private school, or put her on a bus "in dereliction of parental responsibility." Perceptions about schools were influenced by racial stereotypes, for sure, but they were also influenced by independent concerns about travel times, the safety of neighborhoods, and the quality of facilities, all of which made arguments about busing much more complex and difficult to parse than traditional objections to desegregation per se.[45]

Neither protests nor emotional pleas moved Judge Merhige. In August, he approved the school board's revised desegregation plan, which involved busing middle school and high school students and left elementary schools largely untouched. The compromise pleased almost no one. The plaintiffs thought it did not go far enough, and the defendants thought it went too far, too soon. But Judge Merhige held fast. He resisted the plaintiffs' pressure to bus more students, for the school year was fast approaching and buses were in short supply. He also resisted the defendants' suggestion to stay any busing order until the Supreme Court ruled in *Swann*. He acknowledged that the Supreme Court might not approve busing—or "to put it another way...regardless of the fact that segregation exists because governmental policies fostered segregated neighborhood schools, that said neighborhood schools may continue to exist in a segregated manner." But he thought "constitutional deprivations demand[ed] action," and he refused to rule on the basis of a prediction of what the Supreme Court might or might not do.[46]

Judge Merhige nonetheless made it clear that more busing would be ordered in the future, and he told the school board to come up with yet another plan within three months. In the meantime, the plaintiffs and the school board filed separate appeals, and the city council—also a named defendant—sought a stay of the order. The state supported the city council's motion, but the governor, Linwood Holton, expressed his belief that the busing order would not be postponed and called on citizens to aid in the peaceful opening of schools that year.

Holton was a moderate Republican who had no interest in defying court orders. He opposed court-ordered busing and enlisted the state in aid of the defendants' efforts to overturn the busing order. But if the courts decreed busing, he would oblige. Indeed, he took the courageous step of sending his three school-age children to a predominantly black public school in the East End of Richmond, even though the governor's mansion lay on state property and was therefore exempt from the busing order. The move drew national attention and symbolized a significant shift in the state's response to desegregation.[47]

For all the protests and objections, the scope of the busing order was fairly limited. Only twenty-six hundred more students were to be bused than in the previous year. The symbolic importance of busing, however, was greater than its actual impact. Perhaps for both of these reasons, the practical and the symbolic, the 1970–71 school year opened without incident but also with roughly four thousand fewer white students. Some parents created a private, all-white school while others falsified addresses or rented apartments in other areas to avoid busing. Many warned that busing would inevitably lead to an all-black and poor school system, as whites fled either to private schools or the suburbs. But still the buses rolled. Although Richmond police stood at the ready in the event of trouble, there was none. Many parents lent a hand, keeping watch at bus stops and helping to ensure the safety of the children. White newspapers continued to object, however, and offered no encouragement of busing. The *Richmond News Leader* printed an editorial mocking the "silliness" of compulsory busing and deriding federal courts "for punishing the children of the South for the sins of their ancestors."[48]

Expanding Busing and Moving toward Consolidation

After the 1970–71 school year began, the Richmond School Board moved on two fronts. First, in response to Judge Merhige's order, it went back to the drawing board and came up with three new busing plans. Second, it renewed a motion to have Henrico and Chesterfield counties included in the case as defendants, an obvious first step toward consolidation. The seven school board members, three of whom were black, were on their own in making this motion; both the state and the Richmond City Council opposed it. County officials, meanwhile, were not pleased and threatened to retaliate politically and economically, with one Chesterfield official declaring "War is war." An official from Henrico made his feelings even clearer, exclaiming "Richmond can rot in Hell."[49]

Judge Merhige also moved along the same two paths, simultaneously ordering increased busing within Richmond and setting the stage for consolidation. In April 1971, he approved a plan calling for large-scale busing of elementary students beginning in the fall of 1971. Whereas the earlier plan required the school busing of 13,000 students, this one increased the number to 20,500–a bit less than half of the 45,000 students enrolled in the district.[50]

Two weeks after Merhige's order, the Supreme Court issued its decision in *Swann v. Charlotte-Mecklenburg Board of Education*. In a somewhat schizophrenic opinion by Chief Justice Burger, the Court demanded that school districts desegregate to the maximum extent practicable, while simultaneously emphasizing the temporary and limited nature of court relief. The Court was clear, however, where it mattered most: it upheld the use of busing for the purposes of desegregation. The Supreme Court, it seemed, had tacitly thrown its weight behind Judge Merhige's order.[51]

The Court in *Swann* also seemed to open the door to urban-suburban busing. The Charlotte-Mecklenburg school district encompassed both the city of Charlotte and the surrounding suburbs of Mecklenburg County. The busing plan approved in that case featured two-way transportation, with urban black students being bused to white suburban schools and suburban white students to black city schools. If city and suburban students could be part of the same desegregation plan in North Carolina, why not city and suburban students in metropolitan Richmond? Indeed, the Richmond School Board filed a motion two days after the *Swann* decision asking that the Richmond, Henrico, and Chesterfield school districts be merged before the start of the 1971–72 school year. Meanwhile, the *Richmond Times-Dispatch* admitted that it could find only "weak beacons of hope" that the *Swann* opinion did not require merging the three school districts in metropolitan Richmond.[52]

What the board and the *Richmond Times Dispatch* missed, which would come to make all the difference, was the fact that city and suburb in North Carolina were part of the same school district. The Court in *Swann* thus only approved busing within a single school district, which by historical accident encompassed both urban and suburban schools. The Court did not endorse crossing district lines or the more drastic remedy of consolidating school districts. The Court's reluctance to interfere with local control over residents and the ability to exclude outsiders was hinted at a week after *Swann*, when the Court approved a local community's efforts to block the construction of low-income housing. Commentators called the two rulings "schizophrenic," but they missed the fact that *Swann* did not challenge but instead respected existing municipal boundaries.[53]

Those focused on practicalities rather than legalities would have insisted on suburban participation, as it was crucial to making busing work in Richmond and most other metropolitan areas across the country. This explains the Richmond School Board's seemingly inconsistent stance on busing. The board generally opposed busing within Richmond but supported consolidation with

Henrico and Chesterfield counties, to be followed by busing within the new school district. What the board recognized, which Judge Merhige also came to see, was that busing within Richmond alone would be self-defeating. The district was already majority black and would be more so were it not for the annexation in 1970, which accounted for nearly half of all the white students in Richmond. To expand busing within Richmond would just drive more white families to the suburbs. The school board by 1971 thus no longer opposed integration. Indeed, it wanted more rather than less. What it opposed was integration that would be either futile or counterproductive.[54]

Increased busing, and especially the prospect of consolidation, made plenty of people in the Richmond metropolitan area unhappy. But the reaction was noticeably different from what it had been during the era of massive resistance. Indeed, the terms "massive resister" and "interpositionist" were now considered epithets to be avoided. Certainly protests occurred. Many people were vocal and passionate in their opposition to busing and consolidation. But there were no threats of defiance or lawlessness from Virginia's leaders. The governor urged citizens to "play it cool" and insisted that court orders "must be obeyed." Echoing the governor's position, the lieutenant governor made it clear that "Virginia will not be propelled into massive resistance again. . . . Its efforts were futile and very expensive for the present generation of Virginians." This change in attitude boded well for those pushing consolidation. This time, however, the Supreme Court would not be on their side.[55]

Consolidation Hearing

It is difficult to reconstruct now, but in 1971, many people within and outside of Richmond believed that the three school districts would be merged by court order. Some welcomed the prospect. Others dreaded it. But many, if not most, expected it.[56]

The demographics alone pointed to the need for and efficacy of a metropolitan solution. By 1971, the Richmond schools were about 70 percent black, whereas the surrounding counties were over 90 percent white. Richmond had been losing white students since the *Brown* decision in 1954, but the decline accelerated when busing began in 1970. Richmond in 1970 enrolled about forty-four thousand students; the counties enrolled about sixty thousand. A single school system encompassing all three districts would thus enroll roughly a hundred thousand students, two-thirds of whom would be white and one-third black.[57]

The logic and necessity of a metropolitan solution may have been obvious to some, but Henrico and Chesterfield residents were far from swayed. Most were dead set against it. One lawyer for Chesterfield illustrated the emotional nature of the case when he appeared in court wearing a red-striped shirt, breaking from the tradition of most lawyers, including that one, who wore only plain white shirts in court. "The red on this shirt," he told Judge Merhige, "represents my blood and the blood of the children of Chesterfield county." Apparently both were on the line.[58]

The consolidation hearing occurred in August and September 1971. Those who testified in favor of consolidation argued that it was necessary and plausible. A Richmond school official testified that absent consolidation, "white flight into the two 'bedroom' communities will [continue and] kill all effort to desegregate the city." Consolidation was necessary, he continued, for "meaningful integration." As defined by an expert witness, Dr. Thomas F. Pettigrew, professor of education and sociology at Harvard University, meaningful integration required enough minority students to avoid tokenism but not so many as to trigger white flight. The optimal range was pegged at 20 to 40 percent per school.[59]

In an interesting attempt to turn the tables, another expert testified that there was no proven educational advantage to the neighborhood school. Usually, the benefits of neighborhood schools are taken for granted, and those advocating a different assignment system must defend themselves. This expert flipped the question around and found little academic justification for neighborhood schools. He also testified that the proposed bus rides would not interfere with the ability of students to receive a quality education. Surprisingly, the Chesterfield school superintendent, Robert Kelly, agreed on the transportation point. He also made the newsworthy admission that he would seek consolidation if *he* were the superintendent of a heavily black city school system surrounded by two white county systems. After the first week of trial, even the *Richmond Times-Dispatch* had to concede that plaintiffs were "clearly, seemingly commandingly" ahead.[60]

Not much changed in the ensuing weeks. The plaintiffs put on more witnesses who testified about the history of massive resistance and cited instances where Virginia had paid for blacks to attend school out of state. They also described how the state had sponsored all-black regional high schools with attendance zones greater than the Richmond metropolitan region. The idea that crossing district lines or having large attendance zones broke with tradition was thus put to rest. The plaintiffs also received the endorsement of a member of the state board of education, who testified that the board should "assist, not oppose, Richmond School Board efforts to consolidate capital area schools."[61]

One of the last witnesses to testify for the plaintiffs was Dr. Robert E. Lucas, a school superintendent from Princeton, Ohio. He described his experience consolidating the all-white Princeton district with the all-black neighboring district of Lincoln Heights. Lucas explained that, while there was a lot of screaming at first, parents ultimately supported the consolidation and worked to make it successful. The result, he testified, was "the most excitement in education I've ever seen." Parental involvement in the schools increased, student performance improved, and public financing held steady.[62]

Witnesses for Chesterfield and Henrico counties emphasized the importance of local control and the history of poor relations between the counties and the city of Richmond. Chesterfield County's executive secretary, Melvin Burnett, testified that consolidation would ruin parent participation in Chesterfield schools and create immensely difficult school funding problems. He also testified extensively about the county's self-sufficiency, prompting Judge Merhige to wonder aloud when he "would hear about the county's navy."[63]

Other witnesses for the counties denied allegations of intentional housing discrimination and rebutted the notion that desegregation was crucial to educational opportunity. Indeed, one expert witness from the University of Minnesota testified that any attempt to link the quality of education with a diminished black school population was itself racist and imprecise. It was, he testified, "paternalistic of whites to suggest that...black schools are bad schools."[64]

The trial concluded in mid-September, after the start of the 1971 school year. Merhige had hoped to make a decision about consolidation by the end of the calendar year, and he came close to doing so. He released his opinion—all 325 pages of it—on January 10, 1972. By this point, he was receiving around-the-clock police protection due to threats on his life. The opinion did nothing to reduce his need for protection.[65]

Merhige Orders Consolidation

Judge Merhige's opinion was sprawling and relied on at least three different rationales, each more controversial than the last. First, he concluded that the state of Virginia and each of the three school districts had intentionally segregated schools, which was obviously true, and that each had a duty to remedy the past violation. Fulfilling that duty, Merhige concluded, could not be accomplished by busing within Richmond alone, given that the district was already predominantly black and that busing seemed to be driving middle-class whites to the suburbs. Merhige here implicitly acknowledged that busing, begun only two years earlier in Richmond, had been doomed from the start.[66]

The need to provide an effective remedy for past school segregation, Merhige continued, trumped any obligation to respect local political boundaries. He wrote: "The court concludes that the duty to take whatever steps are necessary to achieve the greatest possible degree of desegregation…is not circumscribed by school division boundaries created and maintained by the cooperative efforts of local and central state officials." School district boundaries, in Merhige's view, were simply "matters of political convenience." Indeed, as he pointed out, district lines had been crossed to maintain segregated schools, so there was little ground to argue that they were inviolable.[67]

The second rationale had much broader implications. Judge Merhige recognized that by 1971, the direct cause of most school segregation was the combination of residential segregation and neighborhood schools. Students were assigned to schools near their homes; because neighborhoods were segregated, so, too, were the schools. Judge Merhige concluded that state and local school officials were legally responsible for school segregation that resulted from this dynamic. He reasoned that school officials were both aware of residential segregation and had the power to alter attendance zones and district lines in order to counteract it. If they chose not to do so, Judge Merhige concluded, they ought to be held responsible for their choice.[68]

On this reasoning, it bears emphasizing, it did not matter whether the underlying residential segregation was itself caused by public or private discrimination. Merhige recognized that residential segregation had many causes, some public and some private. He also recognized that the Fourteenth Amendment applied only to "state" action, not to private discrimination. The key state action, in his view, was not the residential segregation itself but the decision by school officials *not* to do anything to combat its effects on school segregation. As he wrote, "school authorities may not constitutionally arrange an attendance zone system which serves only to reproduce in school facilities the prevalent pattern of housing segregation, be it publicly or privately enforced. To do so is only to endorse with official approval the product of private racism."[69]

This view of state responsibility, if accepted by the Court, would blow up the distinction between de facto segregation and de jure segregation. The former was the term reserved for segregation that occurred because of private decisions and was generally thought beyond the reach of the Constitution; the latter referred to segregation by law and was the target of desegregation remedies. Merhige argued, in essence, that there was no such thing as de facto segregation. If accepted, and the de jure-de facto distinction dissolved, both North and South would have the same obligation to desegregate. Judge Merhige recognized as much in his opinion:

When a school board...operating in an area where segregated housing patterns prevail and are continuing, builds its facilities and arranges its zones so that school attendance is governed by housing segregation, it is operating in violation of the Constitution. These conclusions apply in a case where no history of other past intentional
segregation was relied on in order to establish an affirmative duty to desegregate.

In other words, this rationale would apply to school districts across the
country. It was for this reason that *New York Times* columnist Tom Wicker predicted that the decision, if it survived appeal, would "prove not just historic but
cataclysmic, with more and wider practical impact even than the 1954 decision
that started school desegregation."[70]

The third rationale complemented the second. Judge Merhige reasoned, relying on *Brown*, that "if there is to be public education it must, under the Constitution, be afforded to all on an equal basis." He reasoned further that "in a bi-racial
community," which here included the city of Richmond and its suburbs in
Henrico and Chesterfield counties, "meaningful integration is an essential element of securing equality of education." Merhige spoke not of desegregation but
of integration, thus suggesting that states in metropolitan areas across the country had an affirmative duty to integrate their schools as a component of their
obligation to provide an equal education. It was not entirely clear whether this
duty arose because of the benefits of integration or because, under Judge Merhige's approach, the failure to integrate was essentially proof of intent to segregate. But either way, the end result would be the same—an affirmative duty to
achieve a rough racial balance in schools throughout a metropolitan area.[71]

The day after releasing the opinion, Judge Merhige outlined the procedures
to be followed in consolidating the school districts in time for the start of the
next school year, in September 1972. He gave state and county defendants a mere
thirty days to "take all steps and perform all acts necessary to create a single
school division." The enormity of that task is hard to overstate. A new school
board would have to be created, a superintendent and administrative staff hired,
school property transferred to the new school board, and a new funding plan
devised. Judge Merhige gave the defendants ninety days to create student and
faculty assignment plans, as well as devise a transportation plan. He set July 1 as
the deadline for the takeover by the new metropolitan school board.[72]

Reaction

Judge Merhige's opinion attracted local and national attention. Reactions dif-
fered in substance but were equally passionate in tone. The lawyers who had

brought the case praised the decision and expressed optimism about what the case might mean for school desegregation elsewhere in the country. At a news conference two days after the opinion was released, which the *New York Times* covered, NAACP Legal Defense Fund lawyers explained the potential impact of the ruling if upheld by the Supreme Court. It would, they said, lead to metropolitan-wide desegregation decrees, which would combat the racial isolation in urban schools, slow white flight, spread the benefits and burdens of desegregation across not just racial groups but economic ones, and equalize school expenditures across metropolitan regions. The lawyers acknowledged the likelihood of white resistance to Merhige's order, but they defended the order as a logical application of Supreme Court precedent regarding desegregation, as well as a realistic approach that cut through fictions about government responsibility for segregated schools.[73]

Local white papers in Richmond saw neither logic nor wisdom in the opinion. A *Richmond News Leader* editorial, entitled "He Did It," excoriated Merhige for his "harsh, acrimonious, sometimes arrogant" opinion "in which one searches almost in vain for a nugget of good sense." The *Richmond Times-Dispatch* called the judge's decision "pernicious gibberish" and "a nauseating mixture of vacuous sociological theories and legal contradictions. It is insulting to black children in particular, [and] callously indifferent to the interests of all children." The *Richmond Times-Dispatch* was especially outraged that Judge Merhige seemed to mandate a particular racial balance in order for districts to be considered unitary.[74]

The *Richmond Times-Dispatch* also predicted, or perhaps sought to encourage, suburban rebellion. The paper forecast that unless reversed on appeal, the opinion would prompt a grassroots suburban rebellion throughout the nation that "would put an end to destructive federal court attacks upon public schools, once and for all." Protest groups joined forces soon after the release of the opinion, consolidating under the name Richmond Area Coordinating Committee. This umbrella organization sponsored a protest march at the state capitol and a motorcade of thirty-five hundred cars that traveled from Richmond to Washington, D.C., to protest the decision. One Henrico resident explained why he joined the motorcade: "This is middle-class America speaking out. My five-year-old cried when I left this morning, but I told [her] I had to go because it might mean where you go to school. I was a member of the silent majority, until today."[75]

County school board members denounced the decision, as did the parent-teacher associations in both counties. Speakers at neighborhood rallies in the counties proposed boycotts of city-sponsored events and businesses. Some county teachers threatened to resign if the merger were upheld. Students took to the streets waving antibusing posters. And Judge Merhige, according to one historian, "received a barrage of hate mail, obscene phone calls, life insurance policies, and quite a few Fisher Price toy school buses." As Merhige himself described it years later, "every other week or so we received a cryptic letter warning that our son Mark would never live to see age twenty-one. I was burned in effigy, spat upon, and occasionally insulted by people who would deliberately walk out of restaurants whenever my wife and I entered."[76]

It did not help that Merhige sent his own son to a private school. This fact fueled resentment among those who could not afford private school and therefore had to suffer the consequences of his order. It also led to charges that Mehrige was being hypocritical when talking about the importance of integration while sending his son to an exclusive, predominantly white private academy. But Merhige was unbowed. In a nationally televised interview, he declined an invitation to express contrition: "When I'm on the bench I'm a judge and when I'm at home I'm just a father. Mark attends private school because that's where I think he can get the best education, and I make no apologies for it." One might question Mehrige's refusal to acknowledge some tension between his public and private roles, but neither this tension nor his ruling justified the treatment he received, including letters like the following: "Look—You Dirty Bastard, We are sick of you Federal judges playing God. Your knowledge of the law is zero minus a million.... It would be a good idea to look under the hood of your car before starting it. Think about it. You son of a bitch."[77]

Obviously, most who disagreed with the decision did not threaten violence. Less obviously, not all whites disagreed with the decision, and not all blacks supported it. A contingent of white parents who lived in the city supported consolidation for the same reason the school board supported it: without consolidation, Richmond schools would become increasingly poor and black, and the quality of education would suffer. They organized under the name Citizens for Excellent Public Schools and sought to build support for a metropolitan-wide school system. These parents tried to explain that merging with the suburbs was the last chance to "keep our beautiful and wonderful capital city from becoming a ghetto city as many northern cities have become, when white citizens rush to the counties to avoid desegregation."[78]

On the other hand, the Congress of Racial Equality (CORE), which by the late 1960s was dominated by black nationalists, denounced the decision because they believed it would dilute black political power. They attacked consolidation, arguing that it destroyed community control—by which they meant black community control—of local schools. As CORE put it, the merger was "an attempt to offset the clear majority of the black (school) population in Richmond." CORE did not represent the dominant view of the black community in

Richmond, three-fourths of whom supported consolidation when surveyed in 1972. And CORE garnered some strange bedfellows because of its stance. Indeed, both CORE and the National Suburban League filed legal briefs arguing against school district consolidation. Nonetheless, CORE's opposition to consolidation was significant and highly publicized, and it provided useful cover for whites who opposed consolidation and were looking to rebut charges of racism.[79]

State and local officials, for their part, again promised compliance rather than defiance. To be sure, state and county officials expressed their hope that the decision would be overturned on appeal. At the same time, however, they also urged citizens to cooperate. The state board of education set an example by voting both to appeal the decision and to take steps to comply with Judge Merhige's order. When asked by a reporter if the board planned to defy Judge Merhige's decision, the chairman replied: "Are you crazy?"[80]

Even white residents of the counties, though not happy with the decision, did not plan to abandon public schools or move away in response. A surprising 87 percent of Chesterfield and Henrico parents who were surveyed indicated that they would keep their children in a consolidated district if the quality of education did not decline. Whether they were telling the truth is impossible to say for sure, and the significance of the caveat—if educational quality did not decline—was unclear. But it seems unlikely that parents contemplating leaving the school system would fail to say so, given the fact that the decision was being widely protested and threats of departure were a form of protest. So a promise to remain may indeed have been a sincere one. In any event, we will never know what might have happened, because suburban parents were never put to the test. The Court of Appeals made certain of that.[81]

On Appeal

County officials had asked the Court of Appeals for the Fourth Circuit to stay Judge Merhige's consolidation order pending appeal. The appellate court compromised: it stayed the order to consolidate, but it required the counties and the state to continue planning for consolidation. In the meantime, the court expedited the appeal process. While the briefs were being prepared, the district court in the *Milliken* case out of Detroit also ordered busing across school district boundaries. This decision, which would eventually be appealed to the U.S. Supreme Court, intensified the storm over busing, which now cast its shadow across the country. And it drew even more attention to the *Bradley v. Richmond School Board* appeal before the Fourth Circuit.[82]

Oral argument occurred on April 12, 1972. The defendants secured representation by Philip B. Kurland, a renowned constitutional law professor from the University of Chicago, whose participation in the argument testified to the importance of the case. He was selected not just because of his expertise, but also because of his personal history. He was not connected, in any way, to massive resistance, and the defendants believed this would enhance his credibility.

Kurland argued that Merhige's order had no support in precedent and instead represented a "naked power" grab. He ridiculed the notion that integration was necessary for blacks to excel academically, calling it a theory of "white supremacy in the classroom." He also contended that each of the three school districts was already "unitary," meaning that they had all done everything necessary to dismantle the vestiges of the old discriminatory system. The NAACP attorneys, for their part, emphasized the simple fact that city schools would remain predominantly black, and grow more so, as long as the counties operated nearby separate schools that were overwhelmingly white.[83]

Five of the six appellate court judges sided with Kurland and the defendants. The opening line of the opinion, though written as a question, signaled the court's conclusion: "May a United States District Judge compel one of the States of the Union to restructure its internal government for the purpose of achieving racial balance in the assignment of pupils to the public schools?" With the question posed this way, it seemed almost gratuitous that the court immediately answered it: "We think not, absent invidious discrimination in the establishment or maintenance of local government units, and accordingly reverse."[84]

The court of appeals had a much different perspective on the case than did Judge Merhige. He believed that school board officials had a responsibility to counteract residential segregation, regardless of its cause. The court of appeals disagreed, indicating that it would only order consolidation if the counties intentionally worked to keep blacks from living here. Although there was some proof that the counties had done just that, the court of appeals chose to look the other way.[85]

The court thought it impossible to say why most blacks happened to live in Richmond while the counties were overwhelmingly white. "We think that the root causes of the concentration of blacks in the inner cities of America are simply not known," said the court. In its view, a mysterious and unknowable combination of countless, unspecified "economic, political and social" forces produced residential segregation and the concentration of blacks in central cities. These forces drove the residential patterns not only in Richmond but also in "New York, Chicago, Detroit, Los Angeles, [and] Atlanta." Everywhere the court looked, it saw "a growing black population in the central city and a growing white population in the surrounding suburban and rural areas." In something of a non sequitur, the court then observed that "whatever the basic causes" of these demographic patterns might be, "it has not been school assignments." The court concluded its reasoning by suggesting that the issue of housing discrimination was too complicated and unwieldy to be included in a schools case: "That there has been housing discrimination in all three [school districts] is deplorable, but a school case, like a vehicle, can carry only a limited amount of baggage."[86]

Whereas Judge Merhige strained to see state responsibility for housing and school segregation, the appellate judges shielded their eyes so as not to see it. To say that housing discrimination cannot be addressed because a school case "can carry only a limited amount of baggage" is to substitute aphorism for legal analysis. The law recognizes no principle to support the idea that courts can legitimately refuse to consider issues because they are too complicated.

At the same time, however, housing and school segregation were so ubiquitous and inextricable that Judge Merhige's approach, if followed, would open up school systems all across the country to legal challenge and ultimately to judicial control. Moreover, to address school segregation by requiring either the consolidation of districts or cross-district busing was to risk backlash and intense political upheaval. And there would be no end in sight to either judicial control or the controversy it generated, as desegregation decrees would presumably last as long as neighborhoods were segregated, which might be a very long time.

Judge Merhige was willing to weather that storm; he told his biographers that he knew that "the price of busing was high, but I don't think there is any price too high to reach a society where everyone is viewed the way God intended, the way the Constitution intended. Viewed and treated equally." The court of appeals, by contrast, was unwilling to tempt fate, and to assume, as Merhige may have, that what God intended the Constitution required.[87]

A Tie at the Supreme Court

Everyone knew that the decision would be appealed to the U.S. Supreme Court. Speculation began immediately as to whether Justice Powell, appointed in January 1972, would recuse himself because of his past service as chair of the Richmond School Board and member of the state board of education. If Powell recused himself, eight Justices would vote, making a tie vote not just a theoretical possibility but the likely outcome. The three other Nixon appointees—Burger, Blackmun, and Rehnquist—would most likely vote to affirm the court of appeals. The Court's three liberal justices—Marshall, Brennan, and Douglas—would most likely vote to reverse and reinstate Judge Merhige's ruling. If only one of the two moderate justices—Stewart or White—voted with the conservative bloc, the Court would be tied. At the Supreme Court, a tie goes to the court below, meaning that the judgment is affirmed. In an editorial entitled "Oh, Happy Days!" the editors at the *Richmond News Leader* read the tea leaves and seemed confident that the Fourth Circuit's decision would stand.[88]

That is exactly what happened. Justice Powell, as predicted, recused himself. The rest of the Court split four-to-four. The Court did not indicate which justices were on which side. Instead, on May 21, 1973, it issued a nine-word, per curiam opinion stating simply: "The judgment is affirmed by an equally divided court." The decision settled the busing question in Richmond, but it had no precedential value beyond the Richmond case. The showdown over urban-suburban busing would therefore have to await resolution by the Court of what might be called "the other" Bradley case—*Milliken v. Bradley*.[89]

For those in Richmond, however, the game was over, which produced mixed reactions. Governor Holton made no immediate comments about the case, but attorney general Andrew P. Miller expressed pleasure "that the state's position has been affirmed by the Supreme Court of the United States," and relief that the decision had brought "to an end a generation of school litigation in the state." Richmond's superintendent, Thomas C. Little, expressed great disappointment, while Henrico's superintendent, W. E. Campbell, reported that he was "delighted" with the decision. Some members of the Richmond City Council were disappointed by the decision, but not all. Indeed, one councilman, Howard H. Carwile, called the decision "the most glorious victory for human liberty since the American Revolution."[90]

Classrooms across Chesterfield County "literally rocked with cheers" at news of the result, according to one county teacher. The *Richmond News Leader* printed an editorial unsubtly titled "We Won!" and implored: "Let us have no more attempts to impose abstraction on reality. We have all endured enough." State senator Frederick T. Gray, a former Virginia attorney general and lawyer for Chesterfield County, "could scarcely restrain his joy," according to the *New York Times*. "I don't know of any way they can beat us now," he told the *Times*, later adding: "forever is a long time, but I think we've got them licked forever." Senator Gray, like the *Richmond News Leader*'s editorial writers, never specified who "they" and "we" were, leaving to the imagination whether the reference was to Richmonders and county residents or to blacks and whites. It hardly mattered, though, as the groups were tending to become synonymous, at least where schoolchildren were concerned. By 1973, to talk about Richmond schoolchildren was to talk mostly about black students, and to talk about county schoolchildren was to talk about white students.[91]

BEYOND RICHMOND:
MILLIKEN AND SUBURBAN POLITICS

While those in the Richmond metropolitan area either celebrated or mourned the Supreme Court's ruling, residents of the Detroit metropolitan area anxiously awaited a final decision in *Milliken v. Bradley*, which raised similar issues. The demographics of the Detroit metropolitan region were similar to Richmond's. The city was becoming blacker while the surrounding suburbs remained overwhelmingly white; the demographic differences between city and suburb were even more pronounced in the public schools.

One key difference was in the structure of local government. Dozens of small school districts surrounded Detroit, as compared to the two large county systems that surrounded Richmond. This would obviously complicate efforts to integrate metropolitan Detroit, because doing so would involve more independent school districts, each with its own school board, officials, and administrators.[92]

The *Milliken* Case

The Detroit branch of the NAACP filed suit on August 18, 1970, signaling the NAACP's decision to attack segregation outside the South. Northern and western states did not have statutes mandating segregation, but school officials there certainly took steps with the purpose and effect of segregating schools. By 1970, moreover, northern schools were generally more segregated than those in the South.[93]

Detroit itself was a good example. Neither Michigan nor Detroit had ever required segregation by law, but it was clear that state and local officials took numerous intentional steps to keep Detroit schools segregated. It was also clear by 1971 that busing students just within Detroit would be futile; Detroit public schools were already predominantly black. Busing would, if anything, just spur more white flight to the suburbs. Thus, in March 1972, federal district court judge Stephen Roth concluded that "relief of segregation in the public schools of the City of Detroit cannot be accomplished within the corporate geographical limits of the city." He therefore devised a plan that encompassed Detroit and school districts in the surrounding three counties.[94]

The scope of the ruling startled many observers. Whereas Richmond, Henrico County, and Chesterfield County contained three school systems, the three counties surrounding Detroit contained a total of eighty-six independent school districts. Of these, Judge Roth's plan would include fifty-three. Students from all sorts of suburbs—rich and poor, predominantly Catholic and pre-dominantly Jewish—would be bused into Detroit, while students in Detroit would be bused out to the suburbs. At the time, there were 290,000 students in Detroit, and 185,000 thousand of these—or 64 percent—were black. There were 490,000 students in the fifty-three suburban districts, and only 10,000 of them—2 percent—were black. Of these roughly 800,000 students in total, 300,000 would be bused for desegregation purposes. Judge Roth hoped to cre-ate schools across the region with black populations of approximately 25 percent.[95]

The length of the bus trip, on average, would be no more than forty minutes each way. Young children, including those who attended half-day kindergarten, were included in the plan. In a portion of his opinion quoted in the *New York Times*, most likely because it was surprisingly obtuse, Judge Roth wrote that "transportation of kindergarten children of upwards of 45 minutes, one way, does not appear unreasonable, harmful, or unsafe in any way. In the absence of some compelling justification, which does not yet appear, kindergarten chil-dren should be included in the final plan of desegregation." A 90-minute round-trip bus ride for about 180 minutes of school might not have seemed unreason-able to Judge Roth, but most parents probably felt differently.[96]

As surprising as the scope of the plan was its source. Judge Roth was a Hun-garian-born Catholic who grew up in a blue-collar suburb. He was a Democrat but hardly radical. To the contrary, he was relatively conservative and had no previous association with the civil rights movement, making him, as one schol-ar described, "a most unlikely candidate to formulate the most sweeping busing order ever issued." Indeed, Roth's background as an immigrant from a blue-collar Michigan suburb was similar to the backgrounds of those who protested his decision most forcefully.[97]

At trial, the plaintiffs sought to link residential and school segregation. Because residential segregation was itself imposed by the government, they argued, the government should be held responsible for any resulting school segregation. As counsel for the NAACP argued, "racial containment of blacks in Detroit...is not a fortuitous phenomenon, but it is in fact a result of private and public" discrimination. Counsel further argued that "there is an interlock-ing relationship between the racial composition of schools and discrimination with respect to housing opportunities."[98]

The plaintiffs proceeded to present extensive testimony about governmental involvement in residential segregation. Former HUD officials testified about government housing discrimination, which had begun with the FHA in the 1930s and continued to the present. William Price, a former director of the Detroit Urban League, documented discrimination in public housing and

urban renewal. Local workers from civil rights agencies testified to the "severity and ubiquity" of discrimination in housing, while local black real estate brokers recounted their experiences when trying to operate in white neighborhoods. All of these witnesses, whose testimony was not rebutted by the defendants, agreed that the local, state, and federal governments were doing little to overcome the effects of past government actions.[99]

Judge Roth's Opinion

Judge Roth agreed with the plaintiffs and then took their argument a step further. He began by acknowledging the ubiquity of residential segregation: "Residential segregation within the city and throughout the larger metropolitan area is substantial, pervasive, and of long standing. Black citizens are located in separate and distinct areas within the city and are not generally to be found in the suburbs." He acknowledged that private choices and economic factors had played a role in residential patterns, but he concluded that the pattern of residential segregation was, "in the main, the result of past and present practices and customs of racial discrimination, both public and private, which have and do restrict the housing opportunities of black people." He emphasized: "On the record there can be no other finding."[100]

Judge Roth then turned to the question of responsibility. He recognized that both government officials and private citizens engaged in racial discrimination, and that the combination produced residential and school segregation. "Governmental actions and inaction at all levels," he wrote, "have combined, with those of private organizations such as real estate associations and brokerage firms, to establish and maintain the pattern of residential segregation throughout the Detroit metropolitan area." On this basis alone, he logically could have concluded that state and local officials had to correct any school desegregation that resulted from government-produced residential segregation. Judge Roth, however, just like Judge Merhige, believed that the ultimate issue was not whether residential segregation could be blamed on government actions. The real issue was whether to blame local or state school officials for failing to do anything to combat residential segregation—whatever its cause—when assigning students to school.[101]

Judge Roth did not hesitate to do so. He shared Judge Merhige's expansive view of government responsibility. He was willing to hold government officials responsible for the foreseeable consequences of their decisions, which included their decisions *not* to take action. Roth's implicit theory was that failing to address segregation amounted to a conscious choice to perpetuate it, and school

officials should be held accountable for that choice. Thus, at the end of the day, Judge Roth concluded that school officials had a constitutional obligation "to adopt and implement pupil assignment practices and policies that compensate for and avoid incorporation into the school system the effects of residential segregation."[102]

If this meant crossing district lines, so be it. Judge Roth, like Judge Merhige before him, viewed school district lines as nothing more than "matters of political convenience" that surely could not be "used to deny constitutional rights." District lines had been crossed in the past to maintain school segregation in the Detroit metropolitan area, just as they were crossed in Richmond for the same end. If state and local officials were willing to cross school lines to segregate schools, they could hardly complain if courts ordered them to cross those lines to *desegregate* schools. Moreover, as Judge Roth observed, "if the boundary lines of the school districts of the City of Detroit and the surrounding suburbs were drawn today" for the purpose of segregating students, surely they would be deemed unconstitutional. The same should be true, he concluded, of lines that were maintained for the purpose of segregating students.[103]

Nixon's Compromise

Judge Roth's decision generated controversy within and beyond the Detroit metropolitan region. The order to bus across district lines, according to the *Washington Post*, "generated massive resistance in Detroit's predominantly white suburbs. Parents' groups are threatening boycotts and others are working to establish private freedom schools similar to the all-white institutions that began in the South in the face of court-ordered desegregation." Roth's name, like that of Judge Merhige in Richmond, "became a curse" in working-class suburbs, where it was not unusual to see bumper stickers declaring "Roth is a four-letter word." As Rowland Evans and Robert Novak reported in May 1972, "the suburbanite, often a worker in an auto factory, is terrified by the idea of his children being bused into the overwhelmingly black schools of inner Detroit. Fear of violence, of drugs and of the unknown leads these parents to say they will never acquiesce to busing."[104]

Not all opposed Roth's order, but those who supported it were neither as numerous nor intense as those who opposed it. As in Richmond, some whites in Detroit favored busing with the suburbs because they feared that limiting desegregation to Detroit would destroy an already fragile school system. Indeed, the first motion to include the suburbs in the litigation came from a group of white Detroit parents who intervened in the case. Although these parents

strongly supported a metropolitan-wide solution, their numbers were quite small.[105]

A larger group, the African-American community, was split on the issue of busing. Black residents in the Detroit metropolitan area supported busing, but only by a slim 47 to 45 percent margin. Those who supported busing did so, it bears noting, not out of any great desire to send their children to school with white children. They simply believed that suburban schools were better than city ones. Their commitment was thus not to integration per se but to integration as a means to a quality education.[106]

Outside of Detroit, Judge Roth's ruling helped fuel an intense orgy of anti-busing activity on the national level. President Nixon, elected to office on the strength of the suburban vote, led the charge. He delivered his televised speech on desegregation, described in the Introduction, in March 1972, the same month that Judge Roth issued his opinion. Nixon proposed legislation that would prohibit forced busing to achieve racial balance, suggesting that such legislation was consistent with the views of "[t]he great majority of Americans—white and black—[who] feel strongly that the busing of school children away from their own neighborhoods for the purpose of achieving racial balance is wrong." The timing of his speech and its focus on urban and suburban schools suggested that Nixon was worried not just about busing within cities, but also, perhaps primarily, about busing between city and suburban school districts.[107]

Nixon acknowledged the existence of schools in central cities that were "so inferior that it is hypocritical to suggest that the poor children who go there are getting a decent education, let alone an education comparable to that of children who go to schools in the suburbs." But busing city children to suburban schools was not the answer, Nixon argued, because it was wrong to displace children from neighborhood schools. Better to provide greater resources to students in poor city (and rural) schools. Thus Nixon combined his proposal regarding busing with another legislative proposal, entitled the Equal Educational Opportunities Act of 1972, which would direct more funds to the neediest schools. The compromise Nixon offered was quite explicit: students in the city would remain in the city and not be permitted to attend suburban schools; in exchange for staying put, they would get more resources.[108]

Members of Congress, meanwhile, seemed most interested in the "stop the busing" half of Nixon's compromise. They tripped over each other in a rush to introduce measures designed to limit busing, which ranged from constitutional amendments outlawing busing to legislation that would restrict the ability of federal courts to hear desegregation cases. Congress even considered a proposal to deny gasoline to school buses that traveled further than the neighborhood school.[109]

Congress ultimately enacted legislation declaring that "the neighborhood is the appropriate basis for determining public school assignments" and purporting to prevent courts or federal agencies from ordering busing beyond neighborhood schools. The legislation had little practical effect, however, as courts interpreted it to permit busing that was ordered as a remedy for school segregation. Around the same time, Congress passed additional legislation prohibiting federally funded legal services organizations from working on desegregation litigation. This legislation had a good deal more bite, even though it received less publicity than the mostly symbolic busing legislation.[110]

It was not just conservative southerners and their northern sympathizers who opposed busing the suburbs. Antibusing legislation in the early 1970s was just as likely to come from northern moderates and "liberals" whose suburban constituents faced the prospect of busing for school desegregation. The measure to cut gasoline for school buses, for example, came from John Dingell, a Democrat from the Detroit suburbs. Similarly, ostensibly liberal Democrats Joseph Biden from Delaware and Birch Bayh from Indiana each introduced legislation to limit or prohibit cross-district busing for the purpose of school desegregation. They did so in response to political pressure from their suburban constituents. Biden and Bayh were not alone in feeling—and responding to—this pressure. As the New York Times described a vote on an antibusing measure in the summer of 1972, "northern liberals, once in the forefront of the fights for civil rights, spoke feelingly of the need to halt forced busing of children in the placid suburbs and the teeming cities that they represent."[111]

Democrats from Michigan were especially worried. As the Wall Street Journal reported, the possibility of massive busing between suburbs and the inner city caused "panic" not just in the white suburbs but also among "the liberal Democrats who represent Detroit's white neighborhoods and suburbs in the House." All five of these Democrats, who had supported civil rights legislation in the past, now supported antibusing legislation. They expressed their opposition to busing, the Journal reported, in language "reminiscent of stand-in-the-schoolhouse-door Southerners." Representative James O'Hara, for example, had been a floor leader for civil rights bills in the past, but now told his suburban Detroit constituents: "I stand ready to do whatever is necessary by way of further legislation or a constitutional amendment . . . to prevent the implementation of the federal district court's decision on cross-district busing." School desegregation might have been acceptable when limited to the South or confined to urban districts, but when it began to threaten suburban schools, liberal and moderate whites abandoned ship.[112]

The about-face of onetime champions of desegregation and civil rights did not go unnoticed. Ron Dellums, an African-American Democrat from California, blasted his liberal colleagues for trying to prohibit busing. These so-called liberals, Dellums observed, claimed that they could not support busing because if they did, "a real racist" would be sent to Congress in their place. "Well," Dellums concluded, "maybe they should send us a real racist and then we will know what we are dealing with." John Conyers, an African American who represented a heavily black section of Detroit, reached a similar conclusion: "in my judgment, this is not only unbecoming conduct, but it is the height of hypocrisy and cowardice working hand-in-hand."[113]

Dellums and Conyers had a point. Northern liberals who opposed busing once it moved north and into the suburbs were indeed guilty of hypocrisy. But their stance was nonetheless understandable, if not necessarily justifiable; expressing support for cross-district busing really did risk political suicide. As Representative Abner Mikva acknowledged, the issue had northern liberals "scared out of their wits" for good reason. George Wallace, the notorious segregationist and former governor of Alabama, won the Democratic presidential primary in Michigan in 1972 largely because of the busing issue. This followed an effort the previous year to recall Senator Philip Hart of Michigan because he had refused, in contrast to his colleagues in the House, to abandon his support of busing. Given this atmosphere, it is not altogether surprising that members of Congress, especially those from Michigan, generally opposed busing across city-suburban lines.[114]

A similar consensus existed outside of Congress. Polls in the early 1970s consistently revealed strong opposition to busing. Middle-class communities that faced the prospect of busing, according to desegregation expert Gary Orfield, "protested on an unprecedented scale." The mass movement taking to the streets in the early 1970s "marched not under the banner of 'INTEGRATION NOW' but with signs reading 'PRESERVE OUR NEIGHBORHOOD SCHOOLS.'"[115]

On a national level, just as in Detroit, cross-town busing had a few defenders, but they were not as ardent or numerous as the opponents. The black community, as already mentioned, was not of one mind on the issue of busing, either within cities or across city-suburban lines. Many blacks, like many whites, preferred keeping their children within their own neighborhoods to sending them to distant and perhaps hostile schools. Major newspapers also split on this issue. The usually liberal *Washington Post*, for example, editorialized against Judge Roth's decision, calling it "highly questionable...not least on the grounds that it probably won't work."[116]

In this political environment, the appeal of Nixon's compromise was obvious. Suburban whites strongly opposed cross-district busing, while urban blacks offered only mild support at best. At the same time, neither whites nor blacks were opposed, in principle, to providing greater assistance to urban schools. If providing greater funding for urban schools was the price for maintaining the wall between city and suburban districts, it must have seemed like a good bargain to many suburbanites. It certainly seemed like a good bargain to members of Congress, who eventually endorsed the broad outlines of Nixon's compromise and supported legislation that combined a prohibition on busing with a promise of more aid for urban schools. It also seemed like an attractive compromise to those running for president in 1972, including Senator Henry M. Jackson, who proposed a constitutional amendment that would guarantee children two rights: the right to attend their neighborhood school and the right to equal funding within each state.[117]

The only institution still committed to busing, it seemed, was the Supreme Court. As a columnist for the *Washington Post* wrote: "much of the public, the president and much of Congress have all seemingly abandoned the courts" and their aggressive efforts to desegregate the schools. This time, however, the Court blinked. Instead of pushing ahead on the issue of cross-district busing, the Court backtracked and ultimately endorsed the compromise Nixon was offering the rest of the nation. The Court acted to limit cross-town busing shortly after it brought the North and West into the world of court-ordered desegregation.[118]

Keyes and Northern Desegregation

For years, the Court suffered criticism from southerners that its desegregation jurisprudence operated on a double standard, requiring only southern states to integrate their schools. These southerners acknowledged that the South, unlike the North, had explicitly required segregation prior to 1954. They argued, however, that school segregation in both the South and North, at least by 1970, was caused primarily by housing segregation and not by old laws requiring segregation. They further believed that courts were using the hook of past school segregation to force the South, and only the South, to address residential segregation, while allowing the North to ignore the same issue.[119]

The Court brought North and South a bit closer together in a 1973 case from Denver, *Keyes v. School District No. 1.* Colorado had never required school segregation by law as the southern states had, nor had Denver. But school officials in Denver took certain actions, such as redrawing attendance zones, with the intent of segregating schools. The basic question in *Keyes* was whether these actions constituted de jure segregation—that is, segregation imposed by law. The Court answered yes, reasoning that de jure segregation included all actions taken by government officials for the purpose of segregating schools, even if those actions were not mandated by a statute or constitutional provision. State and local governments can act through constitutions and statutes, but they can also act through more informal decisions and policies. To the Court, the latter was no less "state action" than the former.[120]

The Court in *Keyes* did not place the North and South on precisely equal footing. Because southern states explicitly required segregation at the time of *Brown*, the only issue in southern desegregation cases after 1954 concerned the proper remedy. In northern cases, by contrast, a remedy would be available if—and only if—plaintiffs succeeded in demonstrating that school officials engaged in de jure segregation. Importantly, it was not enough for plaintiffs simply to point to the *fact* of school segregation; they had to amass evidence suggesting that school segregation was the result of intentional actions taken by school officials. Whether courts agreed depended in no small measure on their willingness to infer intent from circumstantial evidence, a less-than-scientific process that assured a less-than-uniform approach in northern desegregation cases.[121]

Justice Powell, interestingly enough, wrote a separate opinion in *Keyes* arguing for the abandonment of the de jure–de facto distinction. His reasoning bore more than a passing resemblance to that of Judges Merhige and Roth. Powell contended that school officials had complete control over student assignments; they did not just happen by chance. If schools were segregated by race, he continued, it was perfectly reasonable to hold school officials accountable. The theory, again, was that school officials surely foresaw the consequences of their actions and inactions, and they ought to be held respo;nsible for the decisions they made.[122]

Powell made this argument, which liberal civil rights advocates also advanced, primarily because he disfavored treating the North more leniently than the South when it came to school desegregation. Eliminating the de jure-de facto distinction would put the North and South in the same boat. Powell, however, had no interest in expanding busing, which led him to an uncomfortable position. He wanted to increase the scope of liability for school officials but limit the remedial power of courts.[123]

According to Powell's biographer, John C. Jeffries, Jr., there were five votes on the Court at the time of the *Keyes* decision to abandon the de jure-de facto distinction. Because the other four disagreed with Powell about the use of busing, however, none of them joined Powell's opinion. None of the five, moreover, saw fit to craft an opinion limited to the specific issue of the de jure–de facto distinction, leaving the remedial question to one side. Powell himself never looked back after writing his concurring opinion, and from that point forward he clung to the de jure–de facto distinction. The opportunity to change the law vanished as quickly as it arose in *Keyes v. School District No. 1,* leaving one only to speculate how different the world might look today if the Court had jettisoned the de jure-de facto distinction.[124]

When busing moved north in the early 1970s, it was explosive there not just because it was new, but also because it immediately threatened to include the suburbs. Busing moved north, in other words, at precisely the same time it seemed poised to cross the urban-suburban boundary. Indeed, the Supreme Court's opinion in *Keyes* and the Sixth Circuit's opinion in *Milliken* were released in the same month. *Keyes* made clear that busing was indeed coming to the North, while the Sixth Circuit's decision in *Milliken* made clear that, at least in the Detroit metropolitan region, busing was also coming to the suburbs. Or perhaps one should say coming *for* the suburbs.[125]

The Appellate Court Affirms Judge Roth

The Sixth Circuit endorsed Judge Roth's decision in *Milliken*, thus becoming the first federal appellate court to embrace cross-district busing. The appellate court agreed that "the only feasible desegregation plan involves the crossing of the boundary lines between the Detroit School District and adjacent or nearby school districts for the limited purpose of providing an effective desegregation plan." The court reasoned, like Judge Roth, that "any less comprehensive a solution than a metropolitan area plan would result in an all black school system immediately surrounded by practically all white suburban school systems, with an overwhelmingly white majority population in the total metropolitan area."[126]

The court further agreed with Judge Roth that federal courts possessed the authority to order such relief, reasoning that school boundary lines were "artificial" and could be crossed to remedy constitutional violations. Indeed, to the court of appeals, the question was an easy one. School district lines not only *could* but *should* be crossed, for a simple reason: including the suburbs was necessary to prevent a return to the "separate but equal" era of *Plessy v. Ferguson.* "If we hold that school district boundaries are absolute barriers to a Detroit school desegregation plan," the court wrote, "we would be opening a way to nullify *Brown v. Board of Education*[,] which overruled *Plessy.*"[127]

The court of appeals also endorsed Judge Roth's view of government responsibility, seeing little difference between government action and inaction. The court drew support from two consolidated cases, one from Virginia and the other from South Carolina, decided by the U.S. Supreme Court in 1972. In these cases, *United States v. Scotland Neck Board of Education* and *Wright v. Council of the City of Emporia*, the Court prohibited the redrawing of school boundary lines if the result impeded school desegregation. In each case, smaller, predominantly white districts had been carved out of larger ones that were under desegregation decrees. The Sixth Circuit in *Milliken* reasoned that "if school boundary lines cannot be *changed* for an unconstitutional purpose, it follows logically that existing boundary lines cannot be *frozen* for an unconstitutional purpose." It only followed logically, however, if one accepted the underlying and controversial premise of the court's reasoning: that there was no legal difference between government action and inaction.[128]

The Supreme Court Reverses

The Supreme Court, in a five-to-four decision, reversed the court of appeals. Apparently unafraid of "opening a way to nullify *Brown*," the Court ruled that school district lines could not be crossed to desegregate schools absent proof of an interdistrict violation. The Court reasoned that the scope of the remedy had to match the scope of the violation, which meant that an interdistrict remedy could only be ordered for an interdistrict violation. And an interdistrict violation would only occur, the Court continued, if state or local officials bused students across district lines in order to promote segregation, or if state officials redrew school district lines in order to maintain or increase segregation. In the *Milliken* case itself, the Court concluded, there was very little evidence of an interdistrict violation and therefore no justification for cross-district busing.[129]

Several aspects of the opinion are worth emphasizing. First, all four of the justices appointed by President Nixon—Burger, Blackmun, Powell, and Rehnquist—voted with the majority. Justice Potter Stewart, appointed years earlier by President Eisenhower, supplied the fifth vote. Second, the Court placed a great deal of emphasis on the fact that the school district boundaries in the Detroit metropolitan area had been drawn a century before and had remained largely unchanged. Because the boundaries had not been changed, the Court reasoned, there was no constitutional violation, even though the foreseeable effect of leaving the boundaries intact was to perpetuate school segregation. The Court thus implicitly rejected the notion, embraced by the courts below, that state and local officials should be held responsible for their *in*actions. Third, the Court strongly endorsed the "long" tradition of local control of schools, despite the fact that school districts in Michigan were creatures of the state, not the local, government—and despite recent widespread displacement of local control by state pupil placement boards across the South. Because of the tradition of local control, crossing district boundaries, in the Court's eyes, represented much more than simply crossing artificial boundaries.[130]

Perhaps most important, the Court ducked the issue of residential segregation, just as the Fourth Circuit had in *Bradley v. Richmond School Board*. Judge Roth had rested his decision in part on the ground that state and local officials were responsible for residential segregation within the Detroit metropolitan area. The Sixth Circuit had upheld Roth's decision without relying on this finding, reasoning that the decision could be upheld even absent proof of housing discrimination. The Supreme Court used this as an excuse not to deal with the issue of residential segregation, despite the fact that the Court, unlike the Sixth Circuit, *reversed* Judge Roth's decision. This was a questionable move. It is one thing for an appellate court to ignore alternative rationales for a decision if one alone is sufficient to uphold it. But it is quite another to ignore those alternatives when reversing a decision, because one of those ignored alternatives might justify the ruling below, making reversal inappropriate.[131]

In theory, if state or local officials discriminated with regard to housing and therefore helped cause residential segregation between cities and suburbs, these acts might justify cross-district busing. Whether school officials should be held responsible for the actions of housing officials might pose tricky legal questions for sure. But one could reasonably conclude that a state or local government cannot avoid responsibility for race discrimination by dividing up authority among different agencies.

Ironically, this is how Justice Stewart saw the issue in *Milliken*. He reasoned in a separate, concurring opinion that if state officials had caused segregation among school districts "by purposeful racially discriminatory use of state housing or zoning laws, then a decree calling for transfer of pupils across district lines or for restructuring of district lines might well be appropriate." The irony is that Justice Stewart, having made this concession, refused to take seriously the evidence regarding state responsibility for residential segregation.[132]

Recall that Judge Roth, after hearing extensive testimony on precisely this issue, had concluded that "governmental actions and inaction at all levels, federal, state and local, have combined, with those of private organizations such as real estate associations and brokerage firms, to establish and maintain the pattern of residential segregation throughout the Detroit metropolitan area." Despite this finding, Justice Stewart said that "no record has been made in this case showing that the racial composition of the Detroit school population or that residential patterns within Detroit and in the surrounding areas were in any significant measure caused by governmental activity." By using the phrase "significant measure," Justice Stewart did not completely contradict the record, but he also gave no indication of what sort of proof would be necessary to establish a causal connection between governmental actions, residential segregation, and school segregation.[133]

It seems plain that Justice Stewart, like the other four justices in the majority, either did not know what to make of residential segregation or simply did not want to deal with it. Indeed, just like the Fourth Circuit in *Bradley v. Richmond School Board,* which had argued that "the root causes of the concentration of blacks in the inner cities of America are simply not known," Justice Stewart preferred to think of residential segregation as the product of mysterious forces. He suggested that the heavily black school population in Detroit, surrounded by predominantly white populations in the suburbs, was "caused by unknown and perhaps unknowable factors such as in-migration, birth rates, economic changes, or cumulative acts of private racial fears." Putting aside the oddity of listing examples of "unknown" or "unknowable" factors, conspicuously absent from Justice Stewart's list of potential causes of residential segregation was state action. It would have been wrong to claim that government action was the *only* cause of residential segregation, but to pretend that it was not even *partially* a cause required willful blindness.[134]

The Court decided *Milliken* on the twentieth anniversary of *Brown,* which made it an especially bitter occasion for Justice Marshall. This was the first time since *Brown* that the Court had ruled against plaintiffs in a major desegregation suit, and it was a devastating setback. Marshall knew this and said as much in dissent. "In the short run, it may seem to be the easier course to allow our great metropolitan areas to be divided up" into black and white areas, he wrote, "but it is a course, I predict, our people will regret." Marshall also talked bluntly about the influence of politics and public opinion on the decision. "Today's holding, I fear, is more a reflection of a perceived public mood that we have gone far enough in enforcing the Constitution's guarantee of equal justice than it is the product of neutral principles of law."[135]

A Sigh of Relief

Marshall may well have been correct in suggesting that public opinion influenced the Court in *Milliken,* though the motivations of individual justices necessarily remain in the realm of speculation. What is clear, however, is that the Court did not contradict dominant political sentiment. *Milliken* instead reinforced widespread political activities designed to accomplish the same goal. The Court, like state and federal politicians, acted to protect "local control" of schools. In this context, protecting local control essentially meant protecting the physical independence of the suburban neighborhood school. It also meant protecting the interest of middle-class whites. Just as massive resistance ultimately bent to the interests of middle-class whites, now busing was made to conform to the same interests.[136]

Indeed, "We won!" is precisely what Janice Libon, a housewife living in a Detroit suburb, exclaimed to a neighbor on hearing about the decision in *Milliken*. In an article in the *New York Times* entitled "Many White Parents Now See Their Children as Safe," Libon was pictured on the front porch of her house, with her children on a porch swing and a sign hanging on their picture window declaring: "This family will not be bussed." Another article described the similarly euphoric reaction of Fran Synder, a part-time clerk who lived in suburban Warren, Michigan. "I clapped my hands and said something like 'goodie,'" she recounted. "My kids would have been bused to a bad neighborhood. I was worried. My school's here in the backyard. That's why we moved here."[137]

Reaction among African Americans in the Detroit region and beyond was more mixed. Some were disappointed because they believed their children would have received a better education in suburban schools. Others, including Mayor Coleman Young of Detroit, "shed no big tears for busing." Young and others argued that busing was not really the issue. The issue instead was equal educational opportunity, which could be achieved with greater funding. There was no magic, he asserted, in having white and black kids sit together. Indeed, added Derrick Bell, a civil rights lawyer and soon to be Harvard Law School professor, "insisting on integrating every public school perpetuates the racially demeaning and unproven assumption that blacks must have a majority white presence in order to either teach or learn effectively." W. E. B. Du Bois, who declared decades earlier that the "Negro needs neither integration nor segregation, but education," could not have said it any better.[138]

Milliken II

Having protected the suburbs, the Supreme Court tried to make good on the second half of Nixon's compromise—more funding for urban schools—a few years later. They did so in the same case out of Detroit, which made its way again to the Supreme Court and became known as *Milliken II*. In *Milliken II*, the Court gave both middle-class whites and some black leaders and intellectuals what they wanted: money for urban schools in exchange for suburban (and urban) autonomy. A unanimous Court approved a desegregation plan that entitled students in Detroit to receive additional resources as compensation for being in a district that once intentionally segregated students. The Court reasoned that students in formerly segregated districts suffered educational harms and were therefore entitled to additional resources as a remedy. The connection between past segregation and current educational deficits was not implausible but was difficult to prove with certainty. But in *Milliken II*—unlike in the first *Milliken* decision—the Court was not so demanding about the relationship between right and remedy. Instead, the Court in *Milliken II* emphasized the flexibility and discretion lower courts possess when ordering equitable relief.[139]

The most important part of the decision required the state to help fund these remedial and compensatory education programs, which meant that school districts might actually benefit from being under court-ordered desegregation decrees. In *Milliken II*, for example, the school district remained a nominal defendant, but it had more in common with plaintiffs who, like the district, were interested in securing more funding from the state. At a basic level, it appeared that if the schools were going to be separate as a result of *Milliken*, they might be equal as a result of *Milliken II*—at least as long as the remedial funding continued to flow.[140]

CONSEQUENCES

It is difficult to exaggerate the consequences of *Milliken*, which is easily the most important desegregation decision aside from *Brown*. After *Milliken*, lower courts ordered interdistrict busing in only four metropolitan areas: Little Rock, Indianapolis, Wilmington, and Louisville. Only in these cases did courts find proof of interdistrict violations sufficient to justify an interdistrict remedy. In addition to these court orders, lower federal courts approved a settlement in a St. Louis desegregation case that involved voluntary interdistrict busing. And a small number of metropolitan areas in the South, located mostly in Florida, were integrated by busing because the school districts at issue were like Charlotte-Mecklenburg and encompassed both city and suburb. On the whole, however, suburban school districts received a pass from busing plans.[141]

Without the participation of the suburbs, busing was bound to be a failure. There were too few white students left in most urban districts to make integration meaningful, and the white students who remained were typically poor and often attended inadequate schools. Busing students within the city thus often meant transporting poor white and poor black students from shoddy, single-race schools to shoddy, somewhat integrated schools. In Boston, for example, poor black students from Roxbury were bused to South Boston High, which was previously attended mostly by poor, white Irish Catholics.[142]

As the ensuing riots in Boston indicated, limiting desegregation remedies in this way only heightened opposition and a sense of unfairness among those who were forced to participate. Often, those pushing for desegregation in places like Richmond or Boston—whether they were judges, activists, or politicians—did not send their own kids to public schools in the city. This fueled resentment among those without a real choice about where to live, just as Judge Merhige's decision to send his son to private school had irked those in Richmond without the money to do the same. "We are being asked to do something," said a representative from South Boston, "that all the rest of the world confides they won't do themselves."[143]

Limiting busing to the city was not simply futile and unfair; it was often counterproductive because it provided a strong incentive for continued flight from central cities. Although some middle-class blacks decamped for the suburbs, blacks were generally less able to leave the city for economic and other reasons. The group that fled was disproportionately white—hence the ubiquitous if crude phrase "white flight."

Academics and popular commentators have spilled a great deal of ink arguing over the extent to which school desegregation spurred white flight. There is evidence demonstrating that white flight was an independent phenomenon and occurred in cities, like New York and Atlanta, whose schools were never subjected to extensive desegregation decrees. There is also evidence, however, that desegregation plans added to existing patterns of white flight, at least during the first years of desegregation. Richmond provides a good example of both points. The percentage of white students in Richmond schools began declining in 1929 and continued every year after that. The decrease, however, occurred at a faster rate after 1954 than before 1954, and white enrollment declined dramatically in the few years after busing was implemented in 1971.[144]

Whatever the precise relationship between busing and white flight, the important point to recognize is that the Court unintentionally encouraged white flight with both carrot and stick. Decisions like *Green v. New Kent County*, *Swann v. Charlotte-Mecklenburg Board of Education*, and *Keyes v. School District No. 1* required all-out busing within urban districts that had once segregated their schools by law, which displaced white students from their neighborhood schools and therefore gave middle-class whites a reason to leave. *Milliken*, in turn, protected white suburbs from busing plans and therefore gave middle-class whites a safe place to go. The Court, as some scholars have suggested, might have been better off with either much more busing or much less.[145]

Empirical evidence bears out this hypothesis. School desegregation confined to urban districts generally produced more white flight than desegregation that involved an entire metropolitan area, including the suburbs. One study, for example, indicated that city school districts lost up to twice as many white students as countywide districts when desegregation plans were implemented. This is not surprising. As explained earlier, avoiding a metropolitan-wide desegregation plan was simply harder to do than avoiding one confined to cities.[146]

Milliken, moreover, did not just ensure the separation of white and black students; it also separated middle-class and poor students. Closing off the suburbs meant that city schools would be dominated by students who were primarily poor, whereas suburban schools would be dominated primarily by middle-class ones. Isolating children of poverty was and remains a terrible education policy, as schools of concentrated poverty present the most difficult challenge of all in the world of public education. Indeed, as will be detailed in later chapters, most major education reforms enacted since the time of *Milliken* have been attempts, not very successful, to address this challenge and to close the wide gaps between city and suburban schools.[147]

Milliken also influenced the funding and politics of public education. At the time, suburban districts on average spent about $1,000 per pupil, while Detroit spent roughly $650 per pupil. It was never clear exactly how the finances would be structured under Judge Roth's busing plan, which did not require actual consolidation of districts; indeed, the Supreme Court pointed to the complexity of this task as one reason not to undertake it. But the plaintiffs believed, with justification, that interdistrict busing would lead eventually to the elimination of gross financial disparities between districts. The reason was straightforward: if suburban students were bused into Detroit schools, suburban parents would have a reason to care about funding levels in Detroit schools.[148]

The opposite was also true, and this is why *Milliken* has had a profound influence on the politics of public education. As long as suburban students are safely ensconced in their own districts, suburban parents and their political representatives have much less reason to care about urban schools—whether the issue is funding levels, access to good teachers, safety, or overall educational quality. If anything, their incentive is to limit state funding of urban schools in order to keep state taxes from rising.

Recall that school desegregation originally rested on the fairly old political idea of tying, such that the fate of poor and minority students would be bound to the fate of their advantaged and white peers. School desegregation would accomplish this by placing black students in white schools and vice versa, such that minority students would necessarily benefit from white parents' and legislators' desire to provide for their own children. As one black parent in Richmond explained in the early 1970s: "I pushed so hard for integration because... I've been around long enough to know that if the white child is there, the money will be there."[149]

Milliken precluded the formation of ties—physical, financial, and political—that might have bound urban and suburban schools, students, and parents together. Suburban parents and their representatives might still care about urban schools, but they would have no immediate stake in them. The resulting political dynamic is analogous to the politics of foreign aid. Americans and their representatives may care about what happens in other countries, but they are at least one step removed. As a result, we rarely commit to doing whatever it takes to help other countries succeed; instead, we offer aid sufficient to satisfy our collective conscience or to gain various political favors. State legislatures tend to take the same approach to city school systems, as later chapters explain.[150]

Given the combination of *Milliken* and *Milliken II*, it should come as no surprise that the focus of subsequent desegregation cases, at least in the North and West, shifted away from integration and toward money. Without enough white students enrolled to make integration meaningful, plaintiffs and urban districts instead sought state-funded compensatory programs for minority students in formerly segregated schools. The focus was on the quality of education offered in racially isolated schools, and the hope was that money would help. *Milliken II* funds thus came to supplant rather than supplement racial integration, and the goal of desegregation cases shrank accordingly. The goal was no longer equality of educational opportunity through integration but adequacy through remedial funding. Put differently, the cases became less about integration and more about reparation.[151]

Across the country, in Missouri, New York, Pennsylvania, Maryland, Illinois, Georgia, Ohio, and Arkansas, school desegregation plaintiffs sued state governments for funds to finance "desegregation" plans. As in *Milliken II* itself, these cases often pitted unlikely allies against unusual foes. Civil rights groups representing schoolchildren teamed up with school districts—who were usually defendants in early desegregation cases—in an effort to extract money from unwilling state governments. Plaintiffs and courts thus used these cases like mini versions of school finance cases and sought to redistribute funds from the state to formerly segregated schools. The impact of increased funding is discussed in detail in the next chapter, but suffice it to say here that *Milliken II* money did not make a significant difference in these schools.[152]

CLOSING THE CASE IN RICHMOND

Years after failing in their consolidation efforts, plaintiffs in Richmond followed the national trend and tried to transform their case from one about student integration into one about money. Busing had continued in Richmond under Judge Mehrige's supervision, even after his consolidation order was reversed. But by the mid-1980s, it was painfully obvious that busing was a waste of time. The school system by then was 87 percent black; busing shifted black students from one nearly all-black school to another.

In 1984, the Richmond School Board, which was majority-black, decided that it was time end busing. The board realigned itself with the plaintiffs and went back to court, asking Judge Merhige to halt busing and to order the state to provide *Milliken II* funding to Richmond. Judge Merhige declined the request and went on to conclude that the school system had achieved unitary status and therefore should be released from judicial supervision. Merhige found that no vestiges of past segregation remained in Richmond.[153]

It is impossible to know whether Merhige was chastened by the fact that his earlier opinion was overturned, had a change of heart about the prospects of court-ordered desegregation, or did not believe in substituting money for integration. Whatever the cause, the later Judge Merhige was much different from the earlier one who had ordered consolidation. A once crusading liberal was now a cautious moderate who seemed resigned to the limited reach and authority of courts.

Merhige acknowledged that students in Richmond lagged behind those in Henrico and Chesterfield, which might have formed the basis for *Milliken II* relief. He attributed low achievement levels in Richmond not to race, however, but to concentrated poverty. He recognized "that one of the reasons for the high-poverty rate in Richmond is the inferior education that was provided to blacks under the former dual system." But in contrast to his willingness years before to endorse a far-reaching remedy for past segregation, he was unwilling to extend the court's power here: "It is not within the Court's power," he concluded, "to remedy either the poverty itself or the ancillary effects of such poverty." Thus, despite recognizing that poverty and past segregation were related, he held "that segregation-related poverty is not a factor that can be used to justify the imposition of remedial programs in a school system."[154]

Judge Merhige also rejected the motion for compensatory funding because the state already provided a disproportionate amount of funding to Richmond. Even if Richmond were entitled to compensatory funding, he reasoned, they were essentially already receiving it. School board members acknowledged Richmond's high funding levels, but they argued that even more funding was necessary to help schools overcome the effects of poverty and neglect facing many of their students. Judge Merhige disagreed, and his ruling was affirmed the following year by the Fourth Circuit. In 1987, more than three decades after the *Brown* rulings and with little fanfare, the Richmond school system returned to a system of primarily neighborhood schools.[155]

INEVITABLE?

Today, it may be hard to imagine that *Milliken* could have come out differently or, if it had, that a ruling requiring cross-district busing would have been enforced. More generally, it is simply difficult, because so different from reality, to picture a world in which city and suburban students regularly attend the same schools. But the notion that urban and suburban school systems were destined to remain separate is at least exaggerated, if not simply wrong. Knowing why is important not only because it helps one understand the past better, but also because it helps one think about the future more clearly.

Legal Doctrine

To begin with, the outcome in *Milliken* was certainly not required as a matter of law. As the dissenting opinions pointed out, the legal principle articulated by the Court—that the scope of the remedy must match the scope of the violation—could have justified extending a remedy beyond Detroit's borders, either because the state itself was involved or because without doing so, there would be *no* real remedy. More generally, the Court in *Milliken* latched onto a particularly cramped view of state responsibility, which excused government officials of all but blatant, intentionally segregative acts. Because neither state nor local school officials had taken any steps to segregate suburban schools, the Court reasoned, there was no reason to include them in a desegregation remedy. This view ignored the various steps government officials had taken to keep neighborhoods segregated. More important, it implicitly rejected the view of state responsibility endorsed by Judge Roth in the same case, Judge Merhige in the Richmond case, and Justice Powell in his concurring opinion in *Keyes v. School District No. 1*.

In some ways, the question regarding the scope of state responsibility for segregated schooling has been lost to history. Shortly after *Milliken*, the Supreme Court explicitly decided, in the 1976 case of *Washington v. Davis*, that intent to discriminate must be shown in order to prove an equal protection violation. The Court made clear in subsequent cases, moreover, that intent to discriminate means a desire to achieve disparate treatment—as opposed to simply an awareness of the likely result. In order to prove that school officials intention-ally segregated schools, therefore, plaintiffs would have to show that the offi-cials took actions for the specific purpose and with the specific hope of causing segregation. If they took actions simply with an awareness of the results, that would not be considered intentional segregation. This rule hardened the dis-tinction between de jure and de facto segregation and permanently disposed of the idea that school officials could be held responsible for the foreseeable con-sequences of their actions and inactions.[156]

At the time of the Richmond and Detroit cases, however, the question of how to define state responsibility for segregation remained very much in play. An op-ed in the *Washington Post* in the summer of 1972, written just days after the Fourth Circuit overturned Judge Merhige's consolidation order, captured the legal uncertainty: "the basic question . . . is how much or what kind of action, or inaction, by public officials is required to persuade the courts that the result-ing segregation is the product of unconstitutional state action. It is to this issue that the Supreme Court will have to address itself someday." There is no logi-cally correct answer to that question. Instead, it requires a judgment call, as the Justice Department admitted in its brief before the Supreme Court in *Bradley v. Richmond School Board*. The question, in the words of the brief, remained one of degree and required determining "whether there is a sufficiently proxi-mate and substantially causal relationship" between government action and segregated schools to blame the government for the segregation.[157]

Judge Roth and Judge Merhige thought that as long as state and local school officials knew of segregated housing patterns and failed to counterbalance them in school assignments, those officials should be held responsible for school seg-regation. This was an expansive view of government responsibility, to be sure, though it was also once supported by a majority of justices who decided the *Keyes* case but simply never got together to make that view the law.

Legal theory is one thing, however, and practical considerations are another. Holding state and local officials responsible for any and all school segregation would have led to some fairly dramatic results. Most likely, it would have cre-ated an ongoing duty among school officials to ensure that schools were not segregated. To accept the view of Judge Merhige and Judge Roth, therefore, was to accept the possibility of endless measures, either court or legislature driven, designed to ensure racially integrated schools within particular regions.

Which leads right back to the sense of inevitability that pervades thinking about this issue today: surely parents, whether white or black, would not have stood for a system of student assignments permanently dedicated to the goal of integration. They most certainly would not have stood for integration across the urban-suburban boundary. This much might seem obvious, at least at first blush. But there are some intriguing counterexamples that tug at one's sleeve and beg to be noticed by those prone to accept the conventional wisdom.

A Counterexample

The most interesting counterexample is Charlotte-Mecklenburg in North Carolina, the school district at issue in the famous busing case discussed earlier, *Swann v. Charlotte-Mecklenburg Board of Education*. The City of Charlotte and Mecklenburg County merged school systems in 1960, before busing began. Right away, the importance of historical accident—that is, how district lines have been drawn and redrawn—is clear. Busing could occur throughout the Charlotte metropolitan region because it was a single school district. The same would have been true if Richmond had succeeded in its attempt to annex larger portions of Henrico and Chesterfield counties in the late 1960s and early 1970s.[158]

This did not mean that suburbanites in Mecklenburg County embraced the prospect of court-ordered busing. Far from it. They reacted with the same mixture of outrage and fear that characterized the reactions in metropolitan Richmond and Detroit. White suburbanites embraced the notion of freedom of choice, formed groups to protest court-ordered busing, and convinced their political representatives at the state and national level to pursue ways to limit busing. Buses rolled in 1970 despite the protests and carried students back and forth between the city and the suburbs. White flight was minimal, and most middle-class parents, while not happy about busing, remained committed to public education.[159]

Then something unexpected happened: some middle-class whites voiced support for more busing rather than less. Originally, the affluent suburbs in southeast Mecklenburg County had been left largely untouched by the busing plan. Less affluent whites resented this exemption and argued in favor of a fairer distribution of the busing burden. This in turn changed the politics of busing and produced an interracial coalition that favored more busing over less. It also opened a lot of eyes. As one former opponent of busing acknowledged, there came a time "when ordinary working people experienced what it meant not to be wealthy, a feeling that must be similar to the moment when black people discovered the consequences of not being white."[160]

The district court judge, James B. McMillan, supported the call for more busing rather than less. He was committed to socioeconomic as well as racial integration, believing that class was more important than race when it came to academic achievement. He was also committed to avoiding resegregation, which meant eliminating any white havens from busing. The local newspaper also ultimately endorsed widespread, and seemingly permanent, busing. The *Charlotte Observer* astutely noted in 1973: "If the Supreme Court is becoming the protector of the suburbs and in effect a force for resegregation, the losers will be the cities—not simply because they are turning black but because they will be collecting places for disadvantaged people and inferior, segregated schools." Charlotte-Mecklenburg showed, the *Charlotte Observer* continued, that successful desegregation plans "required suburban inclusion through spatial and socioeconomic remedies."[161]

Charlotte-Mecklenburg School Board members also became supporters of widespread busing, and those who did won reelection in 1974. The community had thus come at least to tolerate busing. A telling poll in 1974 indicated that two-thirds of those surveyed opposed busing away from neighborhood schools, but three-fourths agreed that busing, if it did occur, should be equalized across the entire district. Over time, moreover, the community as a whole came to support the idea of stably integrated schools. As described by historian Matthew Lassiter, an expert on the Charlotte-Mecklenburg experience, two-way integration was at first seen as a "frontal assault on the consensus among the white middle class that a nice home in a safe and segregated suburban neighborhood served by quality public schools was critical to living the good life and the key to their children's futures." Over time, however, "a large majority of white families in Charlotte-Mecklenburg decided that they could reconcile their own versions of the American Dream with enrollment in a comprehensively integrated school system." Indeed, these parents "came to believe that integrated schools were both desirable and essential in a multiracial and decent society."[162]

Throughout the 1970s and 1980s, the Charlotte-Mecklenburg School Board strongly supported comprehensive integration. The Chamber of Commerce touted the schools, and especially the fact that they were stably integrated. When President Reagan campaigned against busing in the Mecklenburg suburbs in 1984, his stump speech went nowhere. Busing kids away from neighborhood schools "makes them pawns in a social experiment that nobody wants," Reagan asserted, adding that "we found out [busing] failed." The crowd greeted these statements with silence, and the next day the *Charlotte-Observer*'s lead editorial began: "You were wrong, Mr. President." It went on to call integrated schools Charlotte-Mecklenburg's proudest achievement.[163]

Well into the 1990s, enrollment in the public schools soared, while the percentage of whites and blacks remained relatively stable throughout the system and within each school. In the late 1990s, however, white parents used the federal courts that had once required busing in Charlotte-Mecklenburg to dismantle the region's desegregation plan, arguing successfully that because Charlotte-Mecklenburg had achieved unitary status, busing for desegregation could no longer be required by the courts—and might actually be unlawful for the legislature to continue on its own. At the start of the new millennium, Charlotte-Mecklenburg returned to neighborhood school assignments with some opportunity for school choice. Because neighborhoods remained largely segregated, the schools became more segregated as well. Busing had become so ingrained in the local culture that most "old-timers" blamed the end of busing on "self-centered newcomers and especially Yankee transplants." The charge was a bit of an exaggeration, but there was some truth to it—and it is nonetheless telling that the desegregation plan was ended not by popular vote but by court decree.[164]

The experience in Charlotte-Mecklenburg is somewhat haunting for those who still believe that schools should be integrated by both class and race. Because the metropolitan region happened to be a single district, the stars aligned there, for well over two decades, to produce schools that were integrated and fairly popular among blacks, whites, the poor, the middle class, and the affluent. The local newspaper, unlike the white papers in Richmond, supported the desegregation plan, which inevitably helped shape white opinion. Yet Charlotte-Mecklenburg was not so different from other metropolitan areas that successful integration could *only* have occurred there and nowhere else. The truth is that integration was never really tried in most other places, at least not in a way that gave it even a fighting chance of success. Charlotte-Mecklenburg is haunting because it suggests that perhaps integration could have worked in other metropolitan areas as well.

What Charlotte-Mecklenburg also indicates is that preferences about integration are not fixed, but are shaped by experience. Initial opposition in Charlotte-Mecklenberg changed to tolerance and then support among many who participated in the desegregation plan. In most places in the country, by contrast, white middle-class parents never seriously confronted the possibility that their children's schools might be significantly integrated for the foreseeable future. Indeed, they fought successfully to limit the reach of school desegregation to avoid such a possibility. This meant that most never had to try to make desegregation work, which is what parents in Charlotte-Mecklenburg were forced to do. Having never been prodded to make desegregation succeed, white middle-class parents elsewhere never had the opportunity or motivation to reconsider their opposition to it.

At first glance, there might seem to be some tension between the idea that middle-class, white parents generally get what they want in education law and policy and the idea that desegregation could have turned out differently. But the ideas are not irreconcilable for the simple reason that the preferences of middle-class, white parents were not unalterable, as the Charlotte-Mecklenburg experience illustrates. Under the right circumstances, it is possible that these parents might have supported more integration rather than less. And it is here, in the shaping of circumstances, that luck played a role.

It is not just that *Milliken* would have come out differently if one justice had switched his vote. More broadly, timing and accident of history influenced the scope of school desegregation at several crucial points. School desegregation, for example, coincided with federal funding for highway construction; the former gave whites a reason to leave the cities, and the construction of highways made commuting from suburbs to cities much easier. Timing was also key in annexation battles. Richmond, for example, had been involved in several attempts in the 1960s to annex portions of Chesterfield and Henrico counties. Richmond even turned down the opportunity to purchase seventeen square miles of land in Henrico County. Had Richmond succeeded in annexing this land, or even larger portions of Chesterfield and Henrico counties, school desegregation might have played out quite differently in that region. After 1970, however, school desegregation was the chief reason why annexation was no longer politically plausible—in Richmond and most metropolitan areas across the country.[165]

In addition, some southern states, like Florida and North Carolina, just happened to include both cities and suburbs in the same countywide school districts. The states with countywide districts drew those boundaries years before school desegregation began; it was purely an accident of history. Yet if more states had followed their lead years ago, there would have been many more opportunities for urban-suburban desegregation, as *Milliken* presented no obstacle to widespread busing within a single district. Had more middle-class, white parents actually experienced integration, who can say with certainty that their opposition to integration would have remain unchanged? The same is true, of course, of black parents, only some of whom supported cross-district integration and, even then, often did so tepidly.

There is an air of inevitability to hindsight. But everyone simultaneously recognizes that chance plays a role in shaping the future. So it is with school desegregation. Its progression looks now as if it had been preordained, at least with regard to urban-suburban districts. But chance helped shape the circumstances under which desegregation unfolded. Middle-class whites, to be sure, got what they wanted when it came to cross-district busing, just like they had before and would again in other battles over education. Yet one can never know whether they would have continued to want the same thing had they been forced to try something else.

CONCLUSION

The prolific English writer and professional curmudgeon G.K. Chesterton once said of Christianity that "the Christian ideal has not been tried and found wanting; it has been found difficult and left untried." The same could be said of desegregation, which was never really tried in most metropolitan areas. For a very brief moment in time, two lower court judges, Merhige in Richmond and Roth in Michigan, seemed willing to tackle the problem by requiring urban-suburban busing. But the enormity of the task was evident to many. Shortly after Judge Roth issued his first busing order in the Detroit case, a telling headline in the *New York Times* read: "Federal Judge, Blaming Virtually All of Society, Finds Detroit School System Deliberately Segregated." Virtually all of society *was* to blame, in one way or another, for the plight of the Detroit schools. But in some ways, that was precisely the problem. It made casting blame solely on the government seem artificial and at the same time made attempts to remedy the intersecting historical injustices seem quixotic.[166]

The Supreme Court in *Milliken*, like the Fourth Circuit in *Bradley v. Richmond School Board*, was unwilling to open the boundaries between urban and suburban school systems. Federal courts, and especially the Supreme Court, are often criticized for being too liberal and too activist, and court involvement in school desegregation is typically cited as a leading example. Court-ordered busing, however, refutes more than it supports that charge. Courts may have been guilty of "liberal activism" in converting the *Brown* rulings into a command to integrate rather than a prohibition against segregation, and by requiring busing to achieve integration. But the limit *Milliken* placed on busing was ultimately more important than the decision to order it in the first place, and that limit was the product of a restrained and conservative Court, not a "liberal activist" one.

We are still living with the consequences of *Milliken* and continued residential segregation. Most African-American students, as well as most Hispanic students, attend urban schools. The urban schools that most attend are both predominantly minority and predominantly poor. Student poverty is typically measured by eligibility for free and reduced-priced lunch. To be eligible for a free lunch, a student's family income must be at or below 130 percent of the poverty level; students whose families earn between 130 percent and 150 percent of the poverty level are eligible for a reduced-price lunch. In 2004–5, 61 percent of the students in the largest urban districts were eligible for a free or reduced-price lunch, compared with 38 percent nationally.[167]

The higher percentage of minorities in an urban school, on average, the higher the percentage of poor students. Indeed, urban schools that are at least 90 percent poor are also, on average, 85 percent minority. Students who attend high-poverty urban schools generally post lower test scores on state, AP, and SAT tests, are less likely to graduate, and are less likely to attend college. They are also less likely to be taught by highly qualified teachers, regardless of whether quality is measured by academic qualifications, experience, or results.[168]

Tee-Jay and the Richmond School District reflect these trends. Eighty-four percent of the students at Tee-Jay are minorities, as are over 90 percent of the students in the Richmond school district. Roughly 75 percent of Richmond students are eligible for free or reduced-price lunch. The reported figure for Tee-Jay students, 44 percent, is considerably lower, but this undoubtedly underestimates the number of poor students there because high school students often do not sign up for lunch programs—so the numbers for all high schools tend to be unusually low given the overall poverty rates in school districts.[169]

Despite the data showing a large gap between urban and suburban schools, the moment for compelled interdistrict integration has passed, just as court-ordered school desegregation is itself fading from view. In a series of cases decided in the 1990s, the U.S. Supreme Court essentially directed lower courts to close out desegregation decrees and return school systems to the control of local and state officials. Some decrees still remain in place, but court-ordered desegregation is clearly in its twilight phase. The Court, meanwhile, has placed new obstacles in the path of school districts that would like to increase integration on their own and without court order. In a 2007 case, *Parents Involved in Community Schools v. Seattle School District No. 1*, the Court placed restrictions on school districts that would like to take steps to voluntarily integrate their schools. School districts still have some ability to consider race in student assignments, as long as they do not classify individual students by race, but the Court's decision makes it easier legally to leave segregated schools alone than to do something about them.[170]

Education reform advocates, for the most part, have also moved beyond segregation as a key issue. Even at the time of *Milliken*, many who cared about urban schools and minority students were already looking for alternative strategies. The first one that caught their imagination was funding. Civil rights advocates, local African-American leaders, school board members, mayors, and black and white intellectuals seemed increasingly to agree that the *real* problem was money. Detroit mayor Young, after telling reporters he "shed no big tears" for the loss in *Milliken*, identified what, to him, was the real problem: unequal resources. "I would like to see state educational fiscal reform," he explained, "so that all schoolchildren throughout the state could receive equal amounts proportionate to their education needs." Many other advocates shared his view and, having given up or turned their backs on integration, looked ahead to equalizing resources.[171]

PART II

PRESENT: SAVE THE CITIES, SPARE

THE SUBURBS

CHAPTER 3

Desegregating Dollars

"We feel a responsibility for others, but we do want to protect the kind of quality our people have come to expect."
    —Betty Menke, president, Scarsdale Board of Education (1972)

In 1968, Derrick Bell was serving as the executive director of the Western Center on Law and Poverty in Los Angeles. Before moving out west, Bell had spent five years working on school desegregation cases as a lawyer with the NAACP Legal Defense Fund. He started his legal career as "a true believer in desegregation," but by 1968 he was beginning to have doubts. More and more, it seemed like money, not segregation, was the real issue. As he later wrote, while a law professor at New York University, "the root of the problem appeared to be the substantial disparities in the resources provided to black students relative to white students."[1]

Bell decided that instead of pushing for more integration, "we should concentrate on desegregating the money." In 1968, he and a colleague helped recruit John Serrano as a plaintiff for a suit challenging California's unequal school finance system. The ensuing case, *Serrano v. Priest*, emerged as the first important victory for school finance plaintiffs, and it set off a slew of similar suits across the country.[2]

The embrace of school finance litigation by Bell and others was at once both ironic and understandable. It was ironic because desegregation began in part as a reaction to the continued failure of efforts to make separate schools equal. Simply suing for equal resources, when *Plessy*'s rule of separate but equal was in force, did not work so well. Integrating schools came to be seen as a better strategy for equalizing resources. But now school funding suits were supposed to make up for the failures of desegregation. In some ways, it seemed like starting all over again.

The embrace of school finance litigation was nonetheless understandable given the disappointing results of school desegregation. By the mid-1960s, integration had lost some of its luster, even to its earlier supporters like Bell. Many despaired over the slow pace and uneven results of court-ordered desegregation. Others came to question the underlying premise of integration: that it was the best means to equalize educational opportunities. Why couldn't black students learn just as much in all-black classrooms?

Under these circumstances, it was only natural that some advocates would switch their focus to school funding, which was grossly unequal in most states. Some school districts spent two to ten times more per pupil than others in the same state. Many of those initially attracted to integration saw it as an indirect way to gain access to more resources for minority students. Given that this strategy did not seem to be working, why not try (again) to go after the resources directly?

In turning away from racial integration and toward school funding, those who embraced school finance reform were essentially embracing the compromise Nixon would propose in his 1972 antibusing speech: let suburban and urban students remain where they are but provide more resources to urban schools. Like Nixon, those who advocated for school funding reform sought to move beyond racial separation as the key issue in the fight for educational equity. Indeed, in some ways they sought to move beyond race itself as the issue, given that school finance reform promised to benefit not just minority students, but all students who attended underfunded schools.

The promise of school finance litigation, however, remains unfulfilled. The litigation has only partially succeeded in court, and even successful lawsuits have not had a major impact on the ground. Litigation based on the federal Constitution was quickly halted by the Supreme Court's 1973 decision in *San Antonio v. Rodriguez*, which upheld Texas's unequal funding system. Richmond native Lewis Powell authored the opinion, which bears the marks of his experiences as a school board member and as a Virginian who lived through court-ordered school desegregation.[3]

Advocates then turned to state constitutions and state courts, filing funding suits in almost every state in the country. Plaintiffs have won only about half of these. Even when plaintiffs succeed on the merits in court, remedies are not always forthcoming. Courts are generally reluctant to order specific remedies, at least at first, and most legislatures are not exactly wild about coming up with their own fixes to a problem they denied existed. This dynamic triggers a tug-of-war between the plaintiffs and the legislature, which in turn typically necessitates several trips back to court. This is especially true in the few cases where urban districts have succeeded in court, which have been unusually long-running and acrimonious.[4]

When legislatures finally respond, they usually provide a bit more state funding to poor school districts while leaving the wealthier districts alone. The latter are usually permitted to devote as much locally raised revenue on their own schools as they would like. They are hardly ever required to share that local revenue with neighboring districts. In this sense, relatively affluent suburban districts have been shielded from the reach of school finance litigation, just as they were spared the burden of school desegregation. This has enabled these schools to remain not only physically separate from urban schools, but financially separate as well.

Despite the hope of advocates, school finance reform has not been an effective substitute for desegregation. The failure to integrate urban schools has left many of them isolated by poverty, and the problems of high-poverty urban schools do not seem solvable by money alone. Indeed, even high-spending urban schools lag behind lower-spending suburban and rural ones. Tee-Jay spends about $4,000 more *per pupil* than Freeman, for example, yet one would be hard pressed to say that Tee-Jay is a better school.[5]

Moreover, even if we were confident that more money could solve the problem, it seems unlikely to materialize. State legislatures are not especially keen to devote additional resources to city schools. This reluctance, it bears noting, seems due at least in part to the continued racial and class segregation between urban and suburban districts. Poor minority students and their families are not especially powerful politically, and representatives of urban areas rarely hold the balance of power in state legislatures. Suburban—and rural— legislators, in turn,have no direct interest in the health of urban schools, and it would not be shocking if at least some were prejudiced against urban schools because of stereotypical assumptions about urban minorities. Most courts, meanwhile, have proven reluctant to do more than tinker at the margins of spending; they have left the political dynamics of funding largely unchanged.[6]

Although school finance litigation has generally not achieved the goals advocates have set for it, it has had one lasting, unintentional impact. In shifting away from race and toward resources, the focus on funding reform has helped narrow the conversation about what to expect from schools. From the outset of the common school movement in the mid-nineteenth century, schools were seen as both academic and socializing institutions, where students would learn not only how to read and write but also how to become good citizens. Integration was consistent with this tradition insofar as it held out the hope that white and black students would learn from one another. When Justice Marshall lamented in his dissenting opinion in *Milliken* that "unless our children begin to learn together, there is little hope that our people will ever learn to live together," he captured the belief that integration could help prepare students to live in a diverse, pluralistic society.[7]

Whether by necessity or design, this socializing aspect of education has been put to one side in the quest for more money. Increasing funding does not and cannot buy integration or racial tolerance; if anything, school finance reform unintentionally entrenches segregation by defining the problem as one of resources rather than racial separation. What money *can* buy, at least in theory, is a better academic education. Not surprisingly, therefore, the ultimate goal of school finance litigation has been to improve academic achievement. And improving academic achievement, usually as measured by scores on standardized tests, has remained the exclusive goal of major education reforms ever since, as we will see in subsequent chapters.

The last two chapters started with Virginia and Richmond and expanded outward to consider national trends. This chapter and the next begin at the national level and work backward to Virginia and Richmond. This chapter covers the early period of school finance litigation, ending with the Supreme Court's decision in *San Antonio v. Rodriguez*. The following chapter describes school finance litigation in state courts and assesses the consequences of that litigation.

There has never been a successful finance suit in Virginia, despite two different attempts—three if one counts the unsuccessful attempt by Richmond, discussed in chapter 2, to secure *Milliken II* funds. Virginia and Richmond nonetheless serve as useful examples of the larger trends in school finance reform. Supporters and opponents of school finance litigation, for different reasons, tend to exaggerate its success in court, but the experience in Virginia brings home the point that a significant number of school finance suits have been rejected. Even without a court victory, however, Richmond schools still spend a good deal more per pupil than those in Henrico County. Richmond schools are thus in roughly the same position as those that have *succeeded* in school finance litigation, which in turn offers the opportunity to study the impact of increased spending on urban education. As this chapter will show, despite greater funding levels, Richmond schools like Tee-Jay still perform worse than their Henrico counterparts like Freeman. The experience in metropolitan Richmond thus provides a sobering example of the limits of school finance reform, at least as currently pursued.[8]

FUNDING BASICS AND THE BASIC PROBLEM

Schools receive funding from states, localities, and the federal government. In the earliest days of "public" education, schools were funded through a mixture of private and local revenues. Over the course of the twentieth century, private funding decreased dramatically, though private contributions still play a marginal role in funding some schools. State contributions, by contrast, increased steadily as states took on more responsibility for education and made greater efforts to equalize the resources available for public schools.[9]

Local, State, and Federal Funding

Today, local and state governments generally contribute about the same amount of funding for education, with localities picking up about 44 percent of the tab and states contributing 47 percent. That said, there are variations both among and within states. Hawaii, for example, has just one district, so the state pays the lion's share of the costs. On the other end of the spectrum, localities provide the bulk of school funding in some states. Within most states, moreover, poorer districts usually contribute a smaller portion of funding than do wealthier districts, which in turn means that the state's share of funding varies as well.[10]

The federal government's financial contribution to public education is small by comparison. This news often comes as a surprise given the increasingly important and intrusive role of the federal government in public education, illustrated most dramatically by the No Child Left Behind Act. The federal government contributes, on average, only about 9 percent of the total costs of public education in each state, though again there are variations. Much of this money is directed toward categorical programs that ostensibly target needy populations, such as poor students, who are funded through Title I, and students with special needs, who are funded through the Individuals with Disabilities in Education Act. Spending on education constitutes only about 2 percent of the federal government's overall budget, while it consumes over 40 percent of all expenditures by localities and over 20 percent of each state's expenditures.[11]

Overall spending on education has increased dramatically over the last half-century. Total expenditures per student have more than quintupled, even after adjusting for inflation. Thus, in today's dollars, average spending per pupil was $1,600 in 1949–50; in 2005, per pupil spending reached $9,400. In total, nearly $500 billion was spent on public education in 2005. The increases in spending are due to a number of factors, including large increases in teachers' salaries, which in turn reflect the fact that women have more employment opportunities today than they did in 1950. (Indeed, an irony of federal antidiscrimination laws, especially Title VII, which prohibits employment discrimination on the basis of gender, is that they made it much harder to find good teachers for low pay.) Increased spending on compensatory programs also accounts for some of the rise, and here special education is by far the most significant and costliest addition. Prior to 1950, indeed prior to 1970, many states simply did not educate students with serious physical or mental disabilities.[12]

Funding increases have not been matched by similarly dramatic advances in student achievement. Commentators disagree over the health of public education and the significance of various indicators such as test scores, graduation rates, and college attendance. Some argue that the entire system is mediocre and lags behind education systems in other countries. Others counter that claims of crisis in public education are overblown and that public schools are fairly strong, at least for some children. No one, however, would claim that there has been anything close to a fivefold increase in quality to match the fivefold increase in expenditures. And no one would claim, as will be discussed in more detail later, that increased expenditures have made urban schools as successful as suburban ones.

Three Kinds of Disparities

Funding disparities come in three varieties—interstate, intradistrict, and interdistrict. Only the last of these three has been the subject of sustained political and legal attention, which is not to say that the others deserve to be neglected. Interstate disparities can be quite severe. In 2005, New York spent, on average, a little more than $14,000 per pupil, while Utah spent only about $5,200 per pupil. Disparities like these, while significant in themselves, mask even greater disparities that exist between low-spending districts in states like Utah and high-spending districts in states like New York. Despite their obvious importance, interstate disparities have generally been ignored in the legal and policy world. Only the federal government could equalize spending among the states. The federal Constitution, however, does not require such equalization, and Congress has never shown much interest in addressing the problem.[13]

At the other end of the spectrum, intradistrict disparities, while usually not as dramatic, certainly exist: some schools in some districts spend more per pupil than others. Before *Brown*, such disparities were rampant and followed racial lines, with all-black schools often funded at much lower levels than all-white schools. Intradistrict disparities are no longer as prevalent, but they continue. Although some researchers have begun to focus attention on these disparities, they remain on the fringes of reform efforts. This inattention is partially due to a lack of solid data about individual school spending. But there is also general acceptance that some students—such as those with disabilities and those living in poverty—need and deserve more resources. The real question, which has only begun to be investigated, is whether intradistrict disparities are due primarily to extra spending on students in need. Early answers suggest perhaps not, but this research has yet to play much of a role in legislative debates or in litigation.[14]

Nearly all of the attention in the area of school finance reform has focused on interdistrict disparities. Outside of Hawaii and the District of Columbia, which do not really count because each has only a single school district, no state has equalized spending among its school districts. The disparities in spending, moreover, have traditionally been severe, with some districts spending two, three, or even ten times more per pupil than others. The prevalence and size of these disparities have diminished in the last thirty years, in part because of school finance litigation, but they continue to exist.[15]

Why Some Districts Spend More Than Others

Interdistrict disparities result from the interplay of three different factors: local property wealth, property tax rates, and state aid. Local funding for schools is typically raised through property taxes. The actual amount raised on the local level is a product of the amount of property wealth in a district and the tax rate. Some districts have more property wealth than others, which enables them to raise more money per pupil at any given tax rate. Indeed, if the differences in property wealth are great enough, property-rich districts can tax themselves at a lower rate and still raise more money than property-poor districts. State aid can be used to eliminate or reduce local funding disparities, leave them untouched, or exacerbate them.[16]

Consider a simple example, limited at first to local funding. Imagine that District A has $100,000 of property wealth per pupil, which means that the total assessed value of property within the district divided by the total number of students in the district results in $100,000 of property value for each student. Imagine that District B has only $50,000 of property wealth per pupil. If both districts tax property at 5 percent, District A will raise $5,000 per pupil, whereas District B will raise only $2,500 per pupil. Now imagine that District A lowers its tax rate to 3 percent while District B retains its 5 percent rate. District A will still raise more money—$3,000 per pupil—than District B, despite taxing itself at a lower rate.

The last example captures the reality in the majority of states, where lower-spending districts generally tax themselves at higher rates than higher-spending districts. Thus, in most states, different levels of property wealth, rather than different tax rates, are the primary cause of local funding disparities. Even where tax rates drive differences in funding, it is important to recognize that the ability of local districts to tax themselves for school funding depends on competing demands for public spending. Not all districts have the same level of competition for public dollars. Cities, for example, typically have greater demands for public services, such as fire and police protection, housing, health care, and welfare, than do middle-class suburbs.[17]

State Aid: The Key Variable

State aid could totally eliminate the effect of local variations in property wealth, but no state has gone that far. There are countless ways that states could structure funding to school districts, and state aid formulas have changed over time. In the past, most states simply provided a flat grant to school districts based on the number of students in the district. Each student received an equal amount of funding, which obviously did nothing to offset the inequalities in local funding.

Today, the most common method of distributing state funding is through what is typically called a foundation program. The details of these programs are varied and can be remarkably complicated, but the basic idea is straightforward. States determine the overall amount of funding per pupil thought necessary to pay for a decent education. This is usually called the foundation amount. The state then determines how much each district should have to pay toward the foundation amount. The state might simply set a uniform minimum property tax rate, or it might use various formulas that are in theory designed to assess each district's ability to raise revenue. Property wealth is a key component in all formulas, but states also consider income levels and other indices of ability to pay. The state then makes up the difference, if any, between the local share and the foundation amount.[18]

To continue with the earlier hypothetical, imagine that the state determines that the foundation amount is $6,000 per pupil. To simplify the example, imagine further that the state requires all districts to tax local property at a minimum of 4 percent. The state will then fund the difference between the amount raised by that tax rate in each locality and the foundation amount. Districts with lower property values will raise less money and therefore will receive more assistance from the state. Going back to District A, which has $100,000 of property wealth per pupil, a 4 percent tax rate will produce $4,000 per pupil, which means that the state would provide $2,000 per pupil to district A. District B, which only has $50,000 per pupil, would receive $4,000 from the state, because it would only be able to raise $2,000 on its own at a 4 percent tax rate.

In theory, this approach could equalize funding, but everything depends on the foundation amount. If the foundation amount were higher than any district would raise on its own, funding across districts would be equal. In reality, however, states tend to set the foundation amount at fairly low levels. This in turn means that most districts will want to spend *more* than the foundation amount. In order to do so, they have to tax themselves at higher rates than the state mandates, which means that local property values and local tax rates still matter a great deal.[19]

The Virginia Formula

Virginia provides a good illustration of the basic point and highlights the complexity of determining local contributions. The state sets a foundation amount, which is the amount of funding per pupil that it believes is necessary to provide an adequate education. It then determines local contributions through something called the Composite Index (CI). The CI represents the percentage of the foundation amount that the locality must provide, or, in other words, the local share. (The local share is a floor, not a ceiling; localities can and do contribute more.) The higher the CI, the less money the district receives from the state.[20]

The CI is a function of ten variables, which include local property values, local adjusted gross income, local taxable sales, state taxable sales, and state adjusted gross income. The CI is supposed to reflect the district's ability to raise revenue, but it is an imperfect measure at best. The formula does not take into account competing demands for local money, nor does it consider differences in costs among districts, due either to wage and price variations or variations among student populations. Those who serve higher percentages of poor students do not, for example, have a lower CI as a result. Richmond and Henrico County have nearly identical CIs—Richmond's is .42 and Henrico's is .46—despite the different student populations they serve, cost differentials in the districts, and different levels of demand for public services.[21]

The fundamental flaw in Virginia's system, however, is the foundation amount. By all accounts, it is unrealistically low. Indeed, all but one district in the entire state—135 out of 136—contribute more than is required by the CI. Many districts spend much more than is required, including Richmond, which contributes 170 percent more than state law mandates. Interestingly, Henrico contributes less per pupil than Richmond, which in turn means that the state funds a slightly larger portion of Henrico's budget than Richmond's. Whether Richmond needs to contribute as much as it does or needs to spend even more is an issue that will be addressed later. For now, however, this brief overview should be sufficient to understand the genesis of school finance litigation, which was designed to eliminate the inequalities that have plagued school funding systems for decades.[22]

IN SEARCH OF A THEORY: EARLY SCHOOL FINANCE LITIGATION

Advocates for school desegregation had a fairly straightforward conception of equal educational opportunity, which was essentially negative: educational opportunity should not be determined on the basis of race, such that African-American students were systematically disadvantaged. The central goal was to break the link between race and educational opportunity. School finance reform advocates, by contrast, have had a much more difficult time articulating their own vision of equal educational opportunity and, in particular, what equal educational opportunity requires with regard to funding. As a result, they have had a harder time figuring out what to ask for, and courts have had an equally difficult time figuring out the proper remedies in school finance cases.

The problems and possibilities were present from the start. Various theories, each of which might become a blueprint for legislative reform and litigation, competed with one another in the late1960s. Three theories proved most important and enduring: (1) equal funding, (2) needs-based funding, and (3) fiscal neutrality.

Equal Funding

In 1968, Arthur Wise, a graduate student at the University of Chicago, proposed the simple idea of equal funding. He called his the "one-dollar, one-scholar theory," picking up on the 1964 apportionment decision in *Reynolds v. Sims*, in which the U.S. Supreme Court adopted the principle of one person, one vote. Wise thought each school in the state should receive the same amount of funding per pupil, period.[23]

Wise's approach was attractive in its simplicity, but it had theoretical and practical problems. Given the differing needs of students, it was not clear why equal educational opportunity should require precisely equal funding. It seemed to violate basic ideas about equality to ignore rather than accommodate relevant differences in need. As a practical matter, moreover, equal funding might hurt urban districts that spent more money but educated a disproportionate share of poor students. In addition, requiring exactly equal spending would either require a dramatic leveling up, which might prove too expensive for most states, or a leveling down, which might prove either politically impossible or self-defeating.[24]

Wise was not an attorney representing clients. He was a graduate student writing his dissertation, so his ideas did not surface in litigation right away. In fact, complete equalization of funding has never been fully embraced. The one-dollar, one-scholar approach has nonetheless remained something of an implicit benchmark against which school funding schemes are measured, and reducing disparities among school districts has remained important in every school funding suit, whether as the chief aim or a subsidiary goal.

Needs-based Funding

Legal aid lawyers came up with their own theory, and theirs was the first actually presented in litigation. These attorneys represented poor students. Not surprisingly, they found Wise's theory unappealing because it offered no way to argue that poor students should receive more funding than middle-income students. Indeed, it prohibited such funding differences. Legal aid lawyers thus favored an alternative approach, which became known as the needs-based theory of equal educational opportunity.[25]

They argued that poor and affluent students should have their education needs met equally, which in turn meant—among other things—that poor students should receive more resources because they had greater needs. Although not styled as such, this theory was really the precursor of the adequacy movement, which is discussed in detail in the next chapter. Meeting the different needs of students is hard to accomplish without reference to some objective outcome goal, unless the aim is the unrealistic one of providing enough resources for each student to maximize his or her individual potential. An obvious goal, as advocates later realized, is an adequate education—that is, students should receive the level of resources they need to obtain an adequate education, which might mean that some students receive more than others if necessary to achieve an adequate outcome.

When first presenting the needs-based theory to courts, however, litigants simply alleged that funding should track the differing needs of the students. As might be expected, courts did not know where to begin. In the two earliest cases, federal courts in Illinois and Virginia rejected the challenges for similar reasons: the plaintiffs offered no manageable standard by which to assess and measure educational need. The court in Virginia, for example, expressed sympathy for the plaintiffs' position, recognizing that the deficiencies in prop-erty-poor districts "are not and cannot be gainsaid" and acknowledging the plaintiffs' "beseeming, earnest, and justified appeal for help." The court also acknowledged that the attempt to provide students "the same educational opportunities . . . is certainly a worthy aim, commendable beyond measure." But the court ultimately concluded that "courts have neither the knowledge, nor the means, nor the power to tailor the public moneys to fit the varying needs of these students throughout the State."[26]

Fiscal Neutrality

At about the same time these decisions were handed down, Professor John Coons at Northwestern University Law School began to frame another theory. He received help from two students, William Clune and Stephen Sugarman, who would themselves go on to become law professors. Their basic idea, which they dramatically styled as "Proposition I," was that school funding in any dis-trict should not be a function of local property wealth. Equal educational opportunity, they argued, required the state to ensure equal access to school funding at the same tax rate. Hence the idea of fiscal neutrality: the funding system would neutralize the influence of local property wealth by enabling all districts to raise the same amount of funding at any given tax rate.[27]

The principle of fiscal neutrality could be satisfied if the state guaranteed exactly equal funding for all districts, as that would sever the link between local wealth and school spending. But fiscal neutrality could also be satisfied by ensuring equal *access* to resources and allowing localities in effect to decide for themselves how much to spend. The mechanics of the latter approach resem-bled the more traditional foundation programs, with one key difference: Instead of establishing a fixed foundation amount, thought sufficient to fund a decent education, states would instead establish a guaranteed tax base (GTB). States would then fund the difference between the amount a locality could raise by applying its tax rate to its tax base, and the amount it could raise if it applied that same tax rate to the GTB.[28]

For example, imagine that a state establishes a GTB of $100,000 per pupil, meaning that all districts can assume they have that much property wealth. Now imagine that District B has a real tax base of $50,000 per pupil. Under a fiscal neutrality program, District B could tax itself at whatever rate it liked, and the state would make up the difference between that tax rate as applied to $50,000 and the same tax rate as applied to $100,000. A 1 percent tax rate would mean that the state would supply the locality with $500 per pupil, because that is the difference between 1 percent of $100,000 ($1,000) and 1 percent of $50,000 ($500). If District B decided to tax itself at 5 percent, state funding would rise to $2,500, as that is the difference between 5 percent of $100,000 ($5,000) and 5 percent of $50,000 ($2,500). In both examples, District B could behave as if it had $100,000 per pupil in property wealth.

In offering their fiscal neutrality theory, Coons, Clune, and Sugarman hoped to solve at least three problems. First, they hoped to change the politics of school funding, which typically pitted poor districts against rich ones. Coons in particular hoped that high-spending districts would become the driving force to ensure that all districts had ample resources. He believed that high-spending districts would have an interest in having the guaranteed tax base set at a high level to avoid having to redistribute locally raised revenues, which might occur if property rich districts had a higher tax base than the GTB. In Coon's view, poor and rich districts would thus work in concert to ensure a high GTB, and in this sense their fates would be tied together.[29]

Second, this theory offered a manageable standard to courts, as compared to the needs-based approach already rejected in two cases. Courts would simply have to ensure that for any given tax rate, all districts in the state could raise the same funding. Courts would not have to determine student need, nor would they have to insist on equal funding for all districts.

Third, fiscal neutrality would respect local control over funding. Coons and his colleagues recognized that local control remained a strong tradition and feared that courts would be reluctant to jettison it. Fiscal neutrality would not require courts to override local control because it would leave to states the decision about how to break the link between local property wealth and school spending. States might mandate equal spending, which would destroy local control. But they could instead, consistent with fiscal neutrality, mandate equal access to funding at any given tax rate. The latter approach would leave to localities control over tax rates and spending.[30]

The idea of fiscal neutrality was also consistent, at least in theory, with providing some districts more funding to compensate for higher costs, due either to location or the demographics of the student population. The bedrock principle of fiscal neutrality was simply that school funding should not be a product of local property wealth, which would not preclude the state from giving more aid to districts that faced higher costs. This aspect of fiscal neutrality theory, however, was often ignored by critics of this approach, and indeed by the courts that favored it.[31]

Fiscal neutrality was not without flaws or critics. To begin, it seemed to replace one arbitrary factor with another, at least from a student's perspective. Instead of local property wealth, local preferences for education spending would determine the amount spent in local schools. Fiscal neutrality would thus respect the wishes of local taxpayers, but it would not necessarily meet the needs of local students. Indeed, fiscal neutrality really promised equity for taxpayers, who could be assured that the same tax rates would result in the same amount of funding for schools. It did not guarantee equity for students.[32]

There were practical and political obstacles as well. If fiscal neutrality were to achieve perfect equality, the GTB would have to be set at the same tax base as the wealthiest school district. This would be financially impossible in most states, as almost every state has some districts that have extraordinarily high property values per pupil. Even if fiscal neutrality programs only sought substantial equality, the GTB would have to be set at the eightieth or ninetieth percentile of local property wealth, which still might be financially unrealistic for many states.

The alternative to setting the GTB at a high level is to use a form of recapture, which is not practically difficult but is politically controversial. The idea is simple enough. The districts with property wealth above the GTB would have to return a portion of funds raised at any given tax rate to reflect the difference between their actual tax base and the guaranteed tax base. It involves the same math, just in reverse. If the GTB were $100,000 per pupil, for example, and a district had $200,000 per pupil in property wealth, if it taxed itself at 1 percent it would have to return $1,000 to the state for redistribution elsewhere. Recapture would effectively equalize spending among districts, but it is not especially popular politically, as we shall see.

Another practical objection came from urban school leaders, who worried that fiscal neutrality might result in less money for city schools, especially if it required wealthier districts to share local funds with poorer districts. The tax base in a number of cities was (and remains) higher than that in some suburbs and in many rural areas; a fiscal neutrality scheme might require cities—already strapped for cash because of high demands for other social services—to tax themselves at higher rates with no increase in money for education. Again, the general idea of fiscal neutrality did not preclude states from offering more assistance to urban districts because of greater needs, but this feature of fiscal neutrality was usually ignored.[33]

While some thought fiscal neutrality might not do enough, especially for poor students, others thought it might prove too much. The main concern was what Coons colorfully described as the "equal sewer" problem. If access to education funding had to be equalized, many wondered, what about other services, such as fire and police protection, welfare, or even health care? Did courts really have the capacity and the authority to restructure the tax and spending schemes of states and localities? Added to this concern about a slippery slope was the underlying uncertainty about the relationship between money and educational opportunity. Was it really the case, some wondered, that more money meant more learning?[34]

Serrano v. Priest (1971)

Despite these shortcomings, fiscal neutrality received a much better reception from courts than did the needs-based theory. The first big victory came in California in *Serrano v. Priest*. The lead plaintiff, John Serrano, Jr., was the father of two boys who had recently moved out of a Mexican-American neighborhood in East Los Angeles. The move was actually prompted by the principal at his sons' elementary school, who called Serrano into his office and told him: "You've got a couple of very bright kids—get them out of East L.A. schools if you want to give them a chance." Serrano took the advice and moved his family to the middle-class suburb of Whittier, California.[35]

Serrano remained troubled by the principal's blunt advice, however, and the broader question of why some schools seemed better equipped than others. When Derrick Bell approached him at a dinner party, Serrano agreed to join a case challenging the unequal funding system in California. At the time, Serrano thought the case was hopeless.[36]

It was not. In August 1971, the California Supreme Court upheld the Serrano complaint. It agreed with the plaintiffs that California's system of school funding, which relied largely on local property tax revenues, violated the equal protection provisions of both the federal and state constitutions. California's funding scheme unlawfully discriminated, the court reasoned, because it made the quality of a child's education dependent on the wealth of the district in which the child lived. In other words, the court agreed with the basic principle of fiscal neutrality. The court also denounced unequal funding as inconsistent with the basic tradition of public education. "By our decision today," the court proclaimed, "we further the cherished idea of American education that in a democratic society free public schools shall make available to all children equally the abundant gifts of learning. This was the credo of Horace Mann, which has been the heritage and the inspiration of this country."[37]

The *Serrano* case helped spark a series of school finance challenges in other states. In a little less than two years following *Serrano*, fifty-two lawsuits had been filed in roughly thirty different states—twenty-seven in federal courts and twenty-five in state courts. Plaintiffs won cases in lower courts in Arizona, New Jersey, Minnesota, Texas, and Kansas. In each of the cases, courts struck down the school funding system without specifying a remedy.[38]

The Lawyer's Committee for Civil Rights Under Law, a public interest organization in Washington, D.C., tried to coordinate plaintiffs' efforts. Armed with a grant from the Ford Foundation, the Lawyer's Committee acted as a clearinghouse and strategy center for lawyers across the country involved in school finance litigation. The Lawyer's Committee, however, could not exercise the same control over school finance litigation that the NAACP Legal Defense Fund (LDF) had exercised over desegregation. The LDF, at least in the early years, was the only game in town. Desegregation cases simply were not brought without their help, which made it easier for the LDF to direct these cases strategically—deciding which ones to bring and when, and which ones to appeal and when.[39]

Not so with regard to school finance cases, which were brought by disparate lawyers who did not have ties to a single organization. Working for legal aid groups, public interest law firms, or simply on their own, not all of these lawyers were willing to take direction from the Lawyer's Committee. As a result, school finance cases were brought in more places over a shorter period of time than desegregation cases had been, and the U.S. Supreme Court confronted a school finance case shortly after litigation efforts began. Indeed, less than two years passed between the California Supreme Court's decision in *Serrano* in 1971 and the U.S. Supreme Court's decision in *San Antonio v. Rodriguez*, a case from Texas. This was not enough time, those involved with the Lawyer's Committee believed, for the Court and the country to get used to the idea of equalizing school resources.[40]

It was a fair point, and it was probably right. Then again, it is not clear, on the basis of thirty subsequent years of school finance litigation in state courts, that any amount of time would have made either the Court or the country comfortable with the idea of equalizing school funding.

THE SUPREME COURT WEIGHS IN:
SAN ANTONIO V. RODRIGUEZ

Arthur Gochman of San Antonio was the lawyer for Demetrio Rodriguez and other parents whose children attended school in the Edgewood school district in Texas. He did not work with the Lawyer's Committee and refused to take their direction. As he told the *Washington Post*: "I filed this suit long before I ever heard of any of these committees and foundations."[41]

Gochman filed his case on July 30, 1968, three years before the *Serrano* decision put school finance litigation on the map. He took the case after friends sought his help for the downtrodden Edgewood school district. Edgewood was a Mexican-American community and one of the poorest in the city of San Antonio. Gochman discovered that the school district was poorly funded despite taxing itself at a high rate.[42]

Things looked even worse when Edgewood was compared to nearby Alamo Heights, a relatively affluent and overwhelmingly white district in the same area. Edgewood had a higher property tax rate than Alamo Heights, but this was not enough to eclipse the vast differences in property wealth between the two districts. Alamo Heights had $45,000 of property value per student, while Edgewood had about one-ninth as much—$5,429. State aid, moreover, did not help matters. The state actually provided Alamo Heights with more money than it did Edgewood, because that aid was tied in part to teacher experience and Alamo Heights had more experienced teachers. The end result was that Alamo Heights spent more than twice as much per pupil than Edgewood. This was a significant disparity, obviously, but it was not the worst in the state. During the same time period, the wealthiest district in the state spent $5,334 per pupil—more than *twenty times* the amount spent by the poorest district: $264.[43]

Gochman brought his case before a special panel of three federal judges, whose ruling could be directly appealed to the U.S. Supreme Court. Two trial court judges and an appeals court judge sat on the panel. They released their decision on Christmas Eve, 1971, just a few months after *Serrano*. These judges, like the California court in *Serrano*, believed it was unconstitutional to allow school funding to be a function of local property wealth. They thus endorsed the same notion of fiscal neutrality that ruled the day in California. But they explicitly refused to prescribe a particular remedy. Instead, they agreed with the plaintiffs' proposal that the legislature could adopt whatever "financial scheme [it] desired so long as the variations in wealth among governmentally chosen districts do not affect spending for the education of any child." The court also gave the legislature two years to come up with a remedy.[44]

The legislature would not need the time. As many predicted, the U.S. Supreme Court decided to hear the case. This did not please the Lawyer's Committee. The Committee believed that prospects for success were low. The Court had recently become more conservative with the addition of four Nixon appointees, and as mentioned, the issue of equalizing school funding was still fairly novel. The Court would not have the benefit of seeing how funding reform worked in several states before deciding whether to mandate equalization across the country.[45]

While the case was pending before the Supreme Court, suburban legislators and citizens began to think harder about what the case might mean for them. School finance reform was initially popular in suburban districts because it seemed to promise some relief from high property taxes. But when suburban-ites considered the alternatives, they began to have second thoughts. In a *New York Times* article entitled "Property Tax Reform Enthusiasm Lags," for example, reporter Linda Greenhouse explained how initial enthusiasm for property tax relief in New York's suburbs had turned to fear that the cure would be worse than the disease. Frederick Shore, who was superintendent of a school district in Long Island, captured the mood of many: "First you say, 'Hooray, finally everyone agrees that the property tax is ridiculous and we're going to get some relief.' Then you start to think 'All right, but what do I have to lose in order to get that relief....I don't want to be hurting myself in order to help my neighbor.' "[46]

Suburban residents expressed particular alarm over the prospect of equal-izing funding by capping local spending. In New York, the state board of educa-tion proposed just such a plan without waiting for a court order. It did not play well in the suburbs. If residents of a local district wanted to spend their own tax money for special programs, many suburbanites believed, they ought to be able to do so. Local leaders recognized the conflict between their own interests and the goal of equalization, and some were apologetic in stating their reservations. But their reservations were nonetheless as clear as they were firm. The president of the Scarsdale Board of Education, Betty Menke, acknowledged the "funda-mental conflict between what's good for everyone and the natural desire of individuals to do the best they can for their own children." She made it plain, however, how she and her constituents would resolve the conflict. "We feel a responsibility for others, but we do want to protect the kind of quality our people have come to expect." Equalization was a nice idea, in other words, but it would be a serious problem if it required too much sacrifice from property-rich districts.[47]

The Opinion

The Supreme Court spared districts like Scarsdale from having to make that sacrifice. In a five-to-four opinion issued in March 1973, the Court rejected the challenge to Texas's unequal school funding scheme. Justice Powell wrote the opinion. He was joined by the same four justices who would make up the majority in the Court's decision in *Milliken v. Bradley* the following year. As in *Milliken*, the Court in *Rodriguez* sought to protect local control. In *Milliken*, preserving local control effectively insulated the suburbs from having to par-ticipate in school desegregation and thus protected the physical independence of suburban districts. Preserving local control in the school finance context protected the financial independence of property-rich suburban districts, which would not be required—at least not by the federal Constitution—to share locally raised revenues. The financial tie that might have bound urban and suburban districts, just like the physical tie of desegregation, was thus cut by the Court in *Rodriguez*.[48]

To reach this result, the Court had to reject the notion that education was a fundamental right. Under existing doctrine, any inequalities with regard to fundamental rights were considered suspect and subjected to intense scrutiny, requiring the government to provide a compelling justification for the inequity. More often than not, attempts at justification failed to satisfy the Court, which meant that the outcome of the case hinged largely on how the Court defined the status of education.

Justice Powell, writing for the Court, acknowledged that education played a vital role in American life. But he did not believe that courts should be involved in the administration of education, and he worried about the implications of recognizing education as a fundamental right. He and his colleagues consequently dismissed the notion that education should be recognized as a fundamental right because of its importance. Instead, the Court reasoned, fundamental rights needed to be tied to the text and history of the Constitution, and education could not be linked in this way. What the Court never explained was the language in *Brown*, in which the Court had stated simply that education, where the state makes it available, "is a right which must be made available to all on equal terms." It is not impossible to reconcile the reasoning in *Rodriguez* with the language in *Brown*, which might be confined to race cases; but rather than attempt to do so, the Court ignored the apparent contradiction.[49]

In declining to recognize education as a fundamental right, the Court expressed concern about what Coons had called the equal sewers problem: if education were considered fundamental because important, what about other important social services like health care, welfare, and housing? What really seemed to trouble the Court, though this is not obvious from the face of the opinion, was the unusual nature of a right to education. The right to education is a positive right: it requires the government to provide something to citizens. The Constitution, however, has traditionally been thought a charter of negative rights—that is, rights that protect *against* governmental interference. The fear among some, and the corresponding hope among others, was that a number of welfare rights might be read into the Constitution if education were given protected status.

The Court's hesitancy to recognize positive rights helps explain, and is highlighted by, an otherwise baffling anomaly. In the very same term that the Court decided *Rodriguez*, it also decided *Roe v. Wade*. In *Roe*, the Court concluded that women have a fundamental right to obtain an abortion, based on a general right to privacy. Whatever else might be said of the right to an abortion or the more general right to privacy, they are surely no easier to link to the text or history of the Constitution than a right to education, a point forcefully made by Justice Marshall in his dissent in *Rodriguez*. But a right to abortion, as opposed to a right to education, is a classic negative right, which basically prevents the government from *interfering* with a decision to obtain an abortion. The government is not obliged to provide abortions, nor, as later cases made clear, is the government obliged to provide financial assistance to women too poor to afford abortions.[50]

Concern about creating welfare rights through constitutional interpretation also influenced the Court's second conclusion in *Rodriguez*: that this case did not involve unconstitutional wealth discrimination. In a series of cases decided in the late 1950s and the 1960s, the Court struck down court fees and poll taxes on the ground that they prevented the poor from exercising important rights like appealing criminal convictions and voting. Many saw the Court inching toward the proposition that discrimination against the poor might be treated similarly to discrimination against racial minorities. Racial discrimination, like discrimination with regard to fundamental rights, also triggered strict scrutiny from the Court, and the Court almost without exception refused to countenance discrimination on the basis of race. When the Court decided *Rodriguez*, some lower courts had already expressed their belief that "it is clear beyond question that discrimination based on poverty is no more permissible than racial discrimination." In truth, the question remained open, and many anticipated that *Rodriguez* would finally settle the matter.[51]

It did and it did not. Although *Rodriguez* came to stand for the proposition that wealth discrimination is not suspect and therefore does not trigger strict scrutiny, in reality the Court did not so much address the question as deflect it. The Court focused, among other things, on the fact that in its earlier decisions, the laws at issue discriminated against a class of *people* clearly defined by their poverty. School funding systems, by contrast, discriminated against property-poor *districts*. To be sure, it was often the case that poor people lived in poor districts, but the correlation was not perfect, and this mismatch prevented the facile conclusion that discriminating against poor school districts necessarily meant discriminating against poor people. Regardless of whether poor *people* might deserve special judicial protection, the Court in *Rodriguez* made clear that poor *school districts* did not.[52]

Having rejected the idea that education was a fundamental right and the notion that unequal funding impermissibly discriminated against the poor, the Court refused to subject Texas's funding scheme to strict scrutiny. Instead, it applied the extremely deferential rational basis test, asking only if the funding scheme was rationally related to a legitimate state interest. The Court identified local control as the relevant state interest. Allowing unequal funding, the Court reasoned, protected local control in two ways: it allowed districts to determine how much to spend on their schools, and it guarded against increased state regulation that might accompany increased state funding.[53]

The Court fleshed out its reasoning by pointing to the numerous practical difficulties that courts would have to confront if the plaintiffs' legal claims were sustained. These concerns reflected Justice Powell's intimate knowledge of administering public education and his experiences on both the Richmond and state boards of education. Two in particular drew sustained attention from the Court, and these same concerns continue to surface in state school finance litigation.

First, the Court confessed great reluctance to interfere with legislative decisions about raising and spending revenues. No system of taxation is perfect, the Court reasoned, and the questions raised by how much to tax and which services to provide are remarkably complex and intertwined. "In such a complex arena in which no perfect alternatives exist," Justice Powell wrote for the Court, it is best "not to impose too rigorous a standard of scrutiny lest all local fiscal schemes become subjects of criticism under the Equal Protection Clause."[54]

Second, the Court discussed the uncertain connection between funding and achievement. Scholars and experts disagreed over "the extent to which there is a demonstrable correlation between educational expenditures and the quality of education." Equally unsettled was the related question regarding the very purpose of public education. The Court was unsure if these questions would ever be settled, but it was sure that it had neither the expertise nor wisdom to settle them. "In such circumstances," the Court concluded, "the judiciary is well advised to refrain from interposing on the States inflexible constitutional restraints that could circumscribe or handicap the continued research and experimentation so vital to finding even partial solutions to educational problems."[55]

Justices White and Marshall dissented. Justice White, whose dissenting opinion was joined by Justices Douglas and Brennan, argued that local control was a fiction in the case of property-poor districts, because state law restricted them from taxing themselves over a certain amount. Local control, in operation, thus did not allow districts to decide for themselves how much to spend on education.[56]

Justice Marshall's dissent, joined only by Justice Douglas, was more sweeping in its rejection of the majority opinion. Marshall believed that education ought to be deemed a fundamental right because of the close nexus between education and the ability to exercise other constitutional rights, such as the right of free speech and the right to participate in the political process. Marshall recognized that his nexus theory might prove too much, but he argued that education was more closely associated with established constitutional rights and therefore could be distinguished from claimed rights to food and shelter. Marshall also took on the majority's skepticism about the connection between funding and educational quality, asking why wealthy districts were so intent on keeping their money if it did not affect educational quality. He also thought the entire issue was somewhat irrelevant: courts should ensure equality of opportunity by equalizing funding; they could not and need not guarantee equal outcomes.[57]

There is some evidence that the Lawyer's Committee was right to worry that the case for school finance reform had been prematurely presented to the Supreme Court. Justice Powell expressed reluctance in the opinion about mandating new funding schemes that "are only recently conceived and nowhere yet tested." (He was blunter in private, writing in a memorandum that the district court was wrong to adopt the "activist scholarship theory of Professors Coon and Sugarman" and expressing great skepticism about "facile new theories" of funding.) Justice Blackmun also commented at the justices' conference, when they met to decide the case, that he wished that lower courts had had more time to wrestle with the issue.[58]

On the other hand, one could argue that the case came too late rather than too early. If the case had been heard a few years earlier, the Court would likely have been more receptive, given that none of the four conservative Nixon appointees would have been on the bench. More broadly, the increasingly controversial and somewhat disappointing experience with school desegregation must have weighed on the justices as they considered the *Rodriguez* case. The bitter public reaction to busing, mandated by *Swann* in 1971, could not have escaped their notice, and it may have made some of them even more reluctant to take on reforming the funding systems in all fifty states. There is no doubt, for instance, that Justice Powell, a southerner intimately involved with school desegregation, feared increased federal control of education. He worried privately that school finance reform would ultimately lead to "national control of education," which he adamantly opposed.[59]

Reaction

Justice Blackmun feared that the decision in *Rodriguez* would be unpopular, but public reaction was fairly muted. Partisans were upset, of course. The National Education Association, for example, charged that the Court had rejected "the idea of equal educational opportunity," and plaintiff Demetrio Rodriguez expressed "deep and bitter resentment" of the justices and those who nominated and confirmed them. But the major newspapers either supported or at least accepted the decision. The *New York Times*, for example, "sympathize[d] with the Court's school ruling" and urged a political fix for school funding systems it called chaotic and unjust. The *Washington Post* supported the outcome, arguing that requiring equal funding might have hurt city schools that needed more money per pupil in order to educate their large portion of poor students. The *Chicago Tribune* blasted the conditions in poor schools but nonetheless supported the decision because it forestalled creating a "uniform mold in the name of guaranteeing equality." In Richmond, the *Times-Dispatch*, true to form, applauded the decision as "pure gold," suggested that money does not really matter, and expressed some hope that this meant the Court would block the consolidation of the Richmond, Henrico, and Chesterfield school districts.[60]

As these editorials indicate, school finance reform directed by the U.S. Supreme Court was not an issue that garnered uniform support, even among liberal-leaning newspapers. In addition to fears about national control of education and the Court's capacity to fix funding, there was uncertainty and disagreement—just as there had been at the very early stages of school finance reform—over what that fix should be. Strictly equal funding? Fiscal neutrality? Needs-based funding? The need to correct the chaos and injustice of funding systems was obvious, but exactly how to do that was unclear. The same is true today.

It is possible that the reaction to *Rodriguez* might have heated up over time, but news of the case was quickly eclipsed by another school finance decision, this one from the New Jersey Supreme Court. Less than two weeks after *Rodriguez* was decided, the New Jersey court struck down its state funding system, relying exclusively on the New Jersey constitution. *Rodriguez*, it appeared, would not be the last word on school finance reform. Instead of ending courts' involvement with the issue, it channeled litigants into state courts, where they have been fighting ever since.[61]

CHAPTER 4

Like a Russian Novel: School Finance Litigation in State Courts

Education law scholar Mark Yudof once compared school finance litigation to a Russian novel: "It's long, tedious, and everybody dies at the end." The comparison is apt. School finance litigation in state courts has been sprawling, complicated, and seemingly endless. All but five states have seen their school funding systems challenged in court, and the highest courts in thirty-six states have issued decisions. Seventeen of these state high courts have ruled for plaintiffs and declared existing funding schemes unconstitutional; nineteen have upheld their respective funding schemes.[1]

Court victories do not always, or even usually, translate immediately into legislative reform. Instead, successful litigation usually only begins a process of political bargaining. Multiple trips back to court are often required before concrete reforms are enacted. In New Jersey, which is the leader in this regard, the state supreme court has issued more than fifteen decisions over the course of its thirty-year involvement in school finance reform. This chapter picks up where the last one left off and traces the somewhat torturous path of school finance litigation in state courts, assessing its impact thus far and gauging its future prospects.

STATE CONSTITUTIONS

School finance suits since *Rodriguez* have been based exclusively on state constitutions. All state constitutions contain education provisions, which require their respective legislatures to create systems of free, public schools and thereby guarantee students the right to attend such schools. The precise language varies, with some constitutions indicating at least vaguely the sort of school system required. Some education clauses, for example, require legislatures to create a "thorough and efficient" system of schools, others a "general and uniform" system, and still others some combination of a general, uniform, thorough, or efficient system. Very few constitutions explicitly require legislatures to provide equal educational opportunities.[2]

These education clauses, sometimes in combination with state equal protection provisions, have formed the basis for modern school finance challenges. In most states, neither the constitutional text nor the drafting history provides much guidance for courts confronted with school finance suits. The language is ambiguous and the history not especially revealing. Perhaps not surprisingly, courts have reached different results even when interpreting similar language.

The constitutions of New Jersey, Maryland, Pennsylvania, Ohio, and West Virginia, for example, all guarantee the right to a "thorough and efficient" education. Courts in these states, however, have interpreted this language quite differently, leading to a wide range of results. Similarly, the strength or specificity of the constitutional language does not correspond with the outcomes in cases. The Georgia Constitution, for example, explicitly states that providing "an adequate education" shall be a "primary obligation of the State." Yet the Georgia Supreme Court held that this provision does not create a judicially enforceable right. The Massachusetts Constitution, by contrast, admonishes the state legislature to "cherish...public schools." Massachusetts' highest court interpreted this opaque language to impose a significant duty on the legislature to provide a sufficient education, the specific components of which the court listed in detail.[3]

Whether courts will intervene thus turns on something other than language and history. Commentators have not been shy about filling in the blanks. Some argue that the cases turn on the political inclinations of the individual judges, with more liberal judges more likely to strike down unequal or inadequate finance systems. Others make the related argument that outcomes depend on whether judges are elected or appointed. Still others suggest that the financial health of the state matters, as there is some evidence that school finance plaintiffs win more readily when the state is flush with money. There is also evidence that the racial composition of the plaintiff districts influences the outcomes, as predominantly minority districts, and especially urban minority districts, win less often than predominantly white ones.[4]

Critics of school finance litigation often argue that only courts ruling for plaintiffs are ignoring the law and engaging in adventurous reasoning, untethered to constitutional text or history. But it is not that simple, as those that rule against plaintiffs are not immune from criticism for departing from traditional doctrinal analysis. The Virginia Supreme Court's 1994 school funding decision, *Scott v. Commonwealth*, is a good example. The court concluded that education is a fundamental right and acknowledged that funding was unequal across the state, which should have led to a victory for plaintiffs. But the court then rejected the idea that the state constitution mandated equal funding.[5]

In doing so, the court misapplied strict scrutiny, which is the test traditionally used to determine whether inequalities with regard to fundamental rights are justified. Instead of faithfully applying this test, the court instead reasoned: "even applying a strict scrutiny test, as urged by the Students...we hold that nowhere does the Constitution require equal, or substantially equal, funding or programs among and within the Commonwealth's school divisions." Strict scrutiny, however, is traditionally applied after it is determined that a fundamental right is at stake and that equal treatment with regard to that fundamental right is therefore required. The point of strict scrutiny is to determine whether the challenged inequality is justified by a compelling state interest. Whether the inequality is justified, moreover, is not a question that can be answered by looking elsewhere in the text of the constitution; it requires weighing the importance of the state's justification. Perhaps the court was just being sloppy, or perhaps it intentionally mangled traditional doctrine to reach a desired outcome—just as courts that rule in favor of school finance plaintiffs are accused of doing. Regardless, the decision can scarcely be described as one that faithfully applied existing legal rules.[6]

The Losing Cases

Regardless of what unspoken factors might motivate courts, whether they rule for or against plaintiffs, those that reject school finance challenges tend to express the same concerns identified by Justice Powell in his opinion in *Rodriguez*. Topping the list is a reluctance to interfere with the legislature's authority to set spending priorities. In light of the vague constitutional language regarding education, these courts conclude that complicated policy questions about school funding should be left to the legislature. The Illinois Supreme Court, for example, was emphatic in concluding that "questions relating to the quality of education are solely for the legislative branch to answer." Similarly, the Florida Supreme Court believed that intervening would "present a substantial risk of judicial intrusion into the powers and responsibilities assigned to the legislature." The Rhode Island Supreme Court was more colorful, and exercised, bluntly refusing to "scal[e] the walls that separate law making from judging."[7]

Some scholars applaud courts that decline to intervene. The position is not indefensible. Faced with ambiguous language and little direction from history, courts have some justification for remaining on the sidelines. At the same time, however, it is not as if constitutional text is always precise or history always clear, leaving little room for debate about constitutional meaning. To the contrary, in most contested cases, the meaning of the text is somewhat up for grabs; this is why the cases are contested. It follows that courts that enforce these provisions, though occasionally subject to criticism for going beyond their proper institutional boundaries, are also acting defensibly. They justifiably take the view that courts exist, at least in part, to enforce their respective state constitutions, even when the meaning of the text is hard to discern.[8]

The concern about enforcing positive rights, moreover, has less purchase in this context, for the simple reason that state constitutions explicitly guarantee the positive right to education. Courts might understandably shy away, as the U.S. Supreme Court did in *Rodriguez*, from recognizing an implicit positive constitutional right. They are on shakier ground, however, in refusing to enforce an explicit constitutional provision, even if it guarantees a right *to* governmental assistance rather than a right *against* governmental interference.

The positive nature of a right to education, however, does lead to more practical problems regarding enforcement. Courts that refuse to strike down funding schemes tend to identify these practical concerns and, in particular, the relationship between funding and achievement. Just like the U.S. Supreme Court in *Rodriguez*, courts that uphold school funding systems tend to express doubt, shared by some education economists, that increased funding will improve academic achievement. Without a clearer link between funding and achievement, these courts conclude, there is little justification to order more spending.

The point is certainly a fair one, and the issue of the relationship between funding and achievement has been the source of endless debate among social scientists. But like the vagueness of constitutional language, it is not obvious that the vagueness of the relationship between funding and achievement is a sufficient justification to uphold unequal or inadequate funding schemes. There can be no doubt that educational opportunities are related at some level to funding. Education costs money. The more money a school system has, for example, the more teachers it can hire, the more it can pay them, and the more it can spend on facilities, curricular offerings, and extracurricular opportunities. If the right at issue is one of *opportunity* rather than *results*, it is not clear why litigants must prove that more money will translate into better results rather than greater opportunities.[9]

In fact, the weakness of this justification for upholding school finance schemes becomes clear when one flips the question around and asks why, if money is not that important, states allow for inequalities. The practical answer, of course, is that parents and citizens in high-spending districts obviously believe that money matters, and they would balk at having to give away local tax dollars in order to equalize funding across the state. That explanation, however, is not itself a justification for unequal spending if, as states and courts sometimes claim, spending is not related to educational quality. In short, courts that uphold school funding schemes may be acting defensibly, but certainly no more than that.

The Winning Cases

Scholars have struggled to categorize successful school finance cases in an effort to make them easier to comprehend, but the cases defy neat categorization. According to the conventional account, successful school finance litigation comes in two varieties: equity cases and adequacy cases. Most early school finance cases were equity cases, so the traditional account continues, with litigants essentially seeking equal funding per pupil or at least equal access to funding through fiscal neutrality. Since 1989, however, most cases have focused on securing adequate resources.[10]

Litigants in so-called adequacy suits, as the name suggests, do not seek equal funding but rather the amount of funding thought necessary to provide an adequate education. The adequacy theory, as mentioned in chapter 3, is in a sense the progeny of the needs-based theory first offered by legal aid lawyers in early school finance cases. The main difference is that contemporary advocates focus more concretely than the legal aid lawyers did on specific outcome goals. Rather than simply arguing that funding should meet the varying but undefined needs of students, adequacy proponents argue that funding should be sufficient to give students a fair opportunity to meet a set of outcome goals. If all goes according to plan, courts in adequacy cases are supposed to define the outcomes that constitute an adequate education, and then work backward to determine the inputs necessary to achieve the desired outcomes. In equity cases, by contrast, the focus is on making the inputs equal, regardless of the effect on outcomes.[11]

If only it were that neat. The cases, however, do not divide chronologically into an early equity era and a modern adequacy era. There are, for example, plenty of recent cases, including ones from Montana, Tennessee, Arkansas, Arizona, Texas, and Vermont, where courts have explicitly recognized a right to equal educational opportunities. Equity cases, in short, are not dead. At the same time, adequacy cases are not that young. There were very early cases, including those out of Washington and West Virginia, that focused on outcome goals and thus looked much more like adequacy than equity cases.[12]

The more fundamental difficulty is with the categories themselves, which tend to obscure rather than reveal what courts are actually doing in these cases. In truth, there is not a clear divide between equity and adequacy cases for the simple reason that courts in all cases tend to converge around the goal of rough comparability. Courts in so-called equity cases rarely require complete equality of resources. Instead, they require "substantial" equality. Courts in so-called adequacy cases, in turn, typically define adequacy in comparative terms and remain focused on resource disparities. To the extent that courts define adequacy as a function of equity, they, too, are essentially requiring something like "substantial" equality of resources—or what I have termed rough comparability.

To be sure, there are differences among the claims made by plaintiffs in school finance suits. Some allege that the problem is a lack of equal funding or equal access to funding; others claim that the funding, at least in some districts, is insufficient. There are also differences in the rationales relied on by courts when striking down funding systems, with some focused more on funding disparities and others more on insufficiencies. These differences are most visible in states where there have been two rounds of school finance litigation based on two different claims. In New York, for example, the court rejected a school finance suit seeking equalized funding, concluding that the state constitution guaranteed not equal funding but only the minimal amount of funding required for a decent education. This implicit invitation to bring another suit, based on a different theory, was accepted, and the second suit was successful in court.[13]

The categories nonetheless tend to break down because equity and adequacy concerns blend together in most decisions. A good example is a 1995 decision by the Wyoming Supreme Court, which ruled that the state had to provide students an equal opportunity for a quality education. While recognizing that localities could spend above the amount required for a quality education, the court emphasized that the definition of a quality education is dynamic and "necessarily will change." Should the definition change because of "local innovation," all students would be "entitled to the benefit of that change as part of a cost-based, state financed proper education." The clear message was that the state could not allow locally driven disparities to grow too large. Put differently, an adequate education was defined as a substantially equal education.[14]

Similar concern for resource disparities is apparent in other so-called adequacy cases. In the second round of litigation in New York, for example, the state's highest court concluded that funding for New York City schools was insufficient, but it reached this conclusion by comparing funding and needs among school districts throughout the state. The court thus focused on disparities in teaching, facilities, instructional materials, and student outcomes that existed between New York City schools and the rest of the state. In explaining and justifying its ruling, the court emphasized that "New York City schools have the *most* student need in the state and the *highest* local costs yet received some of the *lowest* per-student funding and have some of the *worst* results."[15]

As these decisions indicate, courts tend to think of adequacy in relative terms. This is true even when courts explicitly define outcome goals, which are said to be the hallmark of adequacy suits. These goals often include a comparative element. Courts in Wyoming, North Carolina, New Hampshire, and New Jersey, for example, have described the ultimate aim of public education in similar terms: to prepare students to participate as citizens and to compete in the employment market or for admission to higher education. One's ability to compete for employment or college admission depends not only on the sufficiency of one's education, but also on its comparable worth.[16]

The comparative focus in so-called adequacy cases is not altogether surprising, given the nature of education. Education certainly has intrinsic value: students benefit from their own education regardless of the education provided to other students. The value of education, however, is also relative. In the words of economists, education is a positional good: the adequacy of a particular student's education depends in part on the quality of education offered to other students. In this sense, education is a little like tennis practice. Whether a tennis player's preparation is adequate depends in part on the amount and quality of her opponent's preparation. From this perspective, as the Wyoming court implied, adequacy is itself a function of equality.[17]

Court-ordered Remedies

While courts tend to blur the categories in their reasoning, when it comes to the remedial stage, the categories all but disappear. This is true for several reasons. To begin, courts often say little or nothing regarding remedies, at least at first. Whether they find the whole business too complicated or too delicate, given lingering separation of powers concerns, is unclear. What is clear is that most courts initially content themselves with outlawing the current system; they rarely design the replacement, at least not the first time around. This silence leaves legislatures a great deal of room to come up with a remedy, and those remedies, as we shall see, tend to be similar regardless of the underlying theories or rationales in the opinions.

Even when courts are more specific about the remedy, they tend to push toward increased funding and some reduction of disparities. But they hardly ever call for the wholesale elimination of disparities. As mentioned, courts in equity cases tend to require "substantial" equality, not perfect equality. What constitutes substantial equality is usually left to the discretion of legislators, who have an incentive to do the bare minimum required and thus take a cramped view of "substantial." (What courts will ultimately accept as substantial equality of funding, moreover, is undoubtedly influenced by the overall sufficiency of funding; courts are less likely to balk at inequalities above and beyond a level of funding that is itself clearly adequate.) Similarly, in so-called adequacy cases, given the repeated concern for resource disparities and the lack of clear guidance from courts, legislators have an incentive to increase funding in low-spending districts, which has the effect of reducing disparities.

Some courts in more recent decisions have ordered legislatures to conduct "costing-out" studies to determine the resources necessary to afford students an opportunity to receive an adequate education. These studies are supposed to determine the inputs necessary to reach a given set of outcomes. There are numerous ways to conduct such studies, but the two most prominent are the "professional judgment" model and the "successful schools" model. The former relies on the judgment of various professional educators to determine the funding levels required; the latter looks to the funding and resources of a set of "successful" schools. These and other methods remain controversial, with some claiming that they amount to no more than guesses at what sort of resources are needed to improve performance.[18]

At first blush, the costing-out approach seems to represent a clear break from equity cases. Determining the proper level of funding for an adequate education does not, in theory, require a comparative focus. But the costing-out studies do not take place in a vacuum, with no consideration of current spending patterns. This is easiest to see with the successful schools model, which explicitly looks to current spending patterns in existing schools. To the extent these spending patterns become required for other districts, the end result is not much different from the result that would be reached by requiring substantial equality in spending, even though the route is more circuitous. Even with the professional judgment model, those making judgments about funding surely consider funding levels at other schools to ensure that their recommendations are plausible; if they do not, they risk being ignored by courts.

Legislative Responses

Given the general reluctance of courts to specify remedies, legislatures retain a good deal of discretion when it comes time to fix a funding scheme that has been declared unconstitutional. A few legislatures have responded quite quickly and vigorously to a court's declaration that the system needs repair, and they have enacted comprehensive reforms. The Kentucky and Massachusetts legislatures, for example, responded rapidly to court orders, enacting education reforms that addressed both spending and accountability. Both legislatures did so in large part because they had already decided that their funding systems needed reform *before* the courts issued their opinions. Indeed, the Massachusetts legislature had already passed new funding legislation, which was awaiting the governor's signature when the court decision was handed down.[19]

Kentucky and Massachusetts seem like outliers at first glance, but the lesson from these two states is actually generally applicable: legislative responses to court orders are largely influenced by the degree of political support for school finance reform. Politics do not disappear from the equation once courts rule. Unlike Kentucky and Massachusetts, most states are not especially eager to increase funding or to redistribute it, and their opposition shows in their reaction to court decisions. Most legislatures are slow to act; some ignore the decision altogether. Both responses set off an ongoing struggle, sometimes optimistically described as a "dialogue," between the judicial and legislative branches. This interbranch conversation usually requires return trips to court and ultimately ends in one of three ways: a compromise between the court and the legislature, surrender by the legislature, or surrender by the court. Most often, the end result is a compromise.[20]

The end result is never complete equalization of funding, which is perhaps the most important point to recognize. Even the most successful school finance suit—in New Jersey—has not led to school finance equalization across the state. Nor has any other litigation led to fully equal resources, whether dubbed an equity or adequacy suit. In fact, not a single suit has done much to alter the basic structure of school finance schemes. No court, for example, has required that school district boundaries be redrawn in order to equalize the distribution of property wealth in districts. Nor has any court outlawed the use of the local property tax altogether.[21]

When state legislatures finally respond to court decisions, they usually do so by increasing funding for property-poor districts. They either hold steady or increase at a slower rate the state aid given to property-rich districts. This is true whether the suit is styled an equity or an adequacy one; the legislative reaction is usually the same. In time, overall funding levels rise and disparities diminish, but they do not disappear. The end result is that school funding systems in just about every state continue to be unequal and strongly influenced by differing levels of property wealth. Whether the funding is adequate, either before or after a suit, is really anyone's guess.[22]

This is not meant to disparage the significance of school finance litigation. Spending generally increases more in states where plaintiffs have succeeded than in states where they have failed. Similarly, funding becomes more equal in states where plaintiffs succeed than in states where they do not. Funding litigation thus impacts spending decisions. But the magnitude of these changes in most states is modest. A recent study, for example, estimated that favorable school finance judgments led, on average, to a 16 percent decrease in spending disparities between high- and low-spending districts. That leaves a lot of inequality untouched.[23]

The reason for these modest results is not hard to fathom. As discussed earlier, in order to equalize funding, legislatures would have to do one of two things: raise all districts to the level of the highest-spending ones or limit spending in property-rich districts. The first option is financially impractical in most states, which have some districts that spend thousands of dollars more per pupil than the state average because of extremely high property values. The second option is financially feasible but very controversial.

The controversy stems from the fact that limiting spending either requires a cap on all spending or some sort of recapture provision. Neither is popular. Local citizens, and especially parents, dislike being told that they cannot raise and spend local revenues on their own schools. They especially dislike the idea that locally raised revenues might be recaptured and redistributed to the rest of the state.

Localities do not have a state or federal constitutional right to retain local property tax revenues; whether they can do so lies within the political discretion of the state. In terms of fairness, moreover, it seems strange that localities are entitled to keep the property tax revenue of businesses that just happen to locate in one town as opposed to another and earn profits based on employees and customers who live in many different localities. That said, most people seem to think of property taxes as different from other taxes, like those on income. Property taxes seem more like membership dues, given that they are typically devoted to local communities. From that perspective, reluctance to share those revenues is understandable, if not exactly justifiable. It is one thing to raise membership dues to renovate your own clubhouse. It is another thing entirely to raise dues in order to renovate somebody else's clubhouse.[24]

Given this political dynamic, it is not surprising that very few states—even after court-ordered reform—have adopted recapture plans. Those that have, moreover, have engendered intense controversies. Recapture methods are routinely referred to as "Robin Hood" plans in of the few states that have used them, which include Texas, Kansas, and Vermont, and they have sparked public protests and litigation. Donor districts in Texas, for example, claimed that the state had taken their property without compensation. Some donor districts in Kansas threatened to secede from the state. In Vermont, self-professed liberal and well-known novelist John Irving denounced the state's recapture plan, calling it Marxist—which was not meant as a compliment. Other Vermont protestors were more demonstrative. They purchased a used car sold by the chief sponsor of the recapture plan, parked it near the state capitol, and allowed passersby to demonstrate their opposition to the plan by sledge-hammering the car. Legislation was eventually passed in Vermont, but like similar recapture plans, it remains controversial and somewhat vulnerable.[25]

The experiences in states with recapture plans suggest strongly that courts would have to be quite aggressive and remain actively engaged in school funding litigation, over a long period of time, if interested in truly equalizing access to funding. Few courts have shown such zeal or commitment. Even the New Jersey Supreme Court, after more than three decades of fighting for greater funding, finally capitulated in 2009 by returning the issue to legislative control. Even when it was enforcing its own remedy, moreover, the New Jersey court only required increased funding for two dozen districts, out of hundreds in the state. The truth is that courts, or at least some courts, are willing to say funding systems are broken; they are generally much less willing to ensure that legislatures do what it takes to fix them.

IMPACT ON THE GROUND

The impact of school finance litigation can be measured in dollars and cents, and, as discussed, it appears that successful litigation generally leads to increased spending overall and a decrease in spending disparities. There is some debate about the exact size of the impact, with some scholars believing school finance litigation more significant than others. No one, however, believes that this is the only or most important metric by which to measure the success of this litigation. Instead, the question on everyone's mind, whether advocate, scholar, social scientist, or school principal, is whether the increased funding has made much of a difference in terms of academic achievement.

A Limited Yardstick

The focus on academic achievement makes sense, given the nature of school finance reform and one of the purposes of public education. No one doubts that a primary purpose of public education is to impart knowledge and skills to students. The ultimate goal of school finance reform is to improve that process, and the obvious way to measure success is by studying whether academic achievement has improved. At the moment, standardized test scores are the easiest, cheapest, and most widely used measure of the academic performance of schools, and there is no doubt that test scores reveal at least some useful information about a school's academic quality.

The singular focus on test scores, however, does have its limits. From the very start of public education in this country, schools were also supposed to socialize students in the hope of preparing them for citizenship. One way to do this is to educate students from diverse backgrounds in the same school. This idea has a long lineage: a key idea behind the common school movement was that schools would serve rich and poor students alike and together.[26]

The idea of integrating students did not, at least in some states, initially include racial integration. *Brown* effectively broadened the integrative goal of the common school movement to include race as well as class. And indeed, studies of the effects of integration, though initially focused on academic achievement, over time broadened to consider whether attending an integrated school increases the chances that students as adults will live, work, and socialized in more integrated settings. (It does.) The interest in the socializing effects of integration reflected some of the goals of school integration and public education more broadly.[27]

School finance litigation cannot do much to integrate schools along any dimension, at least not directly. It is possible that better-funded schools might become more diverse over time, but any increase in diversity would be an indirect and long-term result at best. Increasing diversity is not, in any event, the goal of school finance reform. The goal is improved academic performance. This is a completely laudable aim, obviously, but it is a narrow one, and it has helped shape expectations about public education. Cause and effect are difficult to pinpoint here, but the end result, as will be apparent in later chapters, is fairly clear: today, there is little talk about the socializing purpose of public education. The conversation is instead dominated by discussion of test scores.[28]

Test scores are also imperfect at measuring what they are supposed to measure: the quality of schools and the academic performance of students. Not all subjects are tested, nor are all skills. The tests themselves vary greatly in quality but tend not to be very demanding. The relationship between performance on state standardized tests and subsequent performance in college or in employment, moreover, remains largely unstudied, so it remains a mystery whether the tests are measuring qualities that translate into long-term success. Whether school funding improves test scores, in short, is an important question, but it leaves one guessing about a host of other relevant questions about school quality and student performance.[29]

Disappointing Results

Notwithstanding those qualifications, test scores do provide at least a rough if incomplete measure of school quality and student performance, and on this measure school finance litigation has been a disappointment. There is not much evidence that school finance reform has significantly boosted test scores. Spending increases resulting from school finance litigation, like spending increases generally, have not typically translated into measured academic improvements. This is especially true in urban, high-poverty, high-minority schools, whose relatively low performance has continued even at relatively high levels of funding.[30]

High-poverty schools, especially high-poverty urban schools, almost always have lower levels of academic achievement than low-poverty schools, regardless of funding levels. Indeed, in a field overflowing with disagreements over methodology and results, educational researchers can at least agree on the fact that high-poverty schools and high academic achievement rarely go hand in hand. A 1997 longitudinal study of forty thousand students, for example, concluded that "the poverty level of the school (over and above the economic status of an individual student) is negatively related to standardized achievement scores." This study confirmed that the "poverty level of certain schools places disadvantaged children in double jeopardy. School poverty depresses the scores of all students in a school where at least half the students are eligible for subsidized lunch, and seriously depresses the scores when over 75 percent of students live in low-income households." A similar study conducted in 1993 found that students in low-poverty schools typically score 50–75 percent higher on reading and math tests than students in high-poverty schools. More recent studies confirm these earlier findings.[31]

In addition to depressing achievement, attending a high-poverty school decreases the odds that students will even graduate. Dropout rates in urban schools are dramatically higher than in non-urban schools. In 2003, none of the nation's ten largest public high school districts graduated more than 60 percent of its students on time. In twenty-one of the largest U.S. cities, most students attend a school where fewer than half of all students graduate within four years, and many drop out altogether. In Indianapolis and St. Louis, all students attend such schools. In some cities, including Detroit, Milwaukee, Cleveland, Baltimore, Oakland, and Atlanta, fewer than half of all students ever graduate. As of several years ago, the dropout rate was close to 90 percent among students who began at certain elementary schools in Chicago.[32]

School finance litigation has hardly made a dent when it comes to high-poverty urban schools. The same is true of legislative programs that have increased spending in urban districts. The question is why. Why has school finance litigation, or increased funding generally, had relatively little impact in urban schools? There are three explanations, which are related and discussed in turn: (1) the funding increases have been insufficient; (2) the money has not been spent wisely; and (3) not all obstacles to improved performance can be overcome with increased funding alone.

Not Enough Money?

Some advocates contend that many school systems, especially urban ones, remain seriously underfunded. To those who believe this, the explanation for the disappointing results of school finance litigation is simple: it has not produced enough funding. The reality, however, is more complicated. It is true that school funding litigation has not produced significant increases in funding, especially for urban districts. It is not obvious, however, that further increases in funding alone would have a huge impact. There are many urban districts, like Richmond, that are relatively well funded as compared to the state average but still perform poorly.

The real problem is that no one actually knows how much funding is necessary to provide all urban students a realistic chance to perform at levels equal to their suburban counterparts. Students have differing needs, which means that schools with different student populations have differing needs. As a general matter, students from lower socioeconomic backgrounds come to school with greater needs than their more advantaged peers. Poorer students, especially in urban areas, generally suffer more from malnutrition, poor health care, a less stable and stimulating home environment, and more exposure to violence and drug use in their neighborhoods. As the New Jersey Supreme Court explained in one of its school finance decisions: "With concentrated poverty in the inner-city comes drug abuse, crime, hunger, poor health, illness, and unstable family situations. Violence also creates a significant barrier to quality education in city schools where often just getting children safely to school is considered an accomplishment." As a result of these obstacles, "many poor children start school with an approximately two-year disadvantage compared to many suburban youngsters. This two-year disadvantage often increases when urban students move through the educational system without receiving special attention."[33]

Special attention requires greater resources. Disadvantaged students simply cost more to educate, requiring additional educational programs and nonacademic services such as health care and counseling. It follows that schools with large concentrations of impoverished students will face greater educational costs, even before considering such additional services like security and counseling, and even without considering the generally higher prices for educational goods and services in cities as opposed to suburban or rural areas. A number of states recognize the greater needs of poor students, at least in theory, and provide additional funding to high-poverty schools. Title I of the original Elementary and Secondary Education Act of 1965, which remains the largest federal investment in education, was initially premised on the idea that poorer students need more funding.[34]

The need for greater-than-average resources in urban schools is clear. The picture becomes murkier, however, when one tries to determine whether city schools already have sufficient funding or whether even more funding would help. The general impression, fueled by Jonathan Kozol's books about the disparities between city and suburban schools and by advocates for urban students, is that all city schools are woefully underfunded. This is a false impression. There is simply not a clear pattern of underfunded urban schools, at least when the state average is the benchmark.[35]

To be sure, city schools are often outspent by some of their wealthy suburban neighbors, and some city schools are indeed seriously underfunded and lack even basic materials and supplies. But most city schools spend above the state average. This holds true even after adjustments are made to take into account the higher costs of providing educational services in urban areas. This does not mean that city schools have sufficient funding, of course, but it does rebut the often-repeated argument that city schools obviously lack sufficient funding. It is not at all obvious that they do.[36]

Existing evidence, moreover, calls into question the extent to which funding levels alone are driving achievement. There is both anecdotal and statistical evidence to suggest that even high levels of funding have not been enough to boost achievement significantly in high-poverty urban schools. The best known anecdote concerns Kansas City. Because of *Milliken II* funding, Kansas City spent nearly *twice* the state average per pupil for several years running but posted only mixed results on tests. What was true in Kansas City was true elsewhere, as *Milliken II* funding generally produced little in the way of academic improvement, even when extremely generous. Similarly, Title I compensatory funds were notoriously ineffective in generating sustained achievement gains, which helped shift the focus of Title I toward testing and accountability.[37]

Studies that compare schools funded at different levels also suggest that spending more money, at least under certain circumstances, does not guarantee improved results. In cities that spent "substantially more than their surrounding suburbs," researchers Gary Orfield and Susan Eaton found that performance was still worse in the city schools. Other studies have found that poor students in middle-class schools achieve at higher levels than poor students in predominantly poor schools, even when the poor schools spend more per pupil.[38]

There is some promising evidence from New Jersey, where high-poverty schools are very generously funded because of the school finance litigation there. The remedy in that case, until very recently, required the legislature to provide poor, mostly minority urban districts with funding equal to that of the highest-spending suburban districts. The students in these urban districts have also been offered additional programs, such as preschool and all-day kindergarten. The end result was a mean spending level, as of 2006, close to $15,000 per pupil, which was substantially higher than most districts in the country. Some evidence suggests that students in these districts are doing well relative to their peers in lower-spending districts. The evidence, however, is recent and follows years of poor results despite high funding levels. It remains unclear whether the funding and the programs it buys are starting to work in New Jersey, or whether this is a slight aberration from an otherwise disappointing track record.[39]

In Virginia, and the Richmond metropolitan area in particular, money has not guaranteed success. For years, Richmond has outspent Henrico by a considerable amount. In 2006, for example, Richmond spent roughly $11,000 per pupil; Henrico spent roughly $7,000. That $4,000 difference per pupil adds up to real money. In a class of twenty students, for example, the spending difference between the districts is $80,000, which is more than the average teacher's annual salary. Despite spending more money, however, there is little evidence that Richmond schools are superior to those in Henrico. To the contrary, on every measurement imaginable—state tests, the National Assessment of Educational Progress, Advanced Placement Tests, the SATs, graduation rates, and college attendance rates—Henrico schools outperform Richmond schools.[40]

The anecdotal evidence from Richmond and elsewhere is consistent with broader statistical studies regarding the relationship between funding and achievement. There is an ongoing and heated debate about this relationship among social scientists, which is often caricatured as a debate over whether "money matters." The caricature is just that, as everyone recognizes that money does matter. The real debate instead concerns two different but related questions. The first is whether there is any systematic relationship between funding and achievement levels. The second is whether certain inputs—such as small class size—reliably produce achievement gains.[41]

To make a very long story short, there is not much of a systematic relationship between funding and achievement levels, as the contrast between Henrico and Richmond suggests. At the same time, however, there is evidence that certain inputs reliably produce achievement gains. In other words, there is evidence—and some consensus—that certain resources, not all of them financial, really matter. Everyone agrees, for example, that middle-class peers matter, as do active and engaged parents. Good teachers and good principals also matter. Some evidence also suggests that reducing class size has a positive effect on student achievement, especially among disadvantaged students. (There remains a need for good teachers, however, as small classes with ineffective teachers are usually worse than larger classes run by good teachers.) And numerous studies show that preschool is a particularly good investment, usually paying for itself in terms of cost savings to the government in the medium and long terms.[42]

There might seem to be some tension between the first and second points. How can there be little evidence of a systematic relationship between funding levels and achievement, whereas there is good evidence that some inputs reliably boost achievement? The answer is twofold: money is not always spent wisely, and money cannot buy everything, which leads to the next two explanations for why increased funding has generally not led to improved performance.

Poor Choices

There is a good deal of evidence to suggest that school districts spend money inefficiently, and that inefficient spending is a particular problem in high-poverty urban school districts. It is undeniable that urban educators and administrators face daunting problems, and many of them are truly heroic in what they accomplish with the amount of funding they have available. It is also undeniable, however, that at least some of those educators and administrators have made unwise and counterproductive decisions on how to spend funds and run their schools and districts. This is as true in Richmond as it is elsewhere.[43]

A case study of the Newark public school system, before it was taken over by the state, provides a good example. In this study, author Jean Anyon described how intense poverty and racial isolation helped create a school system in which political patronage rather than merit was often the basis for the appointment of administrators. In addition, the low social status of parents and their lack of political power meant that teachers and staff did not feel accountable and, indeed, were often abusive to students and dismissive of parents. The teachers and administrators, moreover, "appeared to be resigned to the failure of reform efforts" in the schools. In that context, it is hard to see how increased funding alone would make much of a difference.[44]

Another case study, this one of the St. Louis school system, reached similar conclusions. In poor cities such as St. Louis, "most of the decent paying jobs for

African-Americans are in the public school system," and the temptation toward patronage is often quite high. Indeed, as the authors reported, "over the past thirty years the St. Louis school board has taken better care of many of its employees than it has of the children whose life chances depend on the board's ability to lead." In that setting, dedicated urban educators became "outliers in a field of low expectations," and many have been "eventually swallowed up by the inertia." Studies of schools in Kansas City, Washington, D.C., Detroit, Atlanta, and Baltimore have reached similar conclusions.[45]

At least one Richmond School Board member believes the same is true of the Richmond school system, namely that it is viewed more as a jobs program than as a provider of education. There is little doubt that some money is wasted in Richmond; the only question is how much. Part of the problem is an over-abundance of school facilities. Richmond has too many schools and not enough students. In 2007–8, Richmond operated fifty-four schools, which were designed to accommodate fifty thousand students but housed only about twenty-five thousand. Henrico County, by contrast, in the same year had sixty-nine facilities but nearly twice the number of students.[46]

In addition to too many buildings, Richmond might have too many employees—or at least too many nonteaching employees. Ironically enough, given the comment of the Richmond School Board member, the School Board itself consists of nine members and two clerks, all of whom receive salaries. Henrico County has only five board members and one clerk. The Richmond public schools also have sixty-five assistant principals, whereas Henrico County has sixty-seven—again, for twice the number of students.

Douglas Wilder, who served as mayor of Richmond from 2005–9, believes that Richmond's schools are amply funded and that the real problem is waste and inefficiency. This is not an uncommon refrain among city mayors, but this message comes from a mayor with an unusual background. Wilder previously served as governor of Virginia, and was the first African American in the country elected to a governorship. As mayor, he made it a priority to ensure that money for education in Richmond was well spent, and he was an outspoken critic of the status quo.

"Those who cry about lack of funding," Wilder wrote in the *Richmond Times-Dispatch*, "won't acknowledge that Richmond is the best funded [district] among its peers...and sits among the top 10 of all systems in Virginia." He continued: "We're spending twice as much for half the student population that once numbered 50,000 students. Even allowing for inflation, that makes no sense at all." The *Richmond Times-Dispatch*, perhaps not surprisingly given its conservative orientation, agreed with Wilder that Richmond's "schools need to be run more efficiently. The system employs too much administration, the number of facilities cannot be justified by enrollment, and per-pupil spending seems out of line with peer cities. The mayor is right to demand a leaner school system that focuses money on classroom education."[47]

The maladministration of some urban school systems makes it hard to assess whether their funding is sufficient, as it is difficult to determine the real impact of funding when some of it is being wasted. At the same time, the failure of city schools to translate even generous funding levels into improved academic outcomes lends political and popular strength to the argument that increased funding would be ineffective. Even if more funding would help, therefore, advocates for finance reform have an uphill political battle, as is evidenced by the turn away from funding and toward other measures, such as school choice and standards and testing. These other reforms start from the premise that funding is sufficient and that the problem has to do with incentives among teachers and administrators.

The fact that some money is being wasted in urban school systems also makes it harder to gain support for something that is both necessary and costly: maintenance and renovation of facilities. Facilities costs are not usually included in calculations of per-pupil spending, which can serve to obscure the differences in day-to-day life at urban and suburban schools. Freeman and Tee-Jay are good examples. One would think from comparing spending amounts that Tee-Jay would have a much more pleasant physical environment than Freeman, but that is not the case.

A student at Tee-Jay, whose class I visited, asked me afterward if I was "really interested in what our school is like." After I told her yes, she said, simply: "Check out our bathrooms." I tried, but all the bathroom doors I checked were locked. Apparently, they are open only at certain times during the day. But I understood the student's point from walking around the rest of the building. It is a somewhat depressing place. There are no visible hazards like falling plaster or leaking pipes, and the building is beautiful from the outside. But inside it is dark, and the hallways and classrooms look old and a little neglected. The outdoor athletic facilities are sparse. The locker rooms are on different floors from the gym and have not been renovated since the school opened in the 1930s. Students in the classes I attended shared textbooks or relied on copies of excerpts from books.

Freeman High School is nondescript from the outside and looks like countless other schools in suburbs throughout the United States. Inside, though, it is brighter and has a more modern feel than Tee-Jay. It is not palatial, by any stretch. But the classrooms are well equipped, the athletic facilities are impressive, and each student is provided with a laptop computer. In addition, the school just finished a $20 million renovation project in fall 2009, which followed earlier renovations that the principal describes on the school's website: "With tremendous support of parents, alumni, and the community, funds have been raised to provide state-of-the-art athletic facilities for our students, including a field house, spectator stands, all-weather track, expanded and improved fields, lighting, and concession stands." In addition, "a new magnificent strength train-ing facility was dedicated in May of 2006."

One would not know that Richmond spends more than Henrico by looking around Tee-Jay and Freeman. To the contrary, the experience makes one feel certain that Richmond must have less money than Henrico. Students at Tee-Jay know the feeling, as the complaint about bathrooms at Tee-Jay indicates. Indeed, when I asked students at Tee-Jay what, if anything, was different between their school and Freeman, the first thing they said was that Freeman "has more money." The contrast between the schools is driven home when Tee-Jay students travel to county schools like Freeman for athletic contests. As Dr. Pruden remarked, city students definitely notice that county schools have much better athletic facilities. He believes they cannot help but wonder why "our soci-ety seems to value county kids more than city kids."[48]

In the endless debate over school funding, the atmosphere of a school, and the effect it can have on students and teachers alike, are rarely mentioned. We tend to forget, as an education law scholar once observed, that "schools are not just means to ends, but also places where great numbers of people spend their days." The focus in academic and popular debates, however, is not on what schools feel like but on whether money translates into better academic achievement. Because money has not done so in Richmond, there is not much support for increasing funding for anything, including facilities. It may well be that improving the facili-ties in a district that is struggling academically represents a frill that cannot be afforded. And it is certainly true that more money would be available for facilities if less money were wasted. When walking the halls at Tee-Jay, however, it is hard not to conclude that Dr. Pruden is exactly right: the shoddy facilities in many urban schools send an implicit but strong message about the value placed on the enterprise of urban education and those who participate in it.[49]

What Money Can't Buy

While more money could certainly help improve facilities, there is a fair bit of evidence to suggest that some important resources, more directly related to academic achievement, cannot be purchased. This in turn suggests that more than money is needed to make real improvements in high-poverty urban schools.[50] Of the various reasons why high-poverty schools tend to produce poor academic records, one of the most important appears to be peer influence. In 1966, James Coleman released a mammoth and still controversial report on the nation's schools, entitled *Equality of Educational Opportunity*. The report is best remembered for asserting that school funding exerts little influence on student achievement; instead, an individual student's socioeconomic status is the best predictor of academic success.[51]

Less remembered but equally important was the finding that the socioeconomic status of a student's peers also exerts a significant influence on academic performance. "Student body characteristics," Coleman reported, account for "an impressive percent of variance" in student achievement, and the influence appears greatest on students from disadvantaged backgrounds. Study after study confirms that the social composition of the student body is more highly related to achievement, independent of a student's own social background, than is any other school factor. Education scholars and commentators of every political stripe acknowledge the robustness and consistency of these findings. Simply put, as one researcher reported, "if there is one thing that is more related to a child's academic achievement than coming from a poor household, it is going to school with children from other poor households."[52]

The explanation for the importance of peers is fairly straightforward and somewhat intuitive, though it remains controversial. Students from higher socioeconomic backgrounds, like their parents and teachers, tend to have higher expectations and aspirations regarding academic achievement. In schools, as in other communities, most participants tend to conform to the dominant culture. In schools that are majority middle-class, that culture typically is one that values academic achievement and generally expects students to attend college. This school environment is contagious; it affects most students and thus tends to raise the aspirations and motivation of poor students.[53]

In schools that are majority poor, by contrast, expectations and motivations tend to be lower. Indeed, in poor inner-city schools, which are predominantly minority, researchers have found that the dominant school culture often actively denigrates academic success. Anthropologists and social scientists have identified a distinct culture in many poor, black neighborhoods that is defined primarily by its opposition to conventional middle-class "white" values. As two anthropologists have explained, subordinated minorities, such as black Americans, can "develop a sense of collective identity...in opposition to the social identity of white Americans because of the way white Americans treat them in economic, political, social, and psychological domains, including white exclusion of these groups from assimilation." Once established, this oppositional culture becomes difficult to overcome because it is closely tied to the minority's sense of collective identity and security.[54]

This oppositional culture is not confined to the streets but also exerts an influence within schools, where doing well is associated with "acting white." Anthropologists John Ogbu and Signithia Fordham, who pioneered this field of study, found that children in high-poverty, high-minority schools face tremendous peer pressure to avoid the stigma of "acting white" that attends academic success. The pressure to avoid success is most intense during adolescence. Ogbu and Fordham report that young black students intensely fear being labeled "Oreos" or "Uncle Toms" for performing well in school or even speaking standard English. They further report that some students intentionally fail courses or try to avoid good grades to avoid these labels. This peer pressure, Fordham and other researchers have found, can still exist in integrated schools. But it is at least counterbalanced by a competing culture that supports academic achievement.[55]

Some researchers believe that the oppositional culture identified by Ogbu and Fordham is not particular to racial minorities, but also exists within some poor white communities. This may well be correct, and it may be that class is just as important as race in this context. Even if that is true, however, it does not diminish the problem faced by urban schools, which are both high-poverty and predominantly minority.[56]

This explanation regarding the importance of peers is controversial, and not all accept it, because it seems to blame students or their parents for some moral failing. But recognizing the influence of peers or the existence of an oppositional culture need not be read as casting blame but instead as simply identifying the ways that circumstances shape people, young and old. Starkly different realities face the white, middle-class suburban student and the black, poor, inner-city student. It would be odd, indeed, if those realities did not influence the outlook and behavior of students.

The importance of peers and school culture is not simply the stuff of academic research. To the contrary, it was obvious to the teachers, students, and principals at Tee-Jay and Freeman. When I asked Dr. Pruden, for example, about the performance of poor and minority students at Freeman, student culture was the first thing he discussed. Students who transfer from city schools, he said, often spend the first few weeks out of step with the rest of the student body. "The bell for class might ring," he said, "and the transfer student would linger in the hallway instead of getting to class on time. After a few days, though, this student begins to notice that he's the only one late to class, or he's the only one who hasn't done his homework, and his behavior starts to change." Pruden continued: "Pretty soon, this student is getting to class on time and doing his homework as well."[57]

The Tee-Jay and Freeman students I interviewed also focused, without any prompting, on the influence of student culture. I spoke with a group of Tee-Jay students who were enrolled in the International Baccalaureate (IB) Program, which is a limited program with a competitive admissions process. These students, most of whom were African-American, were at the top of their class academically, and they were a remarkably engaging, thoughtful, and impressive group. This did not make them popular with their peers. They described the intense peer pressure they felt to invest less in and care less about their schoolwork. Other students ridiculed them for reading on the bus, for carrying work home, and for studying for tests, calling them uppity and accusing them of feeling like they were better than everyone else. One African-American girl said some of her African-American peers, not in the IB program, routinely referred to her as that "white girl," apparently because of her academic success and her manner of speaking. "It's not because of the color of my skin," she said, pointing to her dark-skinned arm and saying "I mean, look at me: I'm obviously not white."

The Freeman students I interviewed, by contrast, spoke about the pressure they felt to do well in school, which came from both their parents and their peers. "It's not that I'm super competitive," one student told me, "but I don't like it when my friends do better than me on tests." Another student added, "I feel embarrassed if I have to tell my friends—and they always ask—that I did poorly on a test." These students, all of them white, acknowledged that not every student in the school tried to be a high-achiever, but they also pointed out that striving for academic success was not limited to white students. They described how some students—both white and black—actively disparaged academic achievement, but they emphasized that these students were the exception. "It's ok," they said, "to want to do well in school. People don't make fun of you for that."

Empirical evidence underscores the influence of peers and student culture and, indeed, suggests that they are more important than funding levels—indicating that there are some important school resources that money cannot buy. In addition to the *absence* of much evidence indicating a strong relationship between funding and achievement, there is a consistent line of research indicating that all students benefit from attending majority middle-income schools, and that poor students in particular benefit from doing so. Coleman, again, was one of the first researchers to notice the benefits of socioeconomic integration on poorer students, concluding in his 1966 study that "the environment provided by the student body...has its greatest effect on those from educationally deficient backgrounds."[58]

Subsequent studies have reached similar conclusions. James Rosenbaum, for example, studied the effects of Chicago's well-known Gautreaux program, which allowed some families to move from inner-city Chicago to surrounding suburbs. Rosenbaum compared the students whose families moved to the students whose families remained behind in Chicago. He found that the students who transferred to suburban schools were more likely to be in college preparatory classes, less likely to drop out, and more likely to attend college than those who were left behind.[59]

Robert Crain and Amy Stuart Wells, in their case study of the St. Louis desegregation program, found similar results. Under the St. Louis program, thirteen thousand minority students from the city attended suburban schools during the 1980s and 1990s. City schools received additional funding for traditional and magnet schools. Crain and Wells found that students who transferred to suburban schools outperformed students who remained in city schools, whether traditional or magnet. Suburban transfer students also graduated at twice the rate of those who remained in St. Louis, and they were more likely to attend college.[60]

Another case study from San Francisco points in the same direction. A federal judge in a school desegregation case ordered a study of various desegregation plans. The study found that students from low socioeconomic backgrounds posted significant gains in achievement when they transferred to schools with more advantaged, higher-achieving students. This improvement occurred even though the transfer schools received no additional funding. By contrast, students who remained in city schools populated primarily by low-income students generally showed no academic gains, despite the fact that the city schools received increased funding.[61]

These case studies are bolstered by studies examining larger samples of students. Rita Mahard and Robert Crain, for example, reviewed the results of ninety-three separate studies on the effect of court-ordered desegregation on student achievement. They found that desegregation had moderate, positive effects on black student achievement. More important, they found that desegregation plans that included both cities and suburbs resulted in the greatest academic gains for African-American students. They concluded that racial integration is most effective when it also results in socioeconomic integration.[62]

Consistent with the hypothesis that school culture matters, research also indicates that socioeconomic integration affects student behavior in ways that indirectly spur improvements in academic achievement and attainment. A study by Susan Mayer, for example, found that even after controlling for the students' socioeconomic status, tenth-graders in affluent high schools were less likely to drop out than those who attended poor schools. She also found that tenth-graders in wealthier schools were less likely to have a child than their counterparts in poor schools, and that white students in predominantly black schools were more likely to drop out and have a child than whites in predominantly white schools.[63]

In sum, the research indicates that "one of the most effective ways to improve children's cognitive skills is to put them in an environment with other children who want to acquire cognitive skills and whose families support such learning." More precisely, and perhaps more important, the research shows that "children of low socioeconomic status appear to benefit significantly from exposure to more affluent and highly motivated peers."[64]

Higher-income children, moreover, do not appear to suffer from socioeconomic integration. This sounds too good to be true, and many middle-class parents are unlikely to believe it, which helps explain the traditional opposition to racial and socioeconomic integration in white, middle-class suburban schools. But this is what the research shows, and it is consistent with the hypothesis that school culture matters and influences behavior. Provided that the school culture remains one of high expectations, where academic achievement and attending college are valued, most students in the school will conform to the majority culture. In addition, numerous studies indicate that integration levels impact poorer students more than middle-class ones. Altogether, the research suggests that the school must remain predominantly middle-class and that the benefits of socioeconomic integration might be lost if the balance tips too far in the direction of poverty.[65]

Majority-middle-income schools are also more likely to have active and engaged parents, which is a key factor in school success. These parents are more likely to set high expectations for their children, which is then translated into the school's culture. These parents, in part because they have more time, are also more likely to volunteer in school, to attend conferences, and to be involved in parent-teacher organizations. These differences among parents, detailed in numerous social science studies, were confirmed by the teachers and principals I interviewed at Tee-Jay and Freeman, who described a strong correlation between socioeconomic status and parental involvement. The current principal at Freeman, Anne L. Poates, for example, marveled at the dedication and commitment of the students' parents. By contrast, the current principal at Tee-Jay, Tanya Roane, lamented the lack of participation and interest in Tee-Jay's Parent-Teacher-Student Association, which she estimated had about 30 members and had met only once in the first five months of the 2009–10 school year.[66]

In addition to being involved in the schools, middle-income and affluent parents are also more likely than poor ones to monitor principals and teachers and to complain when their performance is subpar. As important, they are also more likely than poor parents to have the clout to bring about necessary improvements at the school and district level. All of these interventions can improve the quality of education that students receive. Just like middle-income students, middle-income parents are a valuable resource that money cannot purchase.[67]

It must be stressed again that the point of this research is not to cast blame or find fault with poor students or their parents. In the analogous context of racial desegregation, advocates have been justifiably wary of implying that black students need to sit next to white students in order to learn. Critics from the left and right often accuse desegregation of operating on precisely this premise. But this is a caricature. It misses the broader point that school culture matters, and that high-poverty schools, especially urban ones, generally do not have healthy cultures. There are some exceptions, to be sure. Some relatively successful urban schools—including the Knowledge Is Power Program (KIPP) charter schools, discussed in chapter 6—have fought hard to create a culture of high expectations. But the experience of these schools tends to reinforce the research about the benefits of socioeconomic integration, not call it into question, insofar as the schools that are exceptional have cultures that are themselves exceptional for urban schools.

A Reprise

It is difficult to sort through the strands of social science evidence on this topic and come to a simple, rock-hard answer to the question of why, even at fairly generous funding levels, urban schools still perform worse than suburban schools. That said, some points do stand out. First, money is obviously needed to buy some important resources, like good teachers, that influence student achievement. It is also needed to pay for decent facilities, which can influence achievement indirectly and can more directly influence the quality of student and teacher life. Whether most urban schools have sufficient money right now to pay for everything they need is harder to answer, in part because it is clear that some money is being wasted.

It nonetheless seems safe to conclude that, even with all waste eliminated, many urban schools would still need more funding to pay for some key resources, like high quality teachers and decent facilities, though just how much more they might need is extremely difficult to calculate. In addition, and this is the key point, simply giving high-poverty urban schools more money may still not be enough to close the gap between those schools and low-poverty suburban ones. To the extent that middle-income peers and middle-income parents matter—and research strongly suggests they do—increased funding will only be a partial solution. Indeed, socioeconomic integration, on the whole, may be a more effective—and less costly—way to boost the achievement of low-income students than increasing spending on high-poverty schools. As researcher David Rusk once put it, those interested in boosting achievement should probably focus less on "moving money" and more on moving students.[68]

SCHOOLS, RACE, AND MONEY

Even if Rusk is wrong and significant increases in funding would make a big difference, the continued segregation of urban and suburban students creates political obstacles to securing the necessary funding. To see this, one can start by assuming, for the sake of argument, that large increases in funding would cure the problems of high-poverty urban schools. The obvious question then arises: where will this money come from?

There is no real answer to that question. Urban districts do not have an overabundance of local funds for schools, and state legislatures do not seem inclined to make up the gap. The federal government has recently increased funding for schools, but its share of funding remains relatively low. This leaves courts. But courts have not fought very hard for urban districts. As already described, courts in general have not been especially aggressive in school finance suits, even when they have ruled in favor of plaintiffs. Courts have been particularly unreliable, however, when urban, minority districts have been school finance plaintiffs.

In a study I conducted several years ago, I examined the racial composition and the type (rural, suburban, or urban) of districts involved in school funding suits. I wanted to determine whether there was any correlation between success in court and the demographics of the districts involved. The results were striking: minority districts rarely win school finance suits; urban, minority districts almost never do. A more recent follow-up study by other researchers confirmed the earlier results and found that the pattern repeated itself in later years.[69]

In addition, the relatively few minority districts that succeeded in court encountered more intense and prolonged legislative resistance than did successful white districts. Measuring legislative resistance is necessarily an imprecise endeavor, and a number of potential reasons having nothing to do with race can explain the results. But just as with court decisions, there was a discernible pattern among legislative responses that at least suggests race influenced those responses.[70]

In four states where minority districts succeeded as plaintiffs—New Jersey, Texas, Arizona, and New York—protracted legislative battles ensued, prompting numerous returns to court. In New Jersey, court and legislative battles have been ongoing for more than three decades. The court issued more than fifteen decisions in order to force the legislature to comply and has now seemingly bowed out of the picture in the face of continued legislative resistance. The Texas Supreme Court has issued six rulings, the Arizona court four. The New York courts have not been called on as often, but the school finance case involving New York City schools has lingered for years and prompted numerous legislative battles. In two of these four states, the courts have had to threaten to close the schools to prompt legislative action. In all four, the legislature and public have openly and often fiercely opposed devoting more resources to school districts primarily serving minority students.[71]

White districts have had an easier time translating court victories into legislation. This is not to say that all legislatures have been eager to spend more money in the cases these districts have brought, and some of these districts have encountered stiff legislative resistance. Legislative responses in most states, moreover, have generally been fairly tepid, regardless of the districts involved. Nonetheless, where white districts have been involved, the legislative fights over funding have been relatively mild compared to the battles in states like New Jersey and Texas.[72]

Thus, even if one assumes that city schools could improve if given substantially more funding, there is little reason at the moment to expect such funding to materialize. Most courts seem disinclined to push too hard when only minority districts are involved in litigation. Legislatures, in turn, cannot be expected simply to spend whatever it might take to make city schools successful.

This political reality, it bears repeating, is itself a result of the continued separation of urban and suburban schools. Suburban-dominated state legislatures cannot be expected to support large increases in funding for urban schools because their constituents do not have a stake in those schools. To the contrary, at some point, spending more money on urban schools would require sacrifices in suburban districts, which suburbanites will not support. Recall the frank comment of the Long Island superintendent: "*I don't want to be hurting myself in order to help my neighbor.*" This pretty much captures the politics of educational funding, if not education politics altogether.[73]

The failure to integrate schools, especially urban and suburban ones, has thus created not just academic obstacles—like concentrated school poverty—but political ones as well. School finance litigation has been unable to overcome either set of obstacles. More money does not seem to be a good substitute for more integration, at least along socioeconomic lines. Even if money alone could make all the difference, the very fact of separation makes such funding increases politically unlikely. Put differently, segregation, especially by class, creates a dilemma for urban districts: the separation creates the need for greater resources but also makes it extremely unlikely that that need will be met.

Teachers and Education Politics

The difficulty of securing high-quality teachers for urban schools provides a useful, concrete illustration of this dilemma. Numerous studies confirm that teachers in high-poverty, high-minority, urban schools tend to be less experienced, credentialed, and effective than teachers in predominantly white, middle-class suburban schools. The question is why. One common explanation is that urban schools are quite challenging places to teach and that, all else being equal, teachers will choose schools that are less challenging.[74]

One might think that the solution is to pay (good) teachers more to work in high-poverty urban schools. When I interviewed Dr. Ulschmid, who at the time was the principal of Tee-Jay, she indicated that if she had more money to spend, she would spend it on teachers. It is not obvious, however, that more pay would be sufficient to compensate for the challenges of an urban school. Private schools, for example, are quite successful in attracting good teachers even when they pay less than nearby public schools, which suggests that money alone does not drive the decision about where to teach. Indeed, a better strategy to secure good teachers might be to make the schools less challenging by making them more socioeconomically diverse. The segregation of poor students itself, in other words, may be the real obstacle to attracting high-quality teachers to urban schools.[75]

Even if one assumes, however, that paying teachers more money would lure good ones to urban schools, the increase in teacher pay would have to be fairly substantial. This is one of the lessons that can be drawn from existing experiments in differential pay programs for teachers. A few states offer modest "combat pay" increases to teachers who take on difficult assignments, but these have not been very successful in attracting large numbers of good teachers to difficult schools. Clearly, the additional amounts offered were not enough to change the calculations of most teachers. Just how much more would be necessary remains the subject of speculation, but one group of researchers estimated that teachers would need to be paid as much as 50 percent more than they currently earn in order to take an urban school assignment.[76]

Once we posit that teachers would have to be paid significantly more to teach in urban schools, we bump up against the political reality of funding. At least some of the funding would have to come from the state legislature, but there is little reason to think that suburban-dominated legislatures would be willing to pay whatever it takes to attract high-quality teachers to urban schools. Indeed, to the extent that the supply of these teachers is limited, this is essentially a zero-sum game. It is hard to imagine suburban legislators agreeing to devote funds to lure good teachers away from their constituents. Why would a legislator from Henrico, for example, vote for a bill that would use his constituents' tax dollars to attract teachers out of Freeman and into Tee-Jay?[77]

School finance litigation tries to push against this political dynamic, but it has done little to change it. If anything, school finance litigation has done as much to entrench the current structure of educational opportunity as it has to challenge it. District lines remain as important as ever, and segregation remains widespread and increasing. Many criticize courts and advocates in school finance cases as too aggressive or radical. From another perspective, however, they have been quite conservative, which leads to the last topic of this chapter.

COURTS AND LAWYERS

Conservative Courts

Courts that rule for school finance plaintiffs are often tagged with the label of "activism," just as courts that ordered racial desegregation faced similar accusations. These "liberal, activist" courts are seen by critics as overreaching and meddlesome. Those sympathetic with the plaintiffs' cause, by contrast, tend to see the same courts in more heroic terms, as struggling to fix a real and serious problem. They might accept the activism label but view it as a badge of honor rather than an epithet. Both critics and supporters seem to share the view that courts ruling in favor of school finance plaintiffs are acting aggressively and progressively

In reality, however, these courts have been somewhat conservative, which becomes clear when one considers what they have *not* done. When school litigation first began, many observers believed that courts would outlaw the use of the property tax. The media, for example, portrayed these cases as referenda on the legality of the property tax. Yet not a single court has outlawed the use of local property taxes to fund public schools.[78]

In addition, courts have not questioned district boundaries. One way to equalize funding would be to change boundary lines so that districts have roughly equal property wealth. No court has required legislatures to do this. Similarly, courts have generally refrained from requiring wealthy districts to share local property tax revenues with neighboring districts. In general, property-rich districts remain free to spend as much as they would like on their own schools. Hence, disparities and inadequacies continue.

And they most likely will, for the simple reason that courts in school finance cases have done nothing to change the basic structure and politics of school funding. This is why sustained court involvement is necessary. Even if school districts secure more funding through a court order in year one, for example, in year five their funding needs will have changed. But the legislature will have no more incentive in year five than it did in year one to increase funds. Thus, to meet changing needs, plaintiffs usually have to return to court.

Indeed, in no state has one trip to the courthouse been enough to secure long-term relief. Even in Kentucky and Massachusetts, where legislatures responded quickly and in good faith to school funding decisions, plaintiffs have had to return to court in order to secure additional funding because of changing needs. School finance reform, when court-ordered, is not self-sustaining. Continued success requires continued vigilance on the part of courts, and not all courts are willing to stay involved over the long run. In addition to the New Jersey Supreme Court, courts in Ohio and Alabama explicitly bowed out of the process after multiple rounds of litigation. One suspects that, over time, more courts will follow their lead.[79]

Cautious Advocates

School finance reform advocates are similarly mislabeled as aggressive or radical when, in fact, they have been relatively cautious in their approach to these cases. Especially noteworthy is the widespread embrace of adequacy. Over the last decade or so, many advocates (and commentators) have endorsed adequacy, as opposed to equity, as the goal for school funding suits. Although courts in school funding suits, as described, remain interested in comparability and equity of resources, most advocates and commentators seem determined to have adequacy enshrined as the governing standard.[80]

Those who champion adequacy do so for a number of reasons, which are plausible but not convincing. Some believe that adequacy suits will result in more funding for needier students, though there is no empirical basis for this belief and no reason in theory why equity suits should preclude devoting greater resources to those with greater needs. Others worry that equity suits inevitably lead states to level down spending, though the evidence for this proposition is equally thin. The argument rests almost entirely on California's experience, where overall funding levels dropped while an equity suit, *Serrano v. Priest*, was pending. The connection between these two events, however, is attenuated and remains the subject of an ongoing debate. And regardless of which side in that particular debate is correct, the experience has not been repeated in other states, which makes it difficult to claim that equity suits will inevitably lead to leveling down.[81]

Regardless of their reasons, it is worth noticing that those who embrace adequacy as a goal have essentially abandoned any attempt to link the financial fates of poor and rich districts. Adequacy presupposes that some districts will be able to provide an education that is more than adequate. Thus, instead of seeking to ensure that all districts have access to the same pool of resources, which was the goal of fiscal neutrality, those in favor of adequacy accept the inevitable inequalities that will follow. Indeed, some seek to make a virtue of necessity by arguing that adequacy is superior to equity precisely because it is less threatening to property-rich districts. In the words of one commentator, adequacy is less costly "for the elites who derive the greatest benefits from the existing inequalities, because adequacy does not threaten their ability to retain a superior position." This may well be true, but one could easily argue that this is precisely the problem with adequacy, not a reason to pursue it.[82]

In states where courts have rejected equity claims, a switch in focus to adequacy might be understandable due to the lack of choice. Elsewhere, however, it is puzzling that advocates are ignoring the continued emphasis courts place on disparities in resources among districts. To me, this seems like an attractive invitation. One would think it to plaintiffs' advantage to accept the invitation and to hitch their wagons quite explicitly to property-rich districts. They could then argue that funding levels in those districts should serve as the proper benchmark against which equity *and* adequacy of funding should be judged. States are not about to take money *away* from property-rich districts, so this approach if successful should lead states to level up spending in property-poor districts so that it is at least "substantially equal" or comparable to spending in property-rich districts.

It is also puzzling that advocates have not been more creative in their use of the underlying rights recognized in school funding cases. When courts rule for plaintiffs in school funding suits, they recognize that students have a right to either equal or adequate educational opportunities. The remedy for a violation of that right is almost always translated into funding, but there is no legal or logical reason for that particular translation. One could imagine lawyers asking for a right to transfer to another school that is providing a constitutionally sufficient education, much as lawyers in the pre-*Brown* era of "separate but equal" education requested that black students be able to transfer to white schools if black schools were unequal. One could similarly imagine lawyers asking for socioeconomic integration as a remedy for inadequate schools, given the evidence indicating that predominantly middle-class schools perform better than high-poverty ones.

Very few attorneys, however, have pursued these alternative remedies. The most well-known exception is a famous Connecticut case, *Sheff v. O'Neill*, decided in 1996. In that case, which focused on a state constitutional right to education, the Connecticut Supreme Court ruled that students had a right to attend racially integrated schools. The court relied heavily on a provision in the Connecticut Constitution that spoke directly to racial segregation. Similar provisions exist only in the New Jersey and Hawaii constitutions.

Because of the rarity of these state constitutional provisions, most commentators argued that the experience in *Sheff* could not be repeated outside of Connecticut, New Jersey, and Hawaii. What these commentators missed, however, was the basic point that courts have to define the scope of education rights whenever they rule in favor of plaintiffs in a school "finance" suit. Courts tend to define those rights in dollar terms because that is how lawyers present the cases. The real puzzle is why lawyers present their cases this way instead of arguing for alternatives to funding, especially given the lackluster results of funding litigation thus far.[83]

The answer may be that lawyers, as much as courts, are less radical than some might believe. One suspects that lawyers have remained focused on funding rather than integration, whether racial or socioeconomic, because they believe it is politically easier to secure more funding than more integration. They are probably correct on this point, as the experience in Connecticut—admittedly just one state—indicates. *Sheff*, a case squarely about racial integration, has not actually produced much in the way of increased racial integration. Its main impact so far, ironically enough, has been to encourage the legislature to increase funding for Hartford city schools, undoubtedly as a way to relieve pressure to integrate. School finance attorneys may justifiably believe that it is better to go after what is possible than to tilt at windmills.[84]

At the same time, however, it is important to recognize the limitations of the current approach to school finance reform and indeed the limitations inherent in the reform itself. Unless and until the basic politics of educational opportunity change, attempts to secure increased funding and to translate that funding into real improvement on the ground will meet with halting success at best. By working within the current political reality, rather than trying to change it, courts and school finance lawyers are working at the margins of educational opportunity. Indeed, at the end of the day, they may unintentionally be doing as much as anyone to entrench the current politics and structure of educational opportunity, where poor and minority students remain largely separate from their wealthier and white peers, and where most disparities in opportunity and result follow from that basic fact.

CONCLUSION

School finance litigation and school desegregation cases have followed a similar trajectory. In both sets of cases, advocates initially sought ways to link the fates of disadvantaged and advantaged students. Yet in neither set of cases was this goal achieved. To the contrary, the cases have reinforced the boundaries that separate urban and suburban schools. The U.S. Supreme Court in *Milliken v. Bradley* made the boundary between suburb and city all but impassable for the purpose of desegregation. The Court respected that boundary again in *San Antonio v. Rodriguez* by protecting the ability of some districts to spend more than others. School finance litigation in state courts, even where successful, has not made school district boundaries irrelevant to funding.

In both school finance and desegregation cases, moreover, advocates lowered their sights over time and tried to make the best of what they believed available to them through litigation. The hope of equalizing school funding has given way, increasingly, to calls for adequate funding, just as the attempt to equalize opportunities among white and black students through integration gave way to calls for *Milliken II* funding. School desegregation and school finance litigation thus converged around the goal of providing additional funding to some needy school districts, many of which were—and remain—isolated by race and poverty.

Indeed, the parallel between school finance suits and *Milliken II* relief is striking. Both take as a given—either as a matter of strategy or necessity—that poor and minority districts will remain separate from white and wealthier ones. Both sets of cases channel resources to poor, struggling districts, which are usually in urban or rural areas, while protecting the independence and sanctity of wealthy districts, which are usually located in the suburbs. Save the cities, but spare the suburbs.

Increasing funding, however, has not been a panacea. Far from it. Some school finance reform advocates, just like some who supported *Milliken II* relief, might have hoped that increasing resources would make racial segregation and isolation irrelevant. The forty-year history of school finance litigation shows that this hope was misplaced. School finance litigation has been unable to transcend the effects of segregation and the limited reach of court-ordered desegregation. This is primarily because continued separation on the basis of race has meant continued isolation by class and concentrated poverty in urban schools and urban neighborhoods. Additional funding might help alleviate some of the effects of poverty, but it has not come close to bridging the gap between poor urban and middle-class suburban schools.

This is true even in a place like Richmond, whose schools are funded at a significantly higher level than Henrico County's. Indeed, it does not seem unfair to think of Richmond as representative of districts that have won school finance cases, given the amount the city spends relative to its suburban neighbors. Money has not been enough in Richmond to close the gap between city schools like Tee-Jay and suburban ones like Freeman. The same story is true throughout the country. Those who believe in funding reform might argue that lackluster results are explained by lackluster victories and only moderate increases in funding. They would argue that with more money, perhaps a lot more, real improvements would occur. Even if they were correct—and it is far from clear that they are—the source of that additional funding remains hard to identify.

Others disagree about the importance of funding. And just as earlier advocates turned away from desegregation and toward school finance, some contemporary advocates have turned away from school finance reform and toward measures like school choice and standards and testing. These advocates, as the next several chapters detail, believe the problem is a lack of motivation, not a lack of money.

CHAPTER 5

Limited Choices

Parents in Richmond don't ask for vouchers per se, but a lot of them do ask for their money back.

—Richmond School Board member, 2008

The subject of vouchers and charter schools just doesn't come up in Henrico County. People like the schools their kids are in.

—President, Parent-Teacher-Student Association,
Freeman High School, 2008

To an outsider, the proposal to open the Patrick Henry Charter School in Richmond would hardly seem like a source of controversy. Conceived in 2008 by a group of Richmond parents, the school would cater to elementary students and have an environmental science theme. Like all charter schools, in Virginia and elsewhere, Patrick Henry would be freed from some of the regulations that govern traditional schools, but it would remain a public school and be open to all students in the Richmond school district.[1]

To open the school, the parents needed the Richmond School Board's approval. Under Virginia law, only local school boards can grant permission to create charter schools. Perhaps not surprisingly, very few charter schools have been created, as local school districts are not especially fond of setting up competitors. If the school board approved the proposal, Patrick Henry would be the fourth charter school in the entire state, even though charter school legislation has been on the books for nearly a decade. (Other states have dozens or even hundreds of charter schools.) The school itself would be small and serve just a tiny fraction of Richmond students. The need to obtain school board approval for each charter school, moreover, ensured that opening Patrick Henry would hardly represent the beginning of a charter school juggernaut.

Add a few historical and contemporary facts, and the controversy that erupted becomes much easier to understand. Recall that Virginians relied on school choice, as recently as the 1960s, to thwart school desegregation. Some white students received what were effectively vouchers to attend private academies, while freedom-of-choice plans were used in an effort to maintain segregated schools. To parents and grandparents in their fifties and sixties who were raised in Richmond, this is not ancient history. It is their story.

It did not help that those proposing the Patrick Henry School were overwhelmingly white. This fact added to the already well-developed suspicion of some African-American parents and community leaders that school choice in Richmond is unfair and manipulated by white parents. Indeed, while the charter school proposal was pending, the leader of the Richmond Council of PTAs told a local paper that she believed school choice programs in Richmond were in fact creating a two-tiered system, one catering to the few whites in the public schools and the other serving the black students.[2]

The executive director of the local NAACP chapter, King Salim Khalfani, strongly objected to the charter school. When the school board finally approved it by a five-to-two vote (two members did not vote), he lashed out. He claimed the school would serve as a private haven for white students. He further accused the school board of catering to white families, noting that the vote was "straight up white School Board members plus Uncle Braxton," a critical reference to the board chairman, George Braxton, who is African American. Some countered that these charges were nonsensical. But even critics understood the root cause of the controversy: the history of school choice and racial segregation in Richmond. As A. Barton Hinkle, a columnist for the *Richmond Times-Dispatch*, wrote, Khalfani's claims were "wildly off base—but, given Virginia's toxic racial past, not wholly unexpected. Massive resistance and other racial stains continue to poison the atmosphere decades after their abandonment."[3]

The controversy in Richmond highlights the tricky politics of school choice within urban school districts. Some believe school choice will worsen already high levels of segregation, or at the very least that it will give special privileges to the few white, middle-class families remaining in urban districts. Others believe that school choice, despite its checkered past, is now one of the few lifelines left for students stuck in failing schools. Race, in Richmond and elsewhere, is never far from the surface of debates over choice.

By contrast, school choice does not create much controversy in a suburban district like Henrico County because it is not on the agenda there. No one is seriously proposing charter schools or a voucher program in Henrico. According to the Henrico parents I interviewed, the issue of choice rarely comes up because most parents like the schools their children attend. Indeed, many of them settled in Henrico County *because* of the schools there. Choice may be fine for Richmond, but it is not something for the suburbs, so the thinking goes. What is true in the Richmond metropolitan area is true across the country; choice is a hot topic in urban districts but mostly a non-issue in sub-urban ones.

In addition, there is little discussion in Richmond or elsewhere about increasing opportunities for students to cross district lines to attend school. A few business and religious leaders in Richmond are trying to generate enthusiasm for interdistrict school choice, but the idea has yet to gain purchase. When the idea of interdistrict choice was raised in the past, suburban parents basically "went nuts," according to Lil Tuttle, who served on the state board of education when George Allen was governor in the 1990s. These suburbanites told her that the whole point of moving to the suburbs was "to get away from the problems of urban systems." Why turn around and invite these "problems" to the suburbs?[4]

Not all suburbanites in the Richmond metropolitan area—or elsewhere—share this sentiment, of course, but it nonetheless helps explain a ubiquitous feature of school choice plans: they operate within the confines of a single district, and that district is usually an urban one. The limited scope of school choice plans is rarely discussed. It is usually overshadowed by dire or optimistic predictions about the impact of school choice—especially voucher programs. That nearly all choice plans are geographically limited, however, is the most important and telling fact about them.

To understand why, consider what the world would look like if school choice were universal and all students could choose whatever school they liked—public or private—within a reasonable distance of their homes. The idea is not ridiculous, at least not in theory. School choice tends to be favored either for reasons of equity (all students should have the opportunity to choose a good school) or efficiency (competition will improve all schools). Either way, the more choice, the better. If universal choice existed, however, there would be no right to attend a neighborhood school, and school district lines would not determine placement. If one truly believed in the power of school choice, for example, it would be difficult to deny a student who lived in Richmond the opportunity to choose to attend Freeman High School.

A comprehensive school choice scheme would thus take away the advantage of living in the "right" neighborhood or the "right" school district, because doing so would no longer guarantee admission to the "right" public school. A comprehensive choice scheme would also equalize educational opportunities if structured to provide students equal access to all schools within a reasonable distance of their homes. The fate of all students within a metropolitan area would be tied together by virtue of their being part of a system that offered completely open access to local schools. Indeed, given the radical potential of school choice, it is more than a little curious that choice tends mainly to be associated with political conservatives.

Returning to reality, nothing close to a comprehensive system of school choice exists in Richmond or anywhere else in the country. To the contrary, school choice has been constrained in precisely the same way, and for precisely the same reason, that desegregation and school finance reform have been constrained. In all three contexts, the cardinal rule of educational opportunity has been the same: provide some help to urban students but leave the suburbs alone. In school desegregation, buses to integrate students were halted at the boundaries of suburban districts. In school finance reform, suburban districts have been allowed to go their own way and raise and spend local revenue on their own schools. So it is with school choice: it tends to be available within urban districts but does not threaten the ability of suburban districts to control who attends suburban schools.

The reason is not hard to fathom. Suburban parents are generally satisfied with the public schools their children attend, and they want to protect both the physical and financial sanctity of those schools. School choice can threaten both. It creates the possibility, largely unwelcome, of city students being able to attend suburban schools at local taxpayers' expense. It also raises the possibility that locally raised revenues might exit local school districts if students left to attend private schools or schools in other districts. To the extent that choice threatens the exclusivity and superiority of suburban schools, it also threatens suburban housing values, which are linked to the perceived quality of neighborhood schools. Like suburban parents, suburban homeowners without school-age children thus have a strong, self-interested reason to be wary of school choice.[5]

The pattern of school choice in Richmond and throughout the country reflects these concerns and interests. Public school choice is available in most urban districts, though it remains somewhat controversial, as in Richmond. It is less available in suburban districts like Henrico, and there is little pressure for expansion. There is, finally, almost no serious discussion of ways to promote or expand interdistrict school choice.

Charter schools and the few existing publicly funded voucher programs face similar geographical constraints. Most charter schools are located in urban areas, and most, either by law or policy, cater to students who reside in urban districts. Voucher programs in Milwaukee and Washington, D.C., limit the use of vouchers to private schools within the district. The Cleveland voucher program allows vouchers to be used at either private, city schools or suburban public schools that agree to accept voucher students. None has.

This chapter explains the different types of school choice programs that exist, the features they have in common, and the politics that have shaped them. The chapter that follows assesses the impact of choice programs and the role that courts have played in fights over school choice.

THE SHAPE OF SCHOOL CHOICE

Formal, publicly funded school choice plans come in four main varieties: intra-district and interdistrict public school choice, charter schools, and vouchers. One could also say that the roughly two million homeschoolers exercise a form of school choice, and there can be no doubt that homeschooling is an important trend. Homeschooling is not pertinent to this chapter, however, because homeschoolers do not leave one school for another—they simply leave school altogether. This chapter is focused on the extent to which school choice allows students to attend better schools, either because students choose a better school or because choice improves all schools.

Of all the forms of school choice, publicly funded vouchers for private schools generate the most controversy and receive the most popular and scholarly attention. The attention, however, far outpaces the practical significance of vouchers, which occupy a tiny portion of the school choice universe. Only about thirty-three thousand students currently receive publicly funded vouchers, which represents less than one-tenth of 1 percent of all public school students. More students receive privately funded vouchers, but the numbers are still tiny. Most students who are able to choose a school participate in choice plans that offer options *only* among public schools, and most of these programs limit choices to schools within one district.[6]

Before describing these formal plans in more detail, it is important to recognize that the largest school choice "program" is not formalized at all. This form of school choice occurs when parents select where to live on the basis of the quality of local public schools. It is difficult to pin down exactly how many families exercise this type of choice, but conservative estimates—based on polling—put the number at 25 percent of all public school students, which dwarfs all other choice plans combined. School choice in this guise is rarely discussed. But the fact that such a large number of parents, who tend to be higher on the socioeconomic ladder, have already chosen a school for their children is a crucial starting point in trying to understand the shape of current choice plans, as well as the political dynamics confronting proposals to expand school choice.[7]

Intradistrict Public School Choice

The next most popular form of school choice, after what might be called residential school choice, allows students to attend a non-neighborhood school within a single district. Roughly five million students participate in intradistrict choice plans. That number greatly exceeds the number of students exercising other forms of choice, but it still represents less than 10 percent of all students. Even this relatively modest figure is somewhat misleading, insofar as it exaggerates the impact of intradistrict choice plans, most of which essentially preserve neighborhood school assignments while offering limited alternatives to a fairly small group of students.[8]

Intradistrict school choice programs are quite varied in design and scope. By far the most prevalent type offers students the opportunity to attend a specialized school within the district, or a specialized program at a school outside their normal attendance zone. Both Richmond and Henrico County offer students the opportunity to enroll in specialized programs at high schools outside of their normal attendance zones. For example, Tee-Jay offers the International Baccalaureate (IB) Program, which is a well known, highly regarded, and rigorous course of study that combines regular courses with those focusing on international affairs and foreign cultures. Henrico County high schools each sponsor a program organized around a particular theme, including the arts, technology, and political leadership; the last program is housed at Freeman.[9]

Many of these specialized schools and programs require an application, and they often use selective admissions criteria. The most famous examples outside of Richmond include the Boston Latin School, Bronx Science, and the Lowell High School in San Francisco. The specialized programs in both Richmond and Henrico also require an application, and the admissions process is competitive.

Richmond also hosts three alternative public schools. One is the Franklin Military Academy, which offers a regular course of study and mandatory participation in a Junior Reserve Officer Training Program. The two other alternative high schools, Richmond Community and Richmond Open, also take students from throughout the district. Both require an application, and Richmond Community is specifically geared to serve economically disadvantaged, academically gifted students. Both Richmond Community and Richmond Open are, by all accounts, excellent schools. In fact, both were ranked recently by *U.S. News and World Report* as among the best high schools in the country. Their student populations are primarily African American, and both schools are quite small, each enrolling roughly two hundred students.[10]

Both schools were created in the 1970s, during a period of intense white flight from the district. Some commentators argue that they were created in the hope of stemming that flight by offering a small, rigorous academic environment designed to retain white families who might otherwise head for private schools or the suburbs. Although there is some evidence to support this thesis, it is hard to understand how Community's focus on gifted, poor students was designed to retain white, middle-class families in Richmond. In any event, if keeping white students in Richmond high schools was the purpose of these schools, they were not especially successful. More than three-quarters of the students at both schools are African American. This fact, and the fact that both schools have existed for decades, may help explain why they, unlike the Patrick Henry Charter School, do not seem to generate much controversy today, even though both schools operate much like private schools in a public school setting.[11]

An important variation on the theme of specialized programs and schools are magnet programs and magnet schools. Magnet schools were originally designed to foster integration by attracting white students to city schools, and courts approved their use for this purpose in desegregation decrees. The federal government has also supported magnet schools since 1972, through a modest and little known spending program. The continued existence of this program, even through Republican administrations that were opposed to affirmative action of any kind, is somewhat surprising. The funding is relatively low and has remained stagnant—Congress spent $108 million on it in 1994 and the same amount in 2004—which might help explain the continued existence of the program. That said, it would probably come as surprising news to some members of Congress that the federal government continues to spend money to help schools "offer a special curriculum capable of attracting substantial numbers of students of different racial backgrounds."[12]

Magnet schools initially attracted bipartisan support, and many found the idea of using school choice to achieve racial diversity appealing, especially in contrast to "forced busing." The reality, however, has been more troubling. Because of the demographics of urban school districts, where almost all magnet schools were located, more black students than white ones tended to apply for admission. It followed that more black students were denied admission. Indeed, in some well-publicized instances, local black students were denied admission to magnet schools even though seats set aside for white students remained empty.[13]

A program that was designed to assist African Americans was thus seen by some as one that catered to whites. In a sense, the controversy generated by magnet schools was similar to that created by the Patrick Henry School. Like that charter school in Richmond, magnet schools in many urban areas became embroiled in the complicated racial politics that pervade urban schooling.

Over time, many magnet schools have deemphasized racial integration as a primary goal. The switch in focus in some places was prompted by the demographics of urban districts and the scarcity of white students. The move away from race has also been spurred by changes in the law, which have cast a cloud over the extent to which race can be used as a factor in selecting students, even when integration rather than segregation is the goal.

The U.S. Supreme Court's 2007 decision in *Parents Involved in Community Schools v. Seattle School District*, discussed in chapter 2, may further the trend away from racial considerations in magnet admissions. The opinion in that case suggests that race cannot be the dispositive criterion for assignment to any school, even if the ultimate goal is integration rather than segregation. Magnet schools will thus have to rely on race-neutral characteristics, like geography or socioeconomic status, or have a comprehensive review of each candidate, where race is considered among a number of other factors. As time goes on, magnet schools may become less distinguishable from other specialized programs and schools that never had diversity as one of their goals. Even today, although researchers suggest that there are roughly three thousand magnet schools serving close to two million students, it is difficult to know just how many of these schools retain a strong focus on achieving student diversity.[14]

Magnet and other specialized schools or programs are as interesting for what they do not accomplish as for what they do. They certainly increase public school options for some students. But they do not alter the traditional pattern of neighborhood school assignments. A small percentage of students are given the opportunity to choose a specialized school, but the vast majority of students in these districts remain in neighborhood schools.

Some districts do offer greater opportunities for public school choice. These districts have abandoned neighborhood school assignments and instead require all parents to select a school for their children. Parents list several choices among district schools, and school officials make the final assignments, often with an eye toward creating socioeconomically integrated schools. While still confined to single districts, these controlled choice plans are nonetheless fairly radical in their departure from the traditional neighborhood assignment plan. They are also, probably for just this reason, rare. Developed first in Cambridge, Massachusetts, in 1981, comprehensive choice plans currently exist in little more than a handful of districts nationwide.[15]

Richmond has a modest variation on this theme. It divides the district into three so-called megazones, each of which contains a number of elementary schools. Students are allowed to attend any elementary school within that zone, provided space is available after all students who live in the school's specific attendance zone are enrolled. Open seats are allotted by lottery if demand exceeds supply. For years, Richmond provided transportation to students who chose to attend a non-neighborhood school within their megazone. In 2007, however, the school board cut that item from the budget in order to save money.[16]

The cut generated a good deal of controversy. Local papers carried stories of the hardships it created for families trying to transport their children to schools that they believed would better serve them. It did not go unnoticed that canceling the bus service disadvantaged the disadvantaged, who lacked the means or the time to shuttle their children to and from school. To some, it was further proof that the system of choice in Richmond was really designed to benefit the relatively few middle-class, mostly white families who, it was assumed, would have an easier time getting their own kids to school.[17]

To make matters worse, there are informal and ad hoc ways around the official school choice program in Richmond, and the same is true in other urban districts. Parents and school board members alike acknowledged that in Richmond there is one choice program on paper and another one in reality. The whole system, said one board member, operates on the basis of whom you know. The most frequently cited example was of parents whose children end up in schools outside their megazone. In theory, choice is supposed to be confined to schools within each megazone. In reality, principals and district administrators retain discretion to admit individual students, regardless of where they live. Some parents simply take this route and, rather than participate in a lottery for the more popular schools, just ask the principal or a district administrator for permission to enroll. As one board member explained in an interview, "if you know someone in the superintendent's office or the principal, you get what you want; otherwise, you deal with the written rules."[18]

The same is true for at least some middle schools. In theory, Binford Middle School is the only middle school entitled to accept students from throughout the district. All the other middle schools are supposed to accept only students who reside in their attendance zones. But as one parent explained, the reality is different from the written rules. White students who attend Linwood Holton Elementary School in north Richmond, for example, mostly attend Albert Hill Middle School, which is neither their assigned middle school nor designated as a school of choice. "There's no official policy," said this parent, whose children attended Holton. "White parents just go and knock on the principal's door."[19]

Something similar happens at Tee-Jay, which has a formal program of choice, the IB Program, and an informal one. The informal program is not widely advertised. One searches relevant websites for information in vain, for example, and one school board member I interviewed did not realize the option existed when I first asked about it. According to Tee-Jay principal Barbara Ulschmid, however, she had discretion to admit students from outside the attendance zone as long as space permitted. Because the school was under-enrolled, it had plenty of room for transfer students. When deciding whether to admit such students, Dr. Ulschmid indicated that she considered grades, courses taken, standardized test scores, and discipline. We "always have room," she remarked, "for good students from out of the zone." The qualifier is hard to miss and gives a sense of the principal's latitude, as well as the potential for the unfair treatment of students—or at least the appearance of unfairness.[20]

Just how many parents circumvent the formal system of school choice is impossible to know. No data are available. A fairly widespread assumption, however, is that these parents are mostly white and middle-class and that they manipulate the system to ensure that their children cluster in certain elementary schools. Most complaints, it bears mentioning, are directed toward elementary schools, at least in part because there is a noticeable decline in white enrollment beginning in middle school and continuing through high school.

The two elementary schools in Richmond most often targeted by critics of school choice are Mary Munford and William Fox. In a school system that is nearly 90 percent African American, both schools are predominantly white: Munford's student body is 75 percent white; Fox's is 63 percent. No other elementary school has anywhere close to this percentage of white students. Most have less than 5 percent. What is not clear is how many of the Munford and Fox students live within the relevant attendance zone or at least within the megazone. The fact that at least some parents manipulate the system, however, is enough to fuel suspicion about the very lopsided demographics at these two schools.[21]

The existence of these schools, moreover, bolsters the belief among some that school choice is being used, whether intentionally or not, to segregate students. Some school board members agree that open enrollment has allowed "a type of closet segregation" to continue. Richmond PTA members are more blunt, calling the system "a farce" that has created "a separate, unequal and dual education system" in Richmond.[22]

Controversies like these are repeated in urban districts across the country, which should come as no surprise. Offering limited choices will necessarily leave some families with no choice at all. If some schools are perceived as better than others, charges of unfairness are bound to arise. This is especially true when school choice seems to benefit white, middle-income students and families in urban districts such as Richmond. In their defense, these districts face a real dilemma with regard to such families. Many district leaders, in Richmond and elsewhere, believe with justification that it is important to retain middle-class families in urban school districts. Yet the means of doing so sometimes entails offering them something that poorer and often black families might not receive. At the very least, it creates the impression of favoritism.

Similar controversies have yet to erupt in Henrico County. Aside from the few specialized programs at the high school level, students attend their assigned schools. Expanding school choice, as mentioned earlier, is not on the agenda there. That could change in the near future, however, given the increasing diversity within the district. Henrico recently became a majority-minority district, and the percentage of poor students is also on the rise. As the demographics change, Henrico might also become attracted to the idea of using choice as a means of retaining middle-class families.

One final program of intradistrict school choice bears mention. Under the No Child Left Behind Act (NCLB), students who attend schools that fail to meet annual testing goals for two years in a row are entitled to transfer to another school within the same district that has met these goals. The choice measure was a compromise of sorts, as the Bush administration initially wanted to give students the opportunity to obtain vouchers to private schools. As it stands, the option to transfer is rarely used. In some districts, there are not enough successful schools available to accept transfers. Even where such schools exist, most parents are not exercising their options, either because they are not interested or because the option is not widely known. In Richmond, for example, in one year roughly 9,500 students were eligible to transfer, but only 199—2.1 percent—exercised the option.[23]

Notably absent from the NCLB is the option to transfer to a school in another district. The law does not require outside districts to accept students, nor does it encourage them to do so. Instead, it feebly suggests that school districts unable to provide enough options on their own should, "to the extent practicable, establish a cooperative agreement with other [school districts] in the area for a transfer." The Department of Education, moreover, has made clear that it is uninterested in monitoring this aspect of the law, stating that "it would be inappropriate to regulate in this area of State authority." This is an odd rationale, to say the least, given that the NCLB leaves no stone of state educational authority unturned. At any rate, the basic point, as commentators have observed, is that "inner-city students seeking transfers to suburban schools should hardly hold their breath for 'practicable' cooperative agreements to materialize."[24]

Interdistrict Choice

In contrast to the NCLB, some state programs provide students with more of a chance to transfer across district lines, but the pickings here are still pretty slim. There are roughly three types of interdistrict choice programs: statewide open enrollment plans; limited urban-suburban choice plans created to foster racial integration; and specialized regional schools. None of these programs has led to much movement across district boundaries. The most recent estimates suggest that only about 480,000 students across the country—less than 1 percent of all students—attend public schools outside their home districts.[25]

On paper, most states have open enrollment plans, which ostensibly allow at least some students to attend any school within the state. Some plans apply only to specific districts, while others target specific populations of students, including those who are economically disadvantaged or attending a failing school. Minnesota created the first open enrollment plan in the late 1980s, and other states followed in the 1990s. Virginia is now one of only twelve states that do not offer any formal opportunities to cross district lines.[26]

Despite the ubiquity of open enrollment plans, a number of restrictions and practical obstacles work to limit the options actually available to students. One of the most significant restrictions is that participation by school districts in most state programs is entirely or at least partially optional. District participation is completely optional in twenty-four of the thirty-eight states that have open enrollment plans. In the fourteen states that require at least some district participation, most require only that districts allow students to transfer out; they do not require districts to accept students from other districts. This discrepancy itself is telling. If one makes the reasonable assumption that suburban districts with good schools would more likely receive than lose students to interdistrict transfers, it follows that allowing districts to reject all transfers in effect shields suburban districts from outsiders. All state plans, moreover, give first priority to students living within the district and allow all schools to reject transfers if no space is available.[27]

From a historical perspective, it is easy to understand why existing plans are structured this way. Given the history of interdistrict integration and the intense opposition it aroused, it would be surprising if most state legislatures required districts to accept transfer students. Allowing districts to exclude students when space is not available, moreover, is consistent with the traditional preference for neighborhood schools. Indeed, this limitation is similar to one commonly found in intradistrict plans, like the one in Richmond, which allow for transfers only if space is available after all neighborhood students have enrolled.

These structural limitations significantly reduce the options available to students. In some states, the majority of districts have simply declined to participate. In other states, districts might participate but rely on space limitations to limit the number of transfers allowed. No reliable data are available regarding the actual or reported capacities of districts, so it is difficult to assess how many open seats are not being taken. One cannot know for certain, therefore, whether the low participation rates are due more to a (claimed) lack of space or to lack of interest. Undoubtedly both play a role, but without relevant data, it is impossible to tell which factor is more important.[28]

That said, it is important to recognize that at least relatively high-spending districts have a financial incentive to limit or block the transfer of students into their schools. School financing, as discussed in chapter 3, is organized by district, and disparities in funding exist across districts. Interdistrict transfers thus pose more complicated financial (and political) questions than do intradistrict transfers. Under most existing plans, state aid follows students across district lines, but states typically do not cover the local district's share of school funding. Incoming students can thus represent a significant cost to districts, given that their parents are not taxed by the receiving district. Wealthy districts tend to contribute higher shares of local spending than poorer ones, so these districts in particular would suffer financially from accepting interdistrict transfers.[29]

School districts that view transfer students as a bad bargain can protect themselves quite easily, either by opting out altogether where that is permissible or by claiming not to have space available where opting out is not allowed. The latter strategy is easily exercised, as states do not seem to monitor district capacity and instead allow districts to self-report available space. Notice that this structure conforms precisely to what one would expect after studying school finance litigation. In the context of school finance reform, local districts are rarely required to share local revenues with other districts. Here, they are also shielded from that requirement by rarely if ever being forced to accept transfer students and spend local revenues educating them. And, again, if one assumes, as seems entirely reasonable, that suburban districts would most likely be in the position of accepting transfer students, these provisions essentially protect suburban autonomy.[30]

Even where space is available, additional limitations in most plans make it difficult to attend a school in another district. Most states do not provide funds for transportation. Parents who wish their children to participate thus have to transport their children either directly to the school or to a bus stop within the receiving district. Although some states provide transportation subsidies to low-income families, these subsidies are usually reimbursements, which means that the families must first pay the costs of transportation. In addition, not all states require that information be given to parents about the existence of interdistrict choice programs, let alone the availability of transportation subsidies.[31]

Pursuing interdistrict choice is thus not for the faint of heart. Some parents might find that they have no realistic options if nearby districts do not participate or claim that no space is available. Even where options remain available, parents must learn about the schools and have the resources and time to transport their children across district lines. It is undoubtedly true that many parents would not take advantage of interdistrict choice under the most favorable conditions, but it is also true that most open-enrollment plans are hardly designed to maximize transfers. In truth, many seem more like gestures toward choice, designed as much to protect local district autonomy as to offer parents more options.

Open enrollment plans can also work to aggravate segregation rather than ameliorate it. Most segregation, both racial and socioeconomic, occurs across district lines. It follows that interdistrict choice plans create greater opportunities for meaningful integration than choice plans confined to single districts. It does not follow, however, that those who cross district lines will be a representative sample of students. To the contrary, in some states, those who leave for the suburbs tend to be white, middle-class students currently enrolled in majority-minority and majority-poor schools. Open enrollment policies, in the view of some researchers, are thus "allowing whiter and more affluent students to transfer to white and more affluent school districts."[32]

A good illustration of the limits and drawbacks of open enrollment plans comes from Minnesota, long hailed as a progressive pioneer in the territory of school choice. In 1999, a decade after Minnesota created an open enrollment program, the NAACP sued the state. Like the plaintiffs in the Connecticut case of *Sheff v. O'Neill*, discussed in chapter 4, the Minnesota plaintiffs claimed that the state constitution outlawed school segregation regardless of its cause. The parties to the Minnesota suit ultimately settled. Under the terms of the settlement, suburban districts outside of Minneapolis agreed to make a total of five hundred seats available for low-income city students. The state agreed to pay for transportation.[33]

The case highlighted the deficiencies in the existing open enrollment plan. Open enrollment existed on paper, but it did little to alleviate racial or socioeconomic segregation between Minneapolis and surrounding suburbs. To the contrary, the few students who crossed district lines tended to exacerbate the situation, as most who transferred from city to suburb were white and most who went the other way were black. The larger point, however, is that very few transfers occurred because options were limited and hard to exercise. The state did not require suburban districts to accept city students, nor did it provide any funds for transportation.[34]

Equally striking was the settlement of the case. The plaintiffs initially argued that all students in Minneapolis should have the option to attend any school within the metropolitan region. They settled instead for much less, but even this modest plan generated controversy. Some suburbanites likened it to "forced busing" and objected to the fact that local school revenues would be spent on outsiders. At the same time, however, that a settlement was reached at all does suggest that there was at least *some* tolerance among suburban districts for the enrollment of urban students.[35]

The limited scope of the Minneapolis program is typical of other urban-suburban choice programs that are designed to foster racial integration. These plans represent the second type of interdistrict choice program. Most of them were created decades ago and were designed to foster the voluntary integration of city students with suburban ones by allowing a limited number of city students to attend school in the suburbs. Programs exist in just a few places across the country, including districts around Boston, Hartford, Indianapolis, Rochester (New York), Milwaukee, and St. Louis.[36]

All of the programs, aside from the one in St. Louis, are quite small. Boston's METCO program, for example, began in the 1960s with 220 students and currently allows roughly 3,100 students to attend nearby suburban schools. Hartford's program also began in the 1960s and started with roughly 250 students. It has since expanded because of the Connecticut Supreme Court's decision in *Sheff*; choice is being used to comply with the court's order to ameliorate school segregation between Hartford and its suburbs. Still, only about a thousand city students, which is a small fraction of the total, cross district lines to suburban schools. The programs in Rochester and Milwaukee are similar in scope, involving roughly six hundred and three thousand students, respectively.[37]

The programs are not limited because of insufficient demand. To the contrary, most have waiting lists that are much longer than the list of participants. Twelve thousand students are on the waiting list for Boston's METCO program, for example, which is roughly four times the number of students who participate. Three thousand are on the list for the Rochester program, which is five times the number of participants. The scope of these programs is intentionally limited to ensure sufficient space for district residents and, it appears, to prevent the programs from becoming too threatening or controversial. As Susan Eaton, who studied Boston's METCO system, said of that program, it "operates on terms that suburbanites can accept. It does not greatly alter the status quo of either suburbia's schools or their larger communities."[38]

The only relatively large-scale interdistrict choice program is in St. Louis. This program sprang from the settlement of a school desegregation lawsuit, which many suburbanites reasonably believed would lead to forced busing across district lines. This was one of the rare lawsuits where there seemed sufficient proof of an interdistrict violation to satisfy the requirements of *Milliken v. Bradley* and support an interdistrict remedy. To forestall that result, the state secured agreement from sixteen suburban districts to accept a limited number of city students, with the goal of increasing black enrollment in these districts to somewhere between 15 and 25 percent. The state greased the wheels by providing an "incentive payment" to suburban districts, which equaled the per-pupil cost of education within the suburban districts. The state also paid for transportation.[39]

In the mid-1990s, this program dwarfed all others in size, involving nearly thirteen thousand city students who each year attended suburban schools. This is a large number compared to other programs, but it still only represented about one-fourth of all St. Louis students. The vast majority of students stayed in the city. Most suburban students also stayed put, even though they had the option to attend city magnet schools that were created as part of the court settlement. Only about fifteen hundred of them took advantage of the opportunity.

The St. Louis program has generated mixed reactions over time. Some suburbanites have been less than thrilled by the program and have repeatedly suggested, in words President Nixon would have appreciated, "that the millions of dollars the state pays to bring in nearly 13,000 African-American students would be better spent 'fixing up' the city schools." On the other hand, experience with the program seems to have changed quite a few minds in the suburbs. Opinion polls over the years reveal increasing support for the program among suburban students and residents. Most important, when the suburbs had the chance to opt out of the program, they declined. In 1999, the desegregation settlement was dismantled, state funding for the program was set to diminish over time, and suburban districts were gradually relieved of their obligation to participate. Yet all of them agreed to extend the program for another five years, and thirteen of the sixteen agreed to accept new African-American students during the extension—even though they were receiving significantly less funding from the state.[40]

Many suburban students, moreover, became ardent defenders of the program. In 2004, for example, hundreds of suburban students in the affluent Clayton High School walked out in protest over the school board's tentative decision to bow out of the program. Similar examples of support have been reported for programs in the Boston and Rochester regions, and in each area, more suburban districts have signed on to accept students in recent years.[41]

Despite the show of support in St. Louis and elsewhere, the fact remains that these programs are tiny and are not always embraced where tried. The suburban-urban transfer program in Indianapolis, for example, was court-ordered and is now being phased out. In St. Louis itself, the program has shrunk in recent years and participation is down to about eight thousand students. Whether the program will hold steady or continue to decline is difficult to predict. If state funding continues to fall, it seems likely that more slots will disappear as suburban districts decide not to shoulder the costs of transfers. More generally, there does not seem to be much support in any of these metropolitan areas for significantly expanding existing plans.[42]

Rounding out the picture of interdistrict school choice programs are regional, specialized schools. Some of these are magnet schools, or at least began with the purpose of attracting a diverse student body. The vast majority of magnet schools are open only to students who reside in the district, but a few accept students from elsewhere. Precise numbers are hard to come by, but given that no more than 450,000 students in total cross district lines, it is safe to assume that the number of students attending regional magnet schools is relatively small.

Some regional schools are not designed with integration in mind but are designed to attract talented students or students interested in a particular area of study. In Virginia, for example, there are a number of Governor's Schools, which have particular themes and are designed to attract talented students from across nearby school districts. One is located in Richmond and draws students from more than ten school districts.[43]

The Governor's School in Richmond is 75 percent white and only about 8 percent black, with Asian Americans constituting 12.5 percent of the student body. As might be expected, a predominantly white regional school located in the city of Richmond presents a delicate, if not embarrassing, subject for members of the Governor's School Board. "We've struggled with this for years," said the board chairman recently. "It's something we've always wanted to improve, and we've struggled with how to do it." Indeed, a board member made a pledge nearly a decade earlier, in 1999, to work on the issue. It is still a work in progress.[44]

The contrast between regular Richmond students and Governor's School students continues to draw attention, but the contrast is nowhere near as visible and dramatic as it was when the school first opened in 1991. In that year, there was no separate building available for the school—so it opened in Tee-Jay! The nearly all-white student body of the Governor's School occupied the top floor of Tee-Jay, while the nearly all-black student body of the regular high school occupied the two floors below.[45]

The marriage was rocky from the start and continued to be troubled throughout its ten-year existence. It is one thing to be aware that educational disparities tend to track lines of race and class. It is quite another to see the divide on a daily basis. From the perspective of those who lived it, Governor's School students had more freedom to roam around the school, seemed to have better materials, resources, and teachers, and were obviously much whiter as a group than the regular students at Tee-Jay. Although relations were superficially cordial, controversies erupted fairly regularly and served as a reminder of the unequal status of the programs. Race may have been in the background with regard to most controversies, but it never disappeared from view. When someone from the Governor's School, for example, requested that only Governor's School students be allowed to enter the school through the front door, this was not just an insensitive request but, in light of Richmond's history, a racially charged one.[46]

The Governor's School relocated in 2002 to the old Maggie Walker Building. The unusual proximity of the separate educational worlds of Tee-Jay and the Governor's School gave way to a more comfortable distance, which took some of the edge off of the disparities. But the disparities, while not as obvious, have not disappeared. And the Governor's School seems, at least to some, just another example of the unequal status of education in the Richmond metropolitan area.

In sum, interdistrict choice remains an unfulfilled promise. It can and has been used to increase integration among urban and suburban students. In many places where it has been put to this use, initial controversy and opposition have given way to tolerance and even boosterism. Students who transfer, moreover, tend to improve academically and to set their academic sights higher. On the other hand, interdistrict choice has not been embraced everywhere it has been tried. In addition, existing programs are quite small and do little to diminish the general importance of the urban-suburban boundary in education. And there does not seem to be much support, anywhere, for dramatically increasing the scope of interdistrict choice programs.[47]

Charter Schools

A charter school, as mentioned, is something of a cross between a public and a private school. Allowed only where authorized by state statute, these schools are publicly funded, tuition-free, and nonsectarian. They operate pursuant to a contract—the charter in charter schools—between the school and an agency authorized by the state to grant charters. Depending on the state, that agency might be the local school board, the state board of education, or a third party, such as a college or university.[48]

Charter schools can be opened and operated by any number of groups, including teachers, parents, and private corporations. Some states prohibit for-profit corporations from creating, though not necessarily from operating, a charter school. Charter schools are freed from various regulations governing things like teacher hiring and certification, the curriculum, the school calendar, and the length of the school day. In exchange for this freedom, they are supposed to be held accountable for results. Indeed, the core idea behind charters is to grant greater flexibility to schools in exchange for greater accountability, which includes closure if a school fails to perform adequately. Charter periods vary from between three and fifteen years, though most last for five years. Renewal of the charter, at least in theory, is contingent on the school's performance.[49]

Charter schools can be created from scratch or by "converting" a traditional public school. Some states also allow existing private schools, including religious ones, to convert to charter status, provided that religious observances and exercises drop out of the curriculum. The No Child Left Behind Act also encourages the conversion of persistently "failing" public schools into charter schools.[50]

Unlike interdistrict choice plans, which have grown slowly at best, charter schools are the kudzu of school choice. Minnesota opened the first charter school in 1992. Four years later, 178 charters were operating in seventeen states. Another four years after that, at the turn of the new millennium, roughly two thousand charter schools operated in thirty-four states and the District of Columbia. Today, there are more than four thousand charter schools in forty states plus the District of Columbia. The number of students attending such schools has also grown exponentially. Starting from a few hundred students in 1992, more than a million now attend charter schools—a large number, though it still represents only about 2 percent of the total public school enrollment.[51]

Charter schools tend to be smaller than traditional public schools, enrolling on average about half as many students. Many offer alternative curricula, emphasize particular fields of study, or focus on special student populations, most often students at risk of failure. At least initially, one of the chief attractions of charter schools was the opportunity to innovate and create truly alternative schools. Many drawn to charter schools relished the opportunity to pursue their own vision of the nature and purpose of public education. That opportunity has been constrained at least somewhat by the concurrent rise of the standards and testing movement, discussed in detail in chapter 7. Charter schools are now subject to the same testing regimes facing traditional public schools, which limits their ability to pursue a separate path.[52]

Charter schools have attracted bipartisan support. Republicans and Democrats at both the state and federal level have championed the cause, though not always for the same reasons. Charters are seen by Republicans and Democrats alike as a halfway station between public school choice and voucher programs. Republicans who like voucher programs support charter schools in the hope that they will lead to vouchers. Democrats who oppose vouchers, by contrast, hope that charters will satisfy the demand for school choice and therefore dampen support for vouchers. Regardless of their different motives, Republicans and Democrats have been unified in backing both state and federal spending programs designed to ease some of the financial burdens faced by those who wish to open charter schools. Under a program started in 1994, the federal government now spends more than $200 million annually to help charter schools—about twice the amount of assistance it provides to magnet schools.[53]

State statutes regarding charter schools vary a great deal in terms of funding, who can authorize charter schools, the degree of autonomy granted charter schools, and the number of charters that can be granted, either annually or in total. The variation among statutes means that, in reality, some states are much more hospitable to charter schools than others. This helps explain why charter schools are not distributed evenly across the country but are instead concentrated in California, Arizona, Florida, Texas, and Michigan. It also helps explain why so few charter schools exist in Virginia. Virginia's law, which is routinely tagged by charter supporters as one of the worst in the country, allows for charter schools in theory but then sets up enough roadblocks to ensure that few are actually opened.[54]

Variations among state charter laws make it difficult to generalize, but the statutes and schools themselves share three common features that are relevant for the purposes of this chapter. First, charter schools tend to enroll students from their home districts. A minority of states explicitly limit enrollment to district residents, while most states either require or allow that preference be given to local students. Given that most charter schools report having waiting lists, local residency preferences operate in practice to exclude outside students. Even where nonresidents can attend charter schools, they are rarely provided with transportation, which also works to limit attendance to resident students.[55]

The second common feature of charter statutes involves funding. The details of funding schemes vary both across and within states, depending on whether the charter is granted by a local school board or state agency. In general, however, charter schools are funded with a combination of state and local dollars— money that would otherwise go to regular public schools. Put differently, in districts where charter schools are located, public schools stand to lose a portion of their state and local funding.[56]

The potential loss of funding adds to existing incentives among local school boards to block charter schools. Many school board members already see charter schools as unwelcome competition; the financial threat they represent makes it worse. It should come as no surprise, therefore, that local school boards have proven more reluctant than other agencies to grant charters. It should also be obvious that states—like Virginia—that give local districts exclusive authority to approve charter schools are not committed to helping charter schools flourish. Indeed, giving local school boards complete authority to approve charters is, as one observer noted, akin to allowing "the *New York Times* to decide whether the *Wall Street Journal* can sell papers in New York City." In districts where there is a good deal of support for the local schools, obtaining a charter from a local school board can be especially difficult, if not impossible.[57]

This last point leads to the third and final common feature of charter schools: their location. Most charter schools are located in urban school districts. In some states, this concentration is required or encouraged by charter statutes. At least twelve statutes, for example, require that priority be given to charter schools that serve poor, minority, or low-achieving students, and urban districts have a disproportionate share of each. Virginia's law, for example, until recently required that half of all charter schools in the state cater to "at-risk" students; it still requires that such schools be given priority consideration. Ohio and Missouri go even farther, allowing charter schools *only* in urban districts. Wisconsin is more subtle and simply stacks the deck in favor of opening charter schools in Milwaukee. Several different agencies can grant charters in Milwaukee; everywhere else, only local school boards can grant permission.[58]

In addition to statutory provisions that encourage or require charter schools to locate in urban districts, constituent demand and local politics push in the same direction. Suburbanites, in general, seem less interested in charter schools. In fact, in some suburban districts, charter schools are seen not only as unnecessary but as an insult to local public schools and a threat to property values. A recent fight over a charter school proposal for Glen Cove, an affluent New York suburb, is a good example. As reported in the *New York Times*, a resident explained her opposition this way: "We want to keep our community desirable. The connotation of a charter school is, 'The schools are lousy, they're not meeting the needs of our children.' Our property values will go down, [and] our taxes will increase because we'll need to pay more money to keep up the standards." Another resident echoed the point. "There's nothing wrong with our public schools," she exclaimed, "and I take great offense to people coming in here and telling me otherwise."[59]

Charter schools, of course, can send the same message in urban school districts, and many urban leaders and educators also see charters as a threat to existing public schools. The difference, however, is that urban residents are generally more prepared than their suburban counterparts to admit that their public schools are failing and alternatives are needed. Urban school board members, in turn, generally seem more willing to endorse alternatives, both because of the more obvious need for education reform in urban districts and because the large size of urban districts makes it easier to absorb a few charter schools. Some of the school board members in Richmond who approved the Patrick Henry Charter School, for example, conveyed a "why not" attitude, believing it appropriate to explore alternatives given the less-than-stellar track record of some traditional public schools.[60]

The need to cater to middle-class families also explains the different stances among urban and suburban school officials. Some urban leaders see charter schools as a way of attracting and retaining middle-class families. This use of charter schools can create its own controversy, as the protest over the Patrick Henry School illustrates. But there is undoubtedly a felt need in cities to maintain a middle-class presence in public schools. Many suburbs, by contrast, are already filled with middle-class residents, and charter schools, because of the signals they send about the quality of traditional public schools, may drive some of them away.

Charter schools are thus an interesting political phenomenon. As mentioned, they draw broad and bipartisan support on the national level and in most state legislatures. But charters are not universally embraced at the local level. The general sense one gets, from both the details of state charter laws and trends on the ground, is that charter schools are mostly appropriate for students in failing urban districts. They are rarely viewed or created as a means of offering significant opportunities for interdistrict choice, and they can be greeted with outright hostility when proposed in suburban districts. Charter schools are thus seen by many as an innovative, not to mention relatively low-cost, way of reforming ailing urban school systems. At the same time, they do not pose much of a threat to existing suburban schools.

Save the cities, spare the suburbs. In this sense, charter schools are quite similar to the few existing voucher plans.

Vouchers

Although school vouchers might seem like a new innovation, the basic idea of vouchers—providing funding for students to use at the schools of their choice, whether public or private—is quite old. The intellectual history of vouchers stretches back at least to eighteenth-century luminaries like Adam Smith and Thomas Paine, and to John Stuart Mill in the nineteenth century. Each proposed a system of education funded by the government but not controlled by it. Mill famously argued against requiring that students attend government-run schools, claiming that "a general State education is a mere contrivance for moulding people to be exactly like one another." Contrary to thoroughgoing libertarians, however, Mill thought education should be compulsory and that the government should pay the costs for those too poor to afford private school fees. Government schools should exist, if at all, only as "one among many competing experiments."[61]

These libertarian-inspired calls for tuition vouchers went unheeded in this country for well over a century. The common school movement, inspired by Horace Mann and others, was in some ways a complete rejection of the idea that the government should have only a limited role in education. To the contrary, Mann thought government-run and government-funded schools were the path toward social equality and the creation of good citizens. Tuition vouchers would have seemed antithetical to the central idea behind the common school. Vouchers also would have aided those attending Catholic parochial schools, and those in the Protestant-led common school movement had no interest in providing financial support to the Catholic Church or to its schools, as described in more detail in the next chapter.

The Nobel Prize–winning economist Milton Friedman tried to revive the libertarian case for vouchers in 1955, but his timing could not have been worse. He argued that the government's role in education should be limited to providing tuition vouchers and lightly monitoring private schools. According to Friedman, the government should assure "that the schools meet certain minimum standards such as the inclusion of a minimum content in their programs, much as it now inspects restaurants to assure that they maintain minimum sanitary standards." The analogy to restaurants, in retrospect, was probably not the most effective. Friedman's call for deregulating education, moreover, was accompanied by his call to deregulate the training and certification of doctors, which might have made the former seem as radical as the latter. The real problem, however, was that Friedman's proposal coincided with the use of vouchers to avoid desegregation, which tended to preclude dispassionate consideration of Friedman's idea. His proposal went nowhere for decades.[62]

John Chubb and Terry Moe breathed new life into Friedman's cause in 1990 when they published their surprisingly popular book, *Politics, Markets and America's Schools*. They argued that the market, rather than the government, should control schooling and claimed boldly that "reformers would do well to entertain the notion that choice *is* a panacea" for all that ails education. Despite the attention the book received, both favorable and not, the idea of creating a truly market-driven alternative to the public school system never really caught on.[63]

In the meantime, moreover, another intellectual line in the genealogy of vouchers had begun. A little more than a decade after Friedman's call for vouchers, liberal and progressive reformers associated with the War on Poverty began arguing for their own equity-based versions of a voucher plan. Christopher Jencks and Theodore Sizer, two academics, each proposed voucher schemes in the late 1960s and early 1970s that would create more opportunities for inner-city students to attend either private or good public schools. Instead of simply creating an unregulated market in education, dominated by private schools, Jencks and Sizer wished to create a highly structured voucher scheme that would rely on public and private schools alike. Both proposed giving poorer students a voucher worth more than ones given middle-income students, in order to cover the greater costs of educating poor students and to "bribe" suburban districts into accepting them.[64]

During the same time period, John Coons and Stephen Sugarman also threw their hats into the voucher ring, even though they were simultaneously pursuing school finance reform. This dual pursuit may seem incongruous, at least at first. Like Jenks and Sizer, however, Coons and Sugarman saw vouchers as a way to equalize educational opportunities by expanding the options available to poor students. They, too, endorsed the idea of providing greater funding to poor students. They also believed vouchers would create pressure to equalize access to funding. It would become harder, they thought, to justify locally based inequalities in spending if students were using vouchers to go to public and private schools within and outside their local districts. Or at least the inequalities would become more visible, which might increase pressure to eliminate them.[65]

Neither the market-based version of vouchers nor its equity-based counterpart has been adopted in pure form. Instead, the few existing voucher plans have elements of each. All essentially provide a limited number of vouchers to poor, urban students (thus reflecting a concern with equity) that can be used at local private schools (thus reflecting belief in private, market-based alternatives to public education). Although something of a compromise, it would be wrong to think that these plans represent an intellectual melding of ideas, with the most promising elements from each model combined into one program. Existing voucher programs are the product of political compromise, not political theory.[66]

There are currently four publicly funded voucher programs—in Milwaukee, Cleveland, Washington, D.C., and across the state of Ohio. Each program targets just a small slice of students and limits eligibility either to poor students, those who attend low-performing schools, or those who are both poor and attend low-performing schools.[67]

Milwaukee's program is the oldest and largest of the four. Created in 1990, it offers vouchers to students whose family income does not exceed 175 percent of the federal poverty guidelines. Roughly nineteen thousand students currently receive vouchers worth a maximum of $6,500. The Cleveland program, begun in 1995, gives first priority to students whose family income is below 200 percent of the poverty guidelines. Roughly six thousand students receive a voucher worth, on average, about $2,800. The program in Washington, D.C., started in 2004, offers vouchers worth nearly $7,000 to about nineteen hundred students. To be eligible, family income cannot be greater than 185 percent of the poverty guidelines, and priority is given to low-income students who attend low-performing schools.[68]

The Ohio Educational Choice Scholarship program is the most recent addition to the field and currently the only statewide voucher program. Not all students across the state, however, can participate. To be eligible, students must attend public schools that posted low test scores in two of three consecutive years. No more than fourteen thousand students can receive vouchers in any year, and priority is given to low-income families. Currently, about 6,700 students participate and receive a voucher worth between $4,375 (for K–8 students) and $5,150 (for high school students). Nearly all of the students who participate live in urban districts.[69]

In addition to the four existing plans, two other voucher plans were created in Colorado and Florida, but these were discontinued after courts declared them illegal. Both programs had a structure similar to Ohio's and offered a limited number of vouchers to students in low-performing schools across the state. Colorado's plan capped the total number of students who could participate, and at its peak was projected to include no more than twenty thousand students. Florida's plan did not have an explicit cap, but eligibility limitations worked to severely limit the number of students who could participate. Indeed, a few years after it was created, only fifty-two students were using vouchers to attend private schools.[70]

Given all of the ink that has been spilled over vouchers, it is worth recalling that only about thirty-three thousand students across the country are using publicly funded vouchers. More than twice as many students receive privately funded vouchers, and many more students either attend charter schools or are homeschooled. Indeed, at least forty times as many students are homeschooled as receive publicly funded vouchers.

It is also instructive to consider that most voucher proposals have been rejected, and that every single proposal to create a large-scale voucher program has been soundly defeated. Between 1990 and 1993 alone, for example, fourteen state legislatures considered and ultimately rejected voucher proposals. Voters have not been any more receptive. Voucher or tax-credit initiatives appeared on a number of state ballots in the 1990s, including ones in California, Colorado, Oregon, and Washington. In each case, voters rejected the proposals by wide margins.[71]

School choice proponents have typically blamed these losses on teachers' unions, arguing that the unions generally outspent voucher proponents on initiative campaigns. The well-financed opposition of teachers' unions certainly played a role in the defeat of these initiatives. That cannot serve as the sole explanation, however, because voucher initiatives have failed even when supporters have outspent opponents. In a 2001 voucher campaign in Michigan, for example, supporters of the voucher initiative spent $7 million more than opponents. Nonetheless, a proposal to provide a $3,300 voucher to all students in failing schools—which was projected to include roughly 180,000 students—lost by a wide margin. A more recent campaign in California cost supporters and opponents $30 million each, yet the proposal there, to give all students in the state a $4,000 voucher, was crushed at the polls by a margin of 71 to 29 percent.[72]

Even more recently, in 2007, voters in Utah exercised their rarely used right to repeal legislation that had already been passed. The state legislature had enacted a voucher plan that offered vouchers worth between $500 and $3,000 to all students in the state. Voucher opponents secured enough signatures to put the legislation on the ballot, and 62 percent of those who voted rejected the measure, even though voucher supporters outspent opponents by more than $1 million.[73]

Voucher ballot initiatives failed in Michigan, California, and Utah not only, and perhaps not even primarily, because teachers' unions opposed them. They failed because suburbanites did not support them. In explaining the defeat of an earlier voucher initiative in California, in 1993, John J. Miller, associate director of the pro-voucher Manhattan Institute, said simply: "School choice failed in California because Republicans did not want it." He continued:

> Most suburbanites—the folks who make up the GOP's rank and file—are happy with their kids' school systems. Their children already earn good grades, score well on tests, and gain admission into reputable colleges and universities. Moreover, suburban affluence grants a measure of freedom in choosing where to live and thus provides at least some control over school selection. It's not that suburbanites refuse to admit the country's deep education crisis; they just don't believe the problem affects them personally.[74]

Voucher opponents in California exploited these sentiments by arguing that a statewide voucher program would weaken all public schools by taking money away from them and giving it to families whose children were already in private schools. Voucher opponents used similar tactics, with equal success, in fighting ballot initiatives in Michigan and Utah. They convinced suburbanites that a universal voucher program threatened their interest in maintaining high-quality local schools.[75]

Voucher campaigns have revealed an odd disjuncture between the leadership of the two main political parties and their rank-and-file members. Vouchers are typically associated with the Republican Party, and many Republican leaders do indeed support them. Many suburban members of the Republican Party, however, remain skeptical of large-scale voucher programs. As one high-ranking Republican official explained: "School choice is popular in the national headquarters of the Republican Party but is unpopular among the Republican rank-and-file voters[,] who have moved away from the inner city in part so that their children will not have to attend schools that are racially or socioeconomically integrated." Another person involved in voucher campaigns made a similar point and acknowledged that his "most difficult encounters were casual conversations in living rooms with white, middle to upper-class conservative voters...who expressed deep reservations about vouchers."[76]

Those who have worked on similar campaigns in Virginia have noticed the same dynamic. Everyone I interviewed said that it was difficult to push school choice through the state legislature because suburbanites were not interested in it. Suburbanites were dead set against interdistrict public school choice, while they remained leery of private school choice, uncertain about what the ramifications might be. As one person described, "it was hard to get over the WIFM [What's in it for me?] problem." Suburbanites were pleased with their schools and saw no personal benefit to expanding choice options.[77]

The divide between the leaders and members of the Republican Party helps explain why, when push comes to shove, many Republican officeholders back away from large-scale voucher plans. Governor Pete Wilson, for example, came out in opposition to the 1993 voucher initiative in California. Republican Governor John Engler of Michigan opposed the voucher initiative there, as did Republican senator Spencer Abraham. Governor Christine Todd Whitman in New Jersey toyed with a voucher proposal while in office, but she ultimately let it die in the face of legislative opposition from both Democrats and Republicans.[78]

The recent voucher fight in Utah is especially instructive. Governor Jon Huntsman signed the voucher bill there in 2007, after it passed in the legislature by one vote. When the measure was subsequently put on the ballot for voter review, however, Huntsman all but disappeared. In an article in *Education Week* entitled "Voucher Backers: Where is Governor Huntsman?" voucher supporters criticized Huntsman for laying low during the public campaign. As one state legislator explained: "I think the overall feeling is, 'Where is Governor Huntsman? Where is he and why has he backed away and separated himself from this issue?' Because that's what it appears he's done." The answer, suggested a political scientist at Brigham Young University, was easy: Huntsman didn't "want to be on the losing side."[79]

President George W. Bush showed similar instincts in the brief fight over whether to include vouchers as part of the No Child Left Behind Act. The White House pushed for this initially, but when Congress pushed back, the president quickly dropped the proposal without a fight. He apparently understood, as his overheard comments at a press conference suggested, that many Republicans had no interest in vouchers because their children were already in good schools.[80]

These examples are important to consider when assessing the claim that voucher proposals fail because teachers' unions oppose them. Given the traditional association between teachers' unions and Democratic candidates, it seems highly unlikely that Republican leaders who opposed large-scale voucher plans were trying to court the teachers' unions. More likely, they were responding to the less than enthusiastic message being sent by their suburban constituents.

The voucher issue is equally interesting when one looks across the aisle to the Democratic Party. There is also a gap there between the leadership and some core constituents, although the arrows point in the opposite directions. Democratic Party leaders generally oppose vouchers, and this stance undoubtedly reflects the influence of the teachers' unions. Younger African Americans, however, consistently express fairly strong support for vouchers.[81]

This support is not altogether surprising. Parents are much more likely to support vouchers when they are dissatisfied with their children's public schools, and African Americans are disproportionately represented in failing, urban school systems. This fact, along with the history of vouchers, also helps explain the generational divide among African Americans. Those older than sixty are more likely to oppose than support vouchers. This group is obviously less likely to have children currently enrolled in K-12 schools, and they are more likely to recall the role of vouchers in massive resistance.[82]

There has yet to be much of a grassroots movement for vouchers in Richmond. The *Richmond Times-Dispatch* routinely calls for vouchers and tax credits on its editorial pages. No local group, however, has been a visible or reliable supporter of vouchers. Some local and state leaders nonetheless believe that there is untapped support for the idea. One school board member, when asked, said that she could not recall parents specifically requesting vouchers. She did say, however, that a number of parents have pointed to all of the failures in Richmond schools and told her that they would like their money back. A state legislator, Chris Saxman, who has been a strong proponent of tuition tax credits, also believes that private school choice would be popular among Richmond parents. He recently announced plans to start a grassroots movement in favor of school choice, which he hopes will draw more urban legislators to the cause.[83]

No one, by contrast, is planning to push for vouchers or tax credits in Henrico County. The parents I spoke to found the idea far-fetched for Henrico. One of them, it bears noting, originally lived with her family in Richmond but moved out to Henrico when her children were ready to attend school. She did so because she believed the public schools in Henrico were superior. Like so many other suburban parents, she and her husband had already exercised school choice by moving to Henrico; once there, they understandably saw little need for a formal school choice program.[84]

PULLING TOGETHER THE POLITICS OF CHOICE

The pattern of school choice programs, whether public or private, suggests that suburbanites are the key constituents. Suburbanites strongly support local control over student attendance, as demonstrated by their resistance to interdistrict desegregation. Suburbanites also support local control over local revenues, as demonstrated by the myriad battles over school finance reform and the intense opposition to revenue sharing. Most choice plans, in turn, involve choices within single school districts, and districts where choices are available tend overwhelmingly to be urban ones.

Plans that allow for interdistrict choice are not only less prevalent but almost always contain restrictions designed to protect the autonomy of local school districts. Districts can usually opt out of participating altogether or limit transfers on the basis of lacking space for them. Plans that *require* suburban schools to accept urban students are exceedingly rare and usually quite limited in scope.

Charter schools, by practice or design, are most often found in urban districts and enroll local students. Three of the four voucher plans, meanwhile, specifically target poor, urban students, while the fourth operates much the same way in practice. All four essentially limit the use of vouchers to private schools, mostly if not entirely located in cities.

All of these plans protect the ability of suburban parents to send their children to local public schools, limit the ability of city students to attend suburban schools, and limit the extent to which suburban schools have to spend money on outsiders. At the same time, the plans represent some attempt to reform urban school systems and to improve the opportunities available for students currently stuck in failing city schools. In other words, this is Nixon's compromise all over again: Save the cities, this time through school choice, but spare the suburbs.

At the same time, it is important to recognize that there are not many groups currently working to expand school choice to the suburbs or to use it as a way to increase integration, either along racial or socioeconomic lines. There are few organized groups, for example, working to expand interdistrict public school choice programs. There is plenty of organized support in favor of expanding charter schools and vouchers, but those who support expansion express little interest in using choice to increase racial or socioeconomic integration. They are attracted to the promise of competition or alternative pedagogical approaches, not to the benefits of integration.

Groups that remain committed to integration, by contrast, do not fully embrace school choice in all its forms. Some individuals and foundations, most notably the Century Foundation, embrace public school choice as a means of achieving socioeconomic integration. But they remain opposed to vouchers and are somewhat wary of charter schools. Traditional civil rights groups have steadfastly opposed voucher plans. Several years ago, for example, the NAACP partnered with People for the American Way for the stated purpose of preserving public education. The partnership's main activity, however, was fighting against vouchers. One sees a more local example in the opposition of Richmond's NAACP leaders to the Patrick Henry School.[85]

Absent from the field is any sort of broad-based coalition among those who favor expanding school choice and those who favor increasing integration. One sees tentative steps in this direction: Bill Taylor, a veteran of the civil rights movement and lead litigator in some important desegregation cases, recently coauthored a thoughtful article proposing ways to use charter schools and vouchers to enhance racial and socioeconomic integration. Choice and integration advocates, however, generally remain in divided camps, each somewhat suspicious of the other's activities and motives. Those who favor integration tend to doubt the sincerity of conservatives and libertarians who claim to favor vouchers as a way of helping poor, minority students. Why, they wonder, have these choice advocates suddenly become so concerned about equal opportunity for the poor, and if they *are* so concerned, why are they not also pushing to open good suburban public schools to inner-city students? Conservatives and libertarians, in turn, recoil at the idea of structuring school choice to enhance integration, believing that this involves too much coercion. Given the strength of suburban voters and legislators, it is not clear whether even a strong push toward expanding school choice into the suburbs would be successful. As it stands, however, no one is pushing that hard.[86]

Recent developments in Milwaukee illustrate many of these themes. The story of the Milwaukee voucher program is fairly well known, at least in school choice circles. In the late 1980s, Annette "Polly" Williams, a liberal African-American state legislator, teamed up with Republican leaders to launch a pilot voucher program in Milwaukee. Williams pushed the choice program in part because she was fed up with school desegregation in Milwaukee, which she believed was unfair to blacks and educationally ineffective. Indeed, before proposing the voucher program, she favored carving out an all-black school district in Milwaukee that would be run by African-American leaders.[87]

Williams was not interested in using choice to encourage more integration, nor were her Republican allies. Civil rights groups that remained committed to racial integration, by contrast, opposed the plan. With this line up, it is not surprising that the voucher plan was limited to private schools in the city; no one was pushing to allow vouchers to be used at suburban schools.[88]

Most accounts of the voucher program suggest that it was offered as an alternative to the failed attempt to desegregate Milwaukee's schools, and the participation of Williams is highlighted as proof that African Americans have turned their backs on integration. But this is not exactly right. What never makes it into the conventional tale is that the Milwaukee metropolitan area has operated a voluntary desegregation program for roughly thirty years. Known as the Chapter 220 plan, this program allows a limited number of Milwaukee students to attend suburban schools that have volunteered to accept them, while also allowing some suburban students to attend city magnet schools.[89]

The program began in 1976 as a voluntary measure and then in the mid-1980s was folded into the settlement of a school desegregation case. That settlement expired in the mid-1990s, but the program has continued. It has not exactly thrived, however, and in fact has been curtailed over the years. In 1993, roughly six thousand students participated; now, only about three thousand do.[90]

The cutbacks cannot be explained by a lack of interest on the part of city students and their families—the program has a waiting list. Nor could one say the program has been ineffective. An audit of the program found that students who used Chapter 220 to transfer to the suburbs performed better on statewide tests than those who remained in Milwaukee, including those who tried to transfer but did not win the lottery for participation. There is no evidence that vouchers have been more effective at boosting achievement than Chapter 220. Moreover, a number of suburban students, parents, and officials who were involved in the program have accepted and even embraced it over time.[91]

The cutbacks seem due instead to the cost of the program, as well as a lack of enthusiasm among state legislators for helping city students attend suburban schools. The program is expensive because the state pays both the full per-pupil amount to the receiving districts and a hold harmless amount to Milwaukee, which represents about three-fourths of the amount of state aid Milwaukee would receive if each student remained within the district. The payments to both districts were necessary to secure their support, but the high cost of the program has made it a perpetual target for cutting. Vouchers—which are now worth about $6,500 in Milwaukee—are much less expensive. They also keep city students in the city. Both factors help explain why Chapter 220 has shrunk to cover three thousand students, while the voucher program started with one thousand students and has grown to cover more than eighteen thousand.[92]

The lesson from Milwaukee is not that school integration in general, or urban-suburban integration in particular, is a failure. Nor has it lost all support among African Americans or suburban whites. Milwaukee suggests that there is continued support for such programs, more so among those who have participated in them. At the same time, however, there is obviously stronger support in Milwaukee for school choice limited to inner cities. What is true in Milwaukee is true elsewhere, which helps explain the current shape of school choice programs.

CONCLUSION

One lesson to draw from studying school choice is that politics trump ideology. Despite the ideological appeal of school choice to many conservative Republicans, the politics of education have precluded many of them from embracing it wholeheartedly. The need to court suburbanites outweighs the desire to translate attractive theories into concrete policies. Thus, instead of choice plans that conform to academic theory about the benefits of competition and markets, we have choice plans that conform to the political realities of educational opportunity.

The dominant reality is that suburban local control must be preserved, regardless of the reform. The need to preserve local control has been used by conservative majorities on the U.S. Supreme Court as justification for limiting school desegregation and school finance reform. It would be easy to think on the basis of these examples that protecting local control is a way to limit "liberal" education reforms that would otherwise require measures like racial integration or the equalization of funding. But the example of school choice shows that preserving local control—and, more specifically, protecting the suburbs— can also hamper reforms more closely associated with conservatives than liberals. To be sure, the protection of local control is less visible and explicit in debates about school choice than it has been in court cases about desegregation or school finance. But it has been no less influential. School choice has been shaped in ways that leave suburban local control largely intact. Choice touches, if lightly, some cities, but it mostly steers clear of the suburbs.

What remains to be examined is the impact of choice on the ground and the role that courts have played in this context. What effect will limited school choice programs have on the students who exercise choice and those who remain behind? Will this particular manifestation of Nixon's compromise—offering choice programs as a way to improve city schools while not threatening suburban ones—work to close the urban-suburban gap in educational opportunities? And what, if anything, have courts done to encourage or discourage school choice? It is to these questions that the next chapter is addressed.

CHAPTER 6

The Impact of Choice and the Role of Courts

If the pattern described in the preceding chapter holds, limited school choice plans will be neither a panacea nor much of a threat to the status quo. As this chapter explains in some detail, such programs will, on the whole, do little to boost academic achievement, have only a negligible impact on existing levels of school segregation, and promote relatively little productive competition among schools. This is not to deny that limited school choice plans have real costs and benefits, nor is it to deny that a few choice schools—especially the Knowledge is Power Program (KIPP) charter schools—have managed to "beat the odds" by posting good test scores. The simple, basic point instead is that the costs and benefits of school choice are likely to be as limited as the choice plans themselves. Those costs and benefits, moreover, will be felt almost entirely within urban districts.

This chapter then goes on to address the fairly minor role played by courts in the field of school choice. Unlike in the arenas of school desegregation and school finance, courts have not been in the lead when it comes to school choice. No court, for example, has mandated choice as a remedy for educational failure or recognized a right to school choice as a component of a larger right to equal or adequate educational opportunity. Almost all of the cases brought to court have been challenges to the legality of choice plans. The question courts have faced is whether choice is allowed, not whether it is required. Courts, in short, have played defense, not offense, in this context.

The shift in roles is subtle but important, as it signifies the declining significance of courts, especially federal courts, in contemporary fights over educational opportunity. Courts have not been central to school choice programs, nor, as the next chapter describes, have they played much of a role in the standards and testing movement, which is perhaps the most important contemporary education reform. Unlike the past, legislatures, not courts, are driving the key education reforms today and legislatures, not courts, are defining the contours of educational opportunity.

THE CONSEQUENCES OF
CONSTRAINED CHOICES

If school choice stays on its current path, we should continue to see school choice plans confined to single, mostly urban districts. Within those districts, we should expect to see programs that provide opportunities for some students to attend alternative schools—whether another public school, a charter school, a magnet school, or a private school. The neighborhood school, however, will remain the default assignment and the one most students attend.

If school choice programs remain structured and constrained in these ways, what will their impact be? In discussions regarding the impact of school choice, three issues arise most frequently, and these are the issues taken up here: First, how will school choice effect racial and socioeconomic segregation? Second, what impact will school choice have on the academic achievement of students who choose new schools? Third, what effect will school choice have on the students who remain in their assigned schools?

Racial and Socioeconomic Integration

One of the most controversial questions looming over choice programs is whether they will exacerbate segregation based on race, class, or both. Some of the fear stems from knowledge of the past and the ways school choice was used in the service of segregation. Many older civil rights leaders, for just this reason, remain wary of school choice, especially of vouchers. As Kweisi Mfume, former president of the NAACP, put it in 1999, "vouchers don't educate, they segregate."[1]

Some scholars, like advocates, have also looked backward in order to predict the future. Law professor Betsy Levin, for example, looked at the historical use of choice and imagined a future much like the past, in which choice increases racial and socioeconomic segregation. Levin is not alone in her concerns. Many scholars speculate that school choice, particularly vouchers, will lead to greater racial and socioeconomic isolation. This argument reflects the belief that parents, if given the choice, will chose racially and ethnically homogeneous schools. It also reflects a belief that choice programs will be attractive primarily to those who are relatively informed, motivated, and economically secure, and that these families will use school choice to separate themselves from those who are poorer.[2]

These fears are justified, at least somewhat. Traditionally, when they have had choices, parents have opted for the less diverse school. One of the strongest predictors of white private school enrollment, for example, has been the percentage of black students attending public schools within the district. Similarly, there is plenty of anecdotal evidence, within Richmond and elsewhere, to suggest that affluent families are more likely than poorer ones to take advantage of school choice. This dynamic can create the widely discussed "skimming" effect, where choice schools become filled with the students from the most motivated families.[3]

On the other hand, there is reason to believe that at least some forms of school choice, namely vouchers for private schools, could enhance integration. In many urban districts, there are more white students in private than in public schools. In Richmond, for example, there are roughly seventeen hundred white students within the public school system but almost twice as many in private schools. If vouchers were given to public school students, nearly 90 percent of whom are black, and these students used them to attend existing private schools, it is reasonable to expect integration, not segregation, to increase within Richmond.[4]

Similar opportunities exist in other metropolitan areas throughout the country. Indeed, in many of these areas, minority students—both black and Hispanic—in private schools are less likely to be racially isolated than are minority students in public schools. In Minneapolis-St. Paul, for example, roughly 60 percent of the classmates of the average black private school student are white, compared to only 43 percent of the classmates of black public school students. In Dallas, the comparable figures are 42 percent and 28 percent; in Cleveland, 31 percent to 22 percent; and in Oakland, 29 percent to 19 percent. Additional evidence suggests that students using vouchers in Cleveland, Milwaukee, and Washington, D.C. have ended up in schools that were more racially integrated than the schools they left.[5]

Given current demographics, however, vouchers for private schools can only do so much to enhance racial and socioeconomic integration. It is possible, as I suggest in chapter 8, that a universal system of school choice could change the demographics of urban districts by drawing in more middle-income families to city school districts. (One can rest assured, by contrast, that voucher programs limited to poor students, as most are now, will do little to change the demographics of urban districts because they offer nothing to middle-income families.) If the demographics of urban districts do not change, however, even a universal voucher system would have only slight effects on integration levels. The reason is simple: there are currently not enough middle-income or white students in most urban districts, in public and private schools combined, to create meaningfully integrated schools throughout the district. In other words, if the current private and public school populations in urban districts were blended together, the student body would still be predominantly minority.

Richmond is a good example. White students, overall, make up only 17 percent of the total school population, public and private. Even if Richmond had a universal voucher program and all schools, public and private, were perfectly balanced, only 17 percent of the students in each school would be white. Definitions of integration vary quite a bit, but few would consider schools that are 83 percent minority to be meaningfully integrated. The possibility for meaningful socioeconomic integration is not much greater, given the relatively small numbers of students who are in private schools. Including them within the school system would not make it majority middle-income.[6]

What is true for vouchers is also true for other forms of school choice. Public school choice programs limited to schools within urban districts might have some marginal effects on segregation levels at different schools, but no more than that. The same holds for charter schools in urban districts. In school districts where more than 80 or 90 percent of the students are minority, and most are also poor, the potential for increased segregation or increased integration is obviously limited.

This is not to deny that there could be some movement, in either direction, at the margins. Nor is it meant to downplay the sense of unfairness felt by some when white students in an urban school system cluster at just a few schools, as occurs in the Fox and Munford elementary schools in Richmond. The point is simply that marginal changes in levels of segregation, which garner a tremendous amount of attention, should not distract us from the larger picture. In that picture, the dominant scene is of schools segregated by race and income, with a splash of exceptional, integrated schools here and there. Limited school choice plans will do little to alter the scenery.[7]

Academic Achievement among Students Who Choose

For many involved in the debate about school choice, the ultimate barometer of success or failure is academic achievement, which is inevitably measured by test scores. I address this issue second not because of a quarrel with that ranking of priorities but because academic achievement and the socioeconomic status of schools are closely linked. High-poverty schools rarely achieve at a high level. Thus, knowing that most school choice programs confined to urban school districts will do little to alter the socioeconomic status of the schools is a useful starting point in thinking about the academic impact of school choice.

Before getting to the data, three general points are worth highlighting. First, the debate about school choice, like that over school funding, revolves primarily if not exclusively around test scores. Some studies go beyond test scores and consider parental satisfaction with chosen schools, which is usually relatively high. But these findings tend to be discounted or ignored entirely in debates about school choice. For reasons already explained, test scores offer an imperfect measure, at best, of school quality. At the same time, the focus on test scores reinforces the perception that academic achievement is the sole purpose of education. High-poverty, high-minority charter schools that "beat the odds," for example, are usually applauded because of their test scores, not lamented because of their racial and economic isolation.

Second, belief in the power of school choice rests on a premise that is often unstated and is not fully accepted in other contexts: schools matter. In fights over school funding, conservative opponents of increased funding not only disparage the effectiveness of spending but occasionally raise doubts about the degree to which schools alone can overcome the impact of poverty and family disarray. Some liberal advocates have made similar points, arguing that money would be better spent on social welfare programs like health care, housing, and job training. Yet to believe in school choice as a way to address the problem of urban education, one must believe that schools matter and can make a significant difference. Otherwise, there would be little point to shuffling students around.

Third, the impact of school choice on students who exercise it comes almost entirely from the quality of the chosen school. This might seem like an obvious point, but it is often lost in discussions about the impact of choice programs that involve vouchers or charter schools. In these debates, it sometimes seems as if the magic lies in the very fact of choice, as if student achievement improves during the drive across town from one school to the other. To be sure, the very act of choosing a school may in some instances lead parents and students to become more invested and engaged in education, which can boost achievement. But most of the increase in academic performance, if any, comes from the new school itself. The debate about the impact of "choice" on students who choose, therefore, is really nothing more than a debate about whether some schools are better than others.[8]

This question of school quality can be and has been addressed at both the retail and wholesale levels. On the retail level, the question is designed to focus attention on why a particular school is better than others. What is one charter school doing, for example, to produce better test results than other charter schools serving a similar group of students? On the wholesale level, the question is whether one *type* of school is better than another. More specifically, the question is whether private or charter schools outperform traditional public ones.

The problem that bedevils all attempts to assess the impact of school choice programs is the ubiquitous obstacle of self-selection. To study the impact of schools on student achievement, researchers need to control for all other relevant variables. Studies about charter schools, for example, typically compare students from similar socioeconomic backgrounds. The premise, fully justified, is that students from middle-income and affluent families routinely outperform those from poorer families. If socioeconomic status were not held constant when studying charter schools, it would be hard to know whether test scores differ because of the school or because of the student and the student's family.[9]

The one variable that is difficult to control for is what might be called motivation, on the part of the family, student, or both. Family participation in education and student engagement in school affect academic performance, regardless of where the student attends school. The problem is that students from families who care a lot about education are both more likely do well in any school *and* more likely to leave a bad school for the promise of a better one if given the opportunity. This makes it difficult to assess the impact of school choice. If students who choose to attend a different school outperform those who remain behind, was it the school or the student and her family that made the difference? After all, the students who exercised school choice might have outperformed their peers even if they had remained in the same school.

Some researchers have tried to control for selection bias in various ways. They might, for example, compare students who received a voucher—or a spot in a charter school—with those who applied but were denied, on the theory that applying for a choice school is a proxy for motivation. But some studies do little to nothing to control for this factor, which renders the research a bit unreliable and helps explain why there are so many conflicting studies about the impact of choice.[10]

All of that said, some headway can be made in assessing the likely impact of constrained school choice plans on academic achievement. As discussed, the one fact social scientists of all stripes agree on is that schools of concentrated poverty rarely perform as well as their middle-class counterparts. There are some exceptions to this pattern, where schools with mostly poor students post better-than-average test scores. But there is a reason why reports about such schools, whether in the academic or popular literature, inevitably refer to them as "beating the odds." The odds remain highly stacked against predominantly poor schools.[11]

As currently structured, most school choice programs do little to increase socioeconomic integration. Many urban public school choice programs, for example, offer choices primarily among high-poverty schools. Many charter schools, in turn, simply reproduce schools of concentrated poverty in different buildings. If this pattern holds, school choice may benefit the few students who end up in majority-middle-income schools, and it may produce some more exceptional schools that "beat the odds." But the larger picture will be one of stasis, even for those who do exercise choice.

To be sure, there may be some marginal improvements. Choice schools tend to be smaller than regular public schools, and some have smaller classes, both of which have been found to correlate with increased achievement. Some choice schools have also been able to attract very good teachers, who are drawn to the mission of the school. Some urban public schools are also simply terrible, so improving on them is not a big challenge. In short, there is some reason to expect limited academic gains from school choice, but not much more.[12]

Existing evidence about the impact of school choice programs already points in this direction. The Crain and Wells study of the St. Louis choice program, discussed briefly in chapter 4, is a good example. Students had the option of remaining in a traditional public school, attending an urban magnet school, or attending a suburban school. The magnet schools were predominantly poor; the suburban schools were predominantly middle-income. Students who chose the suburban schools experienced the biggest boost in achievement, followed by those who attended magnet schools. Thus, moving from a traditional urban public school to a magnet school helped, but not as much as moving to a majority-middle-income school.[13]

Evidence regarding charter schools and vouchers is consistent with this pattern. To be sure, the studies of charter schools and voucher programs are filled with methodological debates and contradictory conclusions. For every study finding a gain for some or all students, it seems, another study appears that questions the earlier study's methodology, reruns the numbers, and finds no gain. In addition, and remarkably, researchers have not studied whether the socioeconomic composition of charter or voucher schools influences achievement. For all of these reasons, drawing firm conclusions about the impact of charters and vouchers is difficult.[14]

Nonetheless, it seems fair to make two points. First, neither vouchers nor charter schools have yielded consistent, significant academic benefits. Even the most ardent fans of choice would have to admit that, at best, there are some promising signs and mixed results. Second, on the whole, students using vouchers appear to have benefited more than students attending charter schools. The academic gains among voucher users are not consistent across studies, and they are generally not large. But they seem to be more consistent and larger than those reported for students attending charter schools.[15]

This is just what one would expect from research regarding the importance of a school's socioeconomic status. Charter schools tend to reflect the demographics of the districts in which they are located. It would be surprising, therefore, if these schools consistently posted stronger academic results, especially given the fact that they usually receive less funding than traditional schools. Private schools, by contrast, tend to have a higher proportion of middle-income students than do public schools in the same district. Most voucher programs are not especially generous, so students using vouchers may not all end up in majority-middle-income schools. But they are still more likely to be surrounded by middle-income students from stable families than they would be if they remained in a public school or attended a charter school.[16]

I do not mean to suggest that the socioeconomic composition of schools explains everything, and I acknowledge that my argument is based on an inference from the studies rather than direct empirical testing. The point I am making, however, is fairly modest. Schools of concentrated poverty represent the hardest challenge in education. It would be nothing short of a miracle if those who ran charter, private, or magnet schools had all figured out how to make high-poverty schools succeed, and—enhancing the miracle—to do so with less funding. Evidence from existing programs does not point to a miracle.

Schools That Beat the Odds

Some urban schools of choice have nonetheless succeeded in beating the odds by posting high test scores. They deserve some attention before discussing the impact of school choice on those who remain behind in traditional public schools. What are these schools doing differently from traditional public schools, and could these methods be replicated on a larger scale?

To begin, it is worth noting just how exceptional these "high flying" or "beat the odds" schools really are. The Education Trust is an advocacy group committed to proving that high-poverty, high-minority schools can succeed if given adequate resources and held accountable for results. It published a report several years ago that identified over thirteen hundred schools that were high-poverty, high-minority, and supposedly high-performing. The report received a great deal of attention, especially from conservatives who used it as evidence that those in urban schools could do better if they simply tried harder. It turned out, however, that the definition of "high-performing" was a school where test scores in one subject in one grade in one year were in the top third of all scores in the state. In a subsequent analysis of the data, which used a slightly tighter definition of success—two subjects in two grades over two years—the number of "high-performing" schools dropped from thirteen hundred to *twenty-three*. Under this more stringent definition of success, a mostly white, middle-class school had a one-in-four chance of being high-performing, while a high-poverty, high-minority school had one chance in three hundred.[17]

Still, the exceptional schools are alluring to policymakers and pundits alike. To understand what goes on in them, it is helpful to look at the KIPP charter schools. Created by two alumni of the Teach for America program, KIPP schools serve mostly poor and minority urban students. From one school in Houston in 1994, KIPP has grown to a franchise of eighty-two schools in nineteen states and Washington, D.C., serving roughly twenty thousand students. Of all the charter schools, whether started by teachers, parents, or private education management companies, the KIPP schools have probably received the most attention and the most praise. The KIPP franchise has also spawned similar groups of charter schools, including those under the banners "Achievement First" and "Uncommon Schools," both of which use methods like KIPP's and have posted equally impressive results.[18]

Eighty percent of KIPP students are low income, and 90 percent are African American or Hispanic. KIPP prides itself on proving that "demography does not define destiny," and its results tend to support the claim. Students at KIPP schools perform remarkably well on state tests, much better than their peers at urban public schools and often better than the state average. According to the KIPP website, more than 90 percent of KIPP graduates go on to college preparatory high schools, and 80 percent have enrolled in college.[19]

How do they do it? Some critics contend that they skim better students and more motivated families. There is some evidence that KIPP students, at least at some of the schools, enter with higher test scores than their local public school peers. It is harder to assess the motivation levels of families, but there is also some anecdotal evidence—as well as some logic—to support the claim that families who send their children to KIPP schools care more about education than those who leave them in failing public schools. The ubiquitous self-selection problem thus clouds some of the sparkling results.[20]

That said, scores among KIPP students continue to improve during their time in school, which suggests that the schools are adding value—and that KIPP is correctly seen as a success story in the otherwise bleak world of urban education. The key to KIPP's success appears to come from three principles that guide the schools. First, students spend more time in school. The school day runs from roughly eight A.M. to four P.M., with additional tutoring available after school, and classes are held on Saturday mornings. Summer vacation lasts only about one month.[21]

Second, instruction is very structured and goal oriented. Students are tested frequently. Teachers are trained, retrained, frequently observed and assessed by their principals, and removed if they are not meeting established goals. There is also an emphasis on "team building" among the teachers and principals, and the schools are generally rewarding places to work. They tend to attract young, enthusiastic teachers, many of whom are alumni of Teach for America and are willing to put in fifteen- or sixteen-hour days.[22]

Third, the schools focus on behavior, values, and character. As a *New York Times Magazine* article described: "Using slogans, motivational posters, incentives, encouragements and punishments, the schools direct students in everything from the principles of teamwork and the importance of an optimistic outlook to the nuts and bolts of how to sit in class, where to direct their eyes...and even how to nod appropriately." In particular, the schools use a method called SLANT, which teaches students to "sit up, listen, ask questions, nod and track the speaker with their eyes."[23]

This last principle, of focusing on behavior and character, is in many ways the most interesting. The KIPP schools—as well as Achievement First and Uncommon Schools—are essentially following the example of urban Catholic schools. In his study of private schools, Coleman attributed the success of Catholic schools to the culture that pervaded them, which was characterized by a shared sense of purpose, high expectations, and strict discipline. Take away the religious doctrine, and KIPP schools do not seem much different.[24]

What KIPP schools are doing, in a sense, is intentionally creating the sort of culture and atmosphere that would be taken for granted at a lot of middle-income suburban schools. As David Levin, the cofounder of KIPP, has explained, middle-class students come to school already aware of the SLANT method—though they would not call it that—because they have learned it from their families. The KIPP students, by contrast, "need to be taught these methods explicitly." Levin, like his counterparts at Achievement First and Uncommon Schools, also believes that instilling good behavior, optimism about the future, and a solid work ethic are just as important as teaching students how to do long division.[25]

The obvious question about KIPP schools is whether they can be replicated on a large scale. In considering this question, one has to confront the uncomfortable possibility that the KIPP method may depend on segregation to work. It is difficult to imagine the KIPP program being used in a socioeconomically and racially diverse school, where presumably some students would not need instruction in things like the SLANT method and those who received it might feel resentful for being picked out of the crowd.

Even if we set aside the question of whether KIPP's methods would work in diverse schools, it is not clear that KIPP has the capacity to reach a lot of high-poverty, high-minority schools. KIPP schools currently serve just a tiny sliver of urban students, as do Achievement First and Uncommon Schools. They rely on a small cadre of extremely committed—and talented—teachers and principals, who are willing to work long hours for relatively little pay.

Presumably, at some point, teachers and principals less committed to the social justice mission of KIPP would have to be paid more, perhaps much more, to log the kind of hours now expected. The KIPP teachers are already paid 15 to 20 percent more than traditional public school teachers to compensate them for the extra time they spend at school. Even with this higher pay, a nontrivial number of them still leave after just a few years because of the heavy demands of the job. Perhaps even higher pay would not prevent burnout, but higher pay certainly seems necessary, even if not sufficient, to allow KIPP to expand.[26]

If one grants that higher teacher pay would allow KIPP to expand significantly, however, one is confronted again with the question of where the money would come from. The KIPP schools suggest that it is possible, as a matter of policy, to create high-performing, high-poverty schools. But the question of politics remains, and it is hard at this point to envision the political scenario under which states would provide the resources necessary to allow for a significant expansion of KIPP-like schools.

At the moment, KIPP schools are to inner-city education what the Peace Corps is to the developing world. A Peace Corps volunteer might well succeed, for example, in digging a well in a village that lacked running water or in teaching some children how to read and write. In so doing, the volunteer would show what is possible and would undoubtedly help those who are served. But relying on Peace Corps volunteers alone will not bring economic prosperity and development to impoverished countries; that would require a significant shift in political priorities. So it is with educating city students. KIPP is doing an excellent job of showing what is possible in high-poverty, high-minority urban schools. Simply showing that something is possible on a small scale, however, does not make it politically plausible on a grand scale.

The Students Who Do Not Choose

According to its proponents, school choice will help not only those students who leave one school to attend a better one. It will help all students because schools that lose students will respond by becoming more effective. They might mimic the methods of charter, private, or other public schools that are attracting students and succeeding academically, or they might innovate on their own. Either way, the competition engendered by school choice, so its supporters argue, will spur systemic improvements.

There are really two separate questions regarding the relationship between school choice and competition. The first is whether increased competition generates improvements in schools that face it, and the second is whether school choice plans will foster much competition. The first question has received a lot of attention, and the emerging evidence suggests that there are gains from competition. The second question has not received as much attention, but it is arguably more important, given the constraints on school choice I have already identified. Here, the evidence supports what common sense would suggest: the more limited the choice program, the more limited the competition. And limited competition brings only limited gains.

The faith that choice advocates place in competition is both understandable and a little perplexing. On the one hand, the basic idea that competition improves efficiency is intuitive and underlies faith in markets generally. On the other hand, education is not a typical market, and the exact link between competition and school improvement is not obvious. Nor is that link fully explained by many choice advocates—leaving competition more like a black box than a clearly defined path to school improvement.

Charter or private schools might be forced to close if enough students leave, so the link between competition and outcomes is understandable in those contexts. But competition is also supposed to help traditional public schools. Here the link is harder to discern. It is unlikely that many public schools would be completely shut down because of student departures, so the threat of closure is not very significant. Nor are many jobs on the line, as many teachers and administrators would simply be reassigned rather than fired if their current school lost students. Fleeing students might generate bad publicity for the school, but failing schools are already criticized publicly, so the effect would be marginal at most. Those running or teaching in overcrowded schools, moreover, might actually welcome the departure of some students, regardless of the publicity. There are plausible reasons to worry, finally, that any benefits from competition will be offset by losses, which might occur if school choice programs skim the best students and the most motivated families from some schools and concentrate them in new schools.

Notwithstanding the considerable theoretical uncertainty as to why competition might spur improvement in existing public schools, there is some empirical support for the proposition. The evidence is disputed, as one would by now expect, and it points to modest gains at most. Caroline Hoxby has done the best-known work on the topic, and she found modest but positive effects when she assessed the impact of competition among *public* schools. Additional studies also suggest that competition can boost overall school performance and, in particular, increase high school graduation rates. After reviewing forty published studies conducted between 1972 and 2002 on the effects of competition, two education scholars at Columbia University concluded that "increasing competition—either intradistrict, interdistrict, or from private schools—*may* raise the effectiveness and efficiency of public schools, as well as address other educational objectives." They were quick to point out, however, that "the substantive effect is modest and does not support the contention that market competition will produce radical improvements in educational results."[27]

These scholars also emphasized that "the magnitude of the reform is important," which leads to the second and more important question regarding the impact of competition. Evidence suggests a fairly direct relationship between the scope or intensity of competition and its impact. Case studies of Cleveland and San Antonio, for example, suggest that small-scale choice programs generate little pressure to improve. A study of charter schools in Arizona reached the same conclusion. All of this, of course, makes perfect intuitive sense. The more limited the competition, the less pressure there is to change.[28]

Because most school choice plans, especially those involving vouchers, are currently quite limited, the threat to existing schools is small. It is difficult to detect, for example, much pressure on Richmond public schools because of the open enrollment program or the existence of the small but highly effective Community and Open high schools. It is highly doubtful that the tiny Patrick Henry Charter School, once it opens, will add much pressure for reform. Indeed, Richmond has already faced much greater competitive pressure from the suburbs, which is true of most urban school systems. The loss of substantial numbers of students from Richmond over the years has not prevented many schools in Richmond from declining rather than improving. It is hard to imagine that introducing slightly more school choice within Richmond would suddenly spur significant improvements.

Thus, as is true with both integration and achievement levels, the effects of limited school choice plans on students who remain behind will also be limited. Competition might spur some improvements, but a small dose of competition is not a recipe for a miracle cure or even significant reform. None of this is meant to argue against school choice, and it is certainly not meant to argue against the expansion of school choice. The limited empirical evidence about choice suggests that all forms of school choice offer the promise of some benefit, though choice can certainly generate some costs. In my own view, choice experiments are well worthwhile, as are efforts to increase the scope of school choice. But any optimism about impact of school choice must be tempered by the political realities described in this chapter. Unless and until political incentives change—a topic explored in chapter 8—we will continue to see school choice plans that are limited and are confined to urban areas. Some marginal improvements, along a number of dimensions, may indeed occur, but the impact will be as limited as the programs themselves.

SCHOOL CHOICE AND THE COURTS

As mentioned in the introduction to this chapter, courts have been more reactive than proactive in the school choice context. In school desegregation and school finance litigation, courts were out front, ordering state and local officials to take actions aimed at improving educational opportunities. In the school choice arena, by contrast, legislatures have been leading the way and courts have been following. The only question most courts have addressed, at least thus far, is whether choice programs are constitutionally permissible, not whether they are constitutionally required. This is not to suggest that court decisions have been unimportant; courts still act as crucial gatekeepers, and not all programs have survived constitutional review. But we are nonetheless in a new era, where legislatures, not courts, are setting the terms of the debate over educational opportunity.

Almost all of the legal controversies in the school choice arena have revolved around voucher plans, showing again the outsized influence of this intriguing reform. There have been three different sets of challenges. Two of the three have involved questions about church and state. They have received a great deal of attention but have had relatively little impact. The third set involves more obscure questions of state constitutional law. These challenges have received relatively little attention from scholars but have proven the most potent.

From *Brown* to *Zelman*

The first, big question about vouchers was whether they could be used at religious schools without violating the establishment clause of the Constitution. This clause prohibits any "law respecting an establishment of religion," and in the popular imagination simply requires the separation of church and state. In the Supreme Court's hands, things have been more complicated. The Court has not always drawn a clear or coherent line of separation between religion and government, especially in the context of education. Whether religious schools could participate in voucher programs was rightly seen, given the Court's somewhat bewildering establishment clause jurisprudence, as an important constitutional question. But it was of practical importance as well. Most private schools are sectarian, and most sectarian schools are less expensive than secular ones. Without their inclusion, it would be hard for voucher programs to get off the ground in many areas.[29]

In 2002, the Court ruled in *Zelman v. Simmons-Harris* that including religious schools in voucher programs did not violate the establishment clause. The Court reasoned that public money makes it to private religious schools through the genuine choices of parents, which serve to break the link between church and state. The Court thus upheld the inclusion of religious schools in the Cleveland voucher program.[30]

President Bush hailed the ruling as the *Brown v. Board of Education* of our time, signifying the extent to which even conservative voucher supporters tend to emphasize the equity aspects of choice rather than the privatizing aspects. Libertarian Clint Bolick, for example, who for a time was the litigator-in-chief of the voucher movement, never failed to stress that his clients were poor, mostly minority students. Indeed, he brought busloads of African-American students to court hearings in order to emphasize the point.[31]

In comparing the two, President Bush meant to suggest that *Zelman* was as important as *Brown v. Board of Education* in expanding educational opportunities for poor, minority students. Whether that comparison is fair or not, there is another, more intriguing link between the two decisions. This connection is not well known but is nonetheless important, because it draws together two eras of school reform and illustrates one of the unintended consequences of *Brown*.

To make a long story short, *Brown v. Board of Education* actually helped make the use of vouchers at religious schools constitutional. That is, *Brown* spurred political and social changes that helped make possible the Supreme Court's 2002 decision in *Zelman*. It did so by increasing the popularity of private, religious schools, which in turn changed minds about the desirability of providing public support to such schools.[32]

At the time of *Brown*, most private school students were enrolled in Catholic parochial schools. To provide aid to private schools, therefore, was to provide aid to the Catholic Church. A large and powerful coalition of Protestants, Jews, and public secularists strongly opposed any program that would promote Catholic schools. The Supreme Court essentially sided with this coalition by strictly limiting the ability of states to provide support to private, religious schools. The Court's decisions in this area were sometimes hard to follow, as the Court occasionally allowed incidental aid to flow to religious schools. By and large, however, the Court erected a fairly high wall of separation between church and state.[33]

Brown and subsequent desegregation cases, however, prompted the creation of so-called Christian academies. These were sponsored by a range of evangelical

Protestants and were designed, at least at first, to allow whites to avoid integrated public schools. As these schools grew in number, evangelicals, perhaps not surprisingly, began to change their mind about state aid to religious schools. There are numerous examples of this about-face, but none more explicit (or humorous) than Reverend W.A. Criswell's. The Reverend was pastor of the First Baptist Church of Dallas, the largest congregation in the Southern Baptist Convention. In 1960, prior to the advent of Christian academies, Criswell declared, "It is written in our country's Constitution that church and state must be, in this nation, forever separate and free." By 1984, when Christian academies constituted the fastest growing segment of private education, he had changed his tune. "I believe this notion of the separation of church and state," he said on the *CBS Evening News*, "was the figment of some infidel's imagination."[34]

When Criswell and other evangelical leaders flipped sides on the issue of school aid, their congregations and supporters followed suit. The support of conservative evangelicals transformed the political landscape of school aid. Protestants were no longer united in opposition. In addition, the Protestant groups that now supported such aid (conservative evangelicals) were becoming larger and more powerful, while the groups that remained opposed to such aid (the mainline denominations of Episcopalians, Methodists, and Presbyterians) were losing members and political clout. Conservative evangelicals also formed new and previously unthinkable alliances with Catholic groups in order to promote their cause. As conservative white evangelicals became more politically active and more powerful, the consequences of their realignment grew. Indeed, this group, which constitutes about one-quarter of the electorate, played a crucial role in the election of President Reagan and the first President Bush, who between them appointed all five of the justices in the majority in *Zelman*.[35]

Thus, by the time the Court finally approved the use of vouchers at religious schools, there was a much larger and more active coalition pushing for aid to religious schools, while the traditional opposition had fractured and weakened. In addition, school aid could no longer be seen as aid to a particular church. By the 1997–98 school year, and for the first time in the twentieth century, Catholic schools accounted for less than half of private school enrollment. Other religious schools, most of which were Christian academies, accounted for nearly 35 percent. The increasing prevalence of non-Catholic religious schools made it easier to see school aid as neutral among religions, which has always been a key factor in the Court's establishment clause jurisprudence. Finally, the participation of poor minority students in voucher programs, including the one at issue in *Zelman*, made it possible to see the voucher question as less about religion and more about educational opportunity.

All of these factors combined to make the Court's approval of vouchers, if not inevitable, predictable and understandable. The Supreme Court may not slavishly follow election returns, but it does not operate in a political vacuum. By the time the Court decided the voucher case, church-state politics had changed dramatically, as had the realities of aid to religious schools. So, too, had the Court's members, with conservative justices replacing more liberal ones.

Brown, of course, is not solely responsible for all of these changes. The Court's prayer and Bible reading decisions, and later its decision to protect abortion, also played a role in the growth and maintenance of Christian academies and the political activism of conservative Christians. Other factors have also contributed to the ascendancy of conservatism in American politics and the American judiciary over the last three decades. Nonetheless, it seems fair to identify the Court's approval of vouchers in *Zelman* as an unintended consequence of *Brown*.[36]

Zelman may be like *Brown* in one additional way. *Brown* had relatively little impact for the first decade after the decision was announced. The same seems true, so far, of *Zelman*. Many proponents hoped that once the Court approved the use of vouchers at religious schools, voucher programs would proliferate. But the real constraints on voucher programs have always been political, not legal, and *Zelman* obviously could not remove political constraints. If anything, *Zelman* has done less to remove the real obstacles to voucher programs than to reveal them.[37]

The "Baby Blaine" Amendments and Tax Credits

Voucher opponents initially hoped that the U.S. Supreme Court would outlaw the inclusion of religious schools in voucher programs, which would have created a nationwide ban. When that effort failed, they turned to state constitutions in the hope that bans on religious schools in voucher programs could be obtained state-by-state. Two different provisions, one or both of which appear in most state constitutions, bear on the question. The first explicitly prohibits the use of public funds for the "aid" or "benefit" of religious schools. The second prohibits the "compelled support" of a church or religious institution. Thirty-seven state constitutions contain the former provision; twenty-nine contain the latter. Only three contain neither.[38]

Virginia's constitution has both. Recall that legislators and voters amended the state constitution in 1956 in order to allow public aid to flow to private schools, clearing the way for school closures and the creation of all-white academies to avoid desegregation. The 1956 amendment, however, only allowed aid to go to secular schools; it continued to prohibit aid to religious ones. In addition, the Virginia Constitution states that "no man shall be compelled to frequent or support any religious worship, place, or ministry whatsoever" and prohibits the General Assembly from passing any law "requiring or authorizing any religious society, or the people of any district within this Commonwealth, to levy on themselves or others, any tax...for the support of any church or ministry."[39]

Provisions that bar "aid" to religious schools are sometimes referred to as "no aid" or "Baby Blaine" amendments. They have a checkered past, which voucher supporters emphasize and opponents downplay. In 1875, James G. Blaine, a senator from Maine, proposed amending the U.S. Constitution in order to prohibit aid to private, religious schools. Blaine and many of his supporters were motivated by anti-Catholic bigotry; they sought to close every loophole that might allow aid to flow to Catholic schools. Consistent with the ethos of the time, the amendment also made clear that Bible reading—which was almost always from the Protestant version of the Bible—was permissible in public schools.[40]

The Blaine amendment passed in the House of Representatives but fell just short of the votes needed in the Senate. Although the federal effort failed, many states incorporated similar provisions into their own constitutions, some because Congress required them to do as a condition of their admission to the Union. Hence the label "Baby Blaine" amendments for these provisions. By 1890, twenty-nine of the forty-five states had strongly worded provisions barring aid to religious institutions and schools. Like the original Blaine amendment, many of these provisions were also motivated by anti-Catholic prejudice and religious rivalry.[41]

The point is of more than just historical interest. Fights over no-aid provisions constitute one of the current fronts in the voucher wars, and some combatants are trying to use history to their advantage. Those who support vouchers argue broadly that these state constitutional provisions actually violate the *federal* Constitution because they discriminate against religion. It is impermissible, they contend, for states to offer vouchers to secular private schools but not sectarian ones. They also argue, more specifically, that the bigoted origins of many Baby Blaine amendments provide an independent reason for striking them down, because the amendments were designed not just to discriminate against religion generally but to discriminate against Catholics.[42]

Whether these arguments will ultimately persuade federal courts remains anyone's guess. The Supreme Court made it clear, in a case that postdated *Zelman*, that there is "play in the joints" between the free exercise clause, which bars discrimination against religious groups and practices, and the establishment clause. Aid that is *allowed* by the establishment clause, in other words, is not *required* by the free exercise clause. This means that states that allow vouchers to be used at secular schools are not necessarily required, by the federal constitution, to allow them also to be used at religious schools. The bigoted origins of some no-aid provisions in state constitutions might nonetheless cause the Court to strike them down, which would pave the way for inclusion of religious schools in voucher programs.[43]

Although the Court will inevitably have to resolve these issues, at the moment they remain largely untested. This is because few state courts have relied on Baby Blaine amendments or compelled support clauses to strike down voucher programs. Only two have done so. The Vermont Supreme Court ruled in 1999 that religious schools could not be included in a small voucher program for students who lived in towns that did not have public high schools. More recently, the Arizona Supreme Court ruled that voucher programs for special education students and students in foster care ran afoul of the no-aid provision in the Arizona constitution. In addition, a few other state courts, when asked for an advisory opinion, have indicated that providing vouchers for religious schools would violate their state constitutions. (Some state courts are permitted to provide advisory opinions on pending legislation.)[44]

On the other hand, the Supreme Courts of Ohio and Wisconsin sidestepped no aid and compelled support provisions on their way toward upholding the constitutionality of the Cleveland and Milwaukee voucher programs. They did so by adopting a version of the circuit-breaker theory that the U.S. Supreme Court endorsed in *Zelman*, reasoning that the state was not responsible for money that flowed to private schools. Such money passed through the hands of parents first, and parents—not the state—ultimately decided what to do with that money. Just as public employees are not barred from donating some of their salary to a church, so this line of thinking holds, individuals should not be barred from using vouchers to pay for a religious education. Similarly, when families do use vouchers, the state is not aiding the church or the school; it is aiding the family and specifically the child.[45]

At least that is the argument. Whether other state courts will find it persuasive remains to be seen. In the meantime, the no aid and compelled support clauses in state constitutions, despite their limited use in court, continue to cast a serious shadow over voucher programs. These clauses seem, when read plainly, to create significant obstacles to voucher programs that include religious schools. It is hard to conclude, without engaging in some mental gymnastics, that providing funding to religious schools through vouchers does not provide aid to religious schools or compel the support of taxpayers—who are footing the bill for voucher programs—for religious institutions. Unless these provisions continue to be finessed by courts, or unless their application turns out to violate the federal Constitution, these state constitutional provisions pose a real threat to voucher programs.

Indeed, it is precisely for this reason that some choice advocates, including legislators in Virginia, argue in favor of using tax credits instead. Tax credits (or deductions) can be given to families to offset tuition or other expenses. Alternatively, they can be given to donors—whether individuals or corporations—who provide money for private scholarships. Six states have one or both versions of a tax credit program: Minnesota, Illinois, Iowa, Florida, Arizona, and Pennsylvania.[46]

Supporters believe that tax credits are less vulnerable to legal challenge because they do not involve the outlay of public funds. As a result, the argument continues, tax credits do not constitute state aid to religious schools, nor do they compel the support of taxpayers. There is some superficial appeal to the argument, and indeed the Arizona Supreme Court has made this distinction. The Arizona Constitution provides that "no tax shall be laid or appropriation of public money made in aid of any church, or private or sectarian school." In striking down two voucher programs recently, the court made clear that an earlier decision approving tax credits remained good law. The difference between the programs, the court explained, was that tax credits do not involve an appropriation of state money.[47]

The court's reasoning is not beyond question, and tax credits may ultimately prove to be just as legally vulnerable as voucher programs. Tax credits essentially reimburse individuals or corporations for tuition payments made to religious schools. From a functional perspective, reimbursing individuals for tuition—either through a tax refund or by a reduction in tax liability—is the same as paying for tuition, just indirectly. In addition, once one recognizes that money is fungible, there is little practical difference between a direct expenditure and an exemption from taxation. The bottom line for the state's budget—not to mention the schools' budgets—is the same. Tax credit programs have thus far survived judicial scrutiny, but it is too soon to tell whether the trend will continue. There have been only two court decisions, the one in Arizona and another in Illinois, which also upheld the use of tax credits.[48]

Regardless of their legality, tax credits or tax deductions are not an especially effective way of financing private education, at least not on a broad scale. If the credits or deductions are given directly to families, the families must first pay for the tuition and then seek reimbursement, a process that would likely exclude many of the poor families that voucher supporters would like to target. If the credits or deductions are given instead to those who donate to private scholarship funds, funding for scholarships will obviously depend on the collective action of individual or corporate donors. It seems unlikely that the collective efforts of individuals and corporations would be sufficient to sustain more than relatively small voucher programs. Thus, even if tax credits or deductions prove more legally defensible than publicly financed vouchers, it still seems unlikely that they will have a significant impact.[49]

State Education Clauses: From Defense to Offense?

Aside from the U.S. Supreme Court's opinion in *Zelman*, the two most high-profile voucher decisions came from the Colorado and Florida Supreme Courts. Each court struck down its state's voucher program, and neither court relied on religion clauses to do so. The decisions, both in their reasoning and results, came as something of a surprise to supporters and foes alike. Although these cases received a good deal of media attention, it seems unlikely that either will exert much influence over the fate of voucher programs in other states.[50]

The Colorado decision, *Owens v. Colorado Congress of Parents, Teachers, and Students*, relied on a relatively unusual state constitutional provision that grants some control over schools to local school boards. To be precise, the provision says that local boards of education "shall have control of instruction in the public schools of their respective districts." On its face, this provision would seem irrelevant to a voucher program. Vouchers, after all, would be used in private schools, not public ones, and local boards of education would remain in charge of public schools even if there were a voucher program.[51]

The Colorado Supreme Court, however, has over the years added a gloss to the language of the local control provision and has equated control over locally raised revenues with local control over instruction. The court has reasoned that local boards must be able to control what happens to locally raised education revenues in order to maintain control over instruction in local schools. Whether that link is reasonable or not, it doomed the voucher program for the simple reason that localities were required to contribute funds for the vouchers. This meant that some local funding would go to private schools, which were beyond the control of local boards of education.[52]

This decision is unlikely to reverberate much beyond Colorado. Only five other states have local control provisions in their constitutions. The courts in those states, moreover, will not necessarily equate local control over funding with local control over instruction. Even where they are inclined to do so, there is an easy fix: use only state funds for the voucher. Indeed, the Colorado legislature could have done just that in response to the court's decision, but the delicate political coalition that pushed through the first voucher program could not be sustained for a second fight.

The Florida Supreme Court's decision has the potential to be more far-reaching because it relied on a more common constitutional provision. But the five-to-two decision is poorly reasoned and unlikely to gain many followers. The court ruled that the voucher program at issue violated the state constitutional requirement that the legislature establish a "uniform" system of public schools. All state constitutions, as described in chapter 4, have education clauses, most of which describe the sort of educational system that must be established by using one or more adjectives like "uniform," "thorough," "general," and "efficient." If voucher programs were indeed inconsistent with the legislature's duty to provide a "uniform" or "general" education, they would be illegal in many states.[53]

But it is not clear that there is any inconsistency. The Florida court reasoned that the duty to create a uniform system of public schools precluded the legislature from creating and funding any kind of alternative *in addition to* such a system. The voucher program also violated the uniformity requirement, the court continued, because the curriculum and teachers in private schools were not subject to the same standards that govern public schools. But it is not clear why a duty to create uniform public schools forecloses the creation of limited opportunities to attend private ones; it is not as if students were forced to choose a private school. Indeed, the Wisconsin Supreme Court read a similar provision in its constitution as creating a floor, not a ceiling. "The uniformity clause requires the legislature to provide an opportunity for all children in Wisconsin to receive a free uniform basic education," the court reasoned. "The legislature has done so. The [Milwaukee voucher program] merely reflects a legislative desire to do more than that which is constitutionally mandated." The dissenting justices on the Florida Supreme Court read the Florida Constitution in much the same way.[54]

What made the Florida court's reasoning especially dubious was its treatment of another voucher program that was not directly at issue. Florida had two voucher programs—one for students in failing schools, the other for disabled students. In striking down the former, the court made clear that the latter was constitutional. The court reasoned that the program for disabled students did not create a "systematic" private alternative to the public school system. But it is hard to see how the two programs can be distinguished on this ground, given that only a subset of students were eligible for either program. It is also hard to know why private schools that educate disabled students do not violate the "uniformity" requirement because of their different curricula and teacher certification requirements. The court raised even more eyebrows by granting a preemptive exemption to all other alternative education programs, saying that they "may also be distinguishable in ways not fully explored or readily apparent at this stage." In other words, the court seemed to be saying, it would find ways to distinguish these programs if and when necessary.[55]

Although the court's decision was not especially persuasive, its reliance on the education provision of the state constitution was a master stroke strategically. If the court had relied on the no-aid provision in the state constitution—which was the basis on which the lower court ruled—vouchers could still be used at secular schools, so the ruling would not have completely outlawed the program. In addition, a decision to ban only religious schools from voucher programs would raise a federal issue regarding religious discrimination, and thus the decision could be reviewed and overturned by the U.S. Supreme Court. By relying on the state's education provision, the Florida court was able to prohibit vouchers at religious and secular schools and raise no federal issue. If other state courts are intent on killing voucher programs, the Florida decision might be a model. If they are concerned as well about the soundness of their reasons, the Florida opinion is not an example to follow closely.

As the Florida case indicates, education clauses in state constitutions have thus far been seen mostly as a threat to voucher programs. Properly understood, however, they also constitute an opportunity, which is apparent from the nascent drive to establish a *right* to school choice based on these clauses. The idea is fairly straightforward. Some state courts, in school finance cases, have interpreted education clauses as guaranteeing students a right to adequate or equal educational opportunities. Instead of waiting around for increased funding, the argument continues, students in failing schools should be given the immediate chance to attend better schools, whether private or public.[56]

Only a handful of lawsuits have pursued this strategy. To date, none has succeeded or has even made it very far before being dismissed. This includes a case filed in New Jersey in 2006 by Clint Bolick, which has received a little attention in the media. That case was dismissed by the trial court, and the dismissal was recently upheld on appeal. Despite the lack of success of this approach, not to mention the lack of attention to it, there is little reason in theory why the remedy of school choice should be unavailable for students stuck in schools that are not providing a constitutionally sufficient education. After all, when some African-American students in the *Plessy* era were attending unequal, all-black schools, some courts ordered that they be admitted to white schools. Students who are guaranteed an adequate or equal education by state law should have similar remedial options. If nothing else, allowing urban students the opportunity to choose another school, including suburban schools, might be an especially effective way to focus the attention of suburban legislators on the problems of urban schools, just as the threat of integration motivated southern legislatures to focus on black schools in the 1950s and has focused the attention of the Connecticut legislature on Hartford schools in recent years.[57]

CONCLUSION

Court involvement of the sort just described has the potential to expand the scope of school choice beyond what legislatures have devised. The potential for court-ordered expansion is not huge, of course. If the past is any guide, it is unlikely that courts would be willing to stray too far from dominant political sentiment on this issue. If they remain true to form, courts may also be unwilling to push against suburban interests. But at least some courts, if asked, might be willing to push a bit farther than legislatures would. So far, however, few have been asked to do so.

It is also possible to imagine new coalitions forming to push for expanded school choice programs within urban areas, a possibility I describe more fully in chapter 8. This would be a welcome and potentially fruitful development. On the other hand, if courts continue only to play defense in this context, and if legislatures continue to craft limited choice programs, school choice will remain a sideshow in education law and policy, relevant to a small fraction of students. The radical potential of school choice, like that of school finance and desegregation, will remain contained, and the impact of school choice, for better or worse, will be marginal.

CHAPTER 7

Lowering the Bar:
The Standards and Testing Movement

State test scores, as you know, are all-important here.
—Principal, Tee-Jay High School, 2008

I regard state tests as establishing minimum standards. We teach well above and beyond what is tested.
—Principal, Freeman High School, 2006

Spring in Virginia brings green back to the fields and a hint of the hot weather ahead. It also brings standardized tests to the schools, in numbers that rival the daffodils blooming in gardens around the state. The tests are called the Standards of Learning (SOLs). Students take these tests beginning in elementary school and continuing through high school. In addition to math and reading, the SOLs cover a number of other subjects, including history, science, and geography. High school students must pass a series of these tests in order to graduate.

Schools, in turn, must meet certain testing benchmarks or risk sanction, thanks to the state's accountability system and the federal No Child Left Behind Act (NCLB). For this reason, a good deal of attention is paid to these tests in all schools. There is a noticeable difference in approach, however, among schools.

At Tee-Jay, for example, preparing for the tests is very serious business. When I visited during testing season, motivational posters hung in the halls, test-taking advice was written on the blackboards, and teachers, students, and the principal were all talking about the tests. The announcement board outside the school contained one message: "SOL Testing." In one class I visited, half of the students were in the cafeteria at 10:30 A.M. eating lunch because they were scheduled to take a test later that morning. The other half of the class had taken the test the week before. The group in the cafeteria was expected to have trouble with the test, so they were given additional time to prepare. During the class period, the teacher checked his computer to see if test scores for the first group were in yet; scores get reported quite quickly. Indeed, the principal at the time, Dr. Ulschmid, told me that day that early scores were very promising, which meant a lot to her, given the importance of those scores.

On the same day, I spent time at Freeman High School. It was hard to tell that students there were in the midst of the SOLs. The announcement board outside the school contained nothing about the SOLs; instead, an upcoming concert was featured. The class I visited was engaged in a geography project designed to enrich the students' knowledge of Africa and to help the teacher prepare for a working vacation there in the upcoming summer. I saw no posters about the SOLs, no words of advice, and indeed I heard no discussions about the tests.

This was not altogether surprising. Earlier conversations with Freeman's then-principal, Dr. Pruden, had made it clear that students there were expected to do well on the SOLs, and that teachers minimized the amount of time devoted specifically to preparing for them. Instead of emphasizing test scores or test preparation, Dr. Pruden stressed the rigor of regular classwork, noting with some pride that it was not unusual for a student to pass the SOL but receive a low grade or even fail a class given in the same subject. The tests, he made clear, were quite basic, a point echoed by the students I talked to at Freeman, who uniformly told me they thought the tests were a waste of time. That sentiment was shared by a small group of students at Tee-Jay I interviewed, who were enrolled in the rigorous International Baccalaureate Program there. These honor students told me that the tests were a "piece of cake" and "ridiculously easy" for them.[1]

The student reactions to the SOLs, as well as the different approaches taken by Tee-Jay and Freeman, offer a useful window into the reality, as opposed to the rhetoric, of the standards and testing movement. Standards-based reform rests on the idea that all students should learn similar skills and acquire similar knowledge. Testing is supposed to determine whether the standards are being met. Standards and testing currently dominate the world of public education and the parallel world of education commentary.

Standards-based reform, and the NCLB in particular, rest on the admirable notion that expectations should be high for *all* students. They also rest on the largely unproven but nonetheless plausible belief that sanctions for failure can help boost achievement by increasing the motivation to succeed. By demanding similar results at all schools, standards and testing had the potential to fulfill Nixon's pledge to make city schools as good as suburban ones. Standards and testing also had the potential to tie schools and districts together by subjecting all students within a state to the same standards and the same battery of tests. All schools would be dedicated to achieving the same challenging goals, which implied a commitment to ensure that all students would have the opportunity to reach those goals.

But politics again got in the way. It appears that state legislatures cannot afford, either politically or financially, to set truly challenging goals. Urban districts would have too far to travel, and identifying gaps in achievement creates pressure to close them. In addition, legislatures and local leaders have little to gain and much to lose by calling into question the quality of education at suburban schools, which also creates incentives to set the bar fairly low. Sanctions for failure only exacerbate the problem. Indeed, one of the ironies of the standards and testing movement, and especially the NCLB, is that the very mechanism that has been selected to improve achievement—various sanctions for failure—generates incentives to lower the goals.

This is precisely what has happened: academic goals, at least those measured by tests, have been set at a fairly low level. Good suburban schools, like Freeman, go well beyond these goals, while most urban schools, like Tee-Jay, struggle to meet them. Instead of linking these schools and districts together, standards and testing have essentially driven them apart, much in the same way that tracking drives low- and high-achieving students apart. One set of schools (mostly in suburban areas) downplays the tests, tries to minimize their impact on teaching, and goes beyond what is tested. The other set of schools (mostly in urban areas) focuses a great deal of time and attention on preparing explicitly for the tests.

Despite these stark and significant differences, test results nonetheless are used as the dominant if not sole measure of school success. The standards and testing movement in its current form is thus somewhat disingenuous. Instead of insisting that urban and suburban schools provide educations of similar quality, standards and testing work to define down what it means to provide a quality education. Put differently, and more bleakly, we are not even seriously trying to make urban schools as good as suburban ones; we are just pretending to by playing around with the definition of a quality education. As implemented, therefore, the standards and testing movement is of a piece with school finance reform and school choice. It offers some help to the cities, by trying to ensure that urban students learn the basics, but it imposes relatively few burdens on the suburbs.

Given this state of affairs, it is puzzling that school finance reform advocates see promise in hitching their wagon to the standards and testing movement. As I explain toward the end of this chapter, seeking from courts the funding needed to achieve very basic goals seems somewhat pointless. By contrast, in the few states where the goals are currently set at challenging levels, successful legal claims for funding—just like sanctions—will create perverse incentives for these states to lower their goals.

THE STANDARDS MOVEMENT AND THE
NO CHILD LEFT BEHIND ACT

Standards-based reform centers on the deceptively simple idea that states should set ambitious academic standards and periodically assess students to gauge their progress toward meeting those standards. The movement traces back to the 1983 publication of *A Nation at Risk*, which warned in ominous terms that public schools were being flooded by a "rising tide of mediocrity." Standards-based reform promised to raise the academic bar by requiring all schools within a state to meet uniform, challenging standards. So conceived, standards-based reform would promote not only excellence but equity by requiring all students, not just those in good suburban schools, to meet the same rigorous standards.[2]

Some states, beginning in the late 1980s, created standards that set out what students were expected to know and be able to do in each grade. They also devised tests ostensibly designed to assess results and provide a basis for rewarding or punishing schools and students. The federal government became involved in 1994, and since that time it has become the driving force in the standards and testing movement.[3]

In 1994, Congress enacted both the Goals 2000 Act and the Improving America's Schools Act (IASA). The former offered money to states willing to establish academic standards and conduct regular assessments of students. The latter reauthorized and reoriented Title I of the Elementary and Secondary Schools Act by embracing standards-based reform. In the past, Title I provided funds to support remedial instruction for disadvantaged students. Under the IASA, Title I funds now had to be used to create standards for all students.[4]

In order to receive Title I funds, states had to create "challenging" content and performance standards in at least reading and math, develop assessments that were aligned with those standards, and formulate plans to assist and ultimately sanction failing schools. Standards and assessments for Title I schools had to be the same as those established for all other schools within a state. In this way, the federal government hoped to ensure that states would hold all students to the same high expectations and hold all schools, regardless of their student population, accountable for failure.[5]

The NCLB, passed in 2001, is the latest and most important piece of federal education legislation. Indeed, the Act may be the most significant federal education law in our nation's history. It is certainly the most intrusive. The NCLB follows the same basic approach as the IASA, but it establishes more ambitious goals and places greater constraints on the states. States must still develop "challenging" content and performance standards, now not only in reading and math but also in science. States must also continue to use assessments that are aligned with those standards, and they must hold schools and school districts accountable for failing to meet ambitious achievement goals. But the frequency of tests has increased, and the sanctions for failure have become more severe.[6]

The NCLB requires annual testing in reading and math in grades three through eight. Reading and math must also be tested once in high school. Science was added to the list in 2007, and states now have to test students in science three times between grades three through twelve. The NCLB imposes a greater burden on elementary schools than on high schools, but its impact is felt in high schools as well. In addition, a number of states, including Virginia, require testing of high school students beyond what the NCLB requires. Twenty-three states, again including Virginia, also require students to pass one or more "exit" exams in order to graduate from high school.[7]

Test scores are the fuel that makes the NCLB (and state accountability systems) run. Pursuant to the NCLB, scores are tabulated for schools in the aggregate and also must be disaggregated for a number of subgroups, including migrant students, poor students, disabled students, English-language learners, and students from all major racial and ethnic groups. All of these scores are used to determine whether schools are making "adequate yearly progress" (AYP), which, in turn, is the linchpin of the NCLB.[8]

AYP is tied to whether a sufficient percentage of students each year score at the "proficient" level on state tests in reading, math, and science. The NCLB's ultimate goal is to have all students in every state scoring at the proficiency level by 2014. In the meantime, states must set interim goals that are supposed to rise periodically until 2014 (e.g., 70 percent the first year, 75 percent the third year, and so on). Schools that meet these interim goals are said to make AYP. Importantly, the student population as a whole, as well as each identified subgroup of students, must meet the same proficiency goal. Thus, if AYP requires that 75 percent of students pass a state test, a school will fail to make AYP if 80 percent of its students overall pass the test, but only 60 percent of its poor students do.[9]

The NCLB combines this forced-march stringency regarding performance with utter laxity when it comes to the actual tests themselves. States are free to establish their own standards, create their own tests, and determine for themselves the scores students must receive in order to be deemed "proficient." The harder the tests, or the more difficult the scoring system, the harder it is for schools to make AYP. If you are starting to see a problem here, you are on the right track.

Failing to make AYP is no fun for anyone. All schools within a state must make AYP, regardless of whether they receive Title I funding. Their failure to do

so must be publicized. Although the Act itself does not label such schools "failing," and instead uses the phrase "in need of improvement," local media reports
inevitably use the word "failing." Parents, teachers, and administrators tend to
have the same reaction and treat the failure to make AYP as a scarlet letter. The
principal of an elementary school in Utah, which failed to make AYP one year,
captured the reaction of many: "When principals get the results, they automatically look at the upper-righthand corner to see whether their school made AYP.
I looked at that space and about died."[10]

The Act's direct sanctions are reserved for schools that receive federal Title I
funding. This is only a subset of schools, but it is a surprisingly large one. In
order to maintain broad political support, Title I has spread money around
rather than concentrating it on the neediest schools and districts. The funding
formula makes schools with just a 2 percent poverty rate eligible for funding.
As a result, over half of all schools in the country receive some Title I funding.
Not all of these are in predominantly poor districts. Indeed, it is not uncommon for relatively "poor" schools in predominantly middle-class suburbs to
receive Title I funding.[11]

Schools and districts that receive federal funding and do not make AYP face
increasingly severe sanctions for every consecutive year of failure. After two
years, schools must develop a plan for improvement and are entitled to receive
"technical" assistance. Students in these schools are also allowed to choose
another public school, including a charter school, that has made AYP and is
located within the same district. After three years, students in failing schools are
entitled to receive free tutoring, either from a public or private provider. After
four years, schools must take more drastic measures, such as replacing school
staff. After five years, the ball game is basically over, as states must either convert
the school to a charter school, turn its management over to a private company,
or take over the school themselves.[12]

As a result of these combined state and federal efforts, all states have adopted
standards and standardized tests that drive their curricula and their accountability systems. In recent years, the standards and testing movement has generated a healthy amount of criticism, much of it focused on the NCLB. Critics
charge, among other things, that schools waste too much time teaching to the
test, which has the effect of dumbing down the curriculum in many schools;
that basing accountability on test scores provides an inaccurate measure of
schools and unfairly punishes schools with poor and minority students; and
that the federal government has failed to provide sufficient resources to states
to enable them to meet the demanding requirements of the NCLB. Much of
the criticism, especially of the dominance of standardized tests, comes from the
political left, although there is also some criticism from the right regarding

the unprecedented federal intrusion into an area traditionally reserved to the states.[13]

In light of this recent avalanche of criticism, it may seem hard at first blush to understand why the NCLB received overwhelming bipartisan support in Congress. It may also seem difficult to understand why school finance reform advocates have not joined the chorus denouncing the law. The initial appeal of the NCLB, however, as well as the support it continues to receive from school finance reformers, make sense from a political perspective. Understanding why is important, both because it helps link the NCLB to earlier education reforms and because it sheds light on the gap between the Act's potential and its reality.

THE POLITICAL APPEAL OF STANDARDS, TESTING, AND THE NCLB

As we have already seen, both liberal and conservative reformers have generally chosen the vision of Richard Nixon over that of Horace Mann. Advocates may still believe in the common school ideal, whereby children from all walks of life come together to be educated under one roof. But very few try to make it happen, and most seem convinced that efforts to do so are futile. Both liberals and conservatives appear to have resigned themselves to the seemingly unalterable fact that urban and suburban schools simply educate different groups of students. The only real question is what to do about the students in urban schools, and here liberals and conservatives tend to part ways.

For those on the left, more money tends to be the answer, and courts have been their favored institution. Liberal advocacy groups pushed for compensatory funding in "desegregation" cases after *Milliken II*, and such groups now push for "adequate" funding in state courts. Liberals tend to view urban teachers and administrators as capable and well-meaning but lacking the resources necessary to succeed. For those on the right, greater accountability, either through the market or through political sanctions, is the answer, and legislatures are their preferred institution. Conservatives tend to view urban teachers, teachers' unions, administrators, and the ubiquitous "urban bureaucracy" as bloated and corrupt. To them, urban districts have plenty of money; what they lack are the proper incentives to use that money wisely.

Given this political dynamic, it is not surprising that the NCLB appealed to a broad cross-section of legislators and advocates. The NCLB offered something to each group, with the promise of more to come. Both sides welcomed the embrace of higher standards and raised expectations. (Who wouldn't?) To those on the left, the Act also promised to increase federal funding and to make a priority of improving the performance of traditionally disadvantaged students. To those on the right, the Act promised real sanctions for failure. One of the sanctions also promoted intradistrict school choice, making it a sort of two-for-one provision from the perspective of conservatives. Neither side was completely satisfied, but there was something in the Act for everyone, and the bargain seemed worth the price.[14]

To farsighted advocates on the left and the right, there were additional reasons to support the Act, which are now coming into view. Anyone paying attention to public education could have predicted that the Act would mostly confirm what we already knew: suburban schools outperform urban schools on standardized tests. The NCLB would publicize this information, however, and make it more widely discussed and more easily understood. (It is easy to understand the label "failing.") This is precisely what has happened, as newspapers across the country have reported, with apparent surprise, that the NCLB is showing us just how poorly some urban schools are performing.

How is this information useful to advocates? It sets up the next fight, which is all about how to respond to what we mostly already knew. Those on the left could use this information to bolster their campaign for greater resources. Those on the right could use precisely the same information to bolster their campaign for more market-based accountability. The NCLB, from this perspective, simply set the stage for the real fight, and contending sides in this battle had reason to think that the information generated by the Act would help their cause. Liberals would argue that schools can reform if they have sufficient resources; conservatives would argue that public schools are incapable of reform on their own, which is why we need more market-based alternatives.

This is exactly what both sides are doing now, nearly nine years after the Act's passage. Those on the right are pushing to amend the NCLB to include vouchers for children in "failing" schools. This is part of what Clint Bolick, a prominent voucher proponent, calls the "toehold" strategy of choice advocates. The idea is to start small and to secure limited, politically feasible choice programs for the neediest students, and then to expand these programs over time. One can see evidence of this strategy within the NCLB itself. The Act provides students in schools that fail to make AYP the "right" to transfer to a successful public school in the same district. As anyone could have predicted, that "right" will be meaningless in many districts where there are not enough spots in successful schools. The answer? Push to expand choice to private schools.[15]

Those who advocate for including (only) vouchers might claim, as Bolick does, to be thinking only of the hapless students stuck in failing schools. But their ultimate aim—to inject more market-based competition into the public school arena—is not hard to detect. After all, if the goal is simply to give students more options, why limit the amendment to vouchers? Why not give students the right to transfer to public schools outside of their district and thus include suburban schools in the mix of schools to which urban students can transfer? The answer, though Bolick and other voucher proponents might be reluctant to admit it, seems to be that expanding choices for students is a means to an end, not an end in itself. The end is the greater privatization of public education.

Those on the left, meanwhile, are pursuing political and judicial campaigns for increased resources, and it is here that finance reform advocates come back into play. Both the political appeals and the funding lawsuits sound the same theme: If states and the federal government expect more from schools and students, they have an obligation to provide more resources. The Education Trust, a group that advocates for poor, urban students, makes the argument as clearly as anyone. At the conclusion of a report purporting to document a "funding gap" between schools that serve middle-class students and those that serve poor, minority students, the Education Trust makes the pitch for greater funding. Once academic standards and testing are adopted, the report argues, "these standards create a moral commitment (and, according to most state constitutions, a legal commitment) that policymakers will provide the policies, oversight, *and resources* to meet those standards." The emphasis on resources comes from the report's author.[16]

As the Education Trust report illustrates, some advocates seek to use standards and testing to their advantage not just in the political arena but also in court. It is for this reason that school finance reform advocates have hesitated to criticize standards and testing or the NCLB in particular. Indeed, some—including Michael Rebell, one of the leading advocates for school finance reform and an attorney in the New York funding case—have applauded standards and testing in general and the NCLB in particular. These advocates share Rebell's view that standards and test results provide both a rationale and a benchmark for greater funding.[17]

I will return at the conclusion of this chapter to school finance reform advocates and their effort to use standards and testing to their advantage in court cases. But first it is important to take a closer look at the promise and reality of standards-based reform and the NCLB. In doing so, it will become clear why advocates on both sides of the debate—those who want to use the NCLB for increased funding and those who want to use it to promote choice—are likely to be disappointed.

ADMIRABLE INTENTIONS AND
PLAUSIBLE INTUITIONS

Standards-based reform generally, and the NCLB in particular, promised at first to do what no reform has been able to do over the last half century: link the fate of urban and suburban students by by setting the same challenging goals for all schools within a state. Doing so, it seemed at first blush, would also help raise expectations, especially in urban schools.

This was an admirable idea, at least in the abstract. There is no doubt that many urban schools in the past set relatively low goals for their students. The prevalence of "social promotion" in urban schools, highlighted during President Clinton's term in office, was simply one especially visible manifestation of a systemic problem. Setting low expectations is not a great formula for promoting high achievement. To begin the process of making urban schools more like their suburban counterparts, it makes perfect sense to raise expectations and demand similar outcomes in both sets of schools.

It was also plausible to believe—but no more than this, really—that sanctioning schools for failure would help boost achievement. In theory, sanctions could help generate incentives to meet higher expectations. Most people, most of the time, respond to incentives. How they respond can be tricky to predict, but offering rewards or threatening punishment does tend to motivate.

What is important to recognize, however, is that these assumptions, while plausible, were (and remain) largely untested. Indeed, the evidence regarding the impact of sanctions is generally thin, and the little that exists is mixed. Empirical studies on the effectiveness of high-stakes testing, for example, reach contradictory results. Some find that students do better; others find little change and some bad side effects, including increased dropout rates. Similarly, studies of sanctions imposed on schools, such as replacement of staff or administrators, reach mixed conclusions. Some show improved test scores; others reveal little to no change. This is true for studies of schools taken over by the state and studies of schools taken over by private companies. Even the "success" stories typically reveal fairly small gains. Few reconstituted urban schools, for example, show marked improvements.[18]

The accountability provisions that form a core part of the NCLB and of state testing regimes are thus largely unproven. As one commentator observed of the NCLB's passage, at best one could say that there was "no conclusive evidence that [accountability] did not work." The lack of a solid empirical basis for these provisions is nicely revealed by the quality of debate surrounding the enactment of the NCLB. Both sides tended to rely on aphorism instead of empiricism. Opponents of the legislation, for example, repeatedly pointed out that "[y]ou don't fatten a pig by weighing it more often," drawing apparently from the folk wisdom of farmers. Rod Paige, who was secretary of education at the time of the bill's passage, replied with a sports analogy: "If you want to win a football game, you have to first keep score."[19]

There is nothing wrong, per se, about experimenting with new reforms. But it is important to recognize that sanctions, like choice and funding, do not have a track record of success for improving schools of concentrated poverty. Critics of school funding litigation are quick to point out the lack of evidence suggesting a strong link between increased funding and increased achievement, usually as a way to bolster their case for increasing accountability instead. But it is not as if there is a lot of evidence showing a systematic relationship between increased accountability and increased performance. In fact, there is none.

The case for relying on sanctions to boost achievement thus rests on intuition—and perhaps ideology—as much as anything else. This approach rests on the belief that the problem with some schools has to do with motivation— on the belief that students, teachers, and administrators are not really trying as hard as they might. This is a plausible intuition, but it is equally plausible to believe that the problem lies elsewhere. Indeed, those who believe that more funding is the answer harbor a different intuition: that the problem at bottom is not one of motivation but of deprivation. There is good reason to believe that this is true, at least in some places. There is even better reason to believe that there are multiple causes, including both inadequate motivation and insufficient resources, for the poor performance of high-poverty schools.

Testing students to measure progress in meeting standards is also a completely sensible idea. But sanctioning schools based solely on test scores is a questionable practice, for at least two reasons. First, as already mentioned, tests do not tell us everything we need or want to know about schools, and they never will. Not all skills are or can be tested. It is clear that students need to learn basic skills, like reading and math, but it is equally clear that they need other skills in order to succeed in college or at work. Indeed, employers often mention so-called soft skills like being responsible, having a strong work ethic, being a good leader, and being able to work with a team as equal in importance to academic skills and knowledge. Yet states do not, and perhaps cannot, test these skills.[20]

Similarly, standardized tests rarely assess creativity, complex reasoning ability, or the ability to apply knowledge and skills to a new situation. Tests also do not assess the degree to which students are being prepared for democratic participation and civic responsibility, although these are often identified as crucial missions for public schools. Some of these skills cannot be assessed very easily, and few can be assessed by using a standardized test. To judge schools by test scores alone, therefore, is clearly to miss a lot. Indeed, for all the emphasis on testing, there is relatively little evidence to show a correlation between "passing" state tests and future success in college or in the workforce.[21]

The second reason why sanctioning schools for poor test scores is questionable is that schools are not entirely responsible for those scores, whether good or bad. Poor students begin school behind their middle-income counterparts. Those gaps remain or increase over time, and middle-income students generally outperform poor students at every grade level. When a predominantly middle-income school makes AYP and a high-poverty school does not, part of the explanation lies with the students, not the schools. The middle-income school may deserve less credit, and the high-poverty school less blame, than the NCLB assumes.

To see this, imagine two fourth grade classes, one in a middle-income school and the other in a high-poverty school. Imagine further that the students in the high-poverty school start the year reading at the first-grade level and end the year reading at the third-grade level, while the students in the middle-income school start and end the year reading at the fourth-grade level. The high-poverty school (assuming similar performances throughout the school) would not make AYP, while the middle-income school would, even though fourth-grade students in the former progressed further during the year than students in the latter. In sanctioning the high-poverty school while applauding the middle-income school, the NCLB may be getting it exactly backwards.

PERVERSE INCENTIVES AND THE POLITICS OF IMPLEMENTATION

The incentive structure of the NCLB makes testing even less reliable as a measure of school quality, and here we get to the real problem. Under the NCLB and state accountability systems, schools and districts face sanctions if their students do not pass state tests. At the same time, states remain free under the federal law to design their own tests and determine what scores count as passing—or "proficient," to use the Act's language. Sanctions can create incentives to achieve high goals, but they can also create incentives to game the system. By punishing states for not meeting testing goals that they themselves get to set, the NCLB gives states both the motive and the opportunity to set low goals.

Why members of Congress did not see this (or care about it if they did) is difficult to say for sure, although there are several possible explanations. To begin, the basic structure of the Act is a product of the traditional respect for state control over education. National standards and tests were political nonstarters, which meant that states had to be given authority to set their own. In addition, the Act requires a random sample of fourth- and eighth-grade students in every state to take the National Assessment of Educational Progress (NAEP) tests in reading and math. Many in and outside Congress believed— overly optimistically, it now seems—that discrepancies between NAEP scores and scores on state tests would shame states into setting ambitious goals. Finally, there is no discounting the attraction of a law that appears on its surface to address a problem, even if the law's details leave much to be desired.[22]

That said, the perverse incentives created by the NCLB are hard to miss. Given the sanctions involved, and the publicity they bring to schools, to districts, and ultimately to states, state legislatures have little incentive to establish truly challenging academic goals. The harder the goals are to meet, obviously, the more schools will fail to meet them. It is politically untenable for a legislature to allow a large portion of state schools to be labeled as failing. It is especially risky, politically, to have a significant number of suburban schools with otherwise good reputations labeled as failing.[23]

It would also be risky to create tests or assessment systems that highlight very large gaps between urban and suburban school systems. After all, identifying the gap implies a commitment to close it. If the gap exposed is large, the costs of closing it—whether measured politically or financially—will necessarily be higher.[24]

These political considerations have worked to keep standards and tests from becoming too ambitious. A number of states, for example, have lowered the scores necessary to be considered "proficient" for purposes of the NCLB. State tests are criterion-referenced, not norm-referenced. This means that students are not compared to one another but to a single proficiency benchmark, which they either make or do not make. An important issue, obviously, is just where that benchmark is set.

More than a dozen states have tinkered with their scoring systems in order to increase the number of students who "pass" the tests. Tennessee provides as good an illustration as any other. Several years in a row, Tennessee lowered the number of questions students had to answer correctly in order to be deemed proficient. In 2003, for example, eighth-graders had to answer thirty-six out of seventy questions on the reading test—51 percent—to be considered proficient. In 2004 that number dropped to twenty-nine out of sixty-eight, or 43 percent, and in 2005 the number dropped again to twenty-two out of fifty-five, or 40 percent.[25]

Additional evidence that states have set low bars is found in studies that compare results on state tests with results on the NAEP. The NAEP does not align with any particular state's standards. It is insteaddesigned to test what all students in fourth and eighth grade ought to know and be able to do in reading and math. Comparisons between NAEP scores and scores on state tests are thus imperfect. A state may emphasize somewhat different material than is tested on the NAEP. In addition, the NAEP test is not a high-stakes one, so it is not clear how seriously schools or students treat it. Finally, the scores necessary to be deemed "proficient" on the NAEP are not based on science but rest on the subjective judgment of those who created the test. Some believe that the proficiency bar for the NAEP is unreasonably high. These caveats notwithstanding, the NAEP, commonly dubbed "the nation's report card," provides at least a rough benchmark for assessing the rigor of state tests, if only because the gaps between state and NAEP test results vary across states.[26]

Several years ago, Paul Peterson and Frederick Hess, two prominent education commentators and editors of the periodical *Education Next*, tabulated the differences between the percentage of students deemed proficient on state tests and those deemed proficient on the NAEP. They assigned a letter grade to each state, which reflected how much easier it was for students to pass the state test than the NAEP. An A grade reflected consistency between the two tests, while an F represented a wide divergence. Only three states earned an A; the vast majority received a C or a D. The average difference was 31 percent, meaning that 31 percent more students passed state tests than the NAEP, on average. More recent reports have found similarly wide discrepancies between state and NAEP results.[27]

Although the comparison between the NAEP and state tests is not perfect, the consistency of the pattern provides good reason to suspect that most states have not set very high goals. Looking at the performance of particular states adds to the suspicion. In 2006, for example, Mississippi reported that 89 percent of its fourth-grade students were proficient in reading, which was the highest percentage in the nation. No one honestly believed, however, that Mississippi was really first in the nation in teaching young students to read, and their NAEP scores reinforced the skepticism: only 18 percent of Mississippi fourth-graders were proficient according the NAEP. This placed Mississippi next-to-last in the country in fourth-grade reading scores on the NAEP. Perhaps the NAEP proficiency bar is set too high, but there can be little doubt that Mississippi's proficiency bar is set too low.[28]

A CLOSER LOOK AT VIRGINIA

In Virginia, there is more direct proof that the bar has been set fairly low. When Governor George Allen signed legislation establishing the SOLs (which, confusingly, is the term used for both the standards themselves and the tests), he indicated that these standards established "*minimum* expectations for learning and achievement at each grade level." He also encouraged schools to "rise above these standards." This point was echoed recently by another Virginia governor, Tim Kaine. In a 2006 speech, he acknowledged that "the Standards of Learning have raised the academic floor and enabled many students to reach higher" but emphasized that "the SOLs have always been intended as *minimum* standards for competency." Dr. Pruden, while principal at Freeman High School, also repeatedly emphasized that the SOLs establish minimum standards.[29]

The SOLs, however, are the standards and tests Virginia uses to comply with the NCLB and to assess whether schools are making AYP. The NCLB demands that states establish "challenging standards," and the entire thrust of the legislation is to bring all students to a high level of achievement. Yet in Virginia and elsewhere, the actual standards are set at a basic level. This discrepancy, which is hidden in plain view, exposes the hollow core of the NCLB. As mentioned earlier, standards and testing can only be as good as the standards and tests. Virginia's tests are not terrible. Outside reviewers gave Virginia a score of 3.5 out of 5 for test content and a 3 for test rigor, both of which were slightly above average. But the tests are far from demanding.[30]

In addition to giving tests that are not especially difficult, Virginia is a generous grader. The "proficiency" bar has been set at a fairly low level, and, as in other states, has been lowered over time, at least in some subjects. Students are typically expected, across high school tests, to answer roughly 50 percent of questions correctly in order to be considered proficient. This will undoubtedly seem low to many readers, given that a 50 percent score earns an "F" on the traditional A–F grading scale. Unfortunately, the way the proficiency targets are set does not dispel this impression.[31]

Virginia uses what is called "the modified-Angoff procedure" to determine proficiency targets—or cut scores, as they are often called—which gives the process a patina of scientific precision. This procedure, according to the Virginia Board of Education, "has been widely used on multiple-choice tests for over 25 years." The process is this: "Judges" learn how the standards are set and take sample tests, and then they discuss the meaning of "proficient" and whatever other benchmarks (e.g., "basic" or "advanced") might be used. Judges then "independently examine each question on the test, think of 100 barely proficient students, and estimate the proportion (percent) of barely proficient students who should answer the question correctly."[32]

The judge's individual scores are averaged across test questions for a single cut score, and after repeating the process several times, the judges ultimately make a recommendation to the Virginia Board of Education. The board typically accepts the median proficiency score of the judges. It is hard to know exactly how these judges go about imagining the performance of "barely profi-cient" students, or how (or even why) they determine the percentage of barely proficient students who will answer a particular question correctly—given that by definition these students are supposed to be similar in their abilities. But surely the judges, as well as the board of education, must be aware that demanding higher scores will make more schools look bad. One need not be a conspiracy theorist to believe that this recognition has led to the consistent pattern of only asking students to answer about half of all questions correctly. Indeed, the dynamic in Virginia and other states, as some commentators described, "is reminiscent of shooting an arrow into a wall and then drawing a target around it."[33]

If nothing else, it is clear that there is not much hard science behind the setting of cut scores, which obviously leaves room for other factors to play a role. One state board of education member, for example, said of the decision to set the cut score for history tests at 50 percent that "it would look bad to require less than 30 out of 60, but I would not want more than 30." He went on to say: "In World History I, for example, which starts at the beginning of time and runs through 1500, part of that was the Crusades. Someone could have a really good unit on the Crusades and know it cold, yet there might not be a question on the test. It would be unfair to require more than 50 percent." The gap in logic in this statement is easily bridged by political considerations.[34]

WHAT DO TEST SCORES TELL US?

With all of this understood, it becomes possible to appreciate how little test scores really tell us. Freeman and Tee-Jay serve as useful examples. To graduate from high school, students in Virginia must pass at least six tests—two in English, one in math, one in laboratory science, one in history or social science, and one in an elective. The tests are usually offered for the first time in tenth grade, and students who fail have multiple opportunities to retake the test. Students can earn an advanced degree by passing nine tests. Virginia thus gives a lot of tests, which means that there are a lot of test results.[35]

Freeman and Tee-Jay students are not as far apart on these tests as one might initially expect, at least when the percentage of "passing" students is compared. Looking at 2007–8 results, for example, 90 percent of Tee-Jay students passed the English test, compared to 97 percent of Freeman's students. At Tee-Jay, 89 percent passed math, compared to 92 percent at Freeman. Scores were similarly close in history and science. Freeman outscored Tee-Jay on each test, but usually not by all that much. If one were focusing just on pass rates, which is *precisely* what state and federal accountability systems focus on, Tee-Jay and Freeman compare pretty favorably.[36]

A closer look suggests that the reality is otherwise. On state tests, students can earn a score of "advanced," as opposed to a score of "proficient," by answering more questions correctly. Advanced scores generally require that students answer 70–90 percent of the questions correctly.[37] The gap between students at Tee-Jay and Freeman earning an advanced score is much wider than the gap between those earning a proficient score. In English, for example, there is only a five-point difference in proficiency rates, but a twenty-one-point difference in advanced scores. In Algebra II, there is only a one point difference in proficiency rates, but a twenty-eight-point difference between those who earned advanced scores. Similarly large gaps appear in the advanced scores reported for other tests.[38]

SAT and AP test results also indicate that proficiency rates on the SOLs fail to capture much of the picture. Two-thirds of Freeman juniors took the SAT in 2008, compared to slightly fewer than half of their counterparts at Tee-Jay. The average SAT score at Freeman was 1656, which exceeds the state average of 1522; the average score at Tee-Jay was 1306, well below the state average. A similar portrait is revealed by AP scores. Over 25 percent of Freeman students took an AP exam in 2004. At Tee-Jay, only 15 percent did. The bigger difference was in the scores. The AP exams are scored on a 1–5 scale, with 5 considered outstanding and 3 considered passing. Nearly four in five students (78 percent) at Freeman received a 3 or better. At Tee-Jay, only one in twenty did.[39]

In addition, a higher percentage of Freeman seniors (58 percent in 2008) graduate with an advanced diploma than do Tee-Jay seniors (41 percent in 2008). The overall graduation rates for the two schools, as reported, are similar at around 80 percent, but these figures are not entirely trustworthy. Virginia's method of calculating graduation rates, like that of other states, was unreliable for years because it simply counted the percentage of seniors who graduated, which obviously did not account for those who never made it to their senior year. Virginia adopted a new system in 2008, which will track students through high school and should offer more accurate information, but it will take a few more years before its effects can be determined. In the meantime, it may help to know that state-reported graduation rates are inevitably higher than those calculated by independent researchers. A recent analysis performed for *Education Week*, for example, put the national graduation rate at 70 percent, the rate for suburban districts at 75 percent, and the rate for urban districts at 60 percent. Rates for some urban districts, and especially for some subgroups of students in urban districts—black males, for example—are even lower. It is possible that

both Freeman and Tee-Jay are above average in their actual graduation rates—
and that Tee-Jay in particular is well-above average—but it also seems possible
that the reported rates are not entirely accurate. Time will tell.[40]

A higher percentage of Freeman students also enroll in four-year colleges.
The most recent figures, from 2007, indicated that roughly 70 percent of Freeman graduates planned to attend a four-year college. Less than half—47 percent—of Tee-Jay graduates planned to do so. A larger percentage of Tee-Jay
students than Freeman students planned to attend a two-year college (26 percent versus 18 percent), but overall college attendance rates still pointed in
Freeman's favor. Of all 2007 graduates of Freeman, 88 percent planned to attend
either a two- or four-year college, compared to 73 percent of Tee-Jay students.
Unfortunately, no one has tracked the students since that time to check whether
they followed through on their plans, so these numbers, too, are a bit
unreliable.[41]

These figures alone do not explain their cause. Advanced diploma percentages and college enrollment rates, for example, do not indicate *why* more students at Freeman than Tee-Jay graduate with advanced diplomas and go on to
college. Similarly, the test results do not indicate why more students at Freeman
are taking the SAT and AP tests and why more of them are doing better on
those tests than students at Tee-Jay. These are difficult and, one would think,
critical questions. But they are not even raised if one concentrates solely on
proficiency scores, which give the impression that Tee-Jay is doing pretty well in
comparison to Freeman.

And here we get to the heart of the problem. State and federal accountability
systems all focus on proficiency scores, but these scores do not tell us much
about the quality of education provided at a particular school. We might be
able to conclude that schools with "good" test scores have taught their students
the basics. But we will have no idea, based on proficiency scores alone, how one
school compares to another in going beyond the basics.

The Illusion of Equal Opportunity

Among all of the problems associated with standards and testing, the false
impression conveyed by state test scores is perhaps the most insidious. It is both
too tempting and too easy to lull the public into believing that education is
improving, and that urban schools in particular are getting better, by pointing
to rising test scores. There is little incentive among state or local officials to
emphasize that the tests only cover the basics and that, as a result, they do not
tell us that much. (Governor Allen's and Governor Kaine's comments about the

SOLs were exceptional in this regard, but even these comments indicated that going beyond the SOLs was aspirational rather than strictly required.)

Indeed, instead of emphasizing that the tests determine whether students are minimally competent in some fairly basic skills, states say that students who pass the tests are "proficient" in the subject tested. That does not sound very basic. In addition, states do not exactly go out of their way to explain how proficiency scores are set. Virginia, for example, publishes "report cards" for each school, which contain a good deal of information about passage rates on state tests, but there is nothing in the reports that indicates how cut scores have been calculated. One assumes that many parents would be surprised to learn that answering just half of all questions on an achievement test, which is supposed to measure how much students have learned, is considered a passing score.

The reports also do not mention how many opportunities students have to pass the tests. As explained to me by William Flammia, a teacher who retired from Tee-Jay but still helps with test preparation, students who fail initially have multiple opportunities to retake the tests. Students who fail during the academic year can retake the test within days of their first try. If they fail again, they can retake the test two more times during the summer, after attending a tutoring session that is focused exclusively on passing the test. One has to wonder whether the student who passes the test on his third or fourth attempt has actually learned the material being tested, or has simply learned how to succeed on the test, which is not the same thing.[42]

Social scientists who study education often add to the false impression about the importance of test scores by using these scores as their measurement of school success or failure. These reports then get translated by the media into stories about what works and what does not. All the while, the floor becomes the ceiling and what are really minimum competency tests become, to the media and general public, comprehensive examinations.

The problem goes beyond impressions. The false sense of accomplishment has political ramifications as well. It becomes harder to persuade legislatures that more must be done for schools if test scores are the measure of quality and test scores are high. This is true regardless of the desired reform. Those who want to use the NCLB to secure more funding, for example, as well as those who want to use it to promote more choice will have a harder time making their cases if test scores are the sole measure of success. Both Education Trust and Clint Bolick are thus likely to be disappointed. The same is true for those who believe more effort should be made to bring better teachers into urban classrooms. If test scores are already high and are the accepted proxy for school quality, the case for additional improvements is harder to make. Legislators may be well aware that test scores are misleading, but if that is not widely known, pointing to high test scores is a convenient way to declare success and move on.

I came across a concrete example of this phenomenon in Richmond. A teacher at Tee-Jay told me that the Richmond School District required Tee-Jay to accept more students from outside of its attendance zone because of Tee-Jay's "success" on the SOLs. From the perspective of the school district, Tee-Jay was doing well because of its test scores—or at least it should be treated as if it were doing well because of its test scores. From this teacher's perspective, however, Tee-Jay clearly remained a struggling school, and to ask Tee-Jay to take on even more challenges simply because it posted good test scores for a year or two made no sense at all.

Cities and Suburbs

Many urban schools, like Tee-Jay, struggle to meet the testing goals that have been set for them. Newspapers are filled with stories about "teaching to the test," and teachers report diverting time and attention from subjects that are not tested so as to focus on those that are. This is a phenomenon that affects a lot of schools, but it appears to be pervasive and more intensely felt in high-poverty urban schools than in relatively affluent suburban ones.[43]

High-performing suburban schools seem to have learned to live with standards and testing. Initially, stories of suburban backlash in places like Scarsdale, New York appeared in newspapers around the country. Suburban schools claimed that testing served to cheapen, not enrich, the quality of education offered at local schools. Some commentators thought the early grumblings signaled an impending suburban revolt over testing. But the revolt has not (yet) occurred. In its place, one detects a grudging acceptance and a commitment to minimize the damage by spending as little time as possible on test preparation.[44]

One also sees movement in the Department of Education to give suburban schools a break. In 2008, the department created a pilot program that allows participating states to reduce the sanctions for schools that miss AYP because of a subpar performance by one or more subgroups, as opposed to schools that miss AYP because aggregate test scores are low. The program is not explicitly aimed at suburban schools, but these schools are much more likely than urban schools to miss AYP because of the test scores of a subgroup of students. Indeed, this pilot program seems perfectly tailored to insulate generally good suburban schools from the stigma of having their entire school labeled as "failing," and it is also seems perfectly consistent, if not eerily so, with the "save the cities, spare the suburbs" approach of other reforms.[45]

The contrast in approaches between schools that worry about the tests and schools that are more confident is obvious at Tee-Jay and Freeman, as described briefly in the opening pages of this chapter. Test results, Mr. Flammia told me, are "big-time important" at Tee-Jay, a point confirmed by the principal. Everyone feels the pressure, especially those who teach courses that are tested. As a result, teachers at Tee-Jay tend to teach to the test. Students spend a good deal of time preparing specifically for the test, and there is often not time to do much more than this, especially in the weeks, if not months, before the tests are administered.[46]

Test scores at Tee-Jay have risen over the past several years, and Tee-Jay now outperforms other schools in the district. Those victories have been difficult to achieve, and teachers and administrators are justly proud of the accomplishment. But it is important to put the accomplishment in perspective. The "good" test scores signify that Tee-Jay students are mastering the basics. At Freeman, by contrast, teachers and students alike *expect* that most students will pass the SOL tests. The goal in most classes is to go beyond what is covered by the SOLs.

One might reasonably think it sensible for Tee-Jay to focus on the basics because it must, and for Freeman to go beyond the basics because it can. Why introduce students to sophisticated subjects and skills before making sure they understand the basics? The point is intuitively attractive, although the issue is actually more complicated. Some educational theorists believe that basic and more sophisticated skills and knowledge need to be taught together, with one reinforcing the other. If nothing else, mixing things up a bit, as opposed to ceaseless drilling about the basics, works to retain student interest.[47]

Even if we assume, however, that schools should begin with the basics, the key point to recognize is that some schools begin *and end* with the basics, whereas others go well beyond them. This is not a byproduct of the current regime of standards and testing. It is the direct result. What is worse, this result is being peddled as equitable, when in reality it is anything but.

Standards and testing were designed, in part, to eliminate low-track classes where students were taught a watered-down curriculum that emphasized basic skills and knowledge. But standards and testing, as implemented, have supplemented in-school tracking with across-school tracking. Some schools teach to the tests; other schools teach well beyond them. Indeed, it is not a stretch to suggest that we are back to square one in terms of equalizing educational opportunities. Those who challenged segregation envisioned black and white students attending the same schools to ensure that they would receive the same opportunities—exposed to the same teachers, enrolled in the same courses, expected to do the same level of work. That vision was never fully realized, as even students in integrated schools tended to end up in segregated classrooms. Today, however, the vision itself has largely been abandoned.

Teachers know this. A Maryland teacher who has worked in both a high-poverty, mostly minority school and a wealthy white one described his experiences in a 2007 op-ed in the *Washington Post*. In the school that taught mostly poor and minority students, pressure to raise test scores led to a relentless focus on basic skills and test preparation. "Poor and minority students spend hours repeating 'B buh ball' and two plus two equals four," and "administrators require teachers to strictly adhere to a months-long test-prep program." In the wealthy white school, the students studied the "Underground Railroad, brainstormed plans to save wolves from extinction and performed dances based on retellings of Cinderella. The children learned to think and they loved it." As this teacher pointed out:

> At the end of the year, test results will come out for these two schools. Educators and politicians will trumpet any reduction of the so-called achievement gap. This misses the point. Students will leave these two schools and schools like them with a widely varying set of skills. As the achievement gap is being reduced, another gap is being created. Students in largely wealthy and white schools are learning to ask larger questions; students in poor and minority schools are only being taught to answer smaller ones.

As two (friendly) critics of the NCLB recently concluded, if the law continues unchanged, "rich kids will study philosophy and art, music and history, while their poor peers fill in bubbles on test sheets." The schools with rich kids will "spawn the next generation of tycoons, political leaders, inventors, authors, artists and entrepreneurs. The less lucky masses will see narrower opportunities."[48]

To be sure, bringing low-performing students to the proficiency level on state tests represents a genuine accomplishment in many districts and an improvement over past practices. But even this meaningful improvement, where achieved, still leaves a large gap between the kind of education offered at a typical suburban school and the kind offered at a typical urban school. Proficiency does not guarantee equal opportunity; it promises the basics. President Nixon, in the early 1970s, proposed the compromise of keeping urban and suburban schools separate but working to make them equal. We have compromised his compromise.

A PUZZLING EMBRACE

As mentioned earlier, courts have played a fairly minor role in the standards and testing movement, even less of a role than they have played in school choice battles. There have been a few minor legal challenges to the NCLB, but so far none have succeeded. This is not where the action is or will be, as the legislation is not vulnerable to plausible legal challenges, and no litigants seem interested in persuading courts to *require* standards and testing as part of a student's right to education.[49]

Instead, the real action is in the school finance arena, where some litigants are hoping to use standards and testing to their advantage. In chapter 4, I described the somewhat disappointing results of school finance litigation and questioned whether increased resources could close the achievement gap between urban and suburban schools. Here I want to accept, for the sake of argument, that more money will help and focus instead on the strategic question: Will relying on standards and testing in school finance litigation, as its proponents assume, actually produce more resources for needy schools?

The emerging consensus among advocates and commentators, as discussed in chapter 4, is that school finance litigants should pursue the right to an adequate education, as opposed to the right to equitable resources. Those who believe in adequacy also tend to believe that litigants should rely on state academic standards to help make their case. The theory is straightforward. When enforcing the right to an adequate education, courts must define the right. To do so, they need to identify the outcomes that constitute an adequate education. They must then work backward to determine the resources necessary to achieve those outcomes—or, more precisely, the resources necessary to enable schools and students a fair opportunity to achieve those outcomes.[50]

One obvious difficulty facing courts is how to define an adequate education. Describing the outcomes students should achieve is not only conceptually difficult; it also strains the institutional capacity of courts. Why should courts, as opposed to legislatures, define what we expect children to know and do?

This is where standards and testing come in. Academic standards can relieve courts of the onerous task of defining adequacy, because the standards themselves essentially define what counts as an adequate education. Instead of usurping the legislature's authority, courts can simply enforce the goals the legislature has articulated. Courts that rely on standards would still have some work to do: they would have to determine whether schools are meeting the standards and what remedy to order if schools are falling short. But at least the knotty definitional problem would be solved. This would help school finance plaintiffs, so the theory continues, because courts would be more willing to wade into and remain in school funding disputes if they could rely on a legislative benchmark for adequacy.[51]

Commentators and advocates have high hopes for the marriage of standards and school finance litigation. Peter Schrag, a journalist who recently wrote a book on school finance litigation, nicely captures the mood of optimism. "The effort to raise academic standards and accountability in the public schools," Schrag contends, "and then use those standards to calculate the resources need-ed to achieve them is both a radical idea in American education and probably the most helpful step for poor kids since the *Brown* decision a half-century ago."[52]

Not likely. In fact, and contrary to the conventional wisdom, relying on stan-dards in school finance litigation seems like a poor strategy for plaintiffs, for a number of reasons. To begin, courts that rely on standards to define adequacy will, at some point, consult test scores to determine whether students are meeting the standards and thus receiving an adequate education. Tests do not perfectly match the academic standards in most states, but they offer the best existing proof of whether those standards are being met. Test scores will thus be difficult for courts to ignore.

Reliance on test scores, however, will most likely help defendants, not plain-tiffs. To see why, imagine a state where some school districts spend significantly more than others but test scores nonetheless show that most schools in the state are meeting, or close to meeting, the standards. Under the current approach in most school funding cases, the resource disparities themselves could very well be enough to trigger corrective action by courts. Under a standards-based approach, however, good test scores could lead courts to ignore those dispari-ties. After all, the underlying theory of this approach is that outcomes matter more than inputs. If adequate results, as evidenced by adequate test scores, can be achieved within a system marked by disparate resources, presumably the constitutional standard would be satisfied.

Even if test scores are poor, plaintiffs would not necessarily prevail. They would still have to show that the poor scores were caused at least in part by insufficient funding. Plaintiffs would succeed in their quest for funding if, but only if, that causal link could be established. Thus, poor test scores might not guarantee a victory for plaintiffs, while good test scores might well guarantee a defeat. And we should expect to see plenty of good test scores, given how many states have already made tests easy to pass.

If this assessment seems overly pessimistic, consider three recent decisions from three different states. In 1989, the Texas Supreme Court held that the state constitution, which required the legislature to create an "efficient system" of public schools, demanded substantially equal resources for schools. "In other words," the court held, "districts must have substantially equal access to similar revenues per pupil at similar levels of tax effort." The focus of the opinion was on resource disparities among school districts, and the court made it clear that these "inequalities are...directly contrary to the constitutional vision of effi-ciency." The court indicated that localities could supplement state funding,

provided that the state maintained an "efficient system" of schools by preventing the supplemental funding from generating substantial inequalities among
districts.[53]

By 2005, however, the Texas Supreme Court had altered its focus from disparities in inputs to results. The constitutional standard, the court now emphasized, was "plainly result-oriented," creating "no duty to fund public education
at any level other than what is required to achieve a general diffusion of knowledge." (The last phrase, "general diffusion of knowledge," comes directly from
the state constitution and roughly translates to "an adequate education.")The
court went on to reject the plaintiffs' argument that existing funding disparities, and disparities in educational achievement, were unconstitutional. Why?
Because test scores were rising.[54]

The court recognized that there were still funding disparities, and that funding might not be sufficient to meet all curricular demands. It also recognized
that there were wide gaps in performance, that dropout rates were high, that
relatively few students were prepared to enter college, and that there was a
shortage of highly qualified teachers. But none of this ultimately mattered,
"because the undisputed evidence is that standardized test scores have steadily
improved over time, even while tests and curriculum have been made more
difficult." Because the legislature was not acting arbitrarily in determining the
funding necessary for students to perform well on the tests, the court was
satisfied.[55]

The North Carolina Supreme Court, in a recent decision, also placed a good
deal of emphasis on test scores. The court used these scores, along with other
output measures like graduation rates, to gauge whether the state was meeting
its constitutional requirement. The court acknowledged that a disproportionate number of "at-risk" students failed to achieve proficiency on standardized
tests. But this was not enough to deem the funding system unconstitutional.
The low scores simply suggested a problem. It remained necessary to determine
whether poor test performance was caused by a lack of resources. The plaintiffs,
in other words, still had the burden to "show that their failure to obtain [a constitutionally sufficient] education was due to the State's failure to provide them
with the opportunity to obtain one." Ultimately, the court refrained from ordering the legislature to provide more funds and required only that the state "assess
its education-related allocations" to local schools.[56]

In the most recent funding decision from the Court of Appeals in New York,
that state's highest court, test scores also played a role. The state contended that
rising test scores proved that New York City students were receiving a constitutionally sufficient education. The court's response was telling. The court began
by detailing the resource disparities between New York City schools and the

remainder of the state. The court then indicated that "a showing of good test results and graduation rates among [New York City] students—the 'outputs'—might indicate that they somehow still receive the opportunity" for a constitutionally sufficient education. It went on to conclude that the test scores, contrary to the state's assertion, were not good enough to excuse the input disparities. But notice that the court tacitly accepted the state's premise that decent test scores could excuse inadequate or unequal resources. And notice, too, that it was the *state* that sought to use test scores in order to *defend* the funding system.[57]

These three decisions are cautionary tales for school finance plaintiffs and their attorneys. All suggest that relying on test scores might hurt plaintiffs' chances. If the test scores are good, courts can use them to excuse resource inadequacies and disparities. Even if the test scores are bad, plaintiffs will only succeed if they can prove a connection between funding levels and test scores. Under the approach followed by most school finance courts today, resource disparities in themselves can prove a constitutional violation. It is hard to see, from a plaintiff's perspective, how relying on standards and testing represents an improvement over the current approach.

True believers in the marriage of standards and school finance litigation might respond by arguing that courts do not necessarily need to rely on test scores to define or assess adequacy. Instead, courts could rely on the standards themselves and on costing-out studies to determine the cost of meeting the standards. As described in chapter 4, costing-out studies seek to determine the resources schools need to meet the state's academic standards. Relying on costing-out studies could help plaintiffs because standards are often more ambitious and far-reaching than the tests themselves. Thus, focusing on the resources needed to meet the standards rather than those needed just to pass the tests could lead to greater funding.

This is not a completely implausible scenario. Some courts have already ordered costing-out studies. It is possible that more will. It is also possible, as proponents hope, that courts that order costing-out studies will focus on those studies and ignore or downplay test results.[58]

But it is unlikely. Costing-out studies, after all, are not hard science. At best, they are reasonably good guesses about what schools need to meet state standards. They are inevitably controversial and contested. Legislatures defending current funding schemes have and will continue to offer their own costing-out studies to counter those presented by plaintiffs. A court faced with dueling costing-out studies might very well find solace in the relative certainty of test scores and use these to gauge the adequacy of resources. This is especially true if test scores are already fairly high. A court would have to be strong-willed indeed to order more funding based on estimates of what is needed to meet state standards when test scores suggest that the standards are already being met.

Relying on standards to guide school finance litigation seems particularly unwise for most urban districts. Recall that most urban schools are funded above the state average. Some, like Richmond, are also funded at higher levels than their suburban neighbors. The relatively high amounts spent by districts like Richmond might still be insufficient to provide their students with the chance to succeed at the level of their suburban peers. But if test score disparities among schools in these districts are not especially great, as is true in the Richmond area, and if test scores form the basis of school finance litigation, plaintiffs are going to have an especially difficult time persuading a court that city schools need even more funding.

Relying on legislative standards to define adequacy suffers from at least one additional flaw: it creates perverse incentives for states. As already described, imposing sanctions for failing schools creates incentives for states to lower their sights by making tests easier to pass. Precisely the same incentive would be created if states were forced to provide sufficient resources to ensure an adequate opportunity to meet truly challenging standards and pass truly difficult tests. One way to make education cost less, after all, is to lower the goals. Thus, even if costing-out studies are followed by courts, and even if those studies indicate the need for greater resources, states would still have an out: make education cost less by lowering standards and making tests easier to pass.

Indeed, the parallels between this litigation strategy and the NCLB are striking. School finance litigation that relies on state standards, if successful, tells the state that it must pay what it takes to meet the standards and pass the tests. The NCLB tells states that schools will be sanctioned if schools do not post good test scores. But both approaches ultimately leave it to the state to define the goals they are being forced to meet. Evidence already exists that the NCLB has created perverse incentives to lower academic goals. It is hard to see why "successful" school funding suits would not generate the same incentives.

Considering these parallel problems reveals a dilemma at the heart of the NCLB and related state accountability systems. Assume, as seems reasonable, that it is not enough simply to set challenging goals for schools in the form of robust standards and difficult, meaningful tests. Assume instead that more must be done to ensure that schools can meet these challenging goals. At present, the two favored methods are: (1) use sanctions, or (2) increase funding. Both methods might be necessary, and both might actually work to boost achievement.

At the same time, however, relying on either method creates incentives to lower the goals. States will want to avoid the political fallout of sanctioning too many schools, and they will want to avoid large increases in funding that might be thought necessary if the goals are really challenging. Hence the dilemma: high achievement levels may not be attainable without using sanctions, increasing funding, or both. But the very methods that might be necessary to boost achievement also create incentives to set the achievement bar at a low level.

An obvious escape from this particular dilemma is to reduce the ability of states to manipulate outcome goals. But that is difficult to do without creating national standards and tests, which have so far proven politically impossible to establish. National standards and tests are a perfectly sensible idea in theory, at least in core subjects like reading and math. It seems beyond strange that, in the twenty-first century, students in Florida are expected to know one thing about reading and math and students in Maine something else. The discouraging experience with the NCLB, moreover, has led to increased calls for national standards and tests, and there has been some progress on this front.[59]

But national standards and tests remain politically controversial. Even if sufficient support could be generated for them, it is not as if politics would drop out of the picture. Political considerations, and the fear of making thousands of schools across the country appear inadequate, could very well lead to the creation of national standards and tests that are no more ambitious than most existing state standards and tests. Thus, while national tests and standards might limit the ability of states to game accountability systems, there is no guarantee the federal legislation would be immune from the same pressures states have felt to make schools look good.

CONCLUSION

Standards-based reform sprang from the perception that most, if not all, U.S. schools were setting low expectations in comparison to schools in other countries. Initially, the standards and testing movement looked as though it would put all schools in the same boat and challenge all schools to expect and do more. But because of the political dynamics described earlier, it became apparent quite early on that testing and accountability could not really target all schools. It would cost too much, politically and financially, to set the academic bar so high that only top-performing schools could reach it without expending a good deal more effort (or securing a good deal more resources).

As a result, the bar in most states, including Virginia, has been set at a fairly low level. State tests are not designed to determine whether suburban schools in Henrico County, for example, are really pushing their students to succeed. They are designed to ensure that schools in places like Richmond are teaching their students to read.

In this way, a reform that might have tied urban and suburban schools together has been transformed into yet another one that reinforces the gap that separates them. Standards and testing promise, essentially, that urban students will learn the basics. Meanwhile, suburban students, while not immune from standards and testing, are certainly not limited by them.

The NCLB, while still in effect, is already overdue for reauthorization and—presumably—reconsideration. Politicians from the left and right have criticized the Act in its current form. As the target date for 100 percent proficiency—2014-—gets closer, more and more schools are being judged as "in need of improvement" or, more bluntly, as failing. This has created even more pressure to revise the law, and this pressure will only increase over time, as more schools fail to meet their AYP goals. But how the law will be changed is hard to predict at the moment, given the conflicting assessments of its flaws and the political difficulty of appearing to retreat from the original goal of 100 percent proficiency. ("Leave Some Children Behind" is not exactly a winning slogan politically.)[60]

For now, the way that standards and testing have unfolded illustrates the continued difficulty in achieving Nixon's vision of creating urban schools that are equal in quality to suburban ones. In setting academic goals, state officials seem to have recognized that requiring urban schools to perform at the same academic level as suburban schools was either unrealistic or would cost too much. They have therefore lowered their sights. But they have not done so openly. That, too, would be too costly politically. Instead, they have simply defined away the problem by implying, not just with rhetoric but with accountability systems, that passing basic tests is proof of a quality education.

PART III

FUTURE: DEMOGRAPHY IS OPPORTUNITY

CHAPTER 8

In Search of Ties That Bind

The simple fact is that the Richmond public schools, by and large, serve the segment of the community that has the least clout.

—Richmond parent (2008)

What you don't know, you avoid.

—Tee-Jay Student (2009)

In advocating for common schools 150 years ago, Horace Mann recognized that educating poor and more affluent students together was crucial to the success of those schools. Mann emphasized that if relatively affluent families did not participate in common schools—and instead sent their children to private schools—they would be less likely to support common schools and to ensure that they were of high quality. Mann understood the importance of linking the fates of poor children with those from more affluent families, and the costs of failing to create those links. One hundred years after Mann's crusade, desegregation advocates pursued a similar strategy, recognizing that in a political system dominated by whites, black students needed to be in the same school with white students to have equal opportunities.[1]

Neither Mann's efforts, nor those of desegregation advocates, fully succeeded. To the contrary, the last fifty years have been more about severing ties than creating them, and more about maintaining rather than eliminating the boundaries between urban and suburban schools and districts. Tee-Jay and Freeman are good examples. Despite the proximity of their schools, Freeman and Tee-Jay students have little contact with and almost no knowledge of each other. Indeed, some of the students I spoke with at Freeman did not even know where Tee-Jay was located. The schools occasionally play against each other in sports, but they do not share classes, teachers, or resources.

Efforts to connect these students, or schools in Richmond and Henrico more generally, have either failed or not been pursued. Desegregation remained confined to Richmond; school finance reform faltered in court; and school choice across district lines never received serious consideration. Freeman and Tee-Jay students take the same achievement tests, but these tests do relatively little to ensure that students at the two schools are taught the same material. In short, Tee-Jay and Freeman, like Richmond and Henrico, are separate physically, financially, academically, and politically.

What is true in Richmond is true in metropolitan regions across the country. Middle-income and more affluent families, mostly white, have largely walled themselves off in separate school districts, leaving to others the task of educating low-income students, most of whom are African-American or Hispanic. For fifty years, the law and politics of educational opportunity have operated to protect the schools behind those walls. Court and legislative decisions alike have ensured that those schools do not have to share their resources—whether teachers and principals, funding, or students—with other schools or districts. Efforts to improve city schools have certainly been pursued, but those efforts—whether increased funding or increased choice, liberal reforms or conservative counterproposals—have themselves been shaped and curtailed by the overriding principle that suburban schools be left alone.

Separate has not been equal in Richmond or elsewhere. It never will be. As one Richmond parent astutely observed in an interview, the basic problem is "that the Richmond public schools, by and large, serve the segment of the community that has the least clout. The middle class moves to the suburbs, the upper class goes with private school, and there does not exist any powerful constituency advocating on behalf of the public school system." This observation about Richmond captures a more general truth about the political economy of educational opportunity. Urban school systems lack families with political clout. Poor, mostly minority families generally lack the resources, whether measured in time, education, or political savvy, to be effective advocates at the local or state level. The result is a lack of real accountability at the local level, and a lack of political muscle at the state level.

The wisdom of tying as a political strategy for equalizing educational opportunties has either been lost or rejected as hopeless. But it deserves to be resurrected. If poor and minority students remain separated from middle-income white students, there is every reason to believe that the former will continue to be shortchanged in countless ways, large and small, direct and indirect. There is also every reason to believe that the latter will miss a crucial opportunity to learn from students whose backgrounds differ from their own. As a student at Tee-Jay answered, when I asked if calls for integration seemed condescending or elitist, "the learning goes both ways. We need to deal with each other now or we won't know how to deal with each other when we're older. People are afraid of what they don't know. What you don't know, you avoid."

To be sure, it is unfashionable these days to talk seriously about ways to increase racial and socioeconomic integration. The goal seems not only impossible, but also increasingly beside the point. We live in the age of standards and testing, where academic achievement seems the exclusive goal and test scores are the exclusive barometer of achievement. To talk about integration is to talk about a relic from the past or a distracting frill—something that might be nice, but certainly is not necessary.

The alternatives to integration, however, are not working. Nixon's compromise has not been realized. Urban schools continue to lag behind suburban ones on every measure, including test scores, graduation rates, the quality of teachers, the quality of facilities, academic rigor and expectations, and reputation. This should not come as a surprise. To the contrary, it would be shocking if separating poor and minority students from middle-income white ones turned out to be the ticket to equalizing educational opportunities.

The reality is that a poor student in a middle-income school stands a better chance of succeeding academically than she does in a predominantly poor school, and middle-income students are not harmed by attending school with poor students, provided the school remains majority middle-income. The same is true for racial integration. Although the academic gains are relatively modest for minority students, white students are not harmed by attending school with minority students, and each group can benefit socially from exposure to the other. These findings from social science studies are difficult for some to believe, especially those who benefit from the current structure of educational opportunity. But those are the findings.[2]

Some who believe in integration as a means of equalizing educational opportunities focus solely on socioeconomic, as opposed to racial, integration. There are defensible reasons to do so. The socioeconomic composition of a school matters more to academic achievement than the racial composition. Efforts to increase socioeconomic diversity, moreover, do not trigger the same sort of intensive judicial scrutiny as do efforts to increase racial diversity; under current doctrine, governments have more discretion to consider socioeconomic status than race when making student assignments. In addition, it may well be true, as some suggest, that socioeconomic integration is less controversial politically than racial integration.[3]

All of that said, school districts and schools are not completely prohibited under current law from making efforts to achieve racial diversity, and it would be unwise for them to ignore this issue. It may be sensible, for legal and political reasons, to focus direct efforts on increasing socioeconomic diversity, which if successful will also increase racial diversity in many jurisdictions. But districts should not shy from embracing racial diversity as a goal. To give up entirely on racial diversity is to accept the narrowing of expectations for public schools, which began with school finance litigation and has reached its pinnacle under the NCLB. This is a mistake. Academics should remain paramount, for sure. But to ignore the socializing aspects of education, as if these are trivial concerns, is short-sighted.

In addition, one need only spend time in city and suburban schools like Tee-Jay and Freeman to realize that race still matters. Students in the International Baccalaureate (IB) program at Tee-Jay, who experience racial diversity on a daily basis in their classes, appreciate its value. They laughed or rolled their eyes when I asked if studying for and taking the SOLs, which is supposedly the cornerstone of public education in Virginia, was a valuable exercise. But they did not feel that way about the benefits of diversity. "If I was at an all-white school," one white IB student said to me, "all I'd see is me. What good would that do me?"

Those in Tee-Jay who are not in the IB program, as well as most students at Freeman, do not experience much diversity in their classes. It shows. These students, at both Tee-Jay and Freeman, were much more likely to make stereotypical assumptions on the basis of race (whereas the IB students made fun of such assumptions). At the same time, they were able to predict what others would say about them. Ironically, they were well aware of stereotyping but nonetheless fell victim to it. Students at Tee-Jay, for example, told me they were sure Freeman students would say they were all "ghetto," which is a slang term meant to describe a loud, obnoxious, poorly behaved, low-income African American. Sure enough, when I asked a group of white Freeman students about Tee-Jay, they said: "Isn't that school kind of ghetto?" Freeman students, in turn, predicted that Tee-Jay students would say all of them were white and rich, which also turned out to be an accurate prediction. Interracial contact may not be required to overcome racial stereotypes, but separation is an effective way to foster them.

Even if the goal of increasing socioeconomic and racial diversity is accepted, achieving that goal obviously remains remarkably difficult. Legislatures cannot be counted on, at the moment, to force or even strongly encourage integration. Although a few states and localities have shown some interest in doing so, they remain the exception. Courts are not likely to fill the legislative void. The days of court-ordered integration are indeed behind us, and very few courts—not to mention very few attorneys—seem interested in socioeconomic or racial integration. Crossing or altering district lines to achieve integration is also not an especially plausible strategy at the moment; school district lines, as the previous chapters have shown, remain fiercely guarded.

Change, nonetheless, is coming—not from legislatures or courts, but from demographics and changes in attitudes about the most desirable places to live and about diversity itself. As this chapter describes in some detail, these demographic changes are bringing racial and socioeconomic diversity to the suburbs and more middle-income families back to the city. With these changes come greater opportunities for racial and socioeconomic diversity within schools and school districts. Attitudes and behaviors among young adults aged eighteen to twenty-nine push in the same direction. This generation has embraced diversity as none has before it, which bodes well for future housing patterns.

These changing demographics will inevitably shape the politics of educational opportunity. They offer the chance to forge ties between families with few resources and little political power and those with an ample supply of both. Advocates for improving urban education and equalizing educational opportunities for disadvantaged students should be thinking now about how to nudge these changes in productive directions. Indeed, figuring out creative ways to attract and retain middle-income families in urban districts, for example, or how to manage the increased diversity in suburban districts to avoid another round of white flight from suburb to exurb, may be the single most important task school districts could undertake. If successful, these efforts could transform the politics of education and equalize educational opportunities like no other reform. If they fail, and they may very well, we can expect to see more of the same.

This chapter describes the demographic changes under way, assesses what they might mean for school districts, and suggests ways that school districts might nudge them along or otherwise take advantage of them. Before discussing these possible strategies, the chapter begins with a brief restatement of the problem, to make clear the nature and significance of the challenge and why increasing integration is crucial.

SCHOOLS MATTER

When it comes to academic performance, three factors are most important: student talent, family background, and school quality. Not all students have the same intellectual abilities, and no amount of school improvement will change that. Some students will do better than others because they are more talented. Just as some students are going to be better at basketball and others better at ballet, regardless of the coaching or training they receive, some students are going to be better at math, science, or writing than others.[4]

Student performance also varies depending on the student's family background. Students from affluent and middle-class families, on average, perform better on standardized tests, graduate at higher rates, and are more likely to attend college than students from poor families. These academic differences hold true across the different types of schools students attend. A middle-class student in any school, whether that school is predominantly poor or affluent, will generally do better than a poor student in the same school. This does not mean that middle-income and affluent students are inherently more talented than students from poor families; that idea, which surfaces from time to time, has been demolished by social scientists who find no good evidence of a correlation between social class (or race) and innate capacity to learn. Instead, middle-income and affluent students are more likely to realize their potential because of the resources available to them from their families, whether in the form of a healthy and supportive home environment, access to health care, or high expectations.[5]

School quality is also important. Some schools achieve better results than others, even holding the effects of family income constant. The Knowledge is Power Program (KIPP) charter schools, for example, seem to do a better job of educating poor, urban students than do traditional public schools. In addition, students who move from high-poverty schools to middle-income schools generally improve their academic performance and increase their chances of graduating. Indeed, some studies find that middle-income students in high-poverty schools perform worse than poor students in middle-income schools. If school quality were irrelevant, moving a student from one school to another should not affect achievement.[6]

In discussing the factors that affect school performance, some rely on the image of a three-legged stool, with the legs representing student talent, family background, and school quality. The difficulty with this image is that stools have equal-sized legs, which suggests that each of these factors is equally important. No one knows whether this is the case when it comes to school performance. It is clear that students, families, and schools all matter, but the precise degree of influence each factor has on student performance remains unclear.[7]

Nonetheless, advocacy groups have staked out competing positions based on their view of the data. Some believe that family background is dominant, and thus that more attention and resources should be devoted to fixing families rather than to fixing schools. Other advocates refuse to accept the notion that some students are destined to achieve at low levels because of family background, and they argue that attention should remain focused on the schools themselves. These advocates, which include many of the luminaries in the field of education policy, are currently divided into two camps. One camp argues for what they call a "bolder, broader approach" to education that encompasses social services as well as school reform. The other, which operates under the banner of the "Education Equality Project," argues that school reform should remain the main focus.[8]

The debate between these groups is unlikely to be resolved and is, in any event, more curious than productive. We know that families and schools both matter, but we do not and probably never will know the precise influence of each; it is too much to expect social scientists to be able measure this accurately, given the number of variables involved. Instead of debating whether to focus on schools or social welfare programs, it would be more productive to recognize that both matter and get on with the business of pushing for change in both contexts. At the end of the day, a student is much more likely to reach her potential if she is healthy, well fed, lives in a stable home, and has parents who care about and help with her education. But she will still fall short if she goes to a terrible school. On the other hand, a student who has health problems, is malnourished, and comes from a poor home with disengaged parents is going to have a hard time reaching her potential, regardless of the school she attends. She will nonetheless have a better chance if she attends a good school instead of a terrible one.

THE REAL CRISIS: HIGH-POVERTY SCHOOLS

Not all urban schools are terrible schools. Far from it. But urban schools tend to be worse than those found in middle-class suburbs. More generally, high-poverty schools, especially in urban areas, are consistently the worst in terms of academic performance. This is one of the most consistent findings in the social science literature on education, and it is a proposition accepted by researchers regardless of their political or ideological leanings. Indeed, it is a point beyond reasonable debate.

The low performance of high-poverty schools, it bears emphasizing, is not due solely to the fact that most students in such schools are themselves poor. As mentioned, even students from middle-income families tend to do worse in high-poverty schools than in low-poverty schools. There is something about the school itself that depresses achievement. As a 1997 congressionally authorized study of forty thousand students concluded, the poverty level of the school, "over and above the economic status of an individual student," has a negative impact on achievement.[9]

Over the last fifty years, there have been periods when commentators and politicians have argued that the entire system of public education is in a crisis and that American schools are falling behind those in other countries. When the Soviet Union launched *Sputnik*, for example, some argued that American schools were not adequately training students in math and science. In the early 1980s, the federal government published *A Nation at Risk*, which warned that public schools were being flooded by a "rising tide of mediocrity." Today, we seem to be in another period of doubt and uncertainty about the relative quality of American public schools, as U.S. students reportedly fare worse than foreign students on a number of international measures of achievement and attainment. These studies fuel media reports about the declining state of American education.[10]

A closer look at performance on international tests, however, suggests otherwise. When scores are broken down by income, as well as by race, it becomes clear that many American students are doing quite well, whereas others are doing poorly. White, middle-income students who attend predominantly middle-income schools compare favorably with their foreign peers. Poor, mostly African-American and Hispanic students who attend predominantly low-income schools do not. As one observer noted about the international comparisons: "For those who look carefully at the performance of our schools, the real problem is not that the United States is falling behind, or that the entire system is failing. It is the sorry shape of the bottom 30 percent of U.S. schools, those in urban and rural communities full of low-income children."[11]

International test results thus confirm that the most pressing problem in American education is not its overall quality, although there is undoubtedly room for improvement. The real problem is the performance of high-poverty schools, especially those in urban areas. That is where the crisis lies.

WHY SEPARATE WILL NOT BE EQUAL

The Case for Integration

The single best solution to this crisis is greater socioeconomic and racial diversity within each district and school. Integration, as discussed in the introduction to this chapter, brings both direct and indirect benefits that cannot be replicated by other reforms. Majority-middle-income schools are much more likely than high-poverty ones to have strong principals, talented and engaged teachers, reasonable class sizes, a rich curriculum, high expectations on the part of students and teachers alike, adequate facilities, and active parents. Each of these factors has been shown to be related to academic achievement, especially the first two: good principals and teachers. All of them tend to go together and are intertwined. Adequate facilities, for example, mean a nicer place to work, which adds to the reasons why teachers prefer middle-income schools to high-poverty ones.[12]

Socioeconomic and racial diversity can also bring social benefits to all students by exposing them to others from different backgrounds. Diverse schools, as the students in the IB program at Tee-Jay repeatedly emphasized, can increase understanding and friendship across lines of class and race. This not a guaranteed outcome, of course, and diverse schools can sometimes heighten rather than relieve racial tension, especially when students in integrated schools end up, through tracking, in segregated classes. But it hardly follows, as some seem to imply, that the answer is to keep white and minority students in separate schools; it simply means that some effort is necessary to make diverse schools work. Even if they present challenges, attending diverse schools can better prepare students for their future lives as citizens and workers than can racially and economically homogenous schools.[13]

Diversity can also bring political benefits and greater accountability. Here, parents are the linchpin. Greater socioeconomic diversity within school districts means a critical mass of active and engaged parents, who are more likely to be involved at the school, district, and state level. Middle-income parents are much more likely to volunteer in school, attend teacher-parent conferences, and participate in parent-teacher associations. Social science studies indicate as much, and every teacher and principal I interviewed confirmed the accuracy of the point from their experience. Middle-income parents are also more likely to have the time and political savvy to effectively monitor the decisions of school boards and superintendents, who set policies for the entire district. And they are much more likely to have the clout to fight successfully for resources and to insist on adequate facilities, reasonable class sizes, and rich curriculum.[14]

They are also much more likely to be effective in monitoring principal and teacher performance. The current buzzword in education reform is "accountability," which usually refers to sanctions imposed by states for poor test results. For decades, however, middle-income and affluent parents in suburban districts have done a very good job in holding the relevant actors accountable for providing a decent education. In a study of school effectiveness, for example, researchers found that principals retain greater autonomy to hire and fire teachers, free from district or union influence, in low-poverty suburban schools than in high-poverty urban ones. They attributed much of this to the influence of parents. District administrators, they observed, "tend to leave schools alone when they have parents who are relatively high in status and are cooperatively involved in their children's schools." They are more willing to intervene, by contrast, "in schools with parents who are less educated and who demonstrate less interest in or support for their schools." What is true of administrators is also true of unions; the same study found that "teachers' unions and the constraints they seek [on hiring, transfers, and firing] rapidly gain in influence as parents decline in education, affluence, and occupational status."[15]

Critics and Doubters

Some argue against efforts to increase socioeconomic and racial integration on the ground that it constitutes unwise or inequitable "social engineering," whereas others are sympathetic to the concept but think it politically implausible. Regardless of why they have turned away from integration, these opponents argue instead for fixing high-poverty schools rather than changing their composition. They might point to the KIPP charter schools and others that have succeeded and argue that their methods ought to be replicated on a larger scale. Or they might argue for increased resources as the best solution. To focus instead on integration, these reformers suggest, is to give in to the idea that demography is destiny and to let schools off the hook for failure.[16]

These critics of integration are correct, but only to a point. The fact that some high-poverty schools are successful, at least as measured by test scores, does indeed show academic success is possible in such schools. The critics are also accurate in identifying the political obstacles to creating integrated schools.

What these critics tend to miss, however, is that politics do not drop out of the picture once one gives up on integration. For example, efforts to make high-poverty schools work by devoting more resources to them will also be affected by politics. The current politics of educational opportunity make it unlikely that high-poverty schools, which are often nested within districts of concentrated poverty, are going to get the resources they need in order to make all necessary improvements. As discussed earlier, it is the very separation of poor and minority urban students from white, middle-class suburban students that puts the former at a political disadvantage. That disadvantage does not simply disappear when one turns from one education reform to another.

The field of education reform is filled with debates about the merits of particular reforms. These debates are healthy and informative, as some reforms are certainly more effective than others. But to focus solely on the substance of the reforms without more attention to the political context in which those reforms operate is to miss something crucial. The best reform in the world, on paper, will be useless without sufficient political support to sustain its implementation. For the last fifty years, the law and politics of educational opportunity have not worked to maximize the potential of urban education reforms; they have worked to protect suburban schools. Unless and until that political reality changes, it is unrealistic to expect any reform to produce more than sporadic improvement and the occasional success story in high-poverty, urban school systems. And if the past is any guide, it is equally unrealistic to expect those politics to change if schools and districts continue to remain separated by race and class.

NUDGING CHANGE

Now for the hard part. Creating schools and school districts that are stably integrated by race and income levels might seem like an impossible task, akin to saying that the first step to school improvement is to guarantee permanent world peace. It is certainly easier said than done. But it is not as impossible as it might seem.

Demographic Trends

Indeed, there are some hopeful signs and some unprecedented opportunities. Several demographic trends are changing the composition of metropolitan areas and creating opportunities for integration—both socioeconomic and racial—that have not existed in the past. The most promising approach to creating diverse districts is to think now about how to respond wisely to these demographic changes. School district leaders and advocates, in other words, should think of demography not as destiny, but as opportunity.

The public school population is changing because of a relative increase among racial and ethnic minorities in the general population. Nationwide, the percentage of minority students in public schools is growing and is predicted to become larger than the percentage of white students by 2023. The country as a whole is projected to become majority-minority by 2042. Minority students already outnumber white students in the West, where Hispanic, African-American, and Asian students account for nearly 55 percent of the student population. Most of the growth has been and will continue to be among Hispanic and Asian students. Indeed, by 2050 the overall Hispanic population is predicted to triple, from 47 million to 133 million, which would account for 30 percent of the nation's population; today Hispanics make up 15 percent. At least in some regions of the country, racial and ethnic diversity, which will often mean socioeconomic diversity, are becoming increasingly difficult to avoid simply because of these population changes. Avoiding diverse settings will become even harder in a few decades.[17]

In the meantime, housing patterns are becoming more diverse. The most significant trend in this respect is the increased diversity—along lines of income, race, and ethnicity—in the suburbs. A more nascent trend is the revitalization of some central cities and the increasing number of middle-income families who are remaining there even when their children reach school age. These two changes are blurring the line between cities and suburbs, and they are complicating the traditional image of suburbs as havens for middle-class whites and cities as home to poor, minority, and immigrant families.

Looking first at income levels and poverty, as of 2005, there were roughly 38 million people living in poverty, which is roughly 13 percent of the population. The poverty line in 2005 was defined as an income of $15,753 for a family of three, which is quite low and understates the actual amount of families in real need. It certainly underestimates the number of *students* who are considered "poor," given that the benchmark for those students is eligibility for free or reduced-priced lunch, both of which are explicitly pegged to an amount above the poverty line. Nonetheless, poverty rates provide a useful first glimpse of the location of poor households.[18]

Roughly 23 million of the 38 million individuals who are poor live in the one hundred largest metropolitan areas in the country. In the past, the poor tended to be concentrated in central cities, but this is no longer true. In fact, for the first time ever, most of the poor who live in these metropolitan areas—53 percent— live in the suburbs. As analysts at the Brookings Institution observed, "this 'tipping' of poor populations to the suburbs represents a signal development that upends historical notions about who lives in cities and suburbs."[19]

Equally confounding traditional views about cities and suburbs is the increased racial and ethnic diversity in the suburbs, especially the inner-ring suburbs. In 1990, minority residents—African Americans, Asians, and Hispanics—made up only 19 percent of the suburban populations in the 102 largest metropolitan areas of the country. By 2000, minorities comprised 27 percent of this suburban population. Forty-seven percent of all minorities lived in the suburbs in these areas in 2000, up from 40 percent in 1990. Breaking this figure down by subgroup, 55 percent of Asians, 50 percent of Hispanics, and 39 percent of African Americans in these areas lived in the suburbs.[20]

These shifts are evident in Henrico County and its public schools. Over the last fifteen years, the county has become more diverse both socioeconomically and racially. The percentage of students eligible for free and reduced-price lunch increased by more than three percentage points between 1995 and 2003, from roughly 24.5 percent to roughly 28 percent. During the same time period, overall enrollment in the district grew by 5,600 students; 43 percent of these new students—nearly 2,500—were eligible for free and reduced price lunch. The percentage of minority students has also increased fairly significantly over the last ten years. In 1998, 62 percent of the students in the district were white; in 2008, only 48 percent were.[21]

City populations are also shifting somewhat, though the change here is less dramatic than that in the suburbs. For most of the last century, the white population in large cities declined significantly. In the last several years, however, the rate of departure has slowed in many places and has reversed in others. Eight of the fifty largest cities, including Boston, Seattle, San Francisco, Atlanta, and Washington, D.C., have seen their percentage of white residents increase in 2000–6. Boston is now a majority-white city, and the increase in the percentage of whites over the last six years was the first in nearly a hundred years. Los Angeles, New York, Fort Worth, and Chicago are still losing white residents, but at much lower rates than in the past. In Los Angeles, for example, the share of white population dropped by roughly one-half a percent between 2000 and 2006; it fell by more than 7 percent in the prior decade. As demographer William Frey remarked, the latest census data "suggest...that white flight from large cities may have bottomed out in the 1990s."[22]

A number of factors are responsible for the shift in city populations. Some of the change is due to the effect of more minorities moving out to the suburbs and the increasing number of new immigrants who settle immediately in the suburbs, both of which increase the relative portion of whites in cities. But more middle-income and affluent whites are moving to cities as well. A number of cities have worked over the past decade to create a more attractive environment for residents—cleaning up parks, creating more retail and living space from old factories, and cracking down on street crime. This has brought an influx of young professionals and some empty-nesters, many of whom are white.[23]

Some cities are also seeing a rise in middle-income families with young children. Families with children, in every region of the country, are still more likely to live in suburbs than in cities. But there are some signs that this is beginning to change. A recent article in the *New York Times*, for example, chronicled the growing number of families who have decided to remain in New York, even when it means squeezing into small spaces. In the last six years, the number of white, non-Hispanic professionals with one or more children living in New York City—in one-bedroom apartments—increased 31 percent. As one demographer noted, "there seems to be a large contingent who don't move to the suburbs anymore." They are attracted to the feel of city neighborhoods, which often approximate the feel of small towns, and they appreciate being able to walk places rather than having to drive everywhere.[24]

Richmond reflects some of these trends. The percentage of white students in Richmond public schools is still remarkably low—only about 7 percent. But unlike earlier periods, the white student population is holding steady rather than declining. Between 1998 and 2003, for example, the number of white students in the district declined by 229. Between 2003 and 2008, by contrast, the number declined by only 29. By comparison, the number of black students fell by over eighteen hundred during the last five years. This does not show, obviously, that white, middle-income families are engaged in a mad rush into Richmond schools while black families are fleeing. Richmond remains a predominantly poor, African-American school system. But even small signs of change are worth considering, as they dispel the idea that the district's current racial composition is permanently fixed. These changes also call to mind the fact that the composition of the district has changed quickly in the past, as it shifted over the course of merely two decades from being majority white to overwhelmingly African American.[25]

The wealth gap between cities and suburbs is also shrinking, at least in some regions of the country. City residents are still more likely to be poor than are suburban ones. The combined poverty rate for the one hundred largest cities is roughly 19 percent, while the poverty rate in their suburbs is roughly 9.5 percent. Between 1999 and 2005, however, poverty rates in some cities—mostly in the Northeast—fell, whereas poverty rates grew in the surrounding suburbs. The Northeast still has the largest wealth gap between cities and suburbs of all the regions in the country, but this simply highlights the important regional differences when it comes to urban-suburban wealth disparities. Poverty-rate differences between cities and suburbs in the West and in the South are generally lower than those in the Northeast and Midwest.[26]

The Richmond metropolitan area reflects these trends as well. Between 1999 and 2005, the overall poverty rate in the city actually declined, from 21.4 percent to 18.5 percent. The poverty rate in the surrounding suburbs, by contrast, grew from 6.8 percent to 8.9 percent during the same period. These changes are just beginning to show up in schools. Between 2003–8, the percentage of children eligible for free and reduced-price lunch dropped in Richmond by nearly two percentage points, from 78 percent to 76 percent, while it increased in Henrico by one point, from roughly 28 percent to 29 percent.[27]

Rounding out these trends is the slowing growth of exurban areas. Over the last several decades, suburban development has sprawled farther and farther away from central cities into what were once rural areas. During the 1980s and 1990s, growth in the exurbs outpaced growth in central cities and inner-ring suburbs. The metropolitan population of Pittsburgh, to cite one example, fell by 8 percent during those two decades, but the area of developed land increased by 43 percent. In many metropolitan areas, including Pittsburgh, it looked as though another round of white flight was occurring, this time from suburb to exurb instead of from city to suburb.[28]

The march outward to the exurbs no longer appears inexorable. Housing prices in far-flung suburbs are dropping in many metropolitan areas, while housing prices closer to the urban core are dropping more slowly, holding steady, or continuing to rise, despite the general downturn in the housing market. Higher fuel prices are partially responsible for some of the shift, but consumer preferences also seem to be changing. Surveys indicate that a growing percentage of prospective home buyers are more interested in living closer to the urban core rather than farther out, or at least in being able to live in mixed-use, walkable neighborhoods, which at the moment are more likely to be found in cities or close-in suburbs.[29]

Housing analysts predict that the trend back toward the center will continue. One land use expert suggested in an essay in the *Atlantic Monthly* that "many low-density suburbs and McMansion subdivisions, including some that are lovely and affluent today, may be become what inner cities became in the 1960s and '70s—slums characterized by poverty, crime, and decay." This is an extreme prediction, undoubtedly intended to be provocative, and it is not widely shared by other experts. But there is nonetheless some consensus that a significant shift in housing preferences is under way. As one housing economist put it, there is "an ebbing of this suburban tide." He predicted a "reversal of desirability. Typically, Americans have felt the periphery was most desirable, and now there's going to be a reversion to the center."[30]

These demographic trends do not guarantee, of course, that all school districts in the near future are going to be majority-middle-class and racially and ethnically diverse. The growing diversity in the suburbs, for example, is not uniform; some suburbs are still overwhelmingly white and affluent, while others are predominantly minority and poor. But these shifts nonetheless offer an opportunity to create and sustain districts and schools that are much more diverse than they have been in the past. For reasons already described, this is an opportunity worth seizing.

How to Respond

What school districts should do in response to these demographic changes depends on the starting point within the district. In general, to become more diverse, cities need to attract more white, middle-income families into their districts and into their schools. Suburbs that are becoming more diverse need to hold onto a critical mass of the same families.

Housing and land-use policies obviously have a role to play in attracting or maintaining families. As one commentator has correctly emphasized, "housing policy is school policy." Schools reflect the neighborhoods and districts in which they are located. Jurisdictions interested in diverse schools should ensure that there is a diverse supply of housing options.[31]

In the cities, this means affordable housing not just for the poor but for middle-income families. In the suburbs, the challenge is to create more opportunities for low-income families without driving away middle-income ones. A number of strategies have already been tried, with some modest success. Inclusionary zoning programs, for example, which require suburbs to allow for or subsidize affordable housing, exist in over 130 localities, with a combined total of 12 million residents. In addition, housing vouchers are more readily available for use outside of central cities than they have been in the past.[32]

Programs like these, along with better enforcement of laws barring housing discrimination, are important and should be strengthened where possible. But changing housing markets and demographic shifts have arguably done more to diversify the suburbs than have government programs. Given political resistance to "forced" integration of schools and neighborhoods, trying to nudge along these voluntary demographic shifts may ultimately be more productive than more coercive measures. If nothing else, however, education reformers need to work more closely with land-use and housing experts. Too often, these groups work in isolation. Those interested in improving schools in cities and inner-ring suburbs would do well to concentrate more energy on ways to create housing opportunities, as well as schools and communities, that are attractive and affordable for middle-income families.

At the same time, it is important to recognize that just as housing policy is school policy, school policy is also housing policy. Many families choose where to live because of the quality of the local schools. To attract and retain middle-income families, jurisdictions must do more than pay attention to the local housing stock and community amenities. They need to pay a great deal of attention to school options. What they need to do, in short, is ensure that middle-income families have school options that they find attractive, for the simple reason that if they do not, those families will go elsewhere. And here we get to the heart of the challenge.

Universal Choice in Cities and Poor Suburbs

Meeting this goal, as suggested, requires different strategies for different jurisdictions. In cities and inner-ring suburbs that are predominantly poor, it requires offering families options beyond the neighborhood school. There are simply not enough good neighborhood schools in these jurisdictions to attract a critical mass of middle-income families. It follows, by definition, that there are not enough good public schools in general, which means that choice must extend to charter and private schools. Indeed, many cities already offer an array of choices among public schools. The problem, as a recent report on school choice in New York City concluded, is that there are not enough good schools.[33]

Cities and poor suburbs should therefore offer choices that include charter and private schools, and they should offer these choices to all students. Current voucher programs and charter schools cater mostly to disadvantaged, urban students, and even then serve only a tiny fraction of eligible students. As described in chapter 6, limited programs will have a limited impact. More importantly for present purposes, programs limited to the poor will do nothing to attract middle-income families. If anything, they may help keep them away. Urban and poor suburban districts should thus give all students the right to attend their neighborhood school along with the option of attending any other school—public, charter, or private—within the jurisdiction.

In focusing on school choice within urban districts, I do not mean to suggest that interdistrict choice plans should be ignored. To the contrary, I believe they should be continued and expanded where possible. The last fifty years, however, have shown that forcing residents of one district to open their borders or share their resources is exceptionally difficult. In addition, interdistrict choice programs help the students who participate but do little, especially if limited in scope, to alter education politics; those not in the program still will care primarily if not solely about their own districts. If significant change is going to come, therefore, it will almost certainly have to come from within districts.

The political climate is not especially hospitable to a universal choice program, especially if it includes vouchers, even if all choices are confined to schools within single districts. Public school choice, charter schools, and especially vouchers are all controversial, which helps explain why the programs tend to be limited in most districts. Teachers' unions, which are especially strong in many cities, would fight tooth and nail to prevent a universal choice program that included vouchers. Civil rights groups, who might otherwise be counted on to advocate for poor, minority children, remain leery of school choice and mostly opposed to vouchers.

That said, there is a good deal of popular support within urban jurisdictions for school choice, including vouchers. And choice programs, if limited to single jurisdictions, would inspire little opposition from middle-income and affluent suburban districts. The existence of public and private school choice programs in some cities, as well as the proliferation of charter schools, also indicates that creating choice programs is not exactly the same as tilting at windmills.

The time also seems ripe for adding new members to the coalition in favor of school choice, which currently includes an odd mixture of religious conservative groups, libertarians, and African-American parents. It remains possible that some civil rights groups could be persuaded to join in a fight for expanded choice programs. As mentioned earlier, Bill Taylor, a lion among civil rights advocates, recently coauthored an article arguing for the use of school choice—including vouchers—to promote integration. One swallow does not make a spring, but Taylor is not alone among progressive advocates in supporting school choice as a way to enhance educational opportunities. Moreover, pro-voucher minority groups, like the Black Alliance for Educational Options, are putting pressure on traditional civil rights organizations like the NAACP by stressing that they are out of step with their minority constituents. One could also imagine attracting the support of environmental groups opposed to sprawl; if choice would keep more families in cities and first-ring suburbs, this would reduce even further the demand for development on the outer fringes of suburbia.[34]

The details of any choice program would be crucial, especially if vouchers were involved. Steps should be taken to prevent the clustering of all middle-income and affluent families in certain schools. School districts, for example, could require that all charter and participating private schools set aside at least 20–40 percent of their seats for students eligible for free or reduced-price lunch. (Districts would have a more difficult time, under current constitutional doctrine, justifying similarly precise goals regarding race, and for that reason it is probably wiser at least in this context to concentrate on socioeconomic diversity.) Districts could impose similar requirements on public schools that participate in choice plans and have available space.

These requirements would not prevent some schools, at least initially, from becoming or remaining predominantly poor, but they would at least prevent most schools from completely shutting out the poor. One can easily imagine variations on this theme. Private schools, for example, might be permitted to set tuition at an amount higher than the voucher amount but then be required, in exchange for participating in the voucher program, to set aside at least 20 percent of their seats for those who cannot afford to pay more than the voucher. Regardless of the precise approach, there are numerous ways to structure choice programs to encourage integration rather than segregation, without simultaneously scaring away middle-income families.[35]

Other details would also matter, including transportation and the dollar amount of any vouchers made available. Jurisdictions will differ regarding the need to provide transportation and the cost of doing so. Some are much more densely populated than others. In general, transportation, at least where necessary and feasible, ought to be provided within the district. The voucher amount, in turn, should be high enough to provide real choices for students, but below the current amount spent per pupil in order to offset some of the lost income to public schools. Given economies of scale, there is not a one-to-one ratio between the funding and the costs of educating one student, so losing one student usually represents a real cost to school districts.

The voucher amount should also be somewhat below the current per-pupil spending amount to absorb the costs of additional students, currently in private school, who would be eligible for a voucher. Including these students and their families in a voucher program would undoubtedly be controversial, as some would see it as a subsidy for middle-income and wealthy parents—forgetting, perhaps, that these parents already pay taxes, so giving them a voucher would actually mean that they no longer have to pay twice for school. But excluding them, as existing voucher programs do, seems a mistake, for at least three reasons.

First, leaving this group out would eliminate a strong, natural constituency in favor of a universal choice program. Many parents who currently pay private school tuition would be strong supporters of a program that would defray or eliminate tuition costs. Second, excluding students currently enrolled in private school would save money only in the short run, as new students who enter the system would be eligible for vouchers. This short-term savings is probably not worth the loss of political support. Third, and perhaps most important, including these middle-income parents would give them an immediate stake in the school system, which they currently do not have. They would care most of all about the voucher amount. But they would also care about the rules and regulations of the voucher program, which means that they would care about those making the rules—mayors, school boards, and superintendents.

This public-regarding potential of vouchers is not part of the current debate about vouchers. Instead, the claim usually made, by opponents and supporters alike, is that vouchers will privatize public education. Our public system, however, is already quite private in some important respects. To attend school in a wealthy suburb, for example, one must first pay housing costs as the price of entry. Vouchers would bring a market element to public education and in that sense make it somewhat more private. But it would also make private schools more public by tying those schools, and the families who use vouchers to attend them, to the public system. At the same time, it would increase access to private schools among families who cannot currently afford to pay tuition.[36]

The attention to the voucher part of this proposal should not be taken to mean it is the only component or even the most important. It simply reflects the fact that vouchers are the most complicated—and controversial—aspect. Charter schools and public schools would also be crucial. Indeed, where voucher programs are not politically plausible, or where they would violate state constitutional provisions, it is possible that an expanded system of well-funded charter schools in city districts would be enough to attract a critical mass of middle-income families. For this to happen, however, charter school laws and policies in a number of states would have to be changed. Funding for charter schools, for example, should be increased, and caps on the number of schools, where they exist, should either be lifted or at least raised. Virginia's stingy charter school law is a perfect target for education reformers; the law ought to be changed to encourage rather than discourage charter schools. The ultimate goal, again, is to create attractive options for middle-income families. Private schools can help districts meet this goal, and for this reason, they cannot be ignored. But they do not have a magic formula that guarantees academic success, and they are not indispensable, at least where there is a healthy supply of good charter schools.

One could also imagine the creation of charter schools—or private schools where vouchers are available—that are specifically dedicated to fulfilling the vision of the common school movement. A lot of charter schools cater to disadvantaged students, but very few explicitly seek to create a socioeconomically and racially diverse student body. A great opportunity awaits an educational entrepreneur to create charter or private schools that demonstrate that integrated schools can be successful schools. The powerful and prestigious Gates Foundation, among others, has already devoted substantial resources to improving high-poverty, racially isolated urban high schools. Why not support efforts to create more schools in the vision of the common school movement, where students from diverse families are educated together?[37]

Public schools would also have a key role to play. Magnet schools exist in many urban districts, and they have shown an ability to attract middle-income families. More should be created. Care would have to be taken to avoid the inequities, both real and apparent, that have accompanied urban magnet schools in the past. But increasing options should not and cannot wait until every child is guaranteed his first choice of schools.

In creating new choice programs, whether among traditional, charter, or private schools, districts would be wise to begin by focusing on middle schools. Pockets of predominantly middle-income elementary schools, with substantial or majority white student populations, exist in cities throughout the country, including Richmond. But many middle-income families, especially white ones, leave at the middle-school stage in Richmond and elsewhere. Students I spoke with at Tee-Jay, without any prompting, remarked on this phenomenon, describing how their elementary schools were much more racially and ethnically diverse than either their middle schools or Tee-Jay.

School districts should focus on this transition point and respond to parental concerns. One white Richmond parent, who moved his children to private schools after they attended a public elementary school, told me that he thought the public middle school his children would have attended was a poor fit for them. He indicated that he would have explored other options within the public school system if more had been available. This is just one parent, obviously, but the drop in enrollment between elementary and middle school strongly suggests that increasing options for middle school students should be a priority.

Perhaps the most important general point is that districts should listen to parents who are considering leaving the public school system once their children finish elementary school. Indeed, after explaining his reasons for taking his children out of the Richmond public schools, the parent I interviewed remarked that no one in the Richmond school system ever asked him why he was leaving, even though he had come to know many school board members and administrators.

None of these changes would be easy to accomplish. In some places, a universal choice program—even if it excludes vouchers—will be a nonstarter politically. But if I am right about the importance of middle-income families to the health of a school system, efforts like this need to be pursued. This may seem like a radical proposal, and in some ways it is. But incremental change over the last five decades has not done much to alter the sad state of urban school systems. If nothing else, a proposal like this one at least tries to address what matters: changing the political dynamics of urban school systems by attracting more middle-income families into that system.

Embracing Suburban Diversity

In suburban districts, like Henrico County, that are becoming increasingly diverse, the risk is that they are on their way to becoming overwhelmingly minority and poor, as more families move from the suburbs to the exurbs. This was the traditional pattern within cities during the 1970s. White flight began slowly but then accelerated; as the numbers leaving increased, it created more momentum and pressure on others to leave as well.

In light of this experience, and in light of polls showing that whites and blacks have different preferences regarding the right racial mix in neighborhoods, the notion of a tipping point became conventional wisdom. The basic theory is simple. If the percentage of minority residents rises to a certain level, say 20 percent, this will trigger the beginning of white flight, which will snowball until the neighborhood is completely minority. The first ones to leave will be those who have the least tolerance for diversity. If they are replaced by minority families, that will increase the percentage of minority families in the neighborhood, which will then trigger the departure by whites who had slightly more tolerance for diversity than the first families who left. And so on, until the most tolerant whites finally decide to depart.[38]

The good news is that the tipping point phenomenon does not appear as inevitable as it once did. Over the last two decades, many racially diverse communities have remained stable, and these communities also tend to be economically diverse. In one study of thirty-four metropolitan areas, for example, more than three-fourths of the neighborhoods that were racially mixed in 1980 remained mixed in 1990. A more recent study of residential patterns in sixty-nine large metropolitan areas during the 1990s found similar results: of the neighborhoods that were racially mixed at the start of the decade, 80 percent remained stable.[39]

To be sure, there is still a great deal of residential segregation. Racially mixed neighborhoods are the exception rather than the rule in both cities and suburbs—constituting, for example, only one-third of all neighborhoods in the sixty-nine metropolitan areas studied. Nonetheless, it is clear that while the tipping model is an elegant (if depressing) theory, it does not represent current reality. Instead, as a researcher from the Brookings Institution concluded: "The real story about America's neighborhoods, though far from revealing anything close to a color-blind society, is less pessimistic and more dynamic than we have tended to believe. Integrated neighborhoods may be a minority, but their numbers are growing, and many appear likely to remain racially mixed for many years."[40]

Additional signs about changing racial preferences give cause for some optimism about the possibility of stably integrated school districts. A larger percentage of whites express a willingness to live in racially mixed neighborhoods, and this is especially true among young adults, who seem quite tolerant of diversity. Indeed, in his recent book *The Way We'll Be*, renowned political pollster John Zogby found an unprecedented embrace of diversity among the eighteen- to twenty-nine-year-olds he surveyed. Although he did not include questions about residential choices, other inquiries shed some important light on the degree of racial tolerance among this group. To cite just two examples, 86 percent of adults under thirty-years old approved of interracial marriages, compared to just 30 percent of those over sixty-five. Only 12 percent of those aged eighteen to twenty-nine expressed negative feelings about a member of their family dating someone of a different race, while 40 percent of those aged seventy and older said they would oppose it. These poll findings are reinforced by behavior in dating and marriage. Interracial marriages doubled between 1990 and 2000 and now represent more than 7 percent of all American marriages.[41]

Other polls point in the same direction. A recent survey conducted by the Pew Research Center found that 76 percent of young adults, in the eighteen-to-twenty-nine age group, would prefer to live in a racially diverse community. Only 47 percent of those sixty-five or older share this preference. Another study, conducted by the Center for Information and Research on Civic Learning and Engagement, found similar results. This latter study was based on a number of surveys regarding racial issues conducted over a period of four decades, and it found that "young Americans are the most tolerant age group" and that this age cohort has become more tolerant over time.[42]

This is not to say we have reached the golden age of race relations. The degree of residential integration does yet not match the supposed change in attitudes, although the influx of white professionals into urban areas is being led by younger adults. The gap between polling data and change on the ground could reflect the time lag between changed attitudes and behavior. But it may also reflect the gap between what people say and what they do.

Nonetheless, the possibilities for stably integrated communities and schools are certainly greater than they have been in the past. Those who currently craft education policies, as well as those who write about them, are old enough to have lived through the era of "forced" busing. To them, integration requires coercion, which in turn leads to backlash, sometimes violent, which in turn leads inevitably failure. It is difficult for this group to imagine a future much different from their past. But future generations do not carry this burden, and it makes sense to consider the possibilities created by this fact—to think harder, in other words, about how the world looks to the generation that will soon be in charge.

School districts would be wise to begin that process now by embracing the diversity within their schools, while working hard to show that diverse schools can remain academically rigorous. This was the goal of Dr. Pruden as principal at Freeman High School (and it remains the goal of his successor, Anne Poates). Dr. Pruden recognized the trend toward greater diversity and realized it would only continue. His only option, which he embraced wholeheartedly, was to figure out how to make a diverse school succeed—for all students.[43]

At one level, embracing diversity is just a matter of attitude and public relations, but these are nonetheless important. If school districts treat diversity as a problem rather than an opportunity, it will be perceived as a problem, which eventually will drive middle-income families away. School district leaders should instead emphasize that students in diverse schools can receive a much fuller and richer education, one that is strong on academics but also helps prepare students for the real world, which is becoming more diverse by the year. These leaders should be thinking in particular about how to attract and keep the interest of a new generation of young parents, who seem quite open to the idea of living in diverse rather than homogenous settings.

There are examples here to follow. One of the best is Montclair, New Jersey. For more than three decades, this school district, like the town itself, has been racially and economically diverse. The town's population is roughly 60 percent white and 40 percent minority, and over 20 percent have incomes of less than $35,000. The school district is roughly 50 percent white and 50 percent minority, and roughly 20 percent of the students are eligible for free and reduced-price lunches. These figures have held steady for a fairly long period of time. Montclair prides itself on its commitment to racial and economic diversity, and this has worked to attract people to the town, not drive them away. Indeed, the housing market has been so active that the town leaders are more concerned about maintaining enough affordable housing options than about falling demand. Montclair is not perfect, nor are its schools, which have had to deal with the problem of in-school segregation. But it is a promising model nonetheless, and it cannot be doubted that all students in Montclair are receiving a better education than most of their peers in Newark, Camden, or Jersey City.[44]

Another intriguing example is Montgomery County in Maryland. The district, which is adjacent to Washington, D.C. serves nearly 150,000 students. Roughly sixty percent are racial or ethnic minorities, and many of these students come from poor families. The other forty percent are white and middle-income or affluent. The families live in different parts of the county and, for the most part, attend different schools. But for the last ten years, the district has been committed to raising the performance of all students while simultaneously closing the achievement gap. It has done so by shifting some resources, including teachers, from the middle-income, white schools to the poor, minority ones, and by committing all stakeholders in the district—parents, teachers, principals, and school board members—to the success of all schools.[45]

As detailed in a recent case study, the school system has experienced a good deal of success in meeting its academic goals. Scores are up for all students, while students at the lowest levels have made the greatest gains, which means that overall performance has improved while the achievement gap has narrowed. In addition, the approach has received support from all sectors of the community. School officials convinced parents and homeowners that ensuring the success of all students in the district was not only the right thing to do, but was in their best financial interests, as a healthy district is good for business and good for home values.[46]

There are not many districts like Montclair or Montgomery County at the moment, but there could be many more if demographic trends and preferences continue in the direction they are headed. Montclair, for example, is a close-in, older suburb of New York, and it has attracted families who like its urban feel but desire more space than city apartments afford. There are many suburbs that fit this description, and housing analysts suggest that suburbs with these features are becoming increasingly popular. Montclair's success is obviously due in large part to self-selection. Montclair marketed itself, essentially, as a racially and economically diverse place, and those interested in living in such a place moved there. The high demand for housing there, however, suggests that demand for places like Montclair currently exceeds supply. Coupled with indications that younger adults—the group who will have families soon—value diversity, more suburban municipalities should seriously consider championing their diversity rather than trying to hide it.

Montgomery County is much larger and has a diverse range of neighborhoods, from more urban to more rural. It remains a popular place to live in part because of these diverse housing options, but primarily because of its proximity to Washington, D.C. While Montgomery County has not exactly marketed itself in the way Montclair has, the decade-long effort to achieve both excellence and equity in the schools is getting the district a good deal of favorable attention. It also represents what I propose here: a suburban district embracing rather than downplaying increased student diversity. Like Montclair, Montgomery County is not perfect, and the demographics continue to change as the percentage of poor and minority students increase. Whether the academic gains will continue and the white, middle-income population will stabilize remain to be seen.

As for the schools themselves, more than marketing will be needed to maintain academic standards and rigor. A diverse school creates more opportunities for a full education, but it also presents more challenges, academically and socially, than a school filled solely with white, middle-income students. In-school segregation, for example, either in classes or in social settings like the lunch room, represents a genuine challenge, which must be confronted wisely in order to be resolved. School leaders in increasingly diverse suburbs should be working now to gain knowledge about best practices from other schools that have succeeded with diverse student enrollments. They should also take advantage of the body of academic research about how to manage diverse schools. In short, school leaders need to act now to put programs and practices into place that will ensure the continued success of their schools as they become more diverse.[47]

Intradistrict Diversity

School officials should also consider steps to prevent or rectify imbalances among schools within their districts. Especially in large districts like Henrico County, students from different racial and economic backgrounds are not evenly distributed throughout the district. Some schools remain largely white and middle-income, whereas others are predominantly minority and poor. Deep Run High School in Henrico County, for example, is roughly 82 percent white, 5 percent black, 2 percent Hispanic, and 9 percent Asian. Less than 2 percent of the students are eligible for free and reduced-price lunch. By contrast, Highland Springs High School, also in Henrico, is 10 percent white, 85 percent black, and less than 2 percent Hispanic or Asian. Thirty-three percent of the students are eligible for free and reduced-price lunch.[48]

These imbalances present a real challenge. Socioeconomic and racial diversity are crucially important at the district level, but diversity still matters the most at the school level. It would be an improvement, for example, to have more majority-middle-income districts than we currently have, because a critical mass of middle-income families will alter the political dynamics within the school district and work to improve the resources and efficiency of the district overall. But high-poverty schools within a majority-middle-income district are still going to be at a disadvantage compared to majority-middle-income schools in the same district.

At the same time, however, pressing too hard to achieve a perfect balance might drive a significant number of families away. If students are reassigned from one school to another, for example, this will upset the expectations of existing residents and may cause them to leave. More important, it would signal to potential newcomers that they will not be able to control where their children go to school by purchasing or renting a home in a particular neighborhood. This would be a bad signal to send to parents who have options about where to live and would like to select a school through their choice of residence. A private school, for example, presumably would not try to recruit students by suggesting that they might be reassigned to a totally different private school in a few years.

This does not mean that "forced" socioeconomic integration can never work. Wake County, North Carolina, a school district that encompasses both the city of Raleigh and the surrounding suburbs, assigns students so as to avoid any school becoming more than 40 percent poor, which requires some long bus rides. It also requires changing at least some assignments every year. Despite these inconveniences, the school system has experienced explosive growth over the last several years, adding over fifty thousand students in a decade. At nearly 140,000 students, it is now the largest school district in North Carolina and the eighteenth largest in the country. The overall enrollment is roughly 55 percent white and nearly 30 percent poor.[49]

Wake County is not alone in considering socioeconomic status when assigning students. Over forty districts do so. But almost all of these districts use a system of public school choice, as opposed to mandatory assignments, which is managed to create socioeconomically integrated schools. Some districts use magnet or other specialized schools that have general goals for student diversity. Some, like Cambridge, Massachusetts, have a full system of choice, where parents list their first three options and students are assigned with an eye toward socioeconomic integration.[50]

There are over fifteen thousand school districts across the country. It would be foolish to suggest that none of them could be persuaded to follow Wake County's example and redraw attendance lines whenever necessary to create and maintain socioeconomically—or racially—integrated schools. Most districts, however, should probably consider less coercive methods in order to avoid driving families away; parents with options about schooling want to be able to exercise them. A system of complete choice, where families have no right to attend neighborhood schools, should also be avoided for the same reason: it takes away control from parents. Instead, a system that offers a right to attend a neighborhood school combined with the option to attend a magnet school or specialized program would likely be optimal.

Allowing for a combination of neighborhood schools and school choice is also good insurance for districts experiencing fairly rapid demographic changes. Choice offers parents an option to exercise if they become dissatisfied with their neighborhood schools, and providing this option should make it easier to attract new families. In order to avoid sending a signal that neighborhood schools are in decline, however, districts need to take care in creating and presenting choice options. Charter schools, for example, might need to be avoided in some districts, given past fights about them and the perception that they signal a school system in decline. Public magnet schools, at least at first, might be a better method to signal that more options are being created, both to supplement existing public schools and to encourage—through choice—greater integration within the district.

Changing the Conversation

Urban districts looking to attract white, middle-income families, and suburban districts looking to retain them, also need to broaden the conversation about the purpose of public education. They should do this by highlighting successfully integrated schools—ones that are diverse and post good test scores. There are plenty of reports touting the performance of the few high-poverty, high-minority schools that beat the odds. It is time for districts—and commentators—to highlight diverse schools that succeed academically. School diversity should be defended as a supplement to, not a substitute for, academic rigor. Those who run successful, diverse schools can credibly make the case that diverse schools can and should do more than prepare students for standardized tests; they should also prepare them for life.

Changing the conversation is important because white, middle-income families need to see a benefit to their children from attending diverse schools. Most of the time, reformers speak of these families as assets from whom others will benefit. This is undoubtedly true, but it is also incomplete. White, middle-income students can also benefit from exposure to a diverse group of peers. Unless the benefits of diversity to these students are emphasized, moreover, their parents will remain wary of choosing a diverse school over a homogeneous one.[51]

Colleges and universities can help in this regard. These institutions champion diversity on their campuses and recruit poor and minority students. Many have affirmative action programs that are designed to achieve a diverse student body, and these institutions banded together to successfully defend their affirmative action programs against a constitutional challenge. Presumably these institutions believe diversity is part of providing a well-rounded education to all students.

Leaders of colleges and universities should join the conversation about public education and emphasize the importance of diversity in elementary and secondary schools. In particular, they ought to announce that students who attend diverse schools, whether measured by race, ethnicity, or socioeconomic status, will be given a boost in the admissions process. This is not as far-fetched as it might seem. A recent *New York Times* article described a letter from the dean of admissions at Amherst College, which "said, in effect, that in the emerging multicultural world, colleges are looking for students who can negotiate racially diverse settings and that those who don't will be at a distinct disadvantage in the admissions process." If a critical mass of schools formally announced such a position as official policy, and broadened it to include economic diversity, this would surely attract a great deal of attention. More important, it might alter the calculations of middle-income families regarding the benefits of diverse schools. These families would have a greater incentive to support diversity within their neighborhood schools and more reason to consider diverse magnet and charter schools.[52]

Providing incentives to support diversity is crucial as one part of an effort to alter perceptions about diverse schools. The simple but important truth is that if white, middle-income families come to value diversity, then we will see a good deal of diversity in schools and school districts. If they remain wary of it, we will continue to see only token diversity. Public policy and court decisions, if the past is any guide, are no match for the strong preferences of white, middle-income families. Policy and court decisions tend to bend to meet those preferences, not the other way around.

One final issue is worth mentioning. In championing diversity, school district leaders should speak about diversity in broad terms and avoid any suggestion of quotas for racial or ethnic balance. It might be sensible to establish a clear goal of creating schools where fewer than 50 percent of students are eligible for free and reduced-price lunch, pointing to the reams of social science evidence that suggest that high-poverty schools are especially vulnerable to failure. But any similar effort to establish precise goals for race and ethnicity are most likely illegal under the U.S. Supreme Court's affirmative action and voluntary desegregation decisions, which frown on the use of strict racial quotas.[53]

Even if legal, any effort to achieve a precise racial or ethnic balance, which hints at a quota, is likely to backfire politically. In a world that is no longer black and white, questions about the proper level of racial and ethnic diversity are extremely complicated. How should school diversity be measured? Is a school that is mostly African-American and Hispanic more or less diverse than one that is mostly white and Asian-American? Does diversity require proportional representation of all racial and ethnic groups within a reasonable distance? How should students of mixed racial and ethnic backgrounds—a group that is expected to triple in size and make up nearly 4 percent of the population over the next few decades—be counted? There are few good answers to these questions and others like them, and attempts to answer them will likely do little more than generate controversy.

Again, this is not to suggest that race should be ignored, nor is it to suggest that all efforts to increase racial integration are illegal. Schools and districts can take steps to increase racial integration, as long as they do not have a precise quota in mind. In addition, they can take race into account when setting attendance policies—drawing attendance zones, adopting a choice plan, deciding where to build a new school—as long as they do not admit or reject a particular student solely on the basis of race. Districts and schools are also free to rely on proxies for race, like socioeconomic status, which can indirectly increase racial integration. The point is simply that creating specific racial goals for enrollment would likely be both illegal and counterproductive.[54]

BEYOND INTEGRATION

Integration is not going to happen immediately as a result of demographic changes. In some places, it will not happen at all, or at least not for a very long time. Schools in the poorest areas of central cities, like those in far-flung suburbs, will be resistant to change. Even where it occurs, integration will not be a panacea. Pursuing sensible academic policies and reforms, whether within diverse or homogenous schools, will remain as crucial as it has always been. This is nothing more than common sense, and it may go without saying, but proposals to increase integration seem especially vulnerable to misconstruction and misunderstanding.

So to be perfectly clear: the call for a renewed focus on integration should not be read as a rejection of other reforms as unnecessary or unwise. To be in favor of integration is not to be against reforms like greater accountability for students and teachers, (sensible) standards and testing, increased access to preschool, school choice, merit pay for teachers, smaller class sizes, increased funding for facilities, or detracking—or a host of other promising approaches. This is not the place to identify the perfect menu of substantive policies, even assuming one menu would be right for all districts. The point instead is that we are more likely to see the right policies and reforms, and to see them faithfully implemented, if schools and school districts are less isolated by race and class than they are now. In some ways, this is really just a question of priorities, and my argument, which admittedly is out of fashion, is that integration should remain a top priority. Where integration is not possible right away, and even where it is, the substance of other academic policies will still matter.

COURTS

Readers may have noticed that courts do not play a large role in this chapter. The omission is intentional. As this book has documented, courts have not been especially reliable partners in efforts to restructure educational opportunity, and their importance has diminished over time. Looking ahead, it seems unlikely that this pattern will change substantially.

In particular, it seems safe to conclude that federal courts will remain mostly on the sidelines. Lower federal courts, with prodding from the U.S. Supreme Court, are bowing out of school desegregation, and there is little reason to believe that they will revisit this issue or rethink their rulings. The same is true with regard to school finance reform. It seems implausible, especially in light of all of the state court activity, that the Supreme Court would reconsider *San Antonio v. Rodriguez*. It seems equally unlikely that courts will become much more involved in fights over school choice or standards and testing. Federal courts have no real basis on which to order school choice or mandate that standards and tests be made more challenging. The most they can do—and have done—is determine whether there are legal obstacles to such programs, not whether they are required.

Some state courts will remain involved in school finance reform, and there are ways, suggested in previous chapters, that court involvement could become more effective in this arena. It is not likely, however, that many state courts will take on more fundamental issues like racial or socioeconomic segregation. The Connecticut Supreme Court confronted this issue in *Sheff v. O'Neill*, ruling that the state constitution prohibited even de facto school segregation. *Sheff* was decided in 1996, however, and no other court has followed Connecticut's lead. Even courts that are willing to strike down school funding schemes seem reluctant to move beyond funding to address segregation by race and income.[55]

Two cases decided on the same day in 2003 in New York illustrate this point. In the first case, *Campaign for Fiscal Equity (CFE) v. State*, New York's highest court ruled for the plaintiffs in a traditional school funding suit and ordered the state to provide more funding for New York City's schools. Relying on the education clause of the New York Constitution, the court ruled that students were entitled to a "sound, basic education," which in the court's view was one that prepared them for "meaningful civic participation in contemporary society." The court agreed that city students needed more resources in order to achieve that goal.[56]

In the second case, *Paynter v. State*, the court dismissed a complaint brought by students in the Rochester school district. These students also sought to enforce the state constitutional guarantee of a sound, basic education. Instead of claiming that schools lacked sufficient funding, however, the plaintiffs attacked the economic (and racial) isolation that characterized that district. As in many other metropolitan areas, Rochester students are primarily poor and minority, whereas students in many surrounding suburbs are predominantly white and middle-class. The plaintiffs argued that students could not receive an adequate education under such conditions. In particular, they argued that the concentration of poor students in the Rochester district made it impossible for those students to receive an adequate education.[57]

At first glance, the claim in *Paynter* might seem like a stretch. But consider the reasoning in *Campaign for Fiscal Equity*, the school funding case. The state constitution does not say a word about adequate funding of public schools. For the court to rule for New York City students, it had to infer that city students, without adequate funding, would not be prepared for "meaningful civic participation." This meant that the court had to accept a connection between greater resources and meaningful civic participation, defined either narrowly in terms of academic success or more broadly.

It follows logically that if the plaintiffs in *Paynter* could establish a connection between increased integration and meaningful civic participation, they, too, should have prevailed. To be more precise, their complaint should have been allowed to go forward if such a connection could plausibly be demonstrated by the evidence, which it certainly could be. Indeed, the connection between concentrated poverty and low academic achievement is easier to establish than is the connection between funding and achievement. It is also easy to show that attending a racially and economically diverse school can help prepare students for "meaningful civic participation" in a racially and economically diverse society. In fact, attending a diverse school probably does more in this regard than attending a well-funded but racially or economically homogeneous school.[58]

It is therefore difficult to understand from a legal perspective why the New York court ordered the state, in the funding case, to provide more money for city schools but did not even let the plaintiffs go to trial in Rochester. From a political perspective, however, the two opinions are easy to reconcile. Ordering more money for city schools generates some controversy, but this pales in comparison to the controversy that would be created by a decision that required racial and socioeconomic integration across district lines. The court was unwilling to push against that tide.

The fact that few litigants have attempted to pursue cases like *Sheff* or *Paynter*, while many have pursued school funding cases, suggests that such claims appear implausible even to advocates. To be sure, school finance attorneys, who are already committed to funding as the answer, may be unduly pessimistic, and it may be that more courts would follow Connecticut's lead rather than New York's if asked to do so. There may also be some value to pressing the claim even if courts will reject it, if only to keep some attention on racial and economic isolation. Nonetheless, the reluctance to present these claims is understandable in light of the poor track record of attempts to obtain and enforce court-ordered integration across school district lines. Even *Sheff*, the one "successful" case, has done relatively little to increase integration in the Hartford metropolitan area—and that case was decided more than a decade ago.[59]

Court-ordered integration, whether racial or socioeconomic, thus seems unlikely in the near future. If political opinion changes, and integration is more widely embraced, courts might become more willing to intervene. Courts might well be comfortable pushing legislatures in a direction they are already headed, as some school finance cases indicate. Most observers, for example, believed that the Kentucky Supreme Court was willing to declare the entire system of public education unconstitutional because there was already a great deal of political support for reform. Similarly, litigants are increasingly including claims for access to preschool in school funding suits, and some courts have proven receptive. A decade ago, before state-funded preschool programs became popular, court claims seeking a right to preschool education were non-existent. If socioeconomic integration or racial integration were more widely supported as a critical component of education, perhaps state courts would be more willing to take on the issue.[60]

For the moment, however, it must be recognized that the willingness and ability of courts to effect substantial changes in the structure of educational opportunity are limited. Successful school funding suits, for example, bring more money but leave schools isolated by race and poverty, and they usually leave the root cause of inequality—unequal property wealth among districts—untouched. These suits can be the impetus for marginal changes, not fundamental ones. And so it seems with courts generally in the context of education: they are more willing and able to make marginal rather than fundamental changes.

Judge Merhige, who ordered the consolidation of the Richmond, Henrico, and Chesterfield school systems, passed away recently, and his passing symbolized the end of an era. When he issued his consolidation order in the early 1970s, courts were at the forefront of efforts to equalize educational opportunities, and many hoped that court decrees could create more just and humane school systems. That day has largely passed.

One can never know what school systems in metropolitan areas would have looked like if the U.S. Supreme Court had upheld Judge Merhige's ruling or if *Milliken v. Bradley* had been decided differently. But even if courts had the capacity to bring suburban and urban schools together, they did not—and do not—seem to have the will. Indeed, even Judge Merhige lowered his sights at the end. His final order in the Richmond school desegregation case, rejecting a plea for greater funding to make up for the educational harms from segregated schools, acknowledged and accepted the limits of court involvement in education reform. He recognized that injustices and inequities remained, but he also recognized that they could not all be solved by courts. The problems, he suggested, were too intertwined, entrenched, and complicated to be resolved by court decree. Courts, Mehrige seemed to acknowledge, are good at striking things down and telling legislatures what they cannot do. They are not so good—or so comfortable—at building things, like a well-run and equitable school system. It appears that most other judges, for better or worse, have reached the same conclusion.[61]

CONCLUSION

The demographic changes described in this chapter are just emerging, and it remains to be seen whether they will continue. It is also uncertain whether they can be helped along by some of the measures proposed here, even assuming that those measures or others like them could garner enough support to be pursued. The necessary uncertainty that accompanies the future and attempts to shape it, however, should not cause confusion about the past or the present.

There is a tendency among many commentators and advocates working in the field of education law and policy to downplay the significance of concentrated poverty, not to mention racial isolation. Some are opposed to the notion of socio-economic or racial integration, especially if imposed by a court or legislature. Most others have abandoned the idea as impractical or politically impossible. To these commentators and advocates, demography may not be destiny, but the separation of poor and minority students from their white and middle-class peers certainly seems inexorable. The motivation to downplay the importance of school and district composition is thus not difficult to understand: better to focus on what might be attained than to argue for something beyond reach.

I appreciate but do not subscribe to this approach. Where high-poverty schools and districts are impervious to change, it is vitally important to figure out ways to improve those schools and districts. But it is also important to tell the truth. The truth is that separating the poor and politically powerless in their own schools and districts is antithetical to the idea of equal educational opportunity. In the end, there may not be much that can be done to alter the current pattern of separation, although it is still too early to reach this conclusion. But one should never pretend that this separation is not a problem simply because there are no easy or obvious solutions. Indeed, in the field of education law and policy, it was *the* problem of the last half century, and it remains the central problem of the twenty-first century.

Freeman and Tee-Jay Revisited

William Flammia began teaching at Tee-Jay in 1966. He retired in 2000. He remained involved at Tee-Jay after retirement, helping to prepare students who needed additional assistance to pass the SOL tests. When I interviewed him, I asked him about the biggest changes he had seen over nearly four decades as a teacher. Without hesitation, he identified the students. "When I started teaching in 1966," he reported, "the student body was 95 percent white and mostly middle-class. Some were from blue-collar backgrounds, which meant there was some socioeconomic mixing." Today, that is no longer the case: "Now, most of the kids come from at-risk families—single-family homes, low-income homes, parents with limited educations. They come to school with multiple problems, and it shows. There are behavioral issues I didn't confront as a new teacher, absenteeism. It's a huge challenge."[1]

Mr. Flammia remained involved at Tee-Jay, he said, because he wanted to act as a bridge between the past and the present. When he began, Tee-Jay was one of the best schools in the state, and he believed the school did an excellent job in preparing students to succeed later in life. He still believed the school could do this, and as he said, "that's the main focus that keeps me going." Having seen students from difficult home situations succeed, he remained confident that schools can make a difference.

What frustrated him, though, was that "people in affluent schools have no idea about the struggles that kids in poorer schools face. We tend to live in little pockets—some wealthy, some poor. I hate to see the walls we've built." He was especially frustrated, he said, by the fact that people wrote off Tee-Jay as a bad school. Most people were surprised, he told me, when they learned that more than half of the students who graduated went on to college, and in general they were surprised by the number of successful students. To be sure, Tee-Jay did not succeed at the level of suburban schools like Freeman, but it was not a bad—or dangerous—school, as many in the suburbs assumed.[2]

Freeman has also seen its share of changes. Once all-white and a haven for those seeking to avoid desegregation, the school has become increasingly diverse, with a 25 percent minority enrollment and about the same percentage of poor students. Indeed, when I interviewed Dr. Pruden, he indicated that some parents sent their children to Freeman precisely because they were interested in an integrated school environment. The increased diversity at Freeman, in Dr. Pruden's view, was a challenge but one that was worth it. All of the students received a richer education, and the disadvantaged students conformed to the majority culture, which emphasized and expected academic success. "Most of the kids who come here have been talking most of their lives about college with their parents. The question is where, not whether. The kids who haven't had those conversations at home now have them at school."[3]

Dr. Pruden, having spent substantial time working at both Tee-Jay and Freeman, emerged as a true believer in the power of integration. Teachers at Freeman, he said, are "not miracle workers and those at Tee-Jay are not untalented." The difference was in the student population. It is just much harder to succeed in a school where most of the students come from disadvantaged backgrounds and have had few educational role models. It is not the case, Dr. Pruden emphasized, that poor kids are incapable of succeeding. Instead, it is the sheer number of poor students from disadvantaged homes that makes Tee-Jay such a challenging place. He has heard stories about schools with charismatic leaders and dedicated teachers who have managed to achieve at high levels, but for every one of these, "there are thousands who don't make the grade."[4]

It is not impossible to imagine Tee-Jay becoming more like Freeman, both Mr. Flammia and Dr. Pruden agreed, but the key is to reduce the level of poverty at Tee-Jay. The transformation of Tee-Jay from a predominantly middle-income to a predominantly poor school happened over a relatively brief period, and it would be wrong to think that change will never come again. In fact, Dr. Pruden pointed out, the attendance zone for Tee-Jay High School includes a number of affluent neighborhoods. "If all the parents who sent their kids to private school sent them to Tee-Jay instead," he suggested, "the school would look a lot like Freeman."[5]

Socioeconomic and racial integration are not a cure-alls, both Dr. Pruden and Mr. Flammia emphasized. Integration, they also acknowledged, is a subject that inspires controversy on all sides. Dr. Pruden reported that when the subject of increasing integration came up while he was principal at Tee-Jay, a number of African-American parents were resentful and suspicious. Some believed it was just another effort by whites to take over a predominantly black institution because they assumed it was inferior. Resistance to integration, then or now, is not confined to middle-income whites.

Reducing poverty levels in schools, however, gives schools a better chance to succeed at the goal Mr. Flammia identified: preparing students to succeed in life. Increased diversity can also help all students prepare for a remarkably and increasingly diverse world, as Dr. Pruden emphasized. The basic truth is that we have tried for more than three decades to make schools of concentrated poverty work, and we have largely failed. If the walls that Mr. Flammia despises do not come down, we will likely continue to bang our heads against them. And Tee-Jay and Freeman students, like hundreds of thousands just like them around the country, will remain five miles away, but a world apart.

Introduction

1. *Brown* is reported at 347 U.S. 483 (1954). School enrollment data come from the website SchoolMatters and interviews with principals; see www.schoolmatters.com. Student poverty is higher than officially reported, especially at high school, because many students who are eligible do not participate in free and reduced-price lunch programs. Edward H. Pruden, principal, Freeman High School, interview by the author, Jun. 27, 2006, Richmond, VA.

2. Duke, *School That Refused to Die*; enrollment data from SchoolMatters website, www.schoolmatters.com; Barbara Ulschmid, principal, Thomas Jefferson High School, interview by the author, May 22, 2008, Richmond, VA; and William Russell Flammia, former teacher at Tee-Jay, telephone interview by the author, Jul. 25, 2006.

3. Testing data are for the 2007–8 school year, from School Data Direct, www. schooldatadirect.org. Graduation rates from school report cards issued by Virginia Department of Education, and college attendance rates from "Diploma Graduates and Completers by School, 2007–8," both available at www.doe.virginia.gov.

4. In addition to *Savage Inequalities*, Kozol has published *The Shame of the Nation*, which is something of a sequel and raises many of the same issues initially raised in *Savage Inequalities*.

5. These cases are discussed extensively in chapter 2.

6. For a transcript of Nixon's speech, see *NYT*, 17 Mar. 1972, 22.

7. School desegregation is discussed in chapters 1 and 2.

8. School finance litigation and reform are discussed at length in chapters 3 and 4 again briefly in the last section of chapter 7.

9. It is worth noting that desegregation advocates did not likewise turn to state constitutions after losing in *Milliken I*. No effort was made to fashion arguments for cross-district integration based on state constitutional provisions, even though education clauses in state constitutions could logically form the basis for such arguments. Indeed, the Connecticut Supreme Court concluded in a 1996 decision, *Sheff v. O'Neill*, that the Connecticut Constitution protected the right of students to attend integrated schools. The fact that it took until the 1990s before this opportunity was even pursued gives some indication of the political difficulty of crossing district lines and the degree to which Nixon's compromise was accepted—perhaps as politically inevitable—even by desegregation advocates.

10. On the dominance of suburban legislators in Virginia, see, e.g., *WP*, 12 Sept. 1999, A1. See generally Wolman et al., "The Calculus of Coalitions," 1–6; Allen et al., "State Power, Suburban Interests, and City School Reform," 2–12; Thomas, *United States of Suburbia*, 146.

11. School choice is the subject of chapters 5 and 6.

12. Wildman, "Credit Is Due," 15.

13. Chapter 7 addresses in detail the standards and testing movement, and particularly the NCLB.

14. Pruden, Ulschmid, and Flammia interviews; site and classroom visits in spring 2006, 2007, and 2008.

15. See, e.g., Cremin, *Republic and the School*, 23–24, 31–32; Matthews, *Class Struggle*, 185; Macedo, *Diversity and Distrust*, 16–20; Rothstein and Wilder, *Grading Education*, 14–19; Reese, *America's Public Schools*, 10–44; Jeffries and Ryan, "Political History of Establishment Clause," 362–63.

16. For detailed discussion of these points, see chapters 2 and 4.

17. See Cashin, *Failures of Integration*, 231–34 (arguing that the majority of whites are suburbanites who feel little responsibility for solving the problems of high-poverty schools).

18. Pruden interviews, Jun. 27, 2006, May 13, 2008.

Chapter 1

1. Duke, *School That Refused to Die*, 134.

2. The classic conventional account of school desegregation is Kluger, *Simple Justice*.

3. See Klarman, *From Jim Crow to Civil Rights*, 417.

4. Ibid., 417–19; Lassiter, *Silent Majority*, 23–93.

5. See Irons, *Jim Crow's Children*, 189; Klarman, *From Jim Crow to Civil Rights*, 329–43.

6. Cooper v. Aaron, 358 U.S. 1 (1958) (Little Rock); Griffin v. Prince Edward County, 377 U.S. 218 (1964); Shuttlesworth v. Birmingham Board of Education, 358 U.S. 101 (1958) (upholding pupil placement law); Kelley v. Board of Education of Nashville, 270 F.2d 209 (6th Cir.), cert. denied, 361 U.S. 924 (1959) (Warren, C.J., Douglas, J., and Brennan, J., dissenting) (declining to review decision upholding Nashville's plan, which desegregated a grade at a time and allowed for minority-to-majority transfers).

7. Green v. New Kent County, 391 U.S. 430 (1968).

8. *RTD*, 2 May 2004, A1.

9. Ibid.

10. Harrison v. Day, 106 S.E.2d 636, 642 (Va. 1959); *RAA*, 26 Sept. 1952, 22; *RTD*, 18 May 1954, 6; *RTD*, 16 Jul. 1954, 12.

11. *RTD*, 2 May 2004, A1; Duke, *School That Refused to Die*, 34–91, 99.

12. *RTD*, 18 May 1954, 7; *RTD*, 2 May 2004, A1; Johnson, *Douglas Southall Freeman*.

13. Plessy v. Ferguson, 163 U.S. 537 (1896); Pratt, *Color of Their Skin*, 15–20; Duke, *School That Refused to Die*, 10.

14. Quotes from Anderson, "Education of Blacks in the South," 451. See also Duke, *School That Refused to Die*, 10.

15. Anderson, "Education of Blacks in the South," 454–55.

16. Klarman, *From Jim Crow to Civil Rights*, 43–47; Kluger, *Simple Justice*, 134–35; Wilkinson, *From* Brown *to Bakke*, 19; Myrdal, *American Dilemma*, 339; *RTD*, 18 May 1954, 6; Davison, *Jim Crow Moves North*, 163–66, 191–92.

17. Hill quoted in Ryan, "Schools, Race, and Money," 258.

18. Patterson, *Civil Rights Milestone*, 11; Pratt, *Color of Their Skin*, 17; Donohue, III et al., *Social Action*, 3–4; Ryan, "Schools, Race, and Money," 258.

19. Carter, "Reexamining *Brown*," 617.

20. Ibid.; Middleton, "*Brown v. Board:* Revisited," 29; Minow, "School Finance," 395–96; Liebman, "Implementing *Brown*," 396.

21. Klarman, *From Jim Crow to Civil Rights*, 290–91; Bell, "*Brown v. Board of Education*," 524–26; Dudziak, "Desegregation as a Cold War Imperative," 61–120.

22. Du Bois, "Does the Negro Need Separate Schools," 328–35; Patterson, *Civil Rights Milestone*, 8, 240 (noting that John W. Davis, lead attorney for South Carolina in *Brown*, relied on Du Bois's argument in summarizing his case in favor of segregation).

23. Quote from *RAA*, 27 Mar. 1954, 9. Editorial from *RAA*, 22 Aug. 1953, editorial page. For discussion of Du Bois and dissent within the African-American community in the 1950s and later, see Patterson, *Civil Rights Milestone*, xxvi–xxvii, 8–9.

24. Sweatt v. Painter, 339 U.S. 629 (1950).

25. McLaurin v. Oklahoma State Regents, 339 U.S. 637 (1950).

26. Klarman, *From Jim Crow to Civil Rights*, 210–12.

27. Ibid., 292–312; Patterson, *Civil Rights Milestone*, 46–65.

28. Brown v. Board of Education, 347 U.S. 483 (1954); Bolling v. Sharpe, 347 U.S. 497 (1954); Wilkinson, *From* Brown *to Bakke*, 26–27; Patterson, *Civil Rights Milestone*, 52–54, 60–63.

29. Wilkinson, *From* Brown *to Bakke*, 27; Warren quote from Klarman, *From Jim Crow to Civil Rights*, 302.

30. Patterson, *Civil Rights Milestone*, 64–65; Wilkinson, *From* Brown *to Bakke*, 30–31; Hutchinson, "Unanimity and Desegregation," 44, 87.

31. Brown v. Board of Education, 347 U.S. 483, 493 (1954).

32. Ibid., 492–93.

33. Ibid., 493.

34. Ibid., 493–95.

35. Ibid., 495.

36. Bolling v. Sharpe, 347 U.S. 497 (1954). On the desire to avoid antagonizing the South, see, e.g., Patterson, *Civil Rights Milestone*, 65; Wilkinson, *From* Brown *to Bakke*, 31. On the desire to avoid saying anything about interracial marriage, see, e.g., Klarman, *From Jim Crow to Civil Rights*, 321. The decision outlawing bans on interracial marriage was *Loving v. Virginia*, 388 U.S. 1 (1967). On the unlikelihood that the Court was influenced by social science evidence, see, e.g., Goodman, "De Facto School Segregation," 279. Cases outlawing segregation in other public facilities include *Holmes v. City of Atlanta*, 350 U.S. 877

(1955) (public golf courses); *Mayor of Baltimore v. Dawson*, 350 U.S. 877 (1955) (public beaches and bathhouses); and *Gayle v. Browder*, 352 U.S. 903 (1956) (buses).

37. For discussion of critics of the social science evidence cited in note 11 of the *Brown* opinion, which included those friendly and hostile to the opinion, see, e.g., Wilkinson, *From* Brown *to* Bakke, 31–35. On the implications of *Brown*'s focus on harm to blacks from segregation, see Patterson, *Civil Rights Milestone*, xxvi–xxvii; Wilkinson, *From* Brown *to* Bakke, 46–47; Brown, "Has the Supreme Court Allowed," 6; *Missouri v. Jenkins*, 515 U.S. 70, 114–23 (1995) (Thomas, J., concurring).

38. See cases cited in note 36; San Antonio v. Rodriguez, 411 U.S. 1 (1973).

39. Brown v. Board of Education (*Brown II*), 349 U.S. 294, 300–1 (1955).

40. Stanley quoted in *RTD*, 18 May 1954, 9; Almond quoted in Muse, *Virginia's Massive Resistance*, 4; Stanley's view that no desegregation would occur for a year reported in *RTD*, 18 May 1954, 1; State Board decision reported in *RTD*, 30 May 1954, 12.

41. *RTD*, 18 May 954, 14; *RNL*, 18 May 1954, 10.

42. *RNL*, 18 May 1954, 12.

43. Jeffries, *Justice Lewis F. Powell*, 132–33.

44. See Klarman, *From Jim Crow to Civil Rights*, 415. The key decision requiring equal representation was *Reynolds v. Sims*, 377 U.S. 533 (1964).

45. Jeffries, *Justice Lewis F. Powell*, 133; Pratt, *Color of Their Skin*, 3–4; Stanley quoted in Muse, *Virginia's Massive Resistance*, 7. Byrd first coined the phrase "massive resistance," which was quoted in *RNL*, 27 Feb. 1956, 1.

46. Pratt, *Color of Their Skin*, 4–5; Jeffries, *Justice Lewis F. Powell*, 134–35.

47. Almond quoted in *RNL*, 1 Jun. 1955, 7; editorial, *RNL*, 1 Jun. 1955, 13; school construction reported in *RTD*, 3 Jun. 1955, 6 and 4 Jun. 1955, 1; localities' plans to await orders from the state reported in *RTD*, 1 Jun. 1955, 10 and *RNL*, 9 Jun. 1955, 1.

48. Almond v. Day, 89 S.E.2d 851 (Va. 1955).

49. Jeffries reports that the case was brought to test whether the Virginia Constitution "would bar tuition grants to students attending private schools." Jeffries, *Justice Lewis F. Powell*, 596.

50. Picott, "Status of Educational Desegregation in Virginia," 345; Dabney, *Virginia*, 532.

51. Jeffries, *Justice Lewis F. Powell*, 134–35; Pratt, *Color of Their Skin*, 5.

52. *RAA*, 10 Dec. 1955, 1.

53. Jeffries, *Justice Lewis F. Powell*, 134–35.

54. Wilkinson, *Harry Byrd*, 152; *RAA*, 28 Jul. 1956, 1; Jeffries, *Justice Lewis F. Powell*, 136–39; Lassiter, *Silent Majority*, 31–33; Pratt, *Color of Their Skin*, 5–6.

55. Jeffries, *Justice Lewis F. Powell*, 137–38; Pratt, *Color of Their Skin*, 5–6. Kilpatrick later wrote a book on the topic of interposition that elaborated on the editorial he wrote during 1955 and 56. See Kilpatrick, *Sovereign States*.

56. Interposition resolution is reprinted in *Journal of the Senate of Virginia* (1956): 146.

57. Byrd is quoted in *RNL*, 27 Feb. 1956, 1; on the Southern Manifesto, see, e.g., Gates, *Making of Massive Resistance*, 123, Kluger, *Simple Justice*, 752.

58. The Stanley, Gray, and Byrd meetings were reported in Muse, *Virginia's Massive Resistance*, 27–28. Byrd actually said in a speech that "if Virginia surrenders, the rest of the South will go down too." Quoted in Wilkinson, *From* Brown *to* Bakke, 83.

59. Friddell, *Colgate Darden*, 157–66; *RAA*, 8 Sept. 1956, 9; Dabney, *Virginia*, 537.

60. Membership of the Pupil Placement Board is discussed in Pratt, *Color of Their Skin*, 22. The Court referred to the tradition of local control in *Milliken v. Bradley*, 418 U.S. 717 (1974), in which it prohibited interdistrict busing absent a showing of interdistrict segregation.

61. Pratt, *Color of Their Skin*, 9; Wilkinson, *From* Brown *to* Bakke, 82–83.

62. Pratt, *Color of Their Skin*, 7–8; Jeffries, *Justice Lewis F. Powell*, 135; Lassiter, *Silent Majority*, 31–43.

63. Patterson, *Civil Rights Milestone*, 109–13; Klarman, *Jim Crow to Civil Rights*, 326–29; Irons, *Jim Crow's Children*, 180–84.

64. Patterson, *Civil Rights Milestone*, 110–112; Irons, *Jim Crow's Children*, 181–82.

65. Cooper v. Aaron, 358 U.S. 1 (1958).

66. Irons, *Jim Crow's Children*, 187; Patterson, *Civil Rights Milestone*, 112.

67. Jeffries, *Justice Lewis F. Powell*, 136–37; Lassiter, *Silent Majority*, 33.

68. The Richmond Committee is described in *RTD*, 10 Jan. 1959, 3. On the open-schools movement generally, see Lassiter, *Silent Majority*, 33–35; Lassiter and Lewis, *Moderate's Dilemma*, 5–80.

69. Lassiter, *Silent Majority*, 29–93; Klarman, *Jim Crow to Civil Rights*, 417.

70. Jeffries, *Justice Lewis F. Powell*, 151; *RTD*, 10 Jan. 1959, 3; Klarman, *Jim Crow to Civil Rights*, 417–18; Muse, *Virginia's Massive Resistance*, 94–98; Kilpatrick quoted in Wilkinson, *Harry Byrd*, 143.

71. Jeffries, *Justice Lewis F. Powell*, 150–53.

72. The federal court opinion is *James v. Almond*, 170 F. Supp. 331 (E.D. Va. 1959); the Virginia Supreme Court opinion is *Harrison v. Day*, 106 S.E.2d 636 (Va. 1959). It is highly unlikely that mere coincidence explains why the two courts issued their opinions on the same day, but I have been unable to confirm the more plausible inference that the courts coordinated with one another.

73. *Harrison*, 106 S.E.2d at 646.

74. Ibid., 647.

75. County School Board of Prince Edward County v. Griffin, 133 S.E.2d 565 (Va. 1963).

76. There is a large interdisciplinary literature about the motivations of judges and justices, much of it focused on federal judges generally and Supreme Court justices in particular. The general divide is over the influence of "law," meaning legal sources like the text, history, and structure of constitutional provisions, versus the influence of "politics," meaning everything from the ideology of individual justices to the tenor of the times. For an especially astute discussion of this issue, see Klarman, *From Jim Crow to Civil Rights*, 446–54. While less attention has been paid to state court judges, some of whom face different incentives because they are elected, there is little reason to believe that they do not struggle with the same choices between law and politics that confront federal judges.

77. Lassiter documents the opposition of middle-class whites to school closures, as well as their acceptance of token integration, in his excellent book *The Silent Majority*. Contemporary polls also indicated that after schools were closed, a "large majority of white citizens" did not support the policy. *RTD*, 9 May 1962, 6. For discussion of how white citizens changed their views about school closures, from support before schools

were closed to opposition once they were closed, see Klarman, *Jim Crow to Civil Rights*, 417–18.

78. Almond's speech is quoted and discussed in, e.g., Wilkinson, *Harry Byrd*, 146–47. His token integration plan was reported in *RTD*, 1 Feb. 1959, 1. The beginning of desegregation was reported in, e.g., *RTD*, 3 Feb. 1959, 1.

79. On the violence that accompanied desegregation in southern states, see Klarman, *Jim Crow to Civil Rights*, 421; Patterson, *Civil Rights Milestone*, 105–13.

80. Powell quoted in *RTD*, 7 May 1959, 4. Powell's opposition to school closings and interposition is reported in Jeffries, *Justice Lewis F. Powell*, 143–56.

81. On residential segregation in Richmond, see, e.g., Silver, *Twentieth-century Richmond*; on residential segregation generally and its relevance for school segregation, see, e.g., Wilkinson, *From* Brown *to* Bakke, 140–45. Powell is quoted in *RTD*, 7 May 1959, 4.

82. Statement from the board members quoted in *SSN*, Jul. 1960, 8; the Richmond School Directory is cited in *Bradley v. School Board*, 317 F.2d 429, 432 (4th Cir. 1963).

83. Gates, *Making of Massive Resistance*, 172; Jeffries, *Justice Lewis F. Powell*, 154–60; *Bradley v. School Board*, 317 F.2d at 431–34.

84. *Bradley v. School Board*, 317 F.2d at 431–38.

85. Ibid., at 432–33; Pratt, *Color of Their Skin*, 29–31; Jeffries, *Justice Lewis F. Powell*, 154–60.

86. Pratt, *Color of Their Skin*, 29–31; Jeffries, *Justice Lewis F. Powell*, 154–60.

87. *Bradley v. School Board*, 317 F.2d at 438.

88. *RNL*, 10 May 1963, 1; *RTD*, 18 Mar. 1964, 1; Pratt, *Color of Their Skin*, 31–45.

89. Wilkinson, *From* Brown *to* Bakke, 80–88; 108–11; Pratt, *Color of Their Skin*, 40–46.

90. Reception of black students in white schools in Richmond discussed in, e.g., Pratt, *Color of Their Skin*, 42–44; Duke, *School That Refused to Die*, 96–98; Jeffries, *Justice Lewis F. Powell*, 170. General problem of discrimination in freedom-of-choice plans discussed in, e.g., Patterson, *Civil Rights Milestone*, 100–101, Wilkinson, *From* Brown *to* Bakke, 86–87. Brock and student quoted in Duke, *School That Refused to Die*, 193.

91. Admission of Swann and Mead reported in *RNL*, 6 Sept. 1960, 1; *RNL*, 7 Sept. 1960, 1. Enrollment figures reported in Pratt, *Color of Their Skin*, 93.

92. Pratt, *Color of Their Skin*, 93.

93. Crockford quoted in ibid., 33.

94. On token integration plans in other southern states, see Klarman, *Jim Crow to Civil Rights*, 321–43; Irons, *Jim Crow's Children*, 189. School enrollment figures from James, "City Limits on Racial Equality," 969–70.

95. Briggs v. Elliot, 132 F. Supp. 776, 777 (E.D.S.C. 1955). For discussion of the Briggs Dictum, see Patterson, *Civil Rights Milestone*, 143–45.

96. *Bradley v. School Board*, 317 F.2d at 348; see generally Wilkinson, *From* Brown *to* Bakke, 78–127.

97. Judge John J. Parker of the Fourth Circuit most famously championed this view. See, e.g., *Briggs*, 132 F. Supp. at 777; Carson v. Warlick, 238 F.2d 724 (4th Cir. 1956), cert. denied, 353 U.S. 910 (1957).

98. The decision was not published but was discussed in *Bradley v. School Board*, 317 F.2d at 432 n. 3.

99. Bradley v. School Board, 7 Race Rel. L. Rep. 713 (E.D. Va. 1962).

100. Patterson, *Civil Rights Milestone*, 113–17.

101. Wilkinson, *From* Brown *to* Bakke, 86, 101–2.

102. Ibid., 80–91; Klarman, *Jim Crow to Civil Rights*, 318–19.

103. Shuttlesworth v. Birmingham Board of Education, 358 U.S. 101 (1958) (upholding pupil placement law). On the reaction of southern politicians to the decision, including the quote from Senator Long, see Klarman, *Jim Crow to Civil Rights*, 331.

104. Kelley v. Board of Education of Nashville, 270 F.2d 209 (6th Cir.), cert. denied, 361 U.S. 924 (1959) (Warren, C.J., Douglas, J., and Brennan, J., dissenting) (declining to review decision upholding Nashville's plan, which desegregated a grade at a time and allowed for minority-to-majority transfers); Klarman, *Jim Crow to Civil Rights*, 332.

105. The percentage of black students in white schools in the eleven southern states is the subject of some dispute, but no sources put the figure at much over 2 percent. Compare, e.g., Wilkinson, *From* Brown *to* Bakke, 102 (citing 2.3 percent) with Patterson, *Civil Rights Milestone*, 113 (citing 1.2 percent). Patterson quote in ibid.

106. See Klarman, *Jim Crow to Civil Rights*, 342; Patterson, *Civil Rights Milestone*, 100.

107. Wilkinson, *From* Brown *to Bakke*, 102–14.

108. Klarman, *Jim Crow to Civil Rights*, 344–442.

109. Kluger, *Simple Justice*, 753–60; Klarman, *Jim Crow to Civil Rights*, 434–36.

110. Green v. New Kent County, 391 U.S. 430, 430–445 (1968).

111. Exchange quoted in Wilkinson, *From* Brown *to* Bakke, 115.

112. *Green*, 391 U.S. at 430–45.

113. Ibid., 440.

114. On the popularity of freedom of choice, see, e.g., *RTD*, 6 May 1964, 10; 27 Jul. 1964; 11 Nov. 1964, 20; Wilkinson, *From* Brown *to* Bakke, 108–9; HEW official quoted in Dunn, "Title VI," 70.

115. Maddox quote from Patterson, *Civil Rights Milestone*, 146; Swann v. Charlotte-Mecklenburg Board of Education, 402 U.S. 1 (1971).

116. Enrollment figures from Pratt, *Color of Their Skin*, 93; the Richmond report (generally referred to as the Sartain Report) is Sartain et al., "Urban Team Study." The release of the "suppressed" report is reported in *RTD*, 28 Nov. 1971, B1.

117. Carmichael and Hamilton, *Black Power*, 54; Kluger, *Simple Justice*, 761–62.

118. Lassiter, *Silent Majority*, 234–35.

119. Eisenhower quoted in Kluger, *Simple Justice*, 753.

Chapter 2

1. Morrow et al., "Man and Woman of the Year: The Middle Americans," *Time*, Jan. 5, 1970, 10–17; Lassiter, *Silent Majority*, 300–304.

2. The prayer and Bible reading decisions were, respectively, *Engel v. Vitale*, 370 U.S. 421 (1962), and *Abington School District v. Schempp*, 374 U.S. 203 (1963). The southern

congressman, George Andrews of Alabama, is quoted in Hodgson, *World Turned Right Side Up*, 168. Integration as an assault on Middle Americans is described throughout Lassiter, *Silent Majority*.

3. Morrow et al., "Man and Woman of the Year," 15; Kerner Commission Report, formally entitled *Report of the National Advisory Commission on Civil Disorders*, 2.

4. Morrow et al., "Man and Woman of the Year."

5. The relevant opinions in the Richmond case, from trial court to Supreme Court, are as follows: Bradley v. Richmond School Board, 338 F. Supp. 67 (E.D. Va. 1972), reversed by Bradley v. Richmond School Board, 462 F.2nd 1058 (4th Cir. 1972), affirmed by equally divided Court, Bradley v. Richmond School Board, 412 U.S. 92, 1973. Milliken v. Bradley is reported at 418 U.S. 717 (1974).

6. The zoning cases were James v. Valtierra, 402 U.S. 137 (1971), which upheld a law that allowed local voters in California to reject low-incoming housing projects through voter referenda; Warth v. Seldin, 422 U.S. 490 (1975), which made it difficult for poor plaintiffs to challenge exclusionary zoning policies; and Village of Arlington Heights v. Metropolitan Housing Development Corporation, 429 U.S. 252 (1977), which established a difficult standard of proof for plaintiffs alleging race discrimination in zoning decisions. Quote from Wilkinson, *From* Brown *to* Bakke, 224.

7. Lassiter, *Silent Majority*, 280–82.

8. On the causes of residential segregation in Richmond, see, for example, Peery, *Racialism and The Politics of Metropolitan Government*, 1–144; Silver, *Twentieth-century Richmond*, 31–34, 109–29; *RTD*, 8 Feb. 1959, D1; 7 Mar. 1959, 10; 30 Dec. 1962, D1. On the causes and extent of residential segregation generally, see, for example, Massey and Denton, *American Apartheid*, 26–114; Ryan, "Schools, Race, and Money," 276–93.

9. On Richmond, see Lassiter, *Silent Majority*, 280–85; Silver, *Twentieth-century Richmond*, 186–97, 142–45; on the FHA generally, see Massey and Denton, *American Apartheid*, 52–57; Jackson, *Crabgrass Frontier*, 203–18.

10. Silver, *Twentieth-century Richmond*, 57–59; Pratt, *Color of Their Skin*, 14–16; Bradley v. Richmond School Board, 338 F. Supp. at 72–74; *RTD*, 13 Dec. 1966, B1; *RAA*, 26 Nov. 1966, 1; *RTD*, 1 Aug. 1966, 6.

11. Pratt, *Color of Their Skin*, 14–15; Bradley v. Richmond School Board, 338 F. Supp. at 72–74.

12. Bradley v. Richmond School Board, 338 F. Supp. at 73–74; Pratt, *Color of Their Skin*, 14–15; Silver, *Twentieth-century Richmond*, 106–10.

13. Briffault and Reynolds, *Cases and Materials on State and Local Government Law*, 210–24; Reynolds, "Rethinking Municipal Annexation Powers," 247–48, 255 n. 28.

14. On the politics of annexation, see generally Silver, *Twentieth-century Richmond*, 233–35; Peery, *Racialism and Politics of Metropolitan Government*; Edwards, *Neighbors and Sometimes Friends*, 44–49; Moeser and Dennis, *Politics of Annexation*, 39–40; for contemporary accounts, see, for example, *RTD*, 1 May 1961, 1; *RAA*, 2 Sept. 1961, 17; *RTD*, 7 Dec. 1961, 12; 19 Jul. 1966, A1; 26 Jan. 1967, 1; *RAA*, 13 Dec. 1969, 1; 10 Jan. 1970, 1. The role of race was explored in a 1971 trial challenging the annexation, details of

which were reported in *RNL*, 14 Sept. 1971, 1; *RTD*, 19 Sept. 1971, B8; 21 Sept. 1971, A1. Fear among blacks about diluted voting power reported in *RTD*, 1 May 1961, 1. On the odd couple opposed to annexation, see generally Lassiter, *Silent Majority*, 280–85. The moratorium and 1979 amendments to the annexation laws are described in Spicer, "Comment, Annexation in Virginia," 819–25; Weschler, "Twenty-fourth Annual Survey of Developments in Virginia Law," 330–35.

15. Lassiter, *Silent Majority*, 305.

16. Background is in Lassiter, *Silent Majority*, 305–7; Ehrlichman memo is in Ehrlichman, *Witness to Power*, 218.

17. White House statement in Nixon, "Federal Policies Relative to Equal Housing Opportunity," Jun. 11, 1971, in *Weekly Compilation of Presidential Documents*, 721–35; Romney's departure is described in Lassiter, *Silent Majority*, 307.

18. *RTD*, 17 Oct. 1970, B1; Bradley v. Richmond School Board, 462 F.2d at 1062; Lassiter, *Silent Majority*, 290.

19. Black enrollment at Freeman is discussed in an article in the student newspaper at Freeman High School, *The Commentator*, 19 Nov. 1971 (on file with author); enrollment at Tee-Jay is discussed in Duke, *School That Refused to Die*, 96–98, 104.

20. Green v. New Kent County, 391 U.S. 430 (1968); *RNN*, 31 Mar. 1966, 14; *RTD*, 22 Nov. 1968, A1.

21. Sartain and Dennis, "Richmond, Virginia: Massive Resistance without Violence," 226; Sartain et al., "Urban Team Study."

22. Powell quote and commentary about it in *NYT*, 22 May 1973, 20.

23. *RNL*, 13 Aug. 1971, 1; Ryan, "Schools, Race, and Money," 272–96.

24. Ryan, "Schools, Race, and Money," 258–60.

25. The dynamic described in this paragraph has been confirmed by experience; generally speaking, the broader the desegregation plan, the more stable the enrollment. See, for example, Welch and Light, *New Evidence on School Desegregation*, 40; Hochschild, *New American Dilemma*, 64; Orfield and Eaton, *Dismantling Desegregation*, 31; Wells and Crain, *Stepping over the Color Line*, 71.

26. Dr. Thomas Little, assistant superintendent of Richmond City Schools, made this argument in his testimony for plaintiffs at the consolidation trial. *RTD*, 17 Aug. 1971, 1.

27. Green, 391 U.S. at 436–39; Swann v. Charlotte-Mecklenburg Board of Education, 402 U.S. 1, 26 (1971).

28. The early history of the litigation is described in Bradley v. Richmond School Board, 345 F.2d at 313–14.

29. Bradley v. Richmond School Board, 9 Race Rel. L. Rep. 219, 221 (E.D. Va. 1964); *RTD*, 4 Apr. 1964, 2.

30. Bradley v. Richmond School Board, 345 F.2d 310.

31. *RNL*, 31 Mar. 1966, 14.

32. *WP*, 20 Feb. 2005, C8; Bacigal, *May It Please the Court*, 1–50; *RTD*, 1 Aug. 1967, B1.

33. Merhige, "Judge Remembers," 23; Bacigal, *May It Please the Court*, 49.

34. Merhige, "Judge Remembers," 25, 29; Bacigal, *May It Please the Court*, 28; *WP*, 20 Feb. 2005, C8.

35. *RNL*, 10 Mar. 1970, 1; Leedes and O'Fallon, "School Desegregation in Richmond," 15; *RTD*, 1 Apr. 1970, B1; 16 Apr. 1970, C1.

36. *RTD*, 12 May 1970, A1; 13 May 1970, B3; Swann v. Charlotte-Mecklenburg Board of Education, 431 F.2d 138 (4th Cir. 1970), affirmed by 402 U.S. 1 (1971).

37. *RTD*, 11 Jun. 1970, C1; 13 Jun. 1970, A1; 23 Jun. 1970, B1.

38. *RTD*, 25 Jun. 1970, C1; 26 Jun. 1970, A1; 26 Jun. 1970, A2; *RNL*, 26 Jun. 1970, 1.

39. *RNL*, 1 Jul. 1970, 1; 1 Jul. 1970, 12; quotations in Lassiter, *Silent Majority*, 285.

40. *RTD*, 7 Jul. 1970, A1; 24 Jul. 1970, A4; 8 Jul. 1970, A10.

41. School Board Minutes, Aug. 20, 1970; *RTD*, 24 Jul. 1970, A1; 25 Jul. 1970, A1; *RNL*, 23 Jul. 1970, 1.

42. *RTD*, 24 Jul. 1970, A14; 25 Jul. 1970, A1; *RNL*, 30 Jul. 1970, 1; *RTD*, 24 Jul. 1970, B1; Lassiter, *Silent Majority*, 285–86.

43. Lassiter, *Silent Majority*, 286; parent quoted in *RNL*, 8 Jul. 1970, 1.

44. Lassiter, *Silent Majority*, 286.

45. The quotation is in Lassiter, *Silent Majority*, 286; for an exceptionally well-balanced and insightful discussion of the difficult issues raised by busing, see Wilkinson, *From Brown to Bakke*, 228–34.

46. *RNL*, 18 Aug. 1970, 1; *RTD*, 18 Aug. 1970, A1; Bradley v. Richmond School Board, 317 F. Supp. at 575.

47. *RTD*, 18 Aug. 1970, A1; *RNL*, 19 Aug. 1970, 1; *RTD*, 19 Aug. 1970, A1; *RNL* 25 Aug. 1970, 1; 26 Aug. 1970, 1; 28 Aug. 1970, 1; *RTD*, 26 Aug. 1970, A8; Pratt, *Color of Their Skin*, 75.

48. *RNL*, 31 Aug. 1970, 1; *RTD*, 1 Sept. 1970, A1; 3 Sept. 1970, B1; 9 Sept. 1970, A1; *RNL*, 31 Aug. 1970, 10; Lassiter, *Silent Majority*, 288–89.

49. *RTD*, 16 Jan. 1971, A1; 5 Nov. 1970, A1; 9 Nov. 1970, A1; 10 Nov. 1970, A1; 15 Nov. 1970, A1; *RNL*, 10 Dec. 1970, 10; 11 Dec. 1970, 4; Lassiter, *Silent Majority*, 290.

50. *RTD*, 6 Apr. 1971, A1; *RNL*, 5 Apr. 1971, 1.

51. Swann v. Charlotte-Mecklenburg Board of Education, 402 U.S. 1 (1971); *RTD*, 21 Apr. 1971, A1.

52. *RTD*, 22 Apr. 1971, C1; 25 Apr. 1971, F6.

53. James v. Valtierra, 402 U.S. 137 (1971); *RAA*, 15 May 1971, 4; *RTD*, 30 Apr. 1970, A15.

54. *RTD*, 18 Jan. 1971, A14; 5 Nov. 1970, A1.

55. *RTD*, 13 Jul. 1971, A10; Lassiter, *Silent Majority*, 288; *RTD*, 22 Apr. 1971, A1.

56. *RTD*, 20 Oct. 1970, A14; 8 Dec. 1970, A1; 21 Apr. 1971, A1; 25 Apr. 1971, F6.

57. *RNL*, 13 Aug. 1971, 1; 17 Aug. 1971, 1; 19 Aug. 1971, 1; *RTD*, 21 Aug. 1971, A1; 22 Aug. 1971, A1; *RNL*, 26 Aug. 1971, 1; *RTD*, 26 Aug. 1971, A1; 27 Aug. 1971, A1, 1 Sept. 1971, A1; 2 Sept. 1971, A1; Pratt, *Color of Their Skin*, 93; Lassiter, *Silent Majority*, 290–91.

58. Quote from William G. Broaddus, assistant attorney general for Virginia, telephone interview by the author, Nov. 2, 2007.

59. *RTD*, 18 Aug. 1971, A1; 19 Aug. 1971, A1.

60. *RNL*, 19 Aug. 1971, 1; *RTD*, 21 Aug. 1971, A1; 22 Aug. 1971, B2.

61. *RNL*, 24 Aug. 1971, 1; *RTD*, 24 Aug. 1971, A1; 26 Aug. 1971, A1.

62. *RNL*, 13 Sept. 1971, 1; *RTD*, 14 Sept. 1971, A1.

63. *RNL*, 1 Sept. 1971, 1; *RTD*, 1 Sept. 1971, A1; 2 Sept. 1971, A1; 3 Sept. 1971, A1.

64. *RTD*, 1 Sept. 1971, A1; 9 Sept. 1971, A1; 10 Sept. 1971, A1; *RNL*, 10 Sept. 1971, 1.

65. *RNL*, 14 Sept. 1971, 1; 11 Jan. 1972, 5; 11 Jan. 1972, 7; *Bradley v. Richmond School Board*, 338 F. Supp. 67.

66. *Bradley v. Richmond School Board*, 338 F. Supp. at 80–82.

67. Ibid., 79–80, 83–84.

68. Ibid., 84–113.

69. Ibid., 84–85.

70. Ibid., 88; *NYT*, 13 Jan. 1972, 41.

71. *Bradley v. Richmond School Board*, 338 F. Supp. at 114–15.

72. *RNL*, 11 Jan. 1972, 1; *RTD*, 12 Jan. 1972, B1.

73. *NYT*, 13 Jan. 1972, 32.

74. *RNL*, 11 Jan. 1972, 12; *RTD*, 11 Jan. 1972, A14.

75. *RTD*, 11 Jan. 1972, A14; 10 Feb. 1972, B1; 11 Feb. 1972, A1; 18 Feb. 1972, A1.

76. Pratt, *Color of Their Skin*, 67–69; Lassiter, *Silent Majority*, 292–93.

77. Bacigal, *May It Please the Court*, 68; Pratt, *Color of Their Skin*, 69.

78. Lassiter, *Silent Majority*, 290–91.

79. *RTD*, 16 Jan. 1972, B1; 27 Jan. 1972, B1; Brief Amicus Curiae for the Congress of Racial Equality, Bradley v. Richmond School Board, No. 72–549, Mar. 31, 1973; Brief Amicus Curiae for the National Suburban League, Bradley v. Richmond School Board, No. 72–549, Mar. 23, 1973.

80. *RNL*, 11 Jan. 1972, 1; *RTD*, 15 Jan. 1972, A1.

81. Survey results reported in Lassiter, *Silent Majority*, 293.

82. *RNL*, 9 Feb. 1972, 1; *RTD*, 9 Feb. 1972, A1; 29 Mar. 1972, A1; Bradley v. Milliken, 338 F. Supp. 582 (E.D. Mich. 1971); Bradley v. Milliken, 345 F. Supp. 914 (E.D. Mich. 1972).

83. *RTD*, 27 Mar. 1972, B1; Pratt, *Color of Their Skin*, 70–71.

84. *Bradley v. Richmond School Board*, 462 F.2d at 1060.

85. *Bradley v. Richmond School Board*, 338 F. Supp. at 84–113.

86. *Bradley v. Richmond School Board*, 462 F.2d at 1066.

87. Bacigal, *May It Please the Court*, 68; Bradley v. Richmond School Board, 462 F.2d at 1069–70.

88. *RTD*, 7 Jun. 1972, B1; *RNL*, 7 Jun. 1972, 1; 7 Jun. 1972, 14.

89. *RNL*, 15 Jan. 1973, 1; Bradley v. Richmond School Board, 412 U.S. 92 (1973).

90. *RNL*, 21 May 1973, 1; *RTD*, 22 May 1973, A1.

91. *RNL*, 21 May 1973, 1; 21 May 1973, 14; *NYT*, 22 May 1973, 20; 14 Oct. 1973, 62.

92. Bradley v. Milliken, 338 F. Supp. 582, 585–87 (E.D. Mich. 1971).

93. Wilkinson, *From* Brown *to* Bakke, 194.

94. *Bradley v. Milliken*, 338 F. Supp. at 586; Bradley v. Milliken, 484 F.2d 215, 220 (6th Cir. 1973).

95. *WP*, 23 Jul. 1972, B6; *NYT*, 15 Jun. 1972, 1, 28.

96. *Bradley v. Milliken*, 448 F.2d at 257; *NYT*, 15 Jun. 1972, 28.

97. Wolf, *Trial and Error*, 18–19; *NYT*, 16 Jun. 1972, 15; *NYT*, 12 Jul. 1974, 33.

98. Wolf, *Trial and Error*, 23–24.

99. Ibid., 25–34.

100. *Bradley v. Milliken*, 338 F. Supp. at 586–87.

101. Ibid., 587–88, 591–92.

102. Ibid., 91–92.

103. *Bradley v. Milliken*, 482 F.2d at 244–45 (quoting Judge Roth's order).

104. *WP*, 22 Aug. 1972, A2; *NYT*, 12 Jul. 1974, 33; *WP*, 12 May 1972, A27.

105. *NYT*, 15 Jun. 1972, 1.

106. *NYT*, 27 Jul. 1974, 60; *WP*, 26 Mar. 1972, B5.

107. For a transcript of Nixon's speech, see *NYT*, 17 Mar. 1972, 22.

108. Ibid.

109. Orfield, *Must We Bus*, 247–72; Ryan and Heise, "Political Economy of School Choice," 2053–54.

110. Equal Educational Opportunities Act of 1974, codified at 20 U.S.C. secs. 1701, 1714 (1994); for court interpretations, see, e.g., United States v. Texas Education Agency, 532 F.2d 380, 394, n. 18 (5th Cir. 1976), vacated on other grounds sub nom. Austin Independent School District v. United States, 429 U.S. 990 (1976); Legal Services Corporation Act, codified at 42 U.S.C. sec. 2996f(b)(9)(1994).

111. Metcalf, *From Little Rock to Boston*, 162–63, 235–37; Orfield, *Must We Bus*, 263, 272–73; *NYT*, 20 Aug. 1972, E3.

112. *WSJ*, 24 Nov. 1971, 14.

113. *NYT*, 20 Aug. 1972, E3; *WSJ*, 24 Nov. 1971, 14.

114. *WP*, 26 Mar. 1972, B5; 27 Sept. 1972, A27; *WSJ*, 24 Nov. 1971, 14. Hart survived the recall effort, which ultimately did not receive sufficient support from voters. *WP*, 25 Jan. 1972, A19.

115. Buncher, *School Busing Controversy*, 207, 210, 228, 231; Orfield, *Must We Bus*, 248; Rubin, *Busing and Backlash*, 92–100, 121–38.

116. Ryan and Heise, "Political Economy of School Choice," 2055; *WSJ*, 24 Nov. 1971 14; *NYT*, 27 Jul. 1974, 60; *WP*, 23 Jul. 1972, B6.

117. *NYT*, 15 Feb. 1972, 33.

118. *WP*, 14 Nov. 1971, 38.

119. See, e.g., Jeffries, *Justice Lewis F. Powell*, 298–301.

120. Keyes v. School District No. 1, 413 U.S. 189, 201–5 (1973).

121. See, e.g., Wilkinson, *From Brown to Bakke*, 198–200.

122. Keyes v. School District No. 1, 413 U.S. at 219–36 (Powell, J., concurring); ibid., 214–17 (Douglas, J., concurring).

123. Keyes v. School District No. 1, 413 U.S. at 241–53; Jeffries, *Justice Lewis F. Powell*, 300–301.

124. Jeffries, *Justice Lewis F. Powell*, 302–6.

125. The Sixth Circuit's opinion was released on Jun. 12, 1973. Bradley v. Milliken, 484 F.2d 215. The Supreme Court issued its decision in *Keyes v. School District No. 1* less than two weeks later, on Jun. 21, 1973. Keyes v. School District No. 1, 413 U.S. at 189.

126. Bradley v. Milliken, 484 F.2d at 249; ibid., 245.

127. Ibid., 249.

128. Ibid., 250 (emphasis added).

129. Milliken v. Bradley, 418 U.S. at 741–53.

130. Ibid.

131. Ibid., 728 n. 7.

132. Ibid., 755 (Stewart, J., concurring).

133. *Bradley v. Milliken*, 338 F. Supp. at 587–88; *Milliken v. Bradley*, 418 U.S. at 756 n. 2.

134. *Bradley v. Richmond School Board*, 462 F.2d at 1064–66; *Milliken v. Bradley*, 418 U.S. at 756 n. 2 (Stewart, J., concurring).

135. Wilkinson, *From Brown to Bakke*, 225–26; *Milliken v. Bradley*, 418 U.S. at 815 (Marshall, J., dissenting); ibid., 814.

136. Ryan and Heise, "Political Economy of School Choice," 2056.

137. *NYT*, 27 Jul. 1974, 60, 26 Jul. 1974, 17.

138. *NYT*, 26 Jul. 1974, 17, 16.

139. Milliken v. Bradley, 433 U.S. 267, 280–88 (1977).

140. Ibid., 288–91; ibid., 292–98 (Powell, J., concurring); Ryan, "Schools, Race, and Money," 261.

141. See Little Rock School District v. Pulaski County Special School District No. 1, 778 F.2d 404 (8th Cir. 1985); United States v. Board of School Commissioners, 637 F.2d 1101 (7th Cir. 1980); Evans v. Buchanan, 582 F.2d 750 (3d Cir. 1978); Newburg Area Council, Inc. v. Board of Education, 510 F.2d 1358 (6th Cir. 1974); Liddell v. Missouri, 731 F.2d 1294 (8th Cir. 1984); Ryan and Heise, "Political Economy of School Choice," 2056.

142. Ryan, "Schools, Race, and Money," 281; Hochschild, *New American Dilemma*, 55; Lukas, *Common Ground*, 17.

143. On the sense of unfairness, see, e.g., Hochschild, *New American Dilemma*, 57, 69; Wilkinson, *From Brown to Bakke*, 193–215; Lukas, *Common Ground*, 244–69.

144. For views about white flight, see, e.g., Armor, *Forced Justice*, 174–94; Rossell, *Carrot or the Stick*, 65–71; Orfield and Eaton, *Dismantling Desegregation*, 316–17; on New York and Atlanta, see "School Desegregation: A Social Science Statement," in Brief Amicus Curiae of NAACP, DeKalb County, Georgia, in support of Respondents Pitts et al., at 6a–7a, Freeman v. Pitts, 503 U.S. 467 (1992) (No. 89–1920), Armor, *Forced Justice*, 72; Orfield and Eaton, *Dismantling Desegregation*, at 94–95; on Richmond, see Pratt, *Color of Their Skin*, 93.

145. Jeffries, *Justice Lewis F. Powell*, 318; Orfield and Eaton, *Dismantling Desegregation*, 96.

146. On the evidence regarding white flight and metropolitan plans, see, e.g., Welch and Light, *New Evidence on School Desegregation*, 40; Hochschild, *New American Dilemma*, 64; Orfield and Eaton, *Dismantling Desegregation*, 316; Wells and Crain, *Stepping over the Color Line*, 831; Rossell, "Analysis of the Court Decisions in *Sheff v. O'Neill*," 1208–17; Rossell and Armor, "Effectiveness of School Desegregation Plans," 267; the study indicating that city-only plans lost twice as many white students as countywide

plans is Rossell and Hawley, "Understanding White Flight," 166; on the limited flight to private schools, see Orfield and Eaton, *Dismantling Desegregation*, 61–63; Frug, "City Services," 61 n. 115; Ryan, "Schools, Race and Money," 283.

147. Orfield and Eaton, *Dismantling Desegregation*, 54; Chemerinsky, "Lost Opportunity," 1011–12; Ryan, "Schools, Race, and Money," 284–96.

148. *NYT*, 28 Sept. 1971, 25; Milliken v. Bradley, 418 U.S. at 743.

149. Parent quoted in Pratt, *Color of Their Skin*, 108–9.

150. See Hochschild and Scovronick, *American Dream and Public Schools*, 2 (noting gap between belief that all children deserve a good education and efforts to ensure that some children maintain advantage over others).

151. Yudof et al., *Educational Policy and the Law*, 535; Orfield and Eaton, *Dismantling Desegregation*, 143–78; Ryan, "Schools, Race and Money," 261–62.

152. The cases include *Missouri v. Jenkins*, 515 U.S. 70 (1995) (Kansas City); *United States v. City of Yonkers*, 96 F.2d 600 (2d Cir. 1996); *Pennsylvania Human Relations Commission v. School District*, 681 A.2d 1366 (Pa. Comm. Ct. 1996); *Reed v. Rhodes*, 934 F. Supp. 1533, 1536 (N.D. Ohio 1996); *Little Rock School District v. Pulaski County Special School District*, 716 F. Supp. 1162, 1190 (E.D. Ark. 1989), rev'd in part, 921 F.2d 1371 (8th Cir. 1990). Similar litigation in Maryland and Illinois is described in *NYT*, 26 Sept. 1996, B6; litigation in Georgia is described in Orfield and Thronson, "Dismantling Desegregation," 770; on the failure of *Milliken II* funding to produce measurable achievement gains, see Ryan, "Schools, Race, and Money," 265–66.

153. Pratt, *Color of Their Skin*, 99; Bradley v. Baliles, 829 F.2d 1308, 1310 (4th Cir. 1987).

154. Bradley v. Baliles, 639 F. Supp. 680, 690–702 (E.D. Va. 1986).

155. Ibid., 699–702; Bradley v. Baliles, 829 F.2d at 1314.

156. The key cases were *Washington v. Davis*, 426 U.S. 229 (1976); *Village of Arlington Heights v. Metropolitan Housing Development Corporation*, 429 U.S. 252 (1977); and *Personnel Administrator of Massachusetts v. Feeney*, 442 U.S. 256 (1977).

157. *WP*, 9 Jun. 1972, A6; Memorandum for United States as *Amicus Curiae*, Bradley v. Richmond School Board, Nos. 72–549, 72–550 (Apr. 13, 1973), at 25.

158. Lassiter, *Silent Majority*, 128.

159. Ibid., 154–73.

160. Ibid., 174.

161. Swann v. Charlotte-Mecklenburg Board of Education, 362 F. Supp. 1223 (1973); *Charlotte Observer*, 1 Jun. 1973; see generally Lassiter, *Silent Majority*, 198–216.

162. Lassiter, *Silent Majority*, 201–2, 217.

163. Ibid., 210–11; *Charlotte Observer*, 9 Oct. 1984.

164. See Belk v. Charlotte-Mecklenburg, 269 F.2d 305 (2001), cert. denied, 535 U.S. 986 (2002).

165. On Richmond's decision regarding the purchase of land in Henrico County, see Edwards, *Neighbors and Sometimes Friends*, 46.

166. Chesterton, *What's Wrong with the World*, 48; *NYT*, 28 Sept. 1971, 1, 25.

167. Council of the Great City Schools, "Beating the Odds," 11; *EW*, Jan. 8, 1998, 56; SchoolDataDirect, www.schooldatadirect.org (2006 statistics); Galster, "Polarization, Place, and Race," 1439. See generally Clotfelter, *After Brown*, 2 (describing trend toward resegregation and racial isolation between 1970 and 2002).

168. See, e.g., Council of the Great City Schools, "Beating the Odds VII," 10; Orfield and Lee, "Why Segregation Matters," 22 (showing racial composition of extreme poverty schools as 16 percent white, 39 percent black, 41 percent Latino, 2 percent Asian, and 1 percent Native American). For discussion of and data about teachers, see chapter 4.

169. Statistics from U.S. Department of Education, National Center for Education Statistics, "Search for Public Schools: Thomas Jefferson High School."

170. Parents Involved in Community Schools v. Seattle School District No. 1, 551 U.S. 701 (2007).

171. *NYT*, 26 Jul. 1974, 17.

Chapter 3

1. First quote from *WP*, 31 Aug. 1975, 1; more details on Bell's career are reported in *NYT*, 10 Jan. 1972, E1; 21 May 1990, A18. Second quote from Bell, *Silent Covenants*, 161.

2. Bell, *Silent Covenants*, 161; *NYT*, 10 Jan. 1972, E1. Bell's employment confirmed by email from Derrick Bell to author, Nov. 2, 2007.

3. San Antonio Independent School District v. Rodriguez, 411 U.S. 1 (1973).

4. For citation to the cases and discussion of remedies, see, e.g., Ryan, "Standards, Testing, and School Finance Litigation," 1229–39; Brown, "Binding Advisory Opinions," 544. The National Access Network, an advocacy group in favor of increasing the equity and adequacy of funding, maintains a website that contains up-to-date information about litigation across the country. See www.schoolfunding.info. Court remedies are discussed in more detail later in this chapter.

5. The challenges facing high-poverty schools are described in detail later in this chapter. Funding figures for Richmond and Henrico schools are available at the website of SchoolMatters: www.schoolmatters.org.

6. On the dominance of suburbs and the resulting political dynamics affecting school funding, see, e.g., Wolman et al., "Calculus of Coalitions," 746; Allen, "State Power, Suburban Interests," 8, 12, 44; Thomas, *United States of Suburbia*, 146; Boeckelman, "Suburban State Legislatures and School Finance," 47; Downs, *New Visions for Metropolitan America*, 45; Gainsborough, *Fenced Off*, 95.

7. Marshall quote from Milliken v. Bradley, 418 U.S. 717, 783 (1974) (Marshall, J., dissenting).

8. Opinions for each of the three Virginia decisions can be found at: (1) Burruss v. Wilkerson, 310 F. Supp. 572 (W.D. Va. 1969); (2) Bradley v. Baliles, 829 F.2d 1308 (4th Cir. 1987); (3) Scott v. Commonwealth, 443 S.E.2d 138 (Va. 1994).

9. See, e.g., Cremin, *American Education*, 193–94; Berne and Steifel, "Conce[...] School Finance Equity," 7–12; Odden and Picus, *School Finance*, 7–11.

10. U.S. Department of Education, National Center for Education Statistics, table 3.1; Hochschild and Scovronick, *American Dream and Public Schools*, 61.

11. Funding data available at U.S. Department of Education, "Fiscal Year 2005 Budget Summary and Background Information"; U.S. Census Bureau, Statistical Abstract of the United States, "State and Local Governments: Revenue and Expenditures by Function: 2003," table 425.

12. On spending figures in 1949–50 and 2005, see U.S. Department of Education, National Center for Education Statistics 2008, table 181. Current overall spending figure from U.S. Census Bureau, "Public Education Finances Report 2005." Rise in overall spending and explanation of causes discussed in, e.g., Hanushek and Rivkin, "Understanding the Twentieth-century Growth in U.S. School Spending," 39–46. For historical treatment of disabled students, see, e.g., Kirp et al., "Legal Reform of Special Education"; Mills v. Board of Education, 348 F. Supp. 866 (D.D.C. 1972).

13. On interstate disparities in funding, see generally Liu, "Interstate Inequality," 2061–72.

14. Yudof et al., *Educational Policy and the Law*, 837–45; Miller and Rubenstein, "Intradistrict Resource Disparities"; Hochschild, "Social Class in Public Schools," 824.

15. See, e.g., Ryan, "Schools, Race, and Money," 260, 266–69; Dayon and Dupre, "School Funding Litigation," 2357–58.

16. See generally Odden and Picus, *School Finance*, 262–319.

17. Ibid., 274; see also Ornstein, "Educational Financing and Government Spending," 342–43. On greater demand for public dollars, sometimes referred to as municipal overburden, see, e.g., Abbott v. Burke, 119 N.J. 287, 355–57 (1990).

18. Odden and Picus, *School Finance*, 283–93; Alexander and Salmon, *Public School Finance*, 200–3.

19. See Odden and Picus, *School Finance*, 285–86.

20. Explanation from Lynn Bragga, director, Department of Budget and Financial Reporting for Richmond Public Schools, Richmond, Va., interview by Ross Goldman, author's research assistant, May 22, 2007.

21. The Virginia Department of Education produces documents that explain the CI formula and that indicate each district's CI. See www.doe.virginia.gov/VDOE/meet-
'2006/SOQminutes06.pdf; www.doe.virginia.gov/VDOE/Finance/Budget/2008–2010
¹ndex.pdf.

¬v of foundation amount discussed in Bragga interview; Angela Ciolfi,
·² Center, Charlottesville, Va., interview by the author, Jan. 26,
¹s of districts and states are found in respective district
¹chools, "School Board's Adopted Budget FY 2008–2009,"
¹ols, "Students First: Maintaining Excellence in Chal-
¹lan 2009/2010," 2.

ols; Reynolds v. Sims, 377 U.S. 533 (1964).

¹ool Finance Litigation in the Name of Equity," 36.

26. Burruss v. Wilkerson, 310 F. Supp. 572, 573–74 (W.D. Va. 1969); McInnis v. Shapiro, 293 F. Supp. 327 (N.D. Ill. 1968).

27. Coons, *Private Wealth and Public Education*, 201–2; Coons, "*Rodriguez*. Redivirus," 4–6; Minorini and Sugarman, "School Finance Litigation in the Name of Equity," 37–38.

28. Coons et al., *Private Wealth and Public Education*, 204–9.

29. Minorini and Sugarman, "School Finance Litigation in the Name of Equity," 38.

30. Ibid., 38.

31. See Coons, "*Rodriguez* Redivirus," 6–8.

32. See, e.g., Michelman, "Supreme Court, 1968 Term," 47–59; *NYT*, 10 Jan. 1972, E1.

33. Minorini and Sugarman, "School Finance Litigation in the Name of Equity," 38.

34. Coons, "*Rodriguez* Redivirus," 12.

35. *L.A. Times*, 31 Dec. 1976, pt. 1, 3; *NYT*, 10 Jan. 1972, E1.

36. Kirp, "Judicial Policy-Making," 84; *NYT*, 10 Jan. 1972, E1.

37. Serrano v. Priest, 487 P.2d 1241, 1266 (Cal. 1971).

38. *WP*, 13 Oct. 1972, A3; 22 Mar. 1973, A16; 4 Apr. 1973, A6; Levin, "Current Trends in School Finance Reform Litigation," 1101; Berke, *Answers to Inequity*, 17.

39. *WP*, 4 May 1972, K2; 22 Mar. 1973, A1.

40. *WP*, 22 Mar. 1973, A1.

41. *WP*, 4 May 1972, K2.

42. Schragger, "*San Antonio v. Rodriguez* and the Legal Geography of School Finance Reform," 90–93.

43. San Antonio v. Rodriguez, 411 U.S. 1, 12–14 and n. 35 (1973).

44. Rodriguez v. San Antonio Independent School District, 337 F. Supp. 280, 284–86 (W.D. Tex. 1971).

45. *WP*, 4 May 1972, K2; 22 Mar. 1973, A1.

46. *NYT*, 19 Dec. 1972, 89.

47. Ibid.

48. San Antonio v. Rodriguez, 411 U.S. 1 (1973). The five justices in the majority in *San Antonio v. Rodriguez* and *Milliken* were Burger, Stewart, Rehnquist, Powell, and Blackmun. All but Stewart were appointed by Nixon. The discussion of local control appears at pages 49–51 of the *Rodriguez* opinion.

49. *Rodriguez*, 411 U.S. at 30–37.

50. Marshall's dissent appears at *Rodriguez*, 411 U.S. at 70–133. The abortion funding decisions were *Maher v. Roe*, 432 U.S. 464 (1977) and *Harris v. McCrae*, 448 U.S. 297 (1980).

51. Court fees cases were *Griffin v. Illinois*, 351 U.S. 12 (1956) (holding it unconstitutional to require poor to pay for trial transcript as part of appeal in criminal case); *Douglas v. California*, 372 U.S. 353 (1963) (holding that poor have right to free appellate counsel in criminal cases). Poll tax case was *Harper v. Virginia State Board of Elections*, 383 U.S. 663 (1966). The most famous article about where the Court might be heading in these cases was Michelman's, which appeared in the *Harvard Law Review* in 1969. See

Michelman, "Supreme Court, 1968 Term." Lower court quote from *Burruss v. Wilkerson*, 301 F. Supp. 1237, 1239 (E.D. Va. 1968).

52. *Rodriguez*, 411 U.S. at 18–29. The Court also reasoned that, unlike in earlier cases, poor people here were not completely deprived of a benefit (like the right to vote) because of their poverty; their complaint was about relative deprivation, not absolute. Ibid.

53. Ibid., 49–55.

54. Ibid., 41.

55. Ibid., 42–44.

56. Ibid., 63–70 (White, J., dissenting).

57. Ibid., 70–133 (Marshall, J., dissenting).

58. The opinion quotation appears at ibid., 55; quotation from the Powell memorandum and description of Blackmun's hesitation from Schragger, "*San Antonio v. Rodriguez* and the Legal Geography of School Finance Reform," 96–98.

59. Powell is quoted in Schragger, "*San Antonio v. Rodriguez* and the Legal Geography of School Finance Reform," 98–99.

60. Ibid., 102 (describing Blackmun's concern and quoting National Education Association); *NYT*, 26 Mar. 1973, 38; *WP*, 22 Mar. 1973, A26; *Chicago Tribune*, 22 Mar. 1973, 16; *RTD*, 23 Mar. 1973, A14.

61. Robinson v. Cahill, 303 A.2d 273 (N.J. 1973).

Chapter 4

1. Yudof, "School Finance Reform in Texas," 499. For description and discussion of school finance cases, see, e.g., Ryan, "Standards, Testing, and School Finance Litigation," 1229–34; Ryan, "Schools, Race, and Money," 266–69.

2. McCusic, "Use of Education Clauses," 319–26, 333–39.

3. The state constitutional provisions are N.J. Const., art. 8, sec. 4; Md. Const., art. 8, sec. 1; Penn. Const., art. 3, sec. 14, Ohio Const., art. 6, sec. 2; W. Va. Const., art. 12, sec. 1. Examples of divergent results include *Abbott v. Burke*, 575 A.2d 359 (N.J. 1990) (overturning finance scheme) and *Hornbeck v. Somerset County Board of Education*, 458 A.2d 758 (Md. 1983) (upholding finance scheme); the Georgia case is reported at *McDaniel v. Thomas*, 285 S.E.2d 156, 166 (Ga. 1981); the Massachusetts case is *McDuffy v. Secretary of Education*, 615 N.E.2d 516, 526, 554 (Mass. 1993).

4. On the influence of politics, see, e.g., Swenson, "School Finance Reform Litigation," 1166–69; on the influence of selection methods for judges, see, e.g., ibid., 1152; on influence of financial health of states, see, e.g., Lundberg, "State Courts and School Funding," 1145–46; on influence of race, see, e.g., Ryan, "Influence of Race in School Finance Reform," 451–57.

5. Scott v. Commonwealth, 443 S.E.2d 138, 142 (Va. 1994).

6. Ibid.

7. Committee for Educational Rights v. Edgar, 672 N.E.2d 1178, 1189 (Ill. 1996); Coalition for Adequacy and Fairness in School Funding v. Chiles, 680 So.2d 400, 408 (Fl. 1996); City of Pawtucket v. Sundlun, 662 A.2d 40, 58 (R.I. 1995).

8. For two collections of essays largely opposed to court intervention, for various reasons, see West and Peterson, *School Money Trials*, and Hanushek, *Courting Failure*.

9. Justice Marshall made a similar point in his dissent in San Antonio Independent School District v. Rodriguez, 411 U.S. 1, 82–90 (1973) (Marshall, J., dissenting).

10. For a description and critique of the standard account, see, e.g., Ryan, "Standards, Testing, and School Finance Litigation," 1229–39; Briffault, "Adding Adequacy to Equity," 25–27.

11. See, e.g., Enrich, "Leaving Equality Behind," 104–15.

12. See Ryan, "Standards, Testing, and School Finance Litigation," 1233–38; Ryan and Saunders, "Foreword to Symposium on School Finance Litigation," 466–68; Briffault, "Adding Equity to Adequacy," 26–27.

13. See Board of Education v. Nyquist, 439 N.E.2d 359 (N.Y. 1982); Campaign for Fiscal Equity v. State, 801 N.E.2d 326 (N.Y. 2003).

14. State v. Campbell County School District, 907 P.2d 1238, 1274 (Wyo. 1995).

15. *Campaign for Fiscal Equity*, 801 N.E.2d at 350.

16. See Claremont School District v. Governor, 703 A.2d 1353, 1356 (N.H. 1997) (stressing that adequate education plays a "seminal role" in ensuring that citizens can successfully participate economically, politically, and socially); Abbott ex rel. Abbott v. Burke, 693 A.2d 417, 428 (N.J. 1997) (defining "adequate education" as one that prepares students to compete economically and contribute to their community); Hoke County Board of Education v. State, 599 S.E.2d 365, 380–81 (N.C. 2004) (defining "sound basic education" as including the ability to function in society, to understand the basic political system, and to succeed in postsecondary education or employment); *Campbell County School District*, 907 P.2d at 1259 (finding that the Wyoming Constitution required the legislature to provide students with a "uniform opportunity to become equipped for their future role as citizens...and competitors both economically and intellectually").

17. For arguments about the relative value of education, see, e.g., Koski and Reich, "When 'Adequate' Isn't," 547; Michelman, "Supreme Court, 1968 Term," 58.

18. For discussion of costing-out orders by courts, see Ryan and Saunders, "Foreword to Symposium on School Finance Litigation," 476–78. For an example, see Campaign for Fiscal Equity v. State, 801 N.E.2d at 360. For descriptions of the various methods used for these studies, see, e.g., Springer and Guthrie, "Politicization of the School Finance Legal Process," 107–16.

19. For discussion of the Kentucky decision, see, e.g., Combs, "Creative Constitutional Law," 367–72; for Massachusetts, see, e.g., Enrich, "Leaving Equality Behind," 176.

20. See Ryan, "Schools, Race, and Money," 267–68; Rebell, "Fiscal Equality in Education," 697–98 (speaking only of difficulties in so-called equity cases); Kaden, "Courts and Legislatures in a Federal System," 1255–59; Kahn, "State Constitutionalism," 468; Note, "Unfulfilled Promises," 1072; Metzler, "Inequitable Equilibrium," 564.

21. The most recent Abbott decision is *Abbott v. Burke*, 917 A.2d 989 (N.J. 2009).

22. For discussion of legislative responses, see, e.g., Berry, "Impact of School Finance Judgments," 213–40.

23. Ibid. Commentators disagree over the precise impact of court decisions on school funding, but no one argues that court decisions have even come close to eliminating all funding gaps or inadequacies. See Evans et al., "Impact of Court-mandated School Finance Reform," 72–98; Heise, "Equal Educational Opportunity," 585–628; Ryan and Heise, "Political Economy of School Choice," 2059.

24. See generally Fischel, *Homevoter Hypothesis*, 1–18.

25. For discussion of reactions in Texas, see Cortez, "Power and Perseverance," 181; Yudof, "School Finance Reform in Texas"; *NYT*, 3 May 1993, A12; for Kansas, see Fischel, *Homevoter Hypothesis*, 120–21; for Vermont, see *EW*, 28 Oct. 1998. The Kansas case was *Unified School District No. 229 v. State*, 885 P.2d 1170, 1194–96 (Kan. 1994). The Texas case is described at *EW*, 18 Apr. 2001, 26. On the threat of secession in Kansas, see Augenblick, "Role of State Legislatures," 89, 98. On the Vermont protest and Irving's comments, see *EW*, 28 Oct. 1998. See generally Hochschild and Scovronick, *American Dream and Public Schools*, 68–70.

26. See Macedo, *Diversity and Distrust*, 45–54; Jeffries and Ryan, "Political History of the Establishment Clause," 316–18; Ravitch, *Troubled Crusade*, 43–81.

27. For discussion of these studies, see Ryan, "Supreme Court and Voluntary Integration," 143–44.

28. Ibid., 143; Ryan, "Charter Schools and Public Education," 405–6. See Forman, "Rise and Fall of School Vouchers," 550–52.

29. For criticisms of the current emphasis on standardized testing, see, e.g., Neil et al., *Failing Our Children*; Kohn, *Case against Standardized Testing*; Ohanian, *One Size Fits Few*; Sacks, *Standardized Minds*; Rothstein, *Class and Schools*, 86.

30. See, e.g., Ryan, "Schools, Race, and Money," 289–94.

31. Puma et al., "Prospects: Final Report on Student Outcomes," 12, 73; Puma et al., "Prospects: Interim Report," 44; see generally Kahlenberg, *All Together Now* 28–37.

32. Greene and Winters, "Leaving Boys Behind"; Balfanz and Legters, "Locating the Dropout Crisis"; Kozol, *Savage Inequalities*, 58.

33. Orfield and Eaton, *Dismantling Desegregation*, 54; Abbott v. Burke, 693 A.2d 417, 433–34 (N.J. 1997).

34. On the additional costs of educating poor students, see, e.g., Anyon, *Ghetto Schooling*, 6–7; on state efforts to cover some of those costs, see *EW*, 8 Jan. 1998, 88, 118, 141, 188, 195, 204, 263. Before Title I became the vehicle for the NCLB, the statement of purpose indicated that "the most urgent need for educational improvement is in schools with high concentrations of children from low-income families." See Improving America's Schools Act of 1994, Pub. L. No. 103–382, tit. I, secs. 101, 108, Stat. 3519 (codified at 20 U.S.C. sec. 6301).

35. Kozol, *Savage Inequalities*; Ryan, "Influence of Race in School Finance Reform," 439–47.

36. For example of deprivation, see, e.g., Meier et al., *Many Children Left Behind*, 7; for general expenditure figures and discussion, see, e.g., Ryan, "Influence of Race in

School Finance Reform," 439–41; Hochschild and Scovronick, *American Dream and Public Schools*, 62.

37. For discussion of the Kansas case and its impact, see, e.g., Orfield and Eaton, *Dismantling Desegregation* 241–63. Studies of the impact of Title I spending include, e.g., Puma et al, "Prospects: Final Report on Student Outcomes," and "Prospects: Interim Report"; Natriello and McDill, "Title I," 31, 33–34; see generally *EW*, 22 Oct. 1997, 16 (discussing additional studies that reached mixed conclusions).

38. Orfield and Eaton study cited in Orfield and Eaton, *Dismantling Desegregation*, 83; Kahlenberg, *All Together Now*, 28, 36–37 (discussing studies regarding performance of poor students in middle-class schools).

39. For the positive recent news, see Goertz and Weiss, "Assessing Success in School Finance Litigation"; for an older, more pessimistic view, see Hanushek and Lindseth, *Schoolhouses, Courthouses, and Statehouses*, 157–65.

40. Data available through SchoolMatters, www.schoolmatters.com.

41. The title of a collection of essays on this topic—*Does Money Matter?*—is a nod to this caricature.

42. The literature is voluminous on this point, and the following citations offer only a sample of some of the best known studies on the topic. On the lack of a systematic relationship, see, e.g., Hanushek, "School Resources and Student Performance," 43–73. On studies showing a positive return on investments in particular resources, see, e.g., Hedges and Greenwald, "Have Times Changed," 74–90; Ferguson, "Paying for Public Education," 488–89. For a good discussion of the existing evidence, see Burtless, "Introduction and Summary," 1–42. For further discussion and citations to additional studies, see Ryan, "Schools, Race, and Money," 291–94. For discussion of and citation to studies regarding the benefits of preschool, see, e.g., Ryan, "Constitutional Right to Preschool," 56–69.

43. *RTD*, 25 Mar. 2007, 23; Keith West, Richmond School Board member, telephone interview by the author, May 21, 2007.

44. Anyon, *Ghetto Schooling*, 3–38, 157–62.

45. Wells and Crain, *Stepping over the Color Line*, 130–31 (St. Louis); Bracey, "Lesson in Throwing Money," 789 (Kansas City); *WP*, 15 Sept. 1996, A1 (Washington, D.C.); Hochschild and Scovronick, *American Dream and Public Schools*, 85 (Detroit, Baltimore, and Atlanta).

46. West interview, May 21, 2007; Angela Anderson, chief of financial reporting, Richmond Public Schools, interview by Ross Goldman, author's research assistant, May 22, 2007; *RTD*, 26 Aug. 2007, B1; 25 Mar. 2007, 23; 7 Aug. 2005, E6.

47. *RTD*, 5 Aug. 2005, E6; 23 Mar. 2007, A14.

48. Edward H. Pruden, principal, Freeman High School, interview by the author, May 13, 2008. A New York education commissioner, quoted in Hochschild and Scovronick, *American Dream and Public Schools*, 65, offered observations very similar to those of Dr. Pruden: "If you ask the children to attend school in conditions where plaster is crumbling, the roof is leaking…that says something to the child about how you diminish the value of the activity and…perhaps of the child himself."

49. Quotation from Minow, "School Finance," 399.

50. Or it at least suggests that money spent on schools alone, as opposed to greater social services, is not going to be sufficient. There is growing recognition that school reform alone will not significantly improve the educational chances of poor students, and that such reform needs to be coupled with investments aimed at making families and communities healthier and more stable. Dr. Pruden echoed these sentiments when asked about the relationship between school funding and academic performance, suggesting that it would probably be wiser to spend additional funding on social services than on schools. Pruden interview, May 13, 2008.

51. Coleman et al., *Equality of Educational Opportunity*.

52. Ibid., 304; Kahlenberg, *All Together Now*, 37, quoting Jonathan Kozol: "Money is not the only issue that determines inequality. A more important factor, I am convinced, is the makeup of the student enrollment, who is sitting next to you in class"; Finn, "Education That Works," 63, 64 (acknowledging that "disadvantaged children [tend] to learn more when they attend...school with middle-class youngsters"); Chubb and Moe, *Politics, Markets, and America's Schools*, 125–29; Hochschild and Scovronick, *American Dream and Public Schools*, 26. Last quote from Trine Tsouderos, "Schools out of Balance: Murfreesboro Rezoning May Fix Inequalities," *Nashville Tennessean*, Dec. 27, 1998, 2A (quoting James Guthrie). See also Zimmer and Toma, "Peer Effects in Private and Public Schools across Countries," 75–92 (examining data from five countries and finding that peer effects are a significant determinant of educational achievement in each country).

53. For discussion of studies confirming these observations, see Kahlenberg, *All Together Now*, 48–58.

54. Fordham and Ogbu, "Black Students' School Success," 181–82.

55. Ibid., 187–98. See also Fordham, "Racelessness." For the view that oppositional culture among black students is worse in integrated schools, see Freyer and Torrelli, "An Emprical Analysis of 'Acting White.'" Fordham and Ogbu's work, not surprisingly, has prompted responses. Some are critical, see, e.g., Cook and Ludwig, "Do Black Adolescents Disparage Achievement," 375, 390, and some are supportive, see, e.g., Ferguson, "Comment," 394–97.

56. See, e.g., Freyer and Torelli, "An Empirical Analysis of 'Acting White.'"

57. Edward H. Pruden, principal, Freeman High School, interview by the author, Jun. 27, 2006.

58. Coleman et al., *Equality of Educational Opportunity*, 304.

59. Rosenbaum, "Black Pioneers," 1198.

60. Wells and Crain, *Stepping over the Color Line*, 148.

61. Orfield and Thronson, "Dismantling Desegregation," 783 (describing study performed by Orfield for case).

62. Mahard and Crain, "Research on Minority Achievement," 103, 111, 118.

63. Mayer, "How Much Does a High School's Racial and Socioeconomic Mix Affect Graduation and Teenage Fertility Rates," 321, 327, 334. See also Wells and Crain, *Stepping over the Color Line*, 340.

64. Murnane, "Evidence, Analysis, and Unanswered Questions," 486 (1981); Yudof et al., *Educational Policy and the Law*, 597.

65. See, e.g., Armor, *Forced Justice*, 71; Crain and Mahard, "Desegregation and Black Achievement," 2; Jencks and Phillips, *Black-white Test Score Gap*, 26; Anderson et al., "Poverty and Achievement," 2–5; Puma et al., "Prospects: Final Report on Student Outcomes," 12; Jonathan Crane, "Effects of Neighborhoods," 317; Willms, "Social Class Segregation," 226; Crane, "Epidemic Theory of Ghettoes," 1241, 1227, 1236, 1240; Coleman et al., *Equality of Educational Opportunity*, 297, 304–5, 22; Hirsch, *Schools We Need*, 45; Battistich et al., "Schools as Communities," 627, 628, 631, 649; Mounts and Steinberg, "Ecological Analysis of Peer Influence," 919–20. See generally, Century Foundation Task Force, *Divided We Fail*, 23–24.

66. Anne L. Poates, principal, Freeman High School, interview by the author, Dec. 10, 2009; Tonya Roane, principal, Thomas Jefferson High school, email to author Dec. 30, 2009.

67. For an extensive discussion of the social science literature on this point, see Kahlenberg, *All Together Now*, 61–67. See also Ryan and Heise, "Political Economy of School Choice," 2107 and n. 337.

68. Rusk, "To Improve Children's Test Scores," 1, 5.

69. Ryan, "Influence of Race in School Finance Reform," 455–57; Edwards and Ahern, "Unequal Treatment in State Supreme Courts," 326–66.

70. Ryan, "Influence of Race in School Finance Reform," 457–72.

71. Ibid., 458–63; for a description of the New York case and its aftermath, see, e.g., Stanczyk, "Public School Finance Litigation," 353–69.

72. Ryan, "Influence of Race in School Finance Reform," 463–71.

73. Quote from *NYT*, 19 Dec. 1972, 89.

74. See, e.g., Kahlenberg, *All Together Now*, 67–72; Hanushek and Rivkin, "Why Public Schools Lose Teachers," 326–54; Jacob, "Challenges of Staffing Urban Schools," 129–53; UNC Center for Civil Rights, "Socioeconomic Composition of the Public Schools," 4–6; Hochschild, "Social Class in Public Schools," 825, 829.

75. Barbara Ulschmid, principal, Thomas Jefferson High School, interview by the author, May 22, 2008.

76. See Prince et al., "Compensation for Teachers," 1–5.

77. See Rothstein, *Class and Schools*, 68 (noting that "middle-class parents would never consent to removing the most effective teachers from their schools and re-assigning them to schools with lower-class children").

78. See, e.g., *NYT*, 19 Dec. 1972, 1, 89 (describing school finance litigation pending before Supreme Court and lower courts as raising the question whether funding schools through the property tax is unconstitutional).

79. On the responsiveness of Kentucky and Massachusetts, see Enrich, "Leaving Equality Behind," 175–77. On subsequent litigation in each state, see, for example, Hancock v. Commissioner of Education, 822 N.E.2d 1134, 1139–40 (Mass. 2005), which rejects a second-generation suit, and Samberg, "Litigation Update" (describing second-generation litigation in Kentucky). On the need for continued involvement, see, e.g., Koski, "Of Fuzzy Standards," 1185; the New Jersey litigation experience is described at Education Law Center, "History of *Abbott*"; the most recent decision is *Abbott v. Burke*, 917 A.2d 989 (N.J.

2009). The Ohio litigation is described at ACCESS, "Ohio Supreme Court Turns Away Legal Challenge." The Alabama decision is *Ex parte James*, 836 So. 2d 813 (Ala. 2002).

80. See, e.g., Rebell, "Educational Adequacy," 218, 237; Enrich, "Leaving Equality Behind," 166–80; Schrag, *Final Test*, 6.

81. William Fischel is the most prominent and tireless proponent of this argument. See, e.g., Fischel, *Homevoter Hypothesis*, 98–128. For a challenge to Fischel's hypothesis, see Stark and Zasloff, "Tiebout and Tax Revolts," 101–63; for Fischel's response, see, e.g., "Did John Serrano Vote for Proposition 13," 887–932. See also Serrano v. Priest, 226 Cal. Rptr. 584, 619 (Cal. App. 1986).

82. Enrich, "Leaving Equality Behind," 180.

83. Sheff v. O'Neill, 678 A.2d 1267 (Conn. 1996); see generally Ryan, "*Sheff*, Segregation, and School Finance Litigation," 542–62.

84. The impact of *Sheff v. O'Neill* is discussed in more detail in chapter 8.

Chapter 5

1. For a description of the proposed charter school, see e.g., Chris Dovi, "A Little Green?" *Style*, Mar. 5, 2008.

2. Chris Dovi, "School Zones Rekindling Segregation," *Style*, Feb. 6, 2008 (quoting Tichi Pinkney-Eppes, president of the Richmond Council of PTAs).

3. Khalfani's statements appear in *Voice*, 3 Jun. 2008. Hinkle's statement appeared in a blog entry, "Even More on Patrick Henry," May 16, 2008, http://barticles.mytimes-dispatch.com/index.php/barticles/comments/even_more_on_patrick_henry/.

4. Lil Tuttle, interview by the author, Jun. 20, 2008.

5. On suburban satisfaction with local schools, see, e.g., Moe, *Schools, Vouchers, and the American Public*, 34–35; on the link between school quality and local property values, see Fischel, *Homevoter Hypothesis*, 1–18; Bogart and Cromwell, "How Much Is a Neighborhood School Worth," 280.

6. For figures regarding various choice programs, including vouchers, see Kahlenberg, *Public School Choice*, 7.

7. For an exceptional discussion of residential school choice, which includes estimates of its use, see Henig and Sugarman, "Nature and Extent of School Choice," 13–17.

8. Figures from Kahlenberg, *Public School Choice*, 7, and Henig and Sugarman, "Nature and Extent of School Choice," 32 n. 8.

9. For discussion of intradistrict school choice, see Ryan and Heise, "Political Economy of School Choice," 2064–65; for information on the International Baccalaureate Program, see www.ibo.org/; for Tee-Jay's International Baccalaureate program, see http://www.richmond.k12.va.us/ib_jefferson/; for Henrico County's specialized high school programs, see www.henrico.k12.va.us/schools/specialty.html.

10. For information about Richmond's alternative high schools, see www.richmond.k12.va.us/indexnew/sub/Directions/schoolmap/other.cfm; for high school rankings, see *U.S. News & World Report*, "America's Best High Schools." The demographic

information regarding Community and Open Schools comes from the National Center on Education Statistics, which emailed the information on request; it can also be found at the SchoolMatters website, www.schoolmatters.com.

11. On the suggestion that the schools were designed to stem white flight, see Duke, *School That Refused to Die*, 121–22. For demographic information, see the sources cited in note 10.

12. For recent, comprehensive reviews of magnet schools, see Frankenberg and Siegel-Hawley, "Forgotten Choice," 6–51; Rossell, "Whatever Happened to Magnet Schools," which also discusses the federal spending program. For more general information about magnet schools, see, e.g., Blank et al., "After 15 Years," 154–58.

13. For information about admissions problems in magnet schools, see Rossell, *Carrot or the Stick*, 41–110; for evidence of tracking within magnet schools and programs, see West, "Desegregation Tool That Backfired," 2567–92; for a story about magnet programs excluding some African-American students, see, e.g., *NYT*, 3 Aug. 1989, A14.

14. Parents Involved in Community Schools v. Seattle School District No. 1, 551 U.S. 701 (2007); Frankenberg and Siegel-Hawley, "Forgotten Choice," 6–51 (suggesting that roughly one-third of magnet schools retain a focus on racial integration).

15. Henig, *Rethinking School Choice*, 111–12; Viteritti, *Choosing Equality*, 58–60; Kahlenberg, *All Together Now*, 116–30; Henig and Sugarman, "Nature and Extent of School Choice," 19.

16. See *RTD*, 17 Sept. 2007, A1.

17. See ibid.

18. Carol Wolf, former Richmond School Board member, interviews by the author, Jun. 4, 2008; Jun. 26, 2008.

19. Richmond parent (who wished to remain anonymous), interview by the author, Apr. 10, 2008.

20. Barbara Ulschmid, principal, Thomas Jefferson High School, interview by the author, May 22, 2008.

21. School data is available at SchoolMatters, www.schoolmatters.com.

22. Chris Dovi, "School Zones Rekindling Segregation," *Style*, Feb. 6, 2008.

23. The relevant provision of the NCLB is codified at 20 U.S.C. sec. 6316(b)(1)(E) (1); the legislative history and transfer figures are from Sunderman et al., *NCLB Meets School Realities*, xxx–xxxi, 44–46, 50–51; Rudalevige, "Politics of No Child Left Behind," 63–69.

24. 20 U.S.C. sec. 6316(b)(11); Department of Education quote from 67 Fed. Reg. 71, 710, 71, 755 (Dec. 2, 2002); final quote from Liu and Taylor, "School Choice to Achieve Desegregation," 804–5.

25. U.S. Department of Education, National Center for Education Statistics, "Schools and Staffing Survey, 1999–2000," table1.03. These are the most recent, reliable figures. See also Holme and Wells, "School Choice beyond District Borders," 156.

26. Education Commission of the States, "State Education Reforms, Open Enrollment," table 4.2; Ryan and Heise, "Political Economy of School Choice," 2066–67.

27. Education Commission of the States, "State Education Reforms, Open Enroll-ment," table 4.2; Holme and Wells, "School Choice beyond District Borders," 161–62. For further information, though slightly outdated, see Bierlien et al., "National Review of Open Enrollment," B1–49.

28. Ryan and Heise, "Political Economy of School Choice," 2067.

29. Ibid., 2067–68; Sugarman, "School Choice and Public Funding," 119–21.

30. Henig and Sugarman, "Nature and Extent of School Choice," 21.

31. Education Commission of the States, "State Education Reforms, Open Enroll-ment"; Bierlien et al., "National Review of Open Enrollment," B2–3.

32. Dillon, "Plotting School Choice," 1–21; Holme and Wells, "School Choice beyond District Borders," 179.

33. See Kahlenberg, *All Together Now*, 175–77; Ryan and Heise, "Political Economy of School Choice," 2069–70.

34. Henig, *Rethinking School Choice*, 167.

35. Ryan and Heise, "Political Economy of School Choice," 2069–70.

36. Ibid., 2070.

37. Ibid., 2071; Dillon, "Plotting School Choice," 16; Eaton, *Other Boston Busing Story*, 4–5; Holme and Wells, "School Choice beyond District Borders," 208–9; Kahlen-berg, *All Together Now*, 152; Viteritti, *Choosing Equality*, 99.

38. Dillon, "Plotting School Choice," 16; Kahlenberg, *All Together Now*, 152; Eaton, *Other Boston Busing Story*, 221.

39. Wells and Crain, *Stepping over the Color Line*, 97–105.

40. Quote from ibid., 336; on dismantlement of the program, see *EW*, 24 Mar. 1999, 3; on suburban reaction, see, e.g., Wells and Crain, *Stepping over the Color Line*, 326; Liu and Taylor, "School Choice to Achieve Desegregation," 811; Holme and Wells, "School Choice beyond District Borders," 185.

41. See, e.g., Carolyn Bower, "Students Stand Up for Diversity," *St. Louis Post-Dispatch*, 23 May 2004, B1; Holme and Wells, "School Choice beyond District Borders," 184–87.

42. Holme and Wells, "School Choice beyond District Borders," 171, 208–9.

43. See Virginia Department of Education, Virginia Governor's School Program, at www.doe.virginia.gov/VDOE/Instruction/Govschools/.

44. For school demographics, see the website of the Governor's School, at www.gsgis.k12.va.us/ourschool/profile.html. First quote from *RTD*, 19 Oct. 2007, B9; for the pledge to address the problem, made a decade ago, see 20 Oct. 1999, B1.

45. Duke, *School That Refused to Die*, 175–78, 198; Pratt, *Color of Their Skin*, 95.

46. Duke, *School That Refused to Die*, 175–76; Edward H. Pruden, principal, Freeman High School, interview by the author, 27 Jun. 2006.

47. See generally, Wells and Crain, *Stepping over the Color Line*; Holme and Wells, "School Choice beyond District Borders."

48. See, e.g., Manno et al., "Beyond the Schoolhouse Door," 736–44.

49. See, e.g., Ryan, "Charter Schools and Public Education," 394–95; Mead and Rotherham, "Sum Greater Than the Parts," 2–5; Fuller, "Growing Charter Schools," 6–8.

50. See, e.g., Ryan, "Charter Schools and Public Education"; Vanourek, *State of the Charter Movement 2005*; 20 U.S.C. sec. 1116(b)(7)–(8).

51. See Ryan and Heise, "Political Economy of School Choice," 2074; Mead and Rotherham, "Sum Greater Than the Parts," 1.

52. Vanourek, "State of the Charter School Movement," 20–31; Ryan, "Charter Schools and Public Education," 394–99; Fuller, "Charter Schools in Political Context," 7, 12.

53. See Peterson, "School Choice," 53; U.S. Department of Education, "Charter Schools Program"; National Alliance for Public Charter Schools, "Federal Charter Schools Program."

54. See generally Education Commission of the States, "State Profiles—Charter Schools"; see also Ryan and Heise, "Political Economy of School Choice," 2074–75. On distribution and Virginia, see, e.g., Center for Education Reform, "Race to the Top for Charter Schools."

55. See, e.g., Ryan and Heise, "Political Economy of School Choice," 2074–75.

56. Mead and Rotherham, "Sum Greater Than the Parts," 12–14; Ryan and Heise, "Political Economy of School Choice," 2075–76.

57. Quote from *Chicago Tribune*, 30 Aug. 2000, 5.

58. Discussion and citation to relevant statutes in Ryan and Heise, "Political Economy of School Choice," 2076–77. Virginia's earlier charter school law was repealed on Apr. 12, 2004 and replaced by the Charter School Excellence and Accountability Act, codified at Va. Code Ann., sec. 22.1–212.11A. For case study of charters in Michigan, indicating charters most likely to open in central-city districts, see Ross, "Charter Schools in Michigan," 146–76.

59. *NYT*, 18 Dec. 2001, A1; see generally Ryan and Heise, "Political Economy of School Choice," 2077.

60. On threat, see, e.g., Kit Wagar, "Lawmakers Ponder Possible Removal of Accreditation," *Kansas City Star*, 20 Oct. 1999, B7; on different views of urban residents, see, e.g., Moe, *Schools, Vouchers, and the American Public*, 147–54and table 5–7. Views of some school board members based on Wolf interviews, Jun. 4, 2008, Jun. 26, 2008, and Keith West, Richmond School Board member, interview by the author, Jun. 25, 2008.

61. See Coons and Sugarman, *Education by Choice*, 18–19; Mill, *On Liberty*, 89.

62. Friedman, *Capitalism and Freedom*, 89.

63. Chubb and Moe, *Politics, Markets and America's Schools*, 217; Bulman and Kirp, "Shifting Politics of School Choice," 46–47.

64. Bulman and Kirp, "Shifting Politics of School Choice," 39–43; Forman, "Secret History of School Choice," 1309–12.

65. Coons and Sugarman, *Education by Choice*; Coons and Sugarman, *Scholarships for Children*.

66. See generally Forman, "Rise and Fall of School Vouchers," 549–604.

67. In addition to the voucher plans discussed in the text, two other types of programs should be mentioned. First, special education students are entitled, by federal law, to attend private schools at public expense if the public schools cannot satisfy their needs. Some states also offer vouchers to special education students. Second, both Maine

and Vermont provide funding to pay for students in rural districts without high schools to attend school elsewhere. Neither type of program, because of its narrower focus, has played much of a role in the intense debate about vouchers for private school.

68. The background and impact of the Milwaukee and Cleveland programs are discussed in Wolf, "Comprehensive Longitudinal Evaluation"; Van Dunk and Dickman, *School Choice and the Question of Accountability*; *EW*, 18 Jun. 2008, 7; 13 Jul. 2005, 23, 25; 28 Jan. 2004, 1, 28; 4 Sept. 2002, 34.

69. *EW*, 13 Jul. 2005, 23.

70. For description of Colorado program, see, e.g., Liu and Taylor, "School Choice to Achieve Desegregation," 815–16; for Florida program, see, e.g., Greene, "Evaluation of Florida A-Plus Program."

71. See Ryan and Heise, "Political Economy of School Choice," 2079–80.

72. The Michigan campaign is described in Moe, *Schools, Vouchers, and the American Public*, 367–68; the California campaign is described in ibid., 366–67; see generally *EW*, 15 Nov. 2000, 14.

73. See, e.g., *EW*, 14 Nov. 2007, 1, 20–21.

74. *WSJ*, 4 Nov. 1993, A14.

75. Ibid.; see also Moe, *Schools, Vouchers, and the American Public*, 359–65; *EW*, 15 Nov. 2000, 14.

76. First quote appears in Cookson, *School Choice*, 68 (quoting Bill Burrow, associate director of the first President Bush's Office on Competitiveness); second quote from *EW*, 6 Sept. 2000, 58.

77. Quote from Tuttle interview.

78. See Ryan and Heise, "Political Economy of School Choice," 2082.

79. *EW*, 28 Sept. 2007 (article published online only, at www.edweek.org).

80. See *NYT*, 13 Jun. 2001, A26; Wildman, "Credit is Due," 15.

81. Cookson, *School Choice*, 39; Peterson, "School Choice," 53; *NYT*, 15 Aug. 2001, A23; Moe, *Schools, Vouchers, and the American Public*, 212–17; Viteritti, *Choosing Equality*, 5; Bulman and Kirp, "Shifting Politics of School Choice," 38.

82. Moe, *Schools, Vouchers, and the American Public*, 212–17; Ryan and Heise, "Political Economy of School Choice," 2082–83.

83. See, e.g., *RTD*, 24 Sept. 2007, A10; 8 Oct. 2004, A14; 21 Jan. 2003, A11; 16 Jul. 2002, A9; 3 Jul. 2002, A13. Wolf interview, Jun. 26, 2008; Chris Saxman, interview by the author, Jun. 20, 2008.

84. Henrico parent (who wished to remain anonymous), interview by the author, Jun. 20, 2008.

85. The Century Foundation's views are captured in Kahlenberg, *Public School Choice*; the NAACP and People for the American Way Partnership is described in Ryan and Heise, "Political Economy of School Choice," 2089. The partnership appears to have disbanded.

86. Liu and Taylor, "School Choice to Achieve Desegregation," 808–23.

87. Wells, *Time to Choose*, 160–61; Bulman and Kirp, "Shifting Politics of School Choice," 48; *EW*, 12 Sept. 1990, 14.

88. See, e.g., Bulman and Kirp, "Shifting Politics of School Choice," 48.

89. Holme and Wells, "School Choice beyond District Borders," 210–11; Wells, *Time to Choose*, 160–61.

90. Stolee, "Milwaukee Desegregation Case," 256–60; Ramney, "Absolute Common Ground," 815–16; Viteritti, *Choosing Equality,* 102.

91. Stolee, "Milwaukee Desegregation Case," 256–60; Viteritti, *Choosing Equality,* 99; Borsuk, "Eyes on Milwaukee for School Choice."

92. Holme and Wells, "School Choice beyond District Borders," 210–11; Ramney, "Absolute Common Ground," 815–16.

Chapter 6

1. Mfume quote from Thomas and Clemetson, "New War over Vouchers," 46.

2. Levin, "Race and School Choice," 226–28; see also, e.g., McCusic, "Law's Role in Distribution of Education," 125–28; MacInnes, "Choosing Segregation," 89–92.

3. Reardon and Yun, "Private School Racial Enrollments," 6–8; see also MacInnes, "Choosing Segregation," 89–92.

4. See Liu and Taylor, "School Choice to Achieve Desegregation," 805–6.

5. Ibid., 805–7.

6. Enrollment figures for public schools in Richmond come from the National Center for Education Statistics (NCES) Common Core of Data, nces.ed.gov/ccd/school-search/. For the private schools, the figures come from NCES's Private School Universe Survey, nces.ed.gov/surveys/pss/privateschoolsearch/.

7. See generally Ryan and Heise, "Political Economy of School Choice," 2092–102.

8. See Hess and Loveless, "How School Choice Affects Student Achievement," 85–98.

9. In a recent report on charter school achievement, for example, the authors of the study explained that they compared charter school students and public school students who were similar in terms of either demographics, English language proficiency, participation in special education or subsidized lunch programs. See Center for Research on Educational Outcomes (CREDO), "Multiple Choices," 1.

10. For further discussion of this problem and possible ways to ameliorate it, see, e.g., Howell and Peterson, *Education Gap*, 143–67; Barrow and Rouse, "School Vouchers: Recent Findings and Unanswered Questions," 2–6.

11. See chapter 4; see also Mid-Continent Center for Research and Learning, "Final Report."

12. See Ryan and Heise, "Political Economy of School Choice," 2108.

13. Wells and Crain, *Stepping over the Color Line*, 148.

14. In three separate studies of data regarding the Milwaukee voucher program, for example, researchers came to different conclusions. The first found no impact; the second found significant gains; the third split the difference and found mixed results. See Ryan and Heise, "Political Economy of School Choice."

15. The literature is voluminous. For a general discussion, though somewhat dated at this point, see, e.g., ibid., 2019–112. For more recent reviews of the literature, see, e.g., Wolf, "School Voucher Programs"; 415–46; Barrow and Rouse, "School Vouchers: Recent

Findings and Unanswered Questions," 6–8; Howell and Peterson, *Education Gap*, 28–185; CREDO, "Multiple Choices," 1–47; National Center for Education Statistics, "Closer Look at Charter Schools," iii–vi, 17–36.

16. See Ryan, "Charter Schools and Public Education," 399; Reardon and Yun, "Private School Racial Enrollments," 6; Kahlenberg, "Problem of Taking Private Voucher Programs to Scale," 54; see Liu and Taylor, "School Choice to Achieve Desegregation," 806–7 (focusing on race rather than family income).

17. See Tough, "What It Takes to Make a Student," 49; see also Harris, "High Flying Schools," 9–30; Kahlenberg, *All Together Now*, xiv–xv; Rothstein, *Class and Schools*, 72–78.

18. Tough, "What It Takes to Make a Student," 50; Knowledge Is Power Program, www.kipp.org/.

19. See "Frequently Asked Questions," Knowledge is Power Program website; see generally, Mathews, *Work Hard. Be Nice.*

20. See Carnoy et al., *Charter School Dust-Up*, 29–32, 51–66; Henig, "What Do We Know," 5–6.

21. Tough, "What It Takes to Make a Student," 50; U.S. Department of Education, Office of Innovation and Improvement, "Successful Charter Schools," 14.

22. Tough, "What it Takes to Make a Student," 69.

23. Ibid., 50, 51.

24. Coleman et al., *High School Achievement*; see also Bryk et al., *Catholic Schools and the Common Good*.

25. Tough, "What It Takes to Make a Student," 69; see generally Kahlenberg, *All Together Now*, 23–76.

26. See, e.g., Mathews, "Inside the Bay Area KIPP Schools" (reporting high teacher turnover); KIPP, "About KIPP," www.kipp.org/ (reporting higher salaries for KIPP teachers).

27. Hoxby, "Does Competition among Public Schools Benefit Students?" 4–5; Belfield and Levin, "Effects of Competition," 293–94.

28. Belfield and Levin, "Effects of Competition," 293–94; Belfield and Levin, *Privatizing Educational Choice*, 44; Hess, *Revolution at the Margins*, 157–60; Greene, *CEO Horizon Scholarship Program*, 30–31; Ryan and Heise, "Political Economy of School Choice," 2113–14.

29. See Ryan and Heise, "Political Economy of School Choice," 2090–91.

30. Zelman v. Simmons-Harris, 536 U.S. 639 (2002); Jeffries and Ryan, "Political History of the Establishment Clause," 284–91.

31. See *WP*, 2 Jul. 2002, A1; Frankel, "Blackboard Jungle," 64–69, 103–5.

32. See Ryan, "*Brown*, School Choice, and the Suburban Veto," 1635–43; Jeffries and Ryan, "Political History of the Establishment Clause," 327–66.

33. Ryan, "*Brown*, School Choice, and the Suburban Veto," 1638–40.

34. Two quotes from Jeffries and Ryan, "Political History of the Establishment Clause," 327.

35. Ibid., 327–66.

36. Ryan, "*Brown*, School Choice, and the Suburban Veto," 1642–43.

37. See *NYT*, 30 Jun. 2002, 3.

38. Goldenzeil, "Blaine's Name in Vain," 63–65.

39. Virginia Constitution, art. 7, sec. 10; art. 2, sec. 16.

40. For competing views, contrast, e.g., Green, "Insignificance of Blaine Amendment," 327–33, with Richardson, "Eradicating Blaine's Legacy of Hate," 1041–50; see also Mitchell v. Helms, 530 U.S. 793, 828 (opinion of Thomas, J.) (describing history of Blaine amendment as giving rise to doctrine "born of bigotry"). See generally Jeffries and Ryan, "Political History of the Establishment Clause," 301–2.

41. See, e.g., Heytens, "School Choice and State Constitutions," 134–41; Jeffries and Ryan, "Political History of the Establishment Clause," 305.

42. See, e.g., Cato Institute, "Washington State's Blaine Amendment Violates the U.S. Constitution."

43. The case was Locke v. Davey, 540 U.S. 712 (2004); for discussion of constitutional issues, see Heytens, "School Choice and State Constitutions," 141–53.

44. Chittenden Town School District v. Vermont Department of Education, 738 A.2d 539 (Vt. 1999); Cain v. Horn, 202 P.3d 1178 (Ariz. 2009); Heytens, "School Choice and State Constitutions," 129–30.

45. Simmons-Harris v. Goff, 711 N.E.2d 203 (Oh. 1999); Jackson v. Benson, 578 N.W.2d 602 (Wis. 1998).

46. For information on tax credit programs, see the website of SchoolChoiceInfo .Org, www.schoolchoiceinfo.org; and the website of the Home School Legal Defense Association, www.hslda.org.

47. *Cain*, 202 P.3d at 1181–85.

48. Kotterman v. Killian, 972 P.2d 606 (Ariz. 1999); Griffith v. Bower, 747 N.E.2d 432 (Ill. App. 2001).

49. See Henig and Sugarman, "Nature and Extent of School Choice," 128, noting that it "is currently unimaginable that private charity could sustain a nationwide private scholarship scheme that would provide choice opportunities for all the low-income families wishing to pursue them."

50. Owens v. Colorado Congress of Parents, Teachers, and Students, 92 P.3d 933 (Colo. 2004); Bush v. Holmes, 919 So.2d 392 (Fl. 2006).

51. *Owens*, 92 P.3d at 935–36; Bolick, "Constitutional Parameters of School Choice," 345.

52. *Owens*, 92 P.3d at 938–44.

53. *Holmes*, 919 So.2d at 405–9.

54. Davis v. Grover, 480 N.W.2d 460, 474 (Wis. 1992); *Holmes*, 919 So.2d at 423–25 (Bell, J., dissenting).

55. *Holmes*, 919 So.2d at 411–12.

56. See, e.g., Bolick, "Constitutional Parameters of School Choice," 348–50.

57. See Crawford v. Davy, No. 137–06 (N.J. Super. Ct. Oct. 4, 2007), affirmed by Crawford v. Davy, No. A-1297–07T2 (N.J. Super. Ct., App. Div., Nov. 23, 2009); Gebhart

v. Belton, 91 A.2d 137 (Del. 1952) (requiring admission of black students to white schools because black schools were not equal to white ones).

Chapter 7

1. Dr. Edward H. Pruden, principal, Freeman High, interview by the author, Jun. 27, 2006.

2. National Commission on Excellence in Education, *Nation at Risk*, 5; Ravitch, *National Standards in American Education*, 52–56; Massell, "Standards-based Reform in the States," 136; Taylor, "Assessment as Means to Quality Education," 312–13.

3. See Liebman, "Implementing *Brown* in the Nineties," 371–73; Ryan, "Standards, Testing, and School Finance Litigation," 1227.

4. Goals 2000: Educate America Act, Pub. L. No. 103–382, 108 Stat. 125 (1994); Improving America's Schools Act of 1994 (IASA), Pub. L. No. 103–82, 108 Stat. 3518; Ryan, "Perverse Incentives," 937.

5. IASA, sec. 6311(b)(1)(A), (C); Ryan, "Perverse Incentives," 939.

6. No Child Left Behind Act (NCLB), secs. 1111(b)(1)(A)-(C), 1111(b)(3), 1116.

7. NCLB, sec. 1111(b)(3); Center on Education Policy, "State High School Exit Exams," 1 (reporting that twenty-three states had exit exams as of August 2008 and that three more states plan to implement them by 2012).

8. NCLB, sec. 1111(b)(3)(C)(xiii).

9. Ibid., secs. 1111(b)(2)(C), (F). To meet AYP, states must also look to graduation rates and at least one additional academic indicator, such as attendance. But graduation rates and the additional indicators do not need to be set at any particular level or increase over time. Ibid., sec. 1111(b)(2)(C)(vi).

10. Ibid., sec. 1116(a)(1). Examples of news stories equating "in need of improvement" and "failing" are collected in Ryan, "Perverse Incentives," 946 n. 66. Quotation from Ripley, "Inside the Revolt over Bush's School Rules," 33.

11. NCLB, sec. 1116(b)(1)(A); Ryan, "Perverse Incentives," 942 and n. 47.

12. NCLB, sec. 1116(b).

13. See, e.g., Neil et al., *Failing Our Children*, Schrag, *Final Test*, 239–40; Elmore, "Testing Trap," 35, 97; Mathis, "No Child Left Behind," 685; *NYT*, 8 May 2006, A20; 26 Mar. 2006, A11; 22 Mar. 2006, B7; *EW*, 5 Jan. 2006, 8, 16.

14. Kantor and Lowe, "From New Deal to No Deal," 491–94.

15. See *WSJ*, 22 Jun. 2006, A17; Borkowski and Sneed, "Will NCLB Improve," 509.

16. Carey, "Funding Gap 2004," 15.

17. See, e.g., Rebell, "Educational Adequacy," 33; Gorman, "Can't Beat 'Em? Sue 'Em," 36–41 (describing why school finance lawyers like Rebell support the NCLB).

18. For research on high-stakes testing, see, e.g., Nichols et al., "High Stakes Testing and Student Achievement," i–ii, 1–2; Jacob, "Accountability, Incentives, and Behavior," 761–96; Jones et al., "Impact of High-stakes Testing," 681–87; Meier, *Many Children Left Behind*, 20–22. Research on the impact of sanctions includes Steiner, "School Restructuring Options"; Hammer, "Corrective Action"; Wong and Shen, "Does School District

Takeover Work"; Ziebarth, "State Takeovers and Reconstitutions," 4–17, Center on Education Policy, "Hope but No Miracle Cures"; Kasi Addison and John Mooney, "School Takeover Leaves Shaky Legacy," *Newark Star-Ledger*, 17 Jul. 2005, 13.

19. First and third quotes from Rudalevige, "Politics of No Child Left Behind," 68. Some version of the "weighing the pig" remark was ubiquitous during debates over the NCLB and in critiques of the Act after passage. For one example, see Barbara Miner, "Money Key to School Reform," *Milwaukee Journal Sentinel*, 20 Dec. 2001, 23A.

20. See, e.g., Buhler, "Growing Importance of Soft Skills in Workplace," 13–16; *EW*, 24 May 2006, 1; Rothstein, *Class and Schools*, 113–17. A voluntary test of "soft skills" is available through the National Work Readiness Council, which issues a National Work Readiness Credential to those who pass the test. See www.workreadiness.com.

21. See, e.g., Rothstein, "Testing Our Patience," 45; Rothstein, "Leaving 'No Child Left Behind' Behind," 50.

22. See Rudalevige, "Politics of No Child Left Behind," 63–69; Ryan, "Perverse Incentives," 943–44.

23. Ryan, "Perverse Incentives," 944–61.

24. See Rothstein, "Leaving 'No Child Left Behind' Behind," 51 (noting that if the NCLB enforced high standards, "the already unacceptably large number of failing schools would be astronomical").

25. See Kumar and Abdullah, "As Test Scores Rise, Standards Are Lowered"; Carey, "Hot Air," 1–5; Peterson and Hess, "Keeping an Eye on State Standards," 28–29; *EW*, 20 Feb. 2002, 1.

26. See Ryan, "Standards, Testing, and School Finance Litigation," 1249; Rothstein, "Testing Our Patience," 45.

27. Peterson and Hess, "Keeping an Eye on State Standards," 28–29; Cronin et al., "Proficiency Illusion"; Carey, "Hot Air," 3–4.

28. Carey, "Hot Air," 4. See generally Cronin et al., "Proficiency Illusion"; Rothstein, *Class and Schools*, 89–92.

29. Board of Education, Commonwealth of Virginia, "Standards of Learning for Virginia Public Schools," i (1995) (message from Gov. George Allen); Kaine, "Competence to Excellence"; Pruden interview, Jun. 27, 2006.

30. See Cross et al., "Grading the Systems," 1–7.

31. *RTD*, 20 Nov. 2003, B5.

32. The process is described in a document produced by the Virginia Department of Education, "Virginia's K–12 Education Reform: Virginia's Standards of Learning Tests," 7–10.

33. Ibid.; Rotherham, "Making the Cut," 6. Quote from Meier, *Many Children Left Behind*, 82.

34. *RTD*, 20 Nov. 2003, B5.

35. Testing requirements are described by the Virginia Department of Education at www.doe.virginia.gov/2plus4in2004.

36. Data from "School Report Cards" for Thomas Jefferson High School and Freeman High School, compiled by Virginia Department of Education, available at www.doe.virginia.gov/VDOE/src (hereafter "Tee-Jay Report Card" and "Freeman Report Card").

37. Even the label "advanced" needs to be placed in context. One teacher explained that she often has to tell parents, somewhat delicately, that just because their son or daughter achieved an "advanced" score on an SOL test does not mean that he or she is eligible for the gifted and talented program.

38. Pruden interview, Jun. 27, 2006; "Tee-Jay Report Card," 9–15; "Freeman Report Card," 9–16.

39. State average SAT score is from the College Board, available at www.professionals.collegeboard.com; data on specific schools from School Data Direct, available at www.schooldatadirect.org.

40. "Freeman Report Card," 16; "Tee-Jay Report Card," 17; on calculating graduation rates, see, e.g., *RTD*, 9 Jul. 2009, A9; *WP*, 9 Oct. 2008, B4. The *EW* graduation rate report is available at www.edweek.org/ew/toc/2009/06/11/index.html. For essays and studies on graduation rates generally, see Orfield, *Dropouts in America*.

41. Figures available at Virginia Department of Education, "Diploma Graduates and Completers by School, 2007–2008."

42. William Russell Flammia, former teacher, interview by the author, Jul. 25, 2006.

43. Hochschild and Scovronick, *American Dream and Public Schools*, 99–100.

44. See, e.g., Traub, "Test Mess."

45. See *NYT*, 23 Mar. 2008, LI2.

46. Flammia interview; see Traub, "Test Mess."

47. See, e.g., Rothstein, *Class and Schools*, 92 (arguing that basic and higher order skills must be taught simultaneously, not sequentially).

48. *WP*, 9 Apr. 2007, A13; Rothstein, "Leaving 'No Child Behind' Behind," 51 (quoting Chester Finn and Diane Ravitch); see also Traub, "Test Mess" (describing different approaches to testing at suburban and urban schools).

49. For discussion of the legal challenges—chiefly one case out of Connecticut and one in the U.S. Court of Appeals for the Sixth Circuit—see, e.g., Umpstead, "No Child Left Behind Act," 193–229; for an up-to-date list of cases, see website maintained by the National School Boards Association, available at www.nsba.org.

50. See Ryan, "Standards, Testing, and School Finance Litigation," 1229–31.

51. See, e.g., Schrag, *Final Test*, 5; Rebell, "Educational Adequacy, Democracy, and the Courts," 235–36; McCusic, "Law's Role in Distribution of Education," 88, 91; Morgan et al., "Establishing Education Program Inadequacy," 568–69.

52. Schrag and Thernstrom, "Must Schools Fail," 49.

53. Edgewood Independent School District v. Kirby, 777 S.W.2d 391, 396–98 (Tex. 1989).

54. Neeley v. West Orange-Cove Consolidated Independent School District, 176 S.W.3d 746, 769–70, 788–90 (Tex. 2005).

55. Ibid., 787–90.

56. Hoke County Board of Education v. State, 599 S.E.2d 365, 383–91 (N.C. 2004).

57. Campaign for Fiscal Equity v. State, 801 N.E.2d 326, 333–40 (N.Y. 2003).

58. On the use of costing-out studies by courts, see, e.g., Springer and Guthrie, "Politicization of the School Finance Legal Process," 105–7.

59. On the growing popularity of national standards, see, e.g., *EW*, 4 Mar. 2009, 1–5.

60. See, e.g., Meier et al., *Many Children Left Behind*, 5 (reporting growing numbers of schools failing to make annual progress).

Chapter 8

1. Mann, "First Annual Report" (1837), in Cremin, *Republic and the School*, 23–24, 31–32; strategy of desegregation advocates discussed in chapter 1.

2. For discussion of these studies, see chapter 4.

3. See generally Kahlenberg, *All Together Now*.

4. See, e.g., Rothstein, "Leaving 'No Child Left Behind' Behind," 51.

5. See, e.g., discussion and sources cited in Hochschild and Scovronick, *American Dream and Public Schools*, 54; Ryan, "Schools, Race, and Money," 287; Kahlenberg, *All Together Now*, 25–28, 49; Rothstein, *Class and Schools*, 17–34. See generally, Lareau, *Unequal Childhoods*.

6. See, e.g., National Center for Education Statistics, "Condition of Education 2002," 58.

7. For a good overview of the factors that influence student performance and an attempt to solve this puzzle, see Chubb and Moe, *Politics, Markets, and America's Schools*, 101–40. See also Belfield and Levin, *Privatizing Educational Choice*, 63 (noting that everyone agrees that families and schools both matter but differ in estimates of impact).

8. For mission statements of the two "camps" in education reform, see Task Force, Broader, Bolder Approach to Education, "Mission Statement"; Education Equality Project, "Mission Statement." For an argument about the need to focus on social services and family poverty, see Rothstein, *Class and Schools*. See also Traub, "What No School Can Do," *New York Times Magazine*, 16 Jan. 2000, 52–57. For an argument about the need to keep attention focused on schools, see, e.g., Hess, *Common Sense School Reform*, 3–22.

9. Puma, "Prospects: Final Report on Student Outcomes," 73.

10. See Ravitch, *Troubled Crusade*, 228–32; National Commission on Excellence in Education, *Nation at Risk*, 5; for an example of a report on the lackluster performance of U.S. students on international tests, see, e.g., *NYT*, 5 Dec. 2001, D8.

11. Matthews, "Bad Rap on the Schools," 15–20; see also *NYT*, 25 Apr. 2008, A27.

12. See, e.g., Ryan, "Schools, Race, and Money," 296–307; Ryan and Heise, "Political Economy of School Choice," 2102–7; see generally Kahlenberg, *All Together Now*.

13. See, e.g., Ryan, "Schools, Race and Money," 301–7.

14. See, e.g., Kahlenberg, *All Together Now*, 61–67; Anyon, *Ghetto Schooling*, 159–61; Chubb and Moe, *Politics, Markets, and America's Schools*, 147–50; Cashin, *Failures of Integration*, 223; Lareau, *Unequal Childhoods*, 242–44.

15. Chubb and Moe, *Politics, Markets, and America's Schools*, 169–79.

16. For an example of the "social engineering" argument, see, e.g., Finn, "Faux Choice"; for an argument that socioeconomic integration is implausible, see, e.g., Witte and Coons, "Try, Try Again," 75–77 (reviewing Kahlenberg, *All Together Now*).

17. Figures on minority student enrollment come from the U.S. Census Bureau, "Current Population Survey," and "American Community Survey." See also CBS News, "Minority Kids Could Be Majority by 2023." Overall population rates reported in Frey, "Census Projects Minority Surge," and *NYT*, 14 Aug. 2008, A1.

18. Berube and Kneebone, "Two Steps Back," 2.

19. Ibid., 4.

20. Frey, "Melting Pot Suburbs," 1–7.

21. Data available from Virginia Department of Education, www.doe.virginia.gov, and National Center for Education Statistics, Common Core of Data, nces.ed.gov/ccd. The data have to be compiled, so there is no single website to cite. Spreadsheets with compiled data on file with author.

22. *WSJ*, 19 Jul. 2008, A1.

23. *NYT*, 9 Oct. 2008, D1; 25 Jun. 2008, A1.

24. *NYT*, 9 Oct. 2008, D1.

25. Data from NCES, Common Core of Data, www.nces.ed.gov/ccd.

26. Berube and Kneebone, "Two Steps Back," 1–21; Swanstrom et al., "Pulling Apart," 1–18.

27. Berube and Kneebone, "Two Steps Back," 15.

28. See, e.g., Leinberger, "Next Slum," 70–75; *NYT*, 25 Jun. 2008, A1; 9 Dec. 2008, A35.

29. See, e.g., *WSJ*, 19 Jul. 2008, A1; Leinberger, "Next Slum"; Frey, "Melting Pot Suburbs," 1–12; *NYT*, 25 Jun. 2008, A1; Frey, "Migration to Hot Housing Markets Cools Off," 1–2.

30. Leinberger, "Next Slum," 70–75; *NYT*, 25 Jun. 2008, A1 (quoting Joe Cortright, housing economist at consulting group Impresa, Inc., in Portland, Oregon).

31. David Rusk has repeatedly pointed out that housing policy is school policy. See, e.g., Rusk, "Housing Policy *Is* School Policy."

32. The topic of affordable and integrated housing is enormous, as is the literature on it. For a helpful, concise overview, see McCusic, "Future of *Brown v. Board of Education*," 1365–75. For discussion of inclusionary zoning in particular, see Rusk, "Nine Lessons for Inclusionary Zoning."

33. See Abdulkadiroglu et al., "New York City High School Match," 364–67.

34. Liu and Taylor, "School Choice to Achieve Desegregation." Liberal commentators Robert Reich and William Raspberry have made similar arguments in support of vouchers. See, e.g., *WSJ*, 6 Sept. 2000, A26 (Reich); *WP*, 16 Jun. 1997, A21 (Raspberry). See also Kahlenberg, *Public School Choice*, 1 ("Well-respected liberal thinkers like Joseph Califano, Andrew Young, Robert Reich, Matthew Miller, Arthur Levine, William Raspberry, Martha Minow, and the editorial page editors of the *Washington Post* have all come around to thinking that vouchers are worth a try."). As Professor James Forman has detailed, moreover, school choice, including voucher programs, has historically attracted the interest of liberal reformers. Forman, "Secret History of School Choice." See also

Moe, *Schools, Vouchers, and the American Public*, 385 (discussing the Black Alliance for Educational Options and predicting that the leadership of civil rights groups, especially as it devolves to younger members, will "abandon its opposition to vouchers and switch sides"); Hochschild and Scovronick, *American Dream and Public Schools*, 113 (making a similar point).

35. There is no shortage of ideas, past and present, for how to structure choice to encourage integration. See, e.g., Liu and Taylor, "School Choice to Achieve Desegregation," 808–11; Gill, "School Choice and Integration," 130–45; Bulman and Kirp, "Shifting Politics of School Choice," 39–43; Forman, "Secret History of School Choice," 1309–12.

36. See Cashin, *Failures of Integration*, 292 (arguing that it is hard to call current financing of school democratic when only those with the means to buy expensive homes can attend excellent schools); see generally Glenn, *Myth of the Common School*.

37. Toward the very end of editing this manuscript, I came across a similar proposal from the Charles Hamilton Houston Institute for Race and Justice at Harvard Law School. See Charles Hamilton Houston Institute for Race and Justice, "Creating Charter Schools That Reduce Segregation in Massachusetts." See also Goldstein, "On Edu Reform" (questioning why Gates, in his support of charter schools, "never talks about integration").

38. The classic statement of the phenomenon comes from Thomas Schelling. See Schelling, "Process of Residential Segregation," 157–84.

39. The two studies are Ellen, "Welcome Neighbors" and Rawlings et al., "Race and Residence," 1–10.

40. Quote from Ellen, "Welcome Neighbors." See generally Maly, *Beyond Segregation*, 35–45; Fasenfest et al., "Living Together," 1–18; Card et al., "Tipping and the Dynamics of Segregation," 177–218; Easterly, "Empirics of Strategic Interdependence."

41. Zogby, *Way We'll Be*, 99.

42. Taylor and Morin, "Americans Claim to Like Diverse Communities"; Olander et al., "Attitudes of Young People toward Diversity."

43. Edward H. Pruden, principal, Freeman High School, interview by the author, Jun. 27, 2006.

44. *NYT*, 22 Mar. 2003, D1.

45. Childress et al., *Leading for Equity* 1–31.

46. Ibid., 1–148.

47. For a review of some research on managing diverse schools, see, e.g., Kugler, *Debunking the Middle-class Myth*.

48. School data come from NCES, Common Core of Data, www.nces.ed.gov/ccd.

49. See Kahlenberg, "Rescuing *Brown v. Board of Education*," 9–13; Silberman, "Wake County Schools," 141–66. Current demographics reported in Wake County Public School System, Demographics Data Center, "Demographics."

50. Kahlenberg, "Rescuing *Brown v. Board of Education*."

51. For one effort to emphasize the *benefits* of diverse schools to middle-class students, see Kugler, *Debunking the Middle-class Myth*.

52. *NYT*, 18 Dec. 2008, A39.

53. See Rothstein, *Class and Schools*, 170 n. 310 (reporting that the "tipping point" for schools is not certain but appears to be somewhere between 40 and 50 percent poor). The two most relevant Supreme Court decisions are *Parents Involved in Community Schools v. Seattle School District No. 1*, 551 U.S. 701 (2007), and *Gratz v. Bollinger*, 539 U.S. 244 (2003).

54. See *Parents Involved*, 551 U.S. 701.

55. Sheff v. O'Neill, 678 A.2d 1267 (Conn. 1996).

56. Campaign for Fiscal Equity v. State, 801 N.E.2d 326, 330, 340 (N.Y. 2003).

57. Paynter v. State, 797 N.E.2d 1225, 1226–28 (N.Y. 2003).

58. The lone dissenting opinion in *Paynter v. State* made similar points. 797 N.E. 2d at 1231–50 (Smith, J., dissenting); see generally Clotfelter, *After* Brown, 188–92 (describing data regarding long-term social benefits of integrated schools); Hochschild and Scovronick, *American Dream and Public Schools*, 41 (same).

59. Aside from *Paynter v. State*, only one other case followed the lead of *Sheff* v. *O'Neill* and sought to enforce a right to attend an integrated school. The case was brought in Minneapolis and resulted in a modest settlement, which is described in chapter 5.

60. For discussion of the political context of the Kentucky case, see, e.g., Combs, "Creative Constitutional Law," 367–72; for discussion of the political appeal of preschool and associated litigation, see Ryan, "Constitutional Right to Preschool."

61. Merhige's obituary appeared, among other places, in *WP*, 20 Feb. 2005, C8. His last opinion in the Richmond desegregation case is reported at *Bradley v. Baliles*, 639 F. Supp. 680 (E.D. Va. 1986).

Epilogue

1. William Russell Flammia, former Tee-Jay teacher, interview by the author, Jul. 25, 2006.

2. Ibid.

3. Edward H. Pruden, principal, Freeman High, interview by the author, Jun. 27, 2006.

4. Ibid.

5. Ibid.

BIBLIOGRAPHY

NEWSPAPERS AND PERIODICALS

Education Week (EW)

New York Times (NYT)

Richmond Afro-American (RAA)

Richmond News Leader (RNL)

Richmond Times-Dispatch (RTD)

Southern School News (SSN)

Wall Street Journal (WSJ)

Washington Post (WP)

BOOKS

Alexander, Kern, and Richard G. Salmon. *Public School Finance*. Needham Heights, Mass.: Allyn and Bacon, 1995.

Anderson, James D. *The Education of Blacks in the South, 1860–1935*. Chapel Hill: University of North Carolina Press, 1988.

Anyon, Jean. *Ghetto Schooling: A Political Economy of Urban Educational Reform*. New York: Teachers College Press, 1997.

Armor, David J. *Forced Justice: School Desegregation and the Law*. New York: Oxford University Press, 1995.

Bacigal, Ronald J. *May It Please the Court: A Biography of Judge Robert R. Merhige, Jr.* Lanham, Md.: University Press of America, 1992.

Ballou, Dale, and Michael Podgursky. *Teacher Pay and Teacher Quality*. Kalamazoo, Mich.: W. E. Upjohn Institute, 1997.

Belfield, Clive R., and Henry M. Levin. *Privatizing Educational Choice: Consequences for Parents, Schools, and Public Policy*. Herndon, Va.: Paradigm, 2005.

Bell, Derrick A., Jr. *Silent Covenants: Brown v. Board of Education and the Unfulfilled Hopes for Racial Reform*. New York: Oxford University Press, 2004.

Berke, Joel. *Answers to Inequity: An Analysis of the New School Finance*. Berkeley: McCutchan, 1974.

Betts, Julian R., and Tom Loveless, eds. *Getting Choice Right: Ensuring Equity and Efficiency in Education Policy*. Washington, D.C.: Brookings Institution Press, 2005.

Briffault, Richard, and Laurie Reynolds. *Cases and Materials on State and Local Government Law*. 6th ed. St. Paul, Minn.: Thomson/West, 2004.

Bryk, Anthony S., Valerie E. Lee, and Peter B. Holland. *Catholic Schools and the Common Good*. Cambridge Mass.: Harvard University Press, 1993.

Buncher, Judith F., ed. *The School Busing Controversy, 1970–1975*. New York: Facts on File, 1975.

Burtless, Gary, ed. *Does Money Matter? The Effect of School Resources on Student Achievement and Adult Success*. Washington, D.C.: Brookings Institution Press, 1996.

Carmichael, Stokely, and Charles V. Hamilton. *Black Power: The Politics of Liberation in America*. New York: Random House, 1967.

Carnoy, Martin, Rebecca Jacobsen, Lawrence Mishel, and Richard Rothstein. *The Charter School Dust-Up: Examining the Evidence on Enrollment and Achievement*. Washington, D.C.: Economic Policy Institute, 2005.

Cashin, Sheryll. *The Failures of Integration: How Race and Class Are Undermining the American Dream*. New York: Public Affairs, 2004.

Century Foundation Task Force. *Divided We Fail: Coming Together through Public School Choice*. New York: Century Foundation Press, 2002.

Chesterton, G. K. *What's Wrong with the World*. New York: Dodd, Mead, 1912.

Childress, Stacey M., Dennis P. Doyle, and David A. Thomas, *Leading for Equity: The Pursuit of Excellence in Montgomery County Public Schools*. Cambridge, Mass.: Harvard Education Press, 2009.

Chubb, John E., and Terry M. Moe. *Politics, Markets, and America's Schools*. Washington, D.C.: Brookings Institution Press, 1990.

Clotfelter, Charles T. *After Brown: The Rise and Retreat of School Desegregation*. Princeton, N.J.: Princeton University Press, 2004.

Coleman, James S. *Equality of Educational Opportunity Study*. Washington, D.C.: United States Department of Education, 1966.

Coleman, James S., Thomas Hoffer, and Sally Kilgore. *High School Achievement: Public, Catholic, and Private Schools Compared*. New York: Basic Books, 1982.

Cookson, Peter W. *School Choice: The Struggle for the Soul of American Education*. New Haven, Conn.: Yale University Press, 1995.

Coons, John E. *Private Wealth and Public Education*. Cambridge, Mass.: Harvard University Press, 1970.

Coons, John E., and Stephen D. Sugarman. *Education by Choice: The Case for Family Control*. Berkeley: University of California Press, 1978.

———. *Scholarships for Children*. Berkeley: Institute of Governmental Studies Press, University of California, Berkeley, 1992.

Cremin, Lawrence A., ed. *The Republic and the School: Horace Mann on the Education of Free Men*. New York: Teachers College Press, 1957.

———. *American Education: The Metropolitan Experience, 1876–1980*. New York: Harper and Row, 1988.

Dabney, Virginius. *Virginia: The New Dominion, A History from 1607 to the Present*. Garden City, N.Y.: Doubleday, 1971.

Donohue, John J., III, et al. *Social Action, Private Choice and Philanthropy: Understanding the Sources of Improvements in Black Schooling in Georgia, 1911–1960*. Cambridge, Mass.: National Bureau of Economic Research, 1998.

Douglas, Davison M. *Jim Crow Moves North: The Battle over Northern School Segregation, 1865–1954*. New York: Cambridge University Press, 2005.

Downs, Anthony. *New Visions for Metropolitan America*. Washington, D.C.: Brookings Institution, 1994.

Duke, Daniel L. *The School That Refused to Die: Continuity and Change at TJ High*. New York: State University of New York Press, 1995.

Eaton, Susan E. *The Other Boston Busing Story: What's Won and Lost across the Boundary Line*. New Haven, Conn.: Yale University Press, 2001.

Edwards, Jack D. *Neighbors and Sometimes Friends: Municipal Annexation in Modern Virginia*. Charlottesville: Center for Public Service, University of Virginia, 1992.

Ehrlichman, John. *Witness to Power: The Nixon Years*. New York: Simon and Schuster, 1982.

Fischel, William A. *The Homevoter Hypothesis: How Home Values Influence Local Government Taxation, School Finance, and Land-use Policies*. Cambridge, Mass.: Harvard University Press, 2001.

Friddell, Guy, and Colgate Darden. *Colgate Darden: Conversations with Guy Friddell*. Charlottesville: University Press of Virginia, 1978.

Friedman, Milton. *Capitalism and Freedom*. Chicago: University of Chicago Press, 1962.

Fuller, Bruce, Richard Elmore, and Gary Orfield, eds. *Who Chooses? Who Loses? Culture, Institutions and the Unequal Effects of School Choice*. New York: Teachers College Press, 1996.

Fuller, Bruce, ed. *Inside Charter Schools: The Paradox of Radical Decentralization*. Cambridge, Mass.: Harvard University Press, 2002.

Gainsborough, Juliet F. *Fenced Off: The Suburbanization of American Politics*. Washington, D.C.: Georgetown University Press, 2001.

Gates, Robin L. *The Making of Massive Resistance: Virginia's Politics of Public School Desegregation, 1954–1956*. Chapel Hill: University of North Carolina Press, 1964.

Gilles, Myriam E., and Risa L. Goluboff, eds. *Civil Rights Stories*. New York: Foundation Press, 2008.

Gittell, Marilyn, ed. *Strategies for School Equity*. New Haven, Conn.: Yale University Press, 1998.

Glenn, Charles Leslie. *Myth of the Common School*. Amherst: University of Massachusetts Press, 1988.

Greene, Jay P. *The CEO Horizon Scholarship Program: A Case Study of School Vouchers in the Edgewood Independent School District, San Antonio, Texas. Final Report*. Washington, D.C.: Mathematica Policy Research, 2001.

Hanushek, Eric A. ed., *Courting Failure: How School Finance Lawsuits Exploit Judges' Good Intentions and Harm Our Children*. Stanford, Calif.: Education Next Books, 2006.

Hanushek, Eric A. and Alfred A. Lindseth. *Schoolhouses, Courthouses, and Statehouses: Solving the Funding-achievement Puzzle in America's Public Schools*. Princeton, N.J.: Princeton University Press, 2009.

Hartman, Chester, ed. *Poverty and Race in America: The Emerging Agendas*. Oxford: Lexington Books, 2006.

Henig, Jeffry R. *Rethinking School Choice: Limits of the Market Metaphor*. Princeton, N.J.: Princeton University Press, 1994.

Hess, Fredrick M. *Revolution at the Margins: The Impact of Competition on Urban School Systems*. Washington, D.C.: Brookings Institution Press, 2002.

———. *Common Sense School Reform*. New York: Palgrave Macmillan, 2004.

Heubert, Jay P., ed. *Law and School Reform: Six Strategies for Promoting Educational Equity*. New Haven, Conn.: Yale University Press, 1999.

Hirsch, E. D., Jr. *The Schools We Need and Why We Don't Have Them*. New York: Doubleday, 1996.

Hochschild, Jennifer L. *The New American Dilemma: Liberal Democracy and School Desegregation*. New Haven, Conn.: Yale University Press, 1984.

Hochschild, Jennifer L., and Nathan Scovronick. *The American Dream and Public Schools*. New York: Oxford University Press, 2004.

Hodgson, Godfrey. *The World Turned Right Side Up: A History of the Conservative Ascendancy in America*. Boston: Houghton Mifflin, 1996.

Howell, William G., and Paul E. Peterson. *The Education Gap: Vouchers and Urban Schools*. Washington, D.C.: Brookings Institution Press, 2002.

Irons, Peter H. *Jim Crow's Children: The Broken Promise of the Brown Decision*. New York: Viking, 2002.

Jackson, Kenneth T. *Crabgrass Frontier: The Suburbanization of the United States*. New York: Oxford University Press, 1985.

Jeffries, John C. *Justice Lewis F. Powell, Jr.* New York: Scribner's, 1994.

Jencks, Christopher, and Meredith Phillips, eds. *The Black-white Test Score Gap*. Washington, D.C.: Brookings Institution Press, 1998.

Johnson, David. *Douglas Southall Freeman*. Gretna, La.: Pelican, 2002.

Kahlenberg, Richard D. *All Together Now: Creating Middle-class Schools through Public School Choice*. Washington, D.C.: Brookings Institution Press, 2001.

———, ed. *Public School Choice vs. Private School Vouchers*. New York: Century Foundation Press, 2003.

———, ed. *Improving on No Child Left Behind*. New York: Century Foundation Press, 2008.

Karoly, Lynn A. *Investing in Our Children: What We Know and Don't Know about the Costs and Benefits of Early Childhood Interventions*. Santa Monica, Calif.: Rand Corporation, 1998.

Kilpatrick, James J. *The Sovereign States: Notes of a Citizen of Virginia*. Chicago: Regnery, 1957.

Klarman, Michael J. *From Jim Crow to Civil Rights: The Supreme Court and the Struggle for Racial Equality*. New York: Oxford University Press, 2004.

Kluger, Richard. *Simple Justice: The History of Brown v. Board of Education and Black America's Struggle for Equality*. New York: Knopf, 1976.

Kohn, Alfie. *The Case against Standardized Testing: Raising the Scores, Ruining the Schools*. Portsmouth, N.H.: Heinemann, 2000.

Kozol, Jonathan. *Savage Inequalities: Children in America's Schools*. New York: Harper Perennial, 1992.

————. *The Shame of the Nation: The Restoration of Apartheid Schooling in America.* New York: Crown, 2005.

Kugler, Eileen Gale. *Debunking the Middle-Class Myth: Why Diverse Schools Are Good for All Kids.* Lanham, Md.: Rowman and Littlefield Education, 2005.

Ladd, Helen F., ed. *Equity and Adequacy in Education Finance: Issues and Perspectives.* Washington, D.C.: National Academy Press, 1999.

Lareau, Annette. *Unequal Childhoods: Class, Race, and Family Life.* Berkeley: University of California Press, 2003.

Lassiter, Matthew D. *The Silent Majority: Suburban Politics in the Sunbelt South.* Princeton, N.J.: Princeton University Press, 2006.

Lassiter, Matthew D., and Andrew B. Lewis. *The Moderates' Dilemma: Massive Resistance to School Desegregation in Virginia.* Charlottesville: University of Virginia Press, 1998.

Loveless, Tom, ed. *Conflicting Missions: Teachers Unions and Educational Reform.* Washington, D.C.: Brookings Institution Press, 2000.

Lukas, J. A. *Common Ground: A Turbulent Decade in the Lives of Three American Families.* New York: Knopf, 1985.

Macedo, Stephen. *Diversity and Distrust: Civic Education in a Multicultural Democracy.* Cambridge, Mass.: Harvard University Press, 2000.

Maly, Michael T. *Beyond Segregation: Multiracial and Multiethnic Neighborhoods in the United States.* Philadelphia: Temple University Press, 2005.

Massey, Douglas S., and Nancy A. Denton. *American Apartheid: Segregation and the Making of the Underclass.* Cambridge, Mass.: Harvard University Press, 1993.

Mathews, Jay. *Class Struggle: What's Wrong (and Right) with America's Best Public High Schools.* New York: Times Books, 1998.

————. *Work Hard. Be Nice: How Two Inspired Teachers Created the Most Promising Schools in America.* Chapel Hill, N.C.: Algonquin Books of Chapel Hill, 2009.

Meier, Deborah. *Many Children Left Behind: How the No Child Left Behind Act Is Damaging Our Children and Our Schools.* Boston: Beacon Press, 2004.

Metcalf, George R. *From Little Rock to Boston: The History of School Desegregation.* Westport, Conn.: Greenwood Press, 1983.

Mill, John Stuart. *On Liberty.* London: Longman, 2006.

Moe, Terry M. *Schools, Vouchers, and the American Public.* Washington, D.C.: Brookings Institution Press, 2001.

Moeser, John V., and Rutledge M. Dennis. *The Politics of Annexation: Oligarchic Power in a Southern City.* Cambridge, Mass.: Schenkman, 1982.

Muse, Benjamin. *Virginia's Massive Resistance.* Gloucester, Mass.: Peter Smith, 1961.

Myrdal, Gunner. *An American Dilemma.* New York: Harper, 1944.

National Commission on Excellence in Education. *A Nation at Risk: The Imperative for Educational Reform: A Report to the Nation and the Secretary of Education, United States Department of Education.* Washington, D.C: National Commission on Excellence in Education, 1983.

Neil, Monty, et al. *Failing Our Children.* Cambridge, Mass.: Fair Test, 2004.

Odden, Allen, and Lawrence Picus. *School Finance: A Policy Perspective.* 4th ed. Boston: McGraw-Hill, 2008.

Ohanian, Susan. *One Size Fits Few: The Folly of Educational Standards*. Portsmouth, N.H.: Heinemann, 1999.

Orfield, Gary. *Must We Bus? Segregated Schools and National Policy*. Washington, D.C: Brookings Institution, 1978.

———, ed. *Dropouts in America: Confronting the Graduation Rate Crisis*. Cambridge, Mass.: Harvard Education Press, 2004.

Orfield, Gary, and Susan E. Eaton. *Dismantling Desegregation: The Quiet Reversal of Brown v. Board of Education*. New York: New Press, 1996.

Orfield, Gary, and Elizabeth H. McBray, eds. *Hard Work for Good Schools*. New York: Century Foundation Press, 2003.

Orfield, Myron. *Metropolitics: A Regional Agenda for Community and Stability*. Washington, D.C.: Brookings Institution Press, 1997.

———. *American Metropolitics: The New Suburban Reality*. Washington, D.C.: Brookings Institution Press, 2002.

Paige, Rod. *The War against Hope: How Teachers' Unions Hurt Children, Hinder Teachers, and Endanger Public Education*. Nashville, Tenn.: Thomas Nelson, 2007.

Pascal, Anthony H., ed. *Racial Discrimination in Economic Life*. Lexington, Mass.: Lexington Books, 1972.

Patterson, James T. *Brown v. Board of Education: A Civil Rights Milestone and Its Troubled Legacy*. New York: Oxford University Press, 2001.

Peery, George J. *Racialism and the Politics of Metropolitan Government: Richmond-Henrico, Merger-Annexation, 1960–1965*. Charlottesville: University of Virginia Press, 1969.

Peterson, Paul E., ed. *The Urban Underclass*. Washington, D.C.: Brookings Institution Press, 1991.

Pratt, Robert A. *The Color of Their Skin: Education and Race in Richmond, Virginia, 1954–1989*. Charlottesville: University Press of Virginia, 1992.

Ravitch, Diane. *The Troubled Crusade: American Education, 1945–1980*. New York: Basic Books, 1983.

———. *National Standards in American Education: A Citizen's Guide*. Washington, D.C.: Brookings Institution Press, 1995.

Ready, Timothy, et al., eds. *Achieving High Educational Standards for All*. Washington, D.C.: National Academy Press, 2002.

Reese, William J. *America's Public Schools: From the Common School to "No Child Left Behind."* Baltimore: Johns Hopkins University Press, 2005.

Report of the National Advisory Commission on Civil Disorders (Kerner Commission Report). New York: Bantam Books, 1968.

Rossell, Christine H. *The Carrot or the Stick for School Desegregation Policy: Magnet Schools or Forced Busing*. Philadelphia: Temple University Press, 1990.

Rossell, Christine H., and Willis D. Hawley, eds. *The Consequences of School Desegregation*. Philadelphia: Temple University Press, 1983.

Rothstein, Richard. *Class and Schools: Using Social, Economic, and Educational Reform to Close the Black-white Achievement Gap*. Washington, D.C.: Economic Policy Institute, 2004.

Rothstein, Richard, et al. *Grading Education: Getting Accountability Right.* Washington, D.C.: Economic Policy Institute, 2008.

Rouse, Cecilia Elena, and Lisa Barrow. *School Vouchers and Student Achievement: Recent Evidence, Remaining Questions.* New York: National Center for the Study of Privatization in Education, 2008.

Rubin, Lillian B. *Busing and Backlash: White against White in an Urban School District.* Berkeley: University of California Press, 1972.

Rury, John L., and Frank A. Cassell, eds. *Seeds of Crisis: Public Schooling in Milwaukee since 1920.* Madison: University of Wisconsin Press, 1993.

Sacks, Peter. *Standardized Minds: The High Price of America's Testing Culture and What We Can Do to Change It.* Cambridge, Mass.: Da Capo Press, 2001.

Schrag, Peter. *Final Test: The Battle for Adequacy in America's Schools.* New York: New Press, 2005.

Silver, Christopher. *Twentieth-century Richmond: Planning, Politics, and Race.* Knoxville: University of Tennessee Press, 1984.

Sindler, Allan, ed. *Policy and Politics in America.* Boston: Little, Brown, 1973.

Sugarman, Stephen D., and Frank R. Kemerer, eds. *School Choice and Social Controversy.* Washington, D.C.: Brookings Institution Press, 1999.

Sunderman, Gail L., James S. Kim, and Gary Orfield. *NCLB Meets School Realities: Lessons from the Field.* Thousand Oaks, Calif.: Corwin Press, 2005.

Thomas, G. Scott. *The United States of Suburbia: How the Suburbs Took Control of America and What They Plan to Do with It.* Amherst, N.Y.: Prometheus, 1998.

Van Dunk, Emily, and Anneliese M. Dickman. *School Choice and the Question of Accountability: The Milwaukee Experience.* New Haven, Conn.: Yale University Press, 2003.

Vanourek, Gregg. *State of the Charter Movement 2005: Trends, Issues, and Indicators.* Washington, D.C.: Charter School Leadership Council, 2005.

Viteritti, Joseph P. *Choosing Equality: School Choice, the Constitution, and Civil Society.* Washington, D.C.: Brookings Institution Press, 1999.

Weekly Compilation of Presidential Documents. Washington, D.C.: Office of the Federal Registrar, National Archives and Records Administration, 1971.

Welch, Finis, and Audrey Light. *New Evidence on School Desegregation.* Los Angeles: Unicon Research Corporation, 1987.

Wells, Amy Stuart. *Time to Choose: America at the Crossroads of School Choice Policy.* New York: Hill and Wang, 1993.

Wells, Amy Stuart, and Robert L. Crain. *Stepping over the Color Line: African-American Students in White Suburban Schools.* New Haven, Conn.: Yale University Press, 1997.

West, Martin, and Paul Peterson, eds. *School Money Trials.* Washington, D.C.: Brookings Institution Press, 2007.

Wilkinson, J. Harvie, III. *Harry Byrd and the Changing Face of Virginia Politics, 1945–1966.* Charlottesville: University Press of Virginia, 1968.

———. *From* Brown *to* Bakke: *The Supreme Court and School Integration: 1954–1978.* New York: Oxford University Press, 1979.

Willie, Charles V., and Susan L. Greenblatt. *Community Politics and Educational Change.* New York: Longman, 1981.

Wise, Arthur E. *Rich Schools, Poor Schools: The Promise of Equal Educational Opportunity.* Chicago: University of Chicago Press, 1968.

Wolf, Eleanor P. *Trial and Error: The Detroit School Desegregation Case.* Detroit: Wayne State University Press, 1981.

Yudof, Mark G., et al. *Educational Policy and the Law.* 4th ed. Belmont, Calif.: West/ Thomson Learning, 2002.

Zogby, John. *The Way We'll Be: The Zogby Report on the Transformation of the American Dream.* New York: Random House, 2008.

ARTICLES, PUBLISHED REPORTS, AND CHAPTERS IN EDITED VOLUMES

Abdulkadiroglu, Atila, Parag A. Pathak, and Alvin E. Roth. "The New York City High School Match." *AEA Papers and Proceedings* 95 (May 2005): 364–67.

Augenblick, John. "The Role of State Legislatures in School Finance Reform." In *Strategies for School Equity*, edited by Marilyn Gittell, 89–100. New Haven, Conn.: Yale University Press, 1998.

Barrow, Lisa, and Cecilia E. Rouse, "School Vouchers: Recent Findings and Unanswered Questions." *Economic Perspectives* 32 (3d Quarter 2008): 2–16.

Battistich, Victor, et al. "Schools as Communities, Poverty Levels of Student Populations, and Students' Attitudes, Motives, and Performance: A Multilevel Analysis." *American Educational Research Journal* 32 (fall 1995): 627–58.

Belfield, Clive R., and Henry M. Levin. "The Effects of Competition between Schools on Educational Outcomes: A Review for the United States." *Review of Educational Research* 72 (summer 2002): 279–341.

Bell, Derrick A., Jr. "*Brown v. Board of Education* and the Interest-Convergence Dilemma." *Harvard Law Review* 93 (Jan. 1980): 518–33.

Berne, Robert, and Leanna Stiefel. "Concepts of School Finance Equity: 1970 to the Present." In *Equity and Adequacy in Education Finance*, edited by Helen F. Ladd, 7–33. Washington, D.C.: National Academy Press, 1999.

Berry, Christopher. "The Impact of School Finance Judgments on State Fiscal Policy." In *School Money Trials*, edited by Martin West and Paul Peterson, 213–40. Washington, D.C.: Brookings Institution Press, 2007.

Blank, Rolf F., Roger E. Levine, and Lauri Steel. "After 15 Years: Magnet Schools in Urban Education." In *Who Chooses? Who Loses? Culture, Institutions and the Unequal Effects of School Choice*, edited by Bruce F. Fuller, Richard Elmore, and Gary Orfield, 154–72. New York: Teachers College Press, 1996.

Boeckelman, Keith. "Suburban State Legislators and School Finance." *Journal of Political Science* 32 (2004): 47–74.

Bogart, William T., and Brian A. Crowmwell. "How Much Is a Neighborhood School Worth?" *Journal of Urban Economics* 47 (Mar. 2000): 280–305.

Bolick, Clint. "The Constitutional Parameters of School Choice." *Brigham Young University Law Review* 2 (Mar. 2008): 335–51.

Borkowski, John W., and Maree Sneed. "Will NCLB Improve or Harm Public Education?" *Harvard Educational Review* 76 (winter 2006): 503–25.

Bracey, Gerald W. "A Lesson in Throwing Money." *Phi Delta Kappan* 79 (Jun. 1998): 789–90.

Briffault, Richard. "Adding Adequacy to Equity." In *School Money Trials*, edited by Martin West and Paul Peterson, 25–54. Washington, D.C.: Brookings Institution Press, 2007.

Brown, George D. "Binding Advisory Opinions: A Federal Courts Perspective on the State School Finance Cases." *Boston College Law Review* 35 (May 1994): 543–68.

Brown, Kevin. "Has the Supreme Court Allowed the Cure for De Jure Segregation to Replicate the Disease?" *Cornell Law Review* 78 (Nov. 1992): 1–83.

Buhler, Patricia M. "The Growing Importance of Soft Skills in the Workplace." *Supervision* 62 (Jun. 2001): 13–16.

Bulman, Robert C., and David L. Kirp. "The Shifting Politics of School Choice." In *School Choice and Social Controversy*, edited by Stephen D. Sugarman and Frank R. Kemerer, 36–67. Washington, D.C.: Brookings Institution Press, 1999.

Burtless, Gary. "Introduction and Summary." In *Does Money Matter*, edited by Burtless, 1–42. Washington, D.C.: Brookings Institution Press, 1996.

Card, David, et al. "Tipping and the Dynamics of Segregation." *Quarterly Journal of Economics* 123 (1) (2008): 177–218.

Carter, Robert L. "Reexamining *Brown* Twenty-five Years Later: Looking Backward into the Future." *Harvard Civil Rights–Civil Liberties Law Review* 14 (fall 1979): 615–24.

Chemerinsky, Erwin. "Lost Opportunity: The Burger Court and the Failure to Achieve Equal Educational Opportunity." *Mercer Law Review* 45 (spring 1994): 999–1015.

Combs, Bert T. "Creative Constitutional Law: The Kentucky School Reform Law." *Harvard Journal on Legislation* 28 (summer 1991): 367–78.

Cook, Philip J., and Jens Ludwig. "Do Black Adolescents Disparage Achievement?" In *The Black-White Test Score Gap*, edited by Christopher Jencks and Meredith Phillips, 375–94. Washington, D.C.: Brookings Institution Press, 1998.

Cortez, Albert. "Power and Perseverance: Organizing for Change in Texas." In *Strategies for School Equity*, edited by Marilyn Gittell, 181–99. New Haven, Conn.: Yale University Press, 1998.

Crain, Robert L., and Rita E. Mahard. "Desegregation and Black Achievement: A Review of the Research." *Law and Contemporary Problems* 42 (summer 1978): 17–56.

———. "Research on Minority Achievement in Desegregated Schools." In *The Consequences of School Desegregation*, edited by Christine H. Rossell and Willis D. Hawley, 103–25. Philadelphia: Temple University Press, 1983.

Crane, Jonathan. "Effects of Neighborhoods on Dropping Out of School and Teenage Childbearing." In *The Urban Underclass*, edited by Paul E. Peterson, 299–318. Washington, D.C.: Brookings Institution Press, 1991.

————. "The Epidemic Theory of Ghettos and Neighborhood Effects on Dropping Out and Teenage Childbearing." *American Journal of Sociology* 96 (Mar. 1991): 1226–59.

Dayton, John, and Anne Dupree. "School Funding Litigation: Who's Winning the War?" *Vanderbilt Law Review* 57 (Nov. 2004): 2351–413.

Du Bois, W. E. B. "Does the Negro Need Separate Schools?" *Journal of Negro Education* 4 (Jul. 1935): 328–35.

Dudziak, Mary. "Desegregation as a Cold War Imperative." *Stanford Law Review* 41 (Nov. 1988): 61–120.

Dunn, James R. "Title VI, the Guidelines and School Desegregation in the South." *Virginia Law Review* 53 (Jan. 1967): 42–88.

Edwards, Yohance C., and Jennifer Ahern. "Unequal Treatment in State Supreme Courts: Minority and City Schools in Education Finance Reform Litigation." *New York University Law Review* 79 (Apr. 2004): 326–66.

Ellen, Ingrid Gould. "Welcome Neighbors? New Evidence on the Possibility of Stable Racial Integration." *Brookings Review* 15 (winter 1997): 18–21.

Elmore, Richard F. "Testing Trap: The Single Largest—and Possibly Most Destructive—Federal Intrusion into America's Public Schools." *Harvard Magazine* 105 (Sept.-Oct. 2002): 35–37, 97.

Enrich, Peter. "Leaving Equality Behind: New Directions in School Finance Reform." *Vanderbilt Law Review* 48 (Jan. 1995): 100–194.

Evans, William N., et al. "Impact of Court-mandated School Finance Reform." In *Equity and Adequacy in Education Finance: Issues and Perspectives*, edited by Helen F. Ladd, 72–89. Washington, D.C.: National Academy Press, 1999.

Ferguson, Ronald F. "Paying for Public Education: New Evidence on How and Why Money Matters." *Harvard Journal on Legislation* 28 (summer 1991): 465–98.

————. "Comment on 'Do Black Adolescents Disparage Achievement?'" In *The Black-White Test Score Gap*, edited by Christopher Jencks and Meredith Phillips, 394–97. Washington, D.C.: Brookings Institution Press, 1998.

Finn, Chester E. "Education That Works: Make the Schools Compete." *Harvard Business Review* 65 (Sept. 1987): 63–68.

Fischel, William A. "Did John Serrano Vote for Proposition 13?" *UCLA Law Review* 51 (Apr. 2004): 887–932.

Fordham, Signithia. "Racelessness as a Factor in Black Students' School Success: Pragmatic Strategy or Pyrrhic Victory?" *Harvard Educational Review* 58 (spring 1988): 54–84.

Fordham, Signithia, and John Ogbu. "Black Students' School Success: Coping with the Burden Of 'Acting White.'" *Urban Review* 18 (Sept. 1986): 176–206.

Forman, James, Jr. "The Secret History of School Choice: How Progressives Got There First." *Georgetown Law Journal* 93 (Apr. 2005): 1287–319.

————. "Rise and Fall of School Vouchers: A Story of Religion, Race, and Politics." *University of California Los Angeles Law Review* 54 (Feb. 2007): 547–604.

Frankel, Alison. "Blackboard Jungle." *American Lawyer* 22 (May 2000): 64–69, 103–5.

Frug, Gerald E. "City Services." *New York University Law Review* 73 (Apr. 1998): 23–96.

Fuller, Bruce. "Growing Charter Schools, Decentering the State." In *Inside Charter Schools: The Paradox of Racial Desegregation*, edited by Bruce Fuller, 1–12. Cambridge, Mass.: Harvard University Press, 2002.

———. "The Public Square, Big or Small? Charter Schools in Political Context." In *Inside Charter Schools: The Paradox of Racial Desegregation*, edited by Bruce Fuller, 12–65. Cambridge, Mass.: Harvard University Press, 2002.

Gill, Brian. "School Choice and Integration." In *Getting Choice Right*, edited by Julian R. Betts and Tom Loveless, 130–45. Washington, D.C.: Brookings Institution Press, 2005.

Gittell, Marilyn. "State Power, Suburban Interests, and City School Reform: A Nine-state Comparative Study." New York: Howard Samuels State Management and Policy Center, Graduate School and University Center, City University of New York, 2001.

Goldenzeil, Jill, "Blaine's Name in Vain: State Constitutions, School Choice, and Charitable Choice." *Denver University Law Review* 83 (2005): 57–99.

Goodman, Frank. "De Facto School Segregation: A Constitutional and Empirical Analysis." *California Law Review* 60 (Mar. 1972): 275–437.

Gorman, Siobhan. "Can't Beat 'Em? Sue 'Em! What Liberal Lawyers Love about Bush's Education Plan." *Washington Monthly* 33 (Dec. 2001): 36–40.

Green, Steven K. "The Insignificance of the Blaine Amendment." *Brigham Young University Law Review* 2 (Mar. 1998): 295–333.

Hanushek, Eric A. "School Resources and Student Performance." In *Does Money Matter?* edited by Gary Burtless, 43–73. Washington, D.C.: Brookings Institution Press, 1996.

Hanushek, Eric A., and Steven G. Rivkin. "Understanding the Twentieth-century Growth in U.S. School Spending." *Journal of Human Resources* 32 (winter 1997): 35–68.

Hanushek, Eric A., John F. Kain, and Steven G. Rivkin. "Why Public Schools Lose Teachers." *Journal of Human Resources* 39 (spring 2004): 326–54.

Harris, Douglas N. "High Flying Schools, Student Disadvantage, and the Logic of NCLB." *American Journal of Education* 113 (May 2007): 367–94.

Hedges, Larry V., and Rob Greenwald. "Have Times Changed? The Relation between School Resources and Student Performance." In *Does Money Matter?* edited by Gary Burtless, 74–92. Washington, D.C.: Brookings Institution Press, 1996.

Heise, Michael. "Equal Educational Opportunity, Hollow Victories, and the Demise of School Finance Equity Theory." *Georgia Law Review* 32 (winter 1998): 543–641.

Henig, Jeffry R., and Stephen D. Sugarman. "The Nature and Extent of School Choice." In *School Choice and Social Controversy*, edited by Stephen D. Sugarman and Frank R. Kemerer, 111–39. Washington, D.C.: Brookings Institution Press, 1999.

Hess, Fredrick M., and Tom Loveless. "How School Choice Affects Student Achievement." In *Getting Choice Right: Ensuring Equity and Efficiency in Education Policy*, edited by Julian R. Betts and Tom Loveless, 85–100. Washington, D.C.: Brookings Institution Press, 2005.

Heytens, Toby J. "School Choice and State Constitutions." *Virginia Law Review* 86 (Feb. 2000): 117–62.

Hochschild, Jennifer L. "Social Class in Public Schools." *Journal of Social Issues* 59 (Dec. 2003): 821–40.

Holme, Jennifer J., and Amy S. Wells. "School Choice beyond District Borders: Lessons for the Reauthorization of NCLB from Interdistrict Desegregation and Open Enrollment Plans," In *Improving on No Child Left Behind*, edited by Richard Kahlenberg, 139–215. New York: Century Foundation, 2008.

Hoxby, Caroline M. "Does Competition among Public Schools Benefit Students and Taxpayers?" *American Economic Review* 97 (Dec. 2007): 2038–55.

Hutchinson, Dennis J. "Unanimity and Desegregation: Decision Making in the Supreme Court, 1948–1958." *Georgetown Law Journal* 68 (Oct. 1979): 1–87.

Jacob, Brian A. "Accountability, Incentives and Behavior: The Impact of High-stakes Testing in the Chicago Public Schools." *Journal of Public Economics* 89 (Jun. 2005): 761–96.

———. "The Challenges of Staffing Urban Schools with Effective Teachers." *Future of Children* 17 (spring 2007): 129–53.

James, David R. "City Limits on Racial Equality: The Effects of City-suburb Boundaries on Public-school Desegregation, 1968–1976." *American Sociological Review* 54 (Dec. 1989): 963–85.

Jargowsky, Paul. "Concentration of Poverty Declined in the 1990s." In *Poverty and Race in America*, edited by Chester Hartman, 79–81. Oxford: Lexington Books, 2006.

James, Ryan E., and John C. Jeffries. "A Political History of the Establishment Clause." *Michigan Law Review* 100 (Nov. 2001): 279–370.

Jones, M. Gail, et al. "The Impact of High-stakes Testing on Teachers and Students in North Carolina." *Phi Delta Kappan* 81 (Nov. 1999): 199–203.

Kaden, Lewis B. "Courts and Legislatures in a Federal System: The Case of School Finance." *Hofstra Law Review* 11 (summer 1983): 1205–60.

Kahlenberg, Richard. "The Problem of Taking Private Voucher Programs to Scale." In *Public School Choice vs. Private School Vouchers*, edited by Kahlenberg, 51–60. New York: Century Foundation Press, 2003.

Kahn, Paul W. "State Constitutionalism and the Problems of Fairness." *Valparaiso University Law Review* 30 (spring 1996): 459–74.

Kantor, Harvey, and Robert Lowe. "From New Deal to No Deal: No Child Left Behind and the Devolution of Responsibility for Equal Opportunity." *Harvard Educational Review* 76 (winter 2006): 474–502.

Kirp, David. "Judicial Policy-Making: The Problem of Inequitable Public School Financing." In *Policy and Politics in America*, edited by Allan Sindler, 82–122. Boston: Little, Brown, 1973.

Kirp, David, et al. "Legal Reform of Special Education: Empirical Studies and Procedural Proposals." *California Law Review* 62 (Jan. 1974): 40–155.

Koski, William S. "Of Fuzzy Standards and Institutional Constraints: A Re-examination of the Jurisprudential History of Educational Finance Reform Litigation." *Santa Clara Law Review* 43 (4) (2003): 1185–298.

Koski, William S., and Rob Reich. "When 'Adequate' Isn't: The Retreat from Equality in Educational Law and Policy and Why It Matters." *Emory Law Journal* 56 (3) (2006): 545–617.

Leedes, Gary C., and James M. O'Fallon. "School Desegregation in Richmond: A Case History." *University of Richmond Law Review* 10 (fall 1975): 1–61.

Leinberger, Christopher B. "The Next Slum." *Atlantic*, Mar. 2008, 70–75.

Levin, Betsy. "Current Trends in School Finance Reform Litigation: A Commentary." *Duke Law Journal* 1977 (Jan. 1978): 1099–137.

———. "Race and School Choice." In *School Choice and Social Controversy*, edited by Stephen D. Sugarman and Frank R. Kemerer, 36–67. Washington, D.C.: Brookings Institution Press, 1999.

Liebman, James S. "Implementing *Brown* in the Nineties: Political Reconstruction, Liberal Recollection, and Litigatively Enforced Legislative Reform." *Virginia Law Review* 76 (Apr. 1990): 349–434.

Liu, Goodwin. "Interstate Inequality in Educational Opportunity." *New York University Law Review* 81 (2006): 2044–128.

Liu, Goodwin, and William L. Taylor. "School Choice to Achieve Desegregation." *Fordham Law Review* 74 (Nov. 2005): 791–823.

Lundberg, Paula. "State Courts and School Funding: A Fifty-state Analysis." *Albany Law Review* 63 (2000): 1101–46.

MacInnes, Gordon. "Choosing Segregation." In *Public School Choice v. Private School Vouchers*, edited by Richard Kahlenberg, 89–92. New York: Century Foundation Press, 2003.

Manno, Bruno V., Chester E. Finn, and Gregg Vanourek. "Beyond the Schoolhouse Door: How Charter Schools Are Transforming U.S. Public Education." *Phi Delta Kappan* 81 (Jun. 2000): 736–44.

Massell, Diane. "Standards-based Reform in the States: Progress and Challenges." In *Education Policy for the Twenty-first Century: Challenges and Opportunities in Standards-based Reform*, edited by Lawrence B. Joseph, 135–68. Chicago: Center for Urban Research and Policy Studies, Irving B. Harris Graduate School of Public Policy Studies, University of Chicago, 2001.

Mathis, William J. "No Child Left Behind: Costs and Benefits." *Phi Delta Kappan* 84 (May 2003): 679–86.

Matthews, Jay. "Bad Rap on the Schools." *Wilson Quarterly* (spring 2008): 15–20.

Mayer, Susan E. "How Much Does a High School's Racial and Socioeconomic Mix Affect Graduation and Teenage Fertility Rates?" In *The Urban Underclass*, edited by Paul E. Peterson, 319–41. Washington, D.C.: Brookings Institution Press, 1991.

McUsic, Molly S. "The Use of Education Clauses in School Finance Reform Legislation." *Harvard Journal on Legislation* 28 (summer 1991): 307–40.

———. "The Law's Role in the Distribution of Education: The Promises and Pitfalls of School Finance Litigation." In *Law and School Reform: Six Strategies for Promoting Educational Equity*, edited by Jay P. Heubert, 88–159. New Haven, Conn.: Yale University Press, 1999.

————. "The Future of *Brown v. Board of Education*: Economic Integration of the Public Schools." *Harvard Law Review* 117 (Mar. 2004): 1334–77.

Mead, Sara, and Andrew J. Rotherham. "A Sum Greater Than the Parts: What States Can Teach Each Other about Charter Schooling." *Education Sector Reports* (Oct. 2007): 1–21.

Merhige, Robert R., Jr. "A Judge Remembers Richmond in the Post-*Brown* Years." *Washington and Lee Law Review* 49 (winter 1992): 23–30.

Metzler, Jeffrey. "Inequitable Equilibrium: School Finance in the United States." *Indiana Law Review* 36 (3) (2003): 561–608.

Michelman, Frank I. "The Supreme Court, 1968 Term—Foreword: On Protecting the Poor through the Fourteenth Amendment." *Harvard Law Review* 83 (Nov. 1969): 7–59.

Mid-Continent Center for Research for Education and Learning. "Final Report: High-needs Schools—What Does It Take to Beat the Odds?" Aurora, Colo.: Mid-Continent Center for Research for Education and Learning, 2002.

Middleton, Michael A. "*Brown v. Board*: Revisited." *Southern Illinois University Law Journal* 20 (fall 1995): 19–39.

Minow, Martha L. "School Finance: Does Money Matter?" *Harvard Journal on Legislation* 28 (summer 1991): 395–400.

Morgan, Martha I. "Establishing Educational Program Inadequacy: The Alabama Example." *University of Michigan Journal of Law Reform* 28 (spring 1995): 559–98.

Morrow, Lance, et al. "Man and Woman of the Year: The Middle Americans." *Time*, Jan. 6, 1970, 10–17.

Mounts, Nina S., and Laurence Steinberg. "An Ecological Analysis of Peer Influence on Adolescent Grade Point Average and Drug Use." *Developmental Psychology* 31 (Nov. 1995): 915–22.

Murnane, Richard J. "Evidence, Analysis, and Unanswered Questions." *Harvard Educational Review* 51 (Nov. 1981): 483–89.

Natriello, Gary, and Edward L. McDill. "Title I: From Funding Mechanism to Educational Program." In *Hard Work for Good Schools*, edited by Gary Orfield and Elizabeth H. Debray, 32–47. New York: Century Foundation Press, 2003.

Nichols, Sharon L., et al. "High Stakes Testing and Student Achievement: Does Accountability Pressure Increase Student Learning?" *Education Policy Analysis Archives* 14 (Jan. 4, 2006): 1–175.

Orfield, Gary, and David Thronson. "Dismantling Desegregation: Uncertain Gains, Unexpected Costs." *Emory Law Journal* 42 (summer 1993): 759–90.

Ornstein, Allan C. "Educational Financing and Government Spending." *Theory into Practice* 17 (Oct. 1978): 341–47.

Peterson, Paul E. "School Choice: A Report Card." *Virginia Journal of Social Policy and Law* 6 (fall 1998): 47–80.

Peterson, Paul E., and Frederick M. Hess. "Keeping an Eye on State Standards: A Race to the Bottom?" *Education Next* 6 (summer 2006): 28–29.

Picott, Rupert J. "The Status of Educational Desegregation in Virginia." *Journal of Negro Education* 25 (summer 1965): 345–51.

Podgursky, Michael J., and Matthew G. Springer. "Teacher Performance Pay: A Review." *Journal of Policy Analysis and Management* 26 (4) (2007): 909–49.

Ranney, Joseph A. "Absolute Common Ground: The Four Eras of Assimilation in Wisconsin Education Law." *Wisconsin Law Review* 3 (1998): 791–822.

Rebell, Michael A. "Fiscal Equality in Education: Deconstructing the Reigning Myths and Facing Reality." *New York University Review of Law and Social Change* 21 (1993): 691–723.

———. "Educational Adequacy, Democracy, and the Courts." In *Achieving High Educational Standards for All,* edited by Timothy Ready, 218–68. Washington, D.C.: National Academy Press, 2002.

Reynolds, Laurie. "Rethinking Municipal Annexation Powers." *Urban Lawyer* 24 (spring 1992): 247–303.

Richardson, Brandi. "Eradicating Blaine's Legacy of Hate: Removing the Barrier to State Funding of Religious Education." *Catholic University Law Review* 52 (summer 2003): 1041–79.

Ripley, Amanda. "Inside the Revolt over Bush's School Rules." *Time,* May 9, 2005, 30–33.

———. "Rhee Tackles Classroom Challenge." *Time,* Nov. 26, 2008, 36–44.

Rosenbaum, James E. "Black Pioneers: Do Their Moves to the Suburbs Increase Economic Opportunity for Mothers and Children?" *Housing Policy Debate* 2 (4) (1991): 1179–214.

Ross, Karen E. "Charter Schools and Integration: The Experience in Michigan." In *Getting Choice Right: Ensuring Equity and Efficiency in Education Policy,* edited by Julian R. Betts and Tom Loveless, 146–75. Washington, D.C.: Brookings Institution Press, 2005.

Rossell, Christine H. "An Analysis of the Court Decisions in *Sheff v. O'Neill* and Possible Remedies for Racial Isolation." *Connecticut Law Review* 29 (spring 1997): 1187–233.

Rossell, Christine H. "Whatever Happened to Magnet Schools? No Longer Famous but Still Intact." *Education Next* 4 (spring 2005): 44–49.

Rossell, Christine H., and David J. Armor. "The Effectiveness of School Desegregation Plans 1968–1991." *American Politics Quarterly* 24 (Jul. 1996): 267–302.

Rothstein, Richard. "Testing Our Patience: Standardized Tests Have Their Uses, but Current Federal Law Uses Testing to Destroy Learning." *American Prospect,* Feb. 2004, 45–47.

———. "Leaving 'No Child Left Behind' Behind." *American Prospect,* Jan.-Feb. 2008, 50–54.

Rubenstein, Ross, and Larry Miller. "Examining the Nature and Magnitude of Intradistrict Resource Disparities in Mid-size School Districts." *Public Budgeting and Finance* 28 (winter 2008): 26–51.

Rudalevige, Andrew. "The Politics of No Child Left Behind." *Education Next* 3 (fall 2003): 63–69.

Rusk, David. "To Improve Children's Test Scores, Move Poor Families." *Assell Report,* Report 11 (Jun.-Jul. 1998): 1–2.

Ryan, James E. "*Sheff*, Segregation, and School Finance Litigation." *New York University Law Review* 74 (May 1999): 529–73.

———. "Schools, Race, and Money." *Yale Law Journal* 109 (Nov. 1999): 249–316.

———. "The Influence of Race on School Finance Reform." *Michigan Law Review* 98 (Nov. 1999): 432–81.

———. "*Brown*, School Choice, and the Suburban Veto." *Virginia Law Review* 90 (Oct. 2004): 1635–47.

———. "The Perverse Incentives of the No Child Left Behind Act." *New York University Law Review* 79 (Jun. 2004): 932–89.

———. "A Constitutional Right to Preschool?" *California Law Review* 94 (2006): 49–99.

———. "The Supreme Court and Voluntary Integration." *Harvard Law Review* 121 (Nov. 2007): 131–57.

———. "Standards, Testing, and School Finance Litigation." *Texas Law Review* 86 (May 2008): 1223–62.

———. "Charter Schools and Public Education." *Stanford Journal on Civil Rights and Civil Liberties* 4 (Oct. 2008): 393–410.

Ryan, James E., and Michael Heise. "The Political Economy of School Choice." *Yale Law Journal* 40 (Jun. 2002): 2043–136.

Ryan, James E., and Thomas Saunders. "Foreword to Symposium on School Finance Litigation: Emerging Trends or New Dead Ends?" *Yale Law and Policy Review* 22 (spring 2004): 463–80.

Sartain, James Auxford, et al. "Implications and Recommendations of Urban Team Study on Resegregation of Northside Schools." (Sartain Report). Richmond Public Schools (1969).

Sartain, James A., and Rutledge M. Dennis. "Richmond, Virginia: Massive Resistance without Violence." In *Community Politics and Educational Change*, edited by Charles V. Willie and Susan L. Greenblatt, 208–36. New York: Longman, 1981.

Schelling, Thomas. "The Process of Residential Segregation: Neighborhood Tipping." In *Racial Discrimination in Economic Life*, edited by Anthony H. Pascal, 157–85. Lexington, Mass.: Lexington Books, 1972.

Schrag, Peter, and Stephan Thernstrom. "Must Schools Fail?: An Exchange." *New York Review of Books* 52 (Feb. 24, 2005): 49–50.

Schragger, Richard. "*San Antonio v. Rodriguez* and the Legal Geography of School Finance Reform." In *Civil Rights Stories*, edited by Myriam E. Gilles and Risa L. Goluboff, 85–110. New York: Foundation Press, 2008.

Silberman, Todd. "Wake County Schools: A Question of Balance." In *Divided We Fail: Coming Together through Public School Choice*, a report of the Century Foundation Task Force, 141–66. New York: Century Foundation Press, 2002.

Spicer, Robert E., Jr. "Comment: Annexation in Virginia: The 1979 Amendments Usher in a New Era in City-county Relations." *University of Richmond Law Review* 14 (summer 1983): 819–43.

Springer, Matthew G., and James W. Guthrie. "The Politicization of the School Finance Legal Process." In *School Money Trials: The Legal Pursuit of Educational Adequacy*, edited by Martin R. West and Paul E. Peterson, 102–30. Washington, D.C.: Brookings Institution Press, 2007.

Stanczyk, Michael T. "Public School Finance Litigation in New York and Massachusetts: The Bad Aftertaste of a Campaign For Fiscal Equity Win in New York." *St. John's Journal of Legal Commentary* 21 (fall 2006): 353–70.

Stark, Kirk, and Jonathan Zasloff. "Tiebout and Tax Revolts: Did *Serrano* Really Cause Proposition 13?" *UCLA Law Review* 50 (Feb. 2003): 801–58.

Stolee, Michael. "The Milwaukee Desegregation Case." In *Seeds of Crisis: Public Schooling in Milwaukee since 1920*, edited by John L. Rury and Frank A. Cassell, 229–68. Madison: University of Wisconsin Press, 1993.

Sugarman, Stephen D. "School Choice and Public Funding." In *School Choice and Social Controversy*, edited by Stephen D. Sugarman and Frank R. Kemerer, 13–35. Washington, D.C.: Brookings Institution, 1999.

Sugarman, Steven D., and Paul A. Minorini. "School Finance Litigation in the Name of Equity." In *Equity and Adequacy in Education Finance: Issues and Perspectives*, edited by Helen F. Ladd, 34–71. Washington, D.C.: National Academy Press, 1999.

Swenson, Karen. "School Finance Reform Litigation: Why Are Some State Supreme Courts Activist and Others Restrained?" *Albany Law Review* 63 (4) (2000): 1147–82.

Taylor, Willam L. "Assessment as a Means to a Quality Education." *Georgetown Journal on Poverty Law and Policy* 8 (summer 2001): 311–20.

Thomas, Evan, and Lynett Clemetson. "A New War over Vouchers: Poor Parents Want Them, but Civil-rights Leaders Are Split." *Newsweek*, Nov. 22, 1999, 46.

Tough, Paul. "What It Takes to Make a Student." *New York Times Magazine*, Nov. 26, 2006, 44–51, 69–72, 77.

Traub, James. "Test Mess." *New York Times Magazine*, Apr. 7, 2002, 46–51, 60, 78.

Traub, James. "What No School Can Do." *New York Times Magazine*, Jan. 16, 2000, 52–57, 68, 81, 90–91.

Umpstead, Regina R. "The No Child Left Behind Act: Is It an Unfunded Mandate or a Promotion of Federal Educational Ideals?" *Journal of Law and Education* 37 (Apr. 2008): 193–229.

"Unfulfilled Promises." Note. *Harvard Law Review* 104 (Mar. 1991): 1072–92.

Weschler, Patrick J. "Twenty-fourth Annual Survey of Developments in Virginia Law, 1978–1979: Municipal Corporations." *Virginia Law Review* 66 (2) (1980): 327–42.

West, Kimberly C. "A Desegregation Tool That Backfired: Magnet Schools and Classroom Segregation." *Yale Law Journal* 103 (Jun. 1994): 2567–92.

Wildman, Sarah. "Credit Is Due: Who Says Conservatives Like Vouchers?" *New Republic* 224 (Feb. 26, 2001): 15–16.

Willms, J. Douglas. "Social Class Segregation and Its Relationship to Pupils' Examination Results in Scotland." *American Sociological Review* 51 (Apr. 1986): 224–41.

Witte, John F., and John E. Coons. "Try, Try Again." *Education Next* 1 (fall 2001): 75–77.

Wolf, Patrick J. "School Voucher Programs: What the Research Says about Parental School Choice." *Brigham Young University Law Review* 2 (Mar. 2008): 415–46.

Wolman, Harold, Margaret Weir, and Todd Swanstrom. "The Calculus of Coalitions: Cities, Suburbs, and the Metropolitan Agenda." *Urban Affairs Review* 40 (Jul. 2005): 730–60.

Wong, Kenneth K., and Francis X. Shen. "Do School District Takeovers Work? Assessing the Effectiveness of City and State Takeovers as a School Board Reform Strategy." State Education Standard 3 (spring 2002): 19–23.

Yudof, Mark. "School Finance Reform in Texas: The *Edgewood* Saga." *Harvard Journal on Legislation* 28 (summer 1991): 499–505.

Zimmer, Ron W., and Eugenia F. Toma. "Peer Effects in Private And Public Schools across Countries." *Journal of Policy Analysis and Management* 19 (Dec. 1999): 75–92.

REPORTS, ARTICLES, AND DATA
AVAILABLE ONLINE

Anderson, Judith, et al. "Poverty and Achievement: Re-examining the Relationship between School Poverty and Student Achievement." Paper presented at the annual meeting of the American Educational Research Association, San Francisco, Apr. 20–24, 992. www.eric.ed.gov/ERICDocs/data/ericdocs2sql/content_storage_01/0000019b/80/24/13/du.pdf.

Balfanz, Robert and Nettie Legters. "Locating the Dropout Crisis: Which High Schools Produce the Nation's Dropouts?" Johns Hopkins University, June 2004. http://www.csos.jhu.edu/tdhs/rsch/Locating_Dropouts.pdf.

Bierlein, Louann, Kim Sheane, and Lori Mulholland. "A National Review of Open Enrollment/Choice: Debates and Description." Morrison Institute, School of Public Affairs, Arizona State University, Jul. 1993. www.hdl.handle.net/2286/asulib:96213.

Berube, Alan. "Metropolitan Poverty in the United States." Paper presented at Poverty and Place Workshop, Cambridge, England, Sept. 28, 2006. www.regionalinnovation.org.uk/object/download/1678/doc/P&P%20-%20Alan%20Berube.pdf.

Berube, Alan, and Elizabeth Kneebone. "Two Steps Back: City and Suburban Poverty Trends 1999–2005." Brookings Institution, Dec. 2006. www.brookings.edu/reports/2006/12poverty_berube.aspx.

"Best High Schools 2009." *U.S. News and World Report*. www.usnews.com/sections/education/high-schools/.

Borsuk, Alan J. "Eyes on Milwaukee for School Choice." *Milwaukee Journal Sentinel*, 21 Aug. 2000. www.schoolchoiceinfo.org/news/index.cfm?action=detail&news_id=570.

Carey, Kevin. "The Funding Gap 2004: Many States Still Shortchange Low-income and Minority Students." Education Trust, fall 2004. www2.edtrust.org/NR/rdonlyres/30B3C1B3–3DA6–4809-AFB9–2DAACF11CF88/0/funding2004.pdf.

———. "Hot Air: How States Inflate Their Educational Progress under NCLB," Education Sector, May 2006. www.educationsector.org/usr_doc/Hot_Air_NCLB.pdf.

CATO Institute. "Washington State's Blaine Amendment Violates the U.S. Constitution." News release, Sept. 10, 2003. www.cato.org/new/09–03/09–10–03r.html.

CBS News. "Minority Kids Could Be Majority by 2023." Mar. 5, 2009. www.cbsnews. com/stories/2009/03/05/national/main4844040.shtml.

Center for Education Reform. "Race to the Top for Charter Schools." Jun. 15, 2009. www. edreform.com/Issues/Charter_Connection/?Race_to_the_Top_for_Charter_Schools.

Center for Research on Education Outcomes, "Multiple Choice: Charter School Performance in 16 States." Jun. 2009. credo.stanford.edu/reports/MULTIPLE_CHOICE_ CREDO.pdf.

Center on Education Policy. "Hope but No Miracle Cures: Michigan's Early Restructuring Lessons." Nov. 2005. www.cep-dc.org/.

———. "State High School Exit Exams: A Move toward End-of-Course Exams." Aug. 2008. www.cep-dc.org/.

Charles Hamilton Houston Institute for Race and Justice. "Creating Charter Schools That Reduce Segregation in Massachusetts." Jul. 10, 2009. www.charleshamilton-houston.org/assets/documents/news/CHHIRJ%20Charter%20Statement.pdf.

Coons, John E. "*Rodriguez* Redivivus." Mar. 2006. www.law.berkeley.edu/files/coons_ paper.pdf.

Council of Great City Schools. "Beating the Odds VII: An Analysis of Student Performance and Achievement Gaps on State Assessments, Results from the 2006–2007 School Year." Apr. 2008. www.cgcs.org/publications/achievement.aspx.

Cronin, John, et al. "The Proficiency Illusion." Thomas B. Fordham Institute, Oct. 2007. www.edexcellence.net/doc/The_Proficiency_Illusion.pdf.

Cross, Richard W., et al., eds. "Grading the Systems: The Guide to State Standards, Tests, and Accountability Policies." Thomas B. Fordham Institute, Jan. 2004. www.edexcel-lence.net/doc/GradingtheSystems.pdf.

Dillon, Erin. "Plotting School Choice: The Challenges of Crossing District Lines, Education Sector." Education Sector, Aug. 26, 2008. www.educationsector.org/research/ research_show.htm?doc_id=702217.

Easterly, William. "Empirics of Strategic Interdependence: The Case of the Racial Tipping Point." National Bureau of Economic Research, working paper no. 15069, Jun. 2009. www.nber.org/papers/w15069.

Education Commission of the States. "State Profiles—Charter Schools." 2009. www.ecs. org/html/educationIssues/CharterSchools/CHDB_intro.asp.

———. "State Education Reforms, Open Enrollment." 2008. mb2.ecs.org/reports/ Report.aspx?id=268.

Education Equality Project. "Mission Statement." 2009 www.educationequalityproject. org/what_we_stand_for/our_mission.

Education Law Center. "History of *Abbott*: Progress toward Equal Educational Opportunity for Urban Students in New Jersey." 2008. www.edlawcenter.org/ELCPublic/ AbbottvBurke/AbbottHistory.htm.

Fasenfest, David, et al. "Living Together: A New Look at Racial and Ethnic Integration in Metropolitan Neighborhoods." Brookings Institution, Apr. 2004. www.brookings. edu/reports/2004/04demographics_fasenfest.aspx.

Finn, Chester. "Faux Choice." *Education Gadfly*, Sept. 26, 2002. www.edexcellence.net/ gadfly.

Frankenberg, Erica, and Genevieve Seigel-Hawley. "The Forgotten Choice: Rethinking Magnet Schools in a Changing Landscape." Civil Rights Project (Nov. 2008): 1–64. www.ops.org/District/Portals/0/MAGNET%20SCHOOLS/Civil%20Rights%20 Project%202008%20report%20.pdf.

Frey, William F. "Melting Pot Suburbs: A Census 2000 Study of Suburban Diversity." Brookings Institution, Jun. 2001. www.brookings.edu/reports/2001/06demogra-phics_frey.aspx.

———. "Migration to Hot Housing Markets Cools Off." Brookings Institution, Mar. 21, 2008. www.brookings.edu/opinions/2008/0321_migration_frey.aspx.

———. "The Census Projects Minority Surge." Brookings Institution, Aug. 18, 2008. www.cbsnews.com/stories/2009/03/05/national/main4844040.shtml.

Fryer, Roland G., Jr., and Paul Torelli, "An Empirical Analysis of 'Acting White.'" National Bureau of Economic Research, working paper no. 11334, May 2005. http://www. nber.org/papers/w11334.

Goertz, Margaret E., and Michael Weiss. "Assessing Success in School Finance Litigation: The Case of New Jersey." Oct. 4, 2007. www.tc.edu/symposium/symposium07/resource.asp.

Goldstein, Dana. "On Edu Reform, Bill Gates v. Harvard Law." Jul. 22, 2009. danagoldstein. typepad.com/dana_goldstein/2009/07/on-edu-reform-bill-gates-v-harvard-law.html.

Governor's School for Government and International Studies, Richmond VA. "Profile." www.gsgis.k12.va.us/ourschool/profile.html.

Greene, Jay P. "An Evaluation of the Florida A-Plus Accountability and School Choice Program." Manhattan Institute for Policy Research, 2001. www.hks.harvard.edu/ pepg/PDF/Papers/Florida%20A+.pdf.

Greene, Jay P., and Marcus A. Winters. "Leaving Boys Behind: Public High School Gradu-ation Rates." *Civic Report* (Apr. 2006). www.manhattan-institute.org/html/cr_48.htm.

Hammer, Patricia Cahape. "Corrective Action: A Look at State Takeovers of Urban and Rural Districts." Jul. 2005. www.eric.ed.gov/ERICDocs/data/ericdocs2sql/content_ storage_01/0000019b/80/1b/af/7d.pdf.

Henig, Jeffrey R. "What Do We Know about the Outcome of KIPP Schools?" Great Lakes Center for Research and Practice, Nov. 2008. www.greatlakescenter.org/docs/Policy_ Briefs/Henig_Kipp.pdf.

Henrico County Public Schools. "Students First: Maintaining Excellence in Challenging Times, Annual Financial Plan 2009/2010." 2009. http://www.henrico.k12.va.us/ administration/finance/budget.html.

Hinkle, A. Barton. "Even More on Patrick Henry." Blog entry, May 16, 2008. barticles. mytimesdispatch.com/index.php/barticles/comments/even_more_on_patrick_henry/.

Holme, Jennifer Jellison, and Meredith P. Richards. "Review of 'Plotting School Choice' and 'In Need of Improvement.'" Education and the Public Interest Center and Education Policy Research Unit, Jan. 27, 2009. epicpolicy.org/thinktank/review-plotting-school-choice.

Kahlenberg, Richard D. "Rescuing *Brown v. Board of Education*: Profiles of Twelve School Districts Pursuing Socioeconomic Integration." *Century Foundation Report*, Jun. 28, 2007. www.tcf.org/list.asp?type=PB&pubid=618.

Kaine, Tim. "Competence to Excellence: Building on Standards of Learning Successes." Remarks to Virginia Board of Education, Richmond, VA, Apr. 26, 2006. Transcript at www.governor.virginia.gov/mediarelations/speeches/2006/EdBoardAddress.cfm.

Kaine, Tim. "Prepared Remarks of Tim Kaine (D-VA)." Presented at New America's Early Intervention Event, Washington, D.C., Jul. 26, 2006. www.newamerica.net/publications/resources/2006/prepared_remarks_of_governor_tim_kaine_d_va.

Kumar, Ruma Banerji & Halimah Abdullah. "As Test Scores Rise, Standards Are Lowered." *Commercial Appeal*, Mar. 5, 2006. www.commercialappeal.com/mca/education/article/0,2673,MCA_22897_ 4515544,00.html.

Map of Attendance Zones for Richmond Public Schools. 2009 www.richmond.k12.va.us/indexnew/sub/Directions/schoolmap/other.cfm.

Matthews, Jay. "Inside the Bay Area KIPP Schools." *WP*, 19 Sept. 2008. www.washingtonpost.com/wp-dyn/content/article/2008/09/19/AR2008091900978.html.

Mid-continent Center for Research and Learning. "Final Report: High-Needs Schools—What Does it Take to Beat the Odds?" Nov. 2005. www.eric.ed.gov/ERICDocs/data/ericdocs2sql/content_storage_01/0000019b/80/1b/b3/6e.pdf.

National Access Network (ACCESS). "Ohio Supreme Court Turns Away Legal Challenge to School Finance System." May 22, 2003. www.schoolfunding.info/states/oh/5–22–03WritofProhib.php3.

National Alliance for Public Charter Schools. "Federal Charter Schools Program." 2008. www.publiccharters.org/node/40.

Neil, Monty, et al. "Failing Our Children: How 'No Child Left Behind' Undermines Quality and Equity in Education." National Center for Fair and Open Testing, May 2004. www.fairtest.org/node/1778.

Olander, Michael, et al. "Attitudes of Young People toward Diversity." Center for Information and Research on Civic Learning and Engagement, Feb. 2005. www.civicyouth.org/PopUps/FactSheets/Attitudes%202.25.pdf.

Orfield, Gary, and Chungmei Lee. "Why Segregation Still Matters: Poverty and Educational Inequality." Harvard Project on Civil Rights, Jan. 2005. www.civilrightsproject.ucla.edu/research/deseg/Why_Segreg_Matters.pdf.

Prince, Cynthia D., et al. "Compensation for Teachers of Hard-to-Fill Subjects and Teachers in Hard-to-Staff Schools." Center for Educator Compensation Reform, Dec. 2007. http://cecr.ed.gov/guides/researchSyntheses/Research%20Synthesis_ Q%20B8.pdf.

Puma, Michael J., et al. "Prospects: The Congressionally Mandated Study of Educational Growth and Opportunity. The Interim Report." Planning and Evaluation Service, U.S. Department of Education (1993): 1–396. http://www.eric.ed.gov/ERICDocs/data/ericdocs2sql/content_storage_01/0000019b/80/13/10/cc.pdf.

———. "Prospects: Final Report on Student Outcomes." Planning and Evaluation Service, U.S. Department of Education (1997): 1–96. http://www.eric.ed.gov/ERICDocs/data/ericdocs2sql/content_storage_01/0000019b/80/15/0a/e8.pdf.

Rawlings, Lynette, et al. "Race and Residence: Prospects for Stable Neighborhood Integration." Urban Institute, Mar. 2004. www.urban.org/UploadedPDF/310985_NCUA3.pdf.

Reardon, Sean F., and John T. Yun. "Private School Racial Enrollments and Segregation." Civil Rights Project, Harvard University, Jun. 2002. www.civilrightsproject.ucla.edu/research/deseg/Private_Schools.pdf.

Richmond Public Schools. "School Board's Adopted Budget FY 2008–2009." June 2008. http://richmond.k12.va.us/indexnew/sub/Departments/Budget_Reporting/docume nts/09BoardsADOPTEDBudgetDETAIL.pdf.

Rotherham, Andrew J. "Making the Cut: How States Set Passing Scores on Standardized Tests." Education Sector, Jul. 2006. www.educationsector.org/usr_doc/EXPCutScores. pdf.

Rusk, David. "Nine Lessons for Inclusionary Zoning." Keynote remarks to the National Inclusionary Housing Conference, Washington, D.C., Oct. 5, 2005. www.gamaliel. org/DavidRusk/keynote%2010–5–05.pdf.

———. "Housing Policy *Is* School Policy." Paper presented to Housing Mobility and Education Forum, Baltimore, Dec. 3, 2007. www.prrac.org/pdf/Rusk.pdf.

Samberg, Matthew. "Litigation Update: Constitution Satisfied in Arkansas, Mixed Ruling in Alaska, Suit Dropped in Kentucky, New Hampshire Meets Court Deadline." National Access Network (ACCESS), Jul. 3, 2007. www.schoolfunding.info/news/litigation/7–3–07litupdate.php3.

Steiner, Lucy M. "School Restructuring Options under No Child Left Behind: What Works When? State Takeovers of Individual Schools." Center for Comprehensive School Reform and Improvement, 2006. www.centerforcsri.org/pubs/restructuring/KnowledgeIssues1StateTakeovers.pdf.

Swanstrom, Todd, et al. "Pulling Apart: Economic Segregation Among Suburbs and Central Cities in Major Metroplitan Areas." Brookings Institution, Oct. 2004. www.brookings.edu/~/media/Files/rc/reports/2004/10metropolitanpolicy_swan-strom/20041018_econsegregation.pdf.

Task Force, A Broader, Bolder Approach to Education. "Mission Statement." 2008. www.boldapproach.org/statement.html.

Taylor, Paul, and Richard Morin. "Americans Claim to Like Diverse Communities, but Do They Really?" Pew Research Center, Dec. 2, 2008. pewresearch.org/pubs/1045/americans-claim-to-like-diverse-communities-but-do-they-really.

UNC Center for Civil Rights. "The Socioeconomic Composition of the Public Schools: A Crucial Consideration in Student Assignment Policy." Jan. 7, 2005 http://www.law. unc.edu/documents/civilrights/briefs/charlottereport.pdf.

U.S. Census Bureau. "American Community Survey." 2007. www.census.gov/acs/www/.

———. "Current Population Survey." 2008. www.census.gov/cps/.

U.S. Department of Education. "Charter Schools Program." www.ed.gov/programs/charter/index.html.U.S. Department of Education, National Center for Education Statistics. "Condition of Education 2002." nces.ed.gov/pubs2002/2002025.pdf.

———. "Schools and Staffing Survey, 1999–2000." 2002. ces.ed.gov/pubSearch/pub-sinfo.asp?pubid=2002313.

———. "Closer Look at Charter Schools." 2006. nces.ed.gov/pubsearch/pubsinfo. asp?pubid=2006460.

———. "Common Core of Data." 2007–8. nces.ed.gov/ccd/schoolsearch/.

———. "Private School Universe Survey." 2007–8. nces.ed.gov/surveys/pss/private-school search/.

———. "Search for Public: Thomas Jefferson High School." 2007–8. nces.ed.gov/ccd/schoolsearch/school_detail.asp?Search=1&SchoolID=510324002070&ID=510324002070.

U.S. Department of Education, Office of Innovation and Improvement. "Successful Charter Schools." Jun. 2004. www.ed.gov/admins/comm/choice/charter/report.pdf.

Virginia Department of Education. "Virginia's K–12 Education Reform: Virginia's Standards of Learning Tests." 2004. 141.104.22.210/VDOE/PolicyPub/EduReform/Infopac4.pdf."/.

———. "Virginia Governor's School Program." 2009. www.doe.virginia.gov/VDOE/Instruction/Govschools.

Wake County Public School System, Demographics Data Center. "Demographics." www.wcpss.net/demographics/index.html.

Wolf, Patrick J. "The Comprehensive Longitudinal Evaluation of the Milwaukee Parental Choice Program: Summary of Baseline Reports." School Choice Demonstration Project, University of Arkansas, Feb. 2008. www.uaedreform.org/SCDP/Milwaukee_Eval/Report_1.pdf.

Ziebarth, Todd. "State Takeovers and Reconstitutions." Education Commission of the States, Apr. 2002. www.ecs.org/clearinghouse/13/59/1359.pdf.

INDEX